EAST KENT

ROAD CAR COMPANY LTD

A Century of Service, 1916–2016

RICHARD WALLACE

THE CROWOOD PRESS

First published in 2016 by
The Crowood Press Ltd
Ramsbury, Marlborough
Wiltshire SN8 2HR

www.crowood.com

British Library Cataloguing-in-Publication Data
A catalogue record for this book is available from the British Library.

ISBN 978 1 78500 100 0

Acknowledgements
This work would not have been possible if it had not been for the M&D and East
Kent Bus Club and its members recording aspects of East Kent operations since the
1950s. In particular, thanks are due to the club's current editor, Nicholas King,
who has provided invaluable assistance in checking and correcting drafts and adding
important information unknown to the author. Without that input this would be
very much a lesser work; any errors are, however, down to the author. Thanks are
also due to Brian Weeden, Barry Ovenden, Geoff Dodson, John (Fred) Wilson,
Phil Drake, David Harman, Mike Ansell and David Morgan, as well as many others
who have provided assistance and historic documents, including the management
of Stagecoach East Kent for permission to use archive material from the former
company. Photographs are individually credited where known but apologies are
made for any incorrect attributions or omissions; these are unintentional. Images
of artefacts and unattributed photographs are credited to the appropriate owner
or custodian of the collection, for example AUTHOR'S COLLECTION. Lastly, thanks are
due to all the author's former East Kent colleagues who made it so much fun and
contributed to making it a really colourful bus company.

Typeset by Jean Cussons Typesetting, Diss, Norfolk

Printed and bound in India by Replika Press Pvt Ltd

CONTENTS

The East Kent route network circa 1966

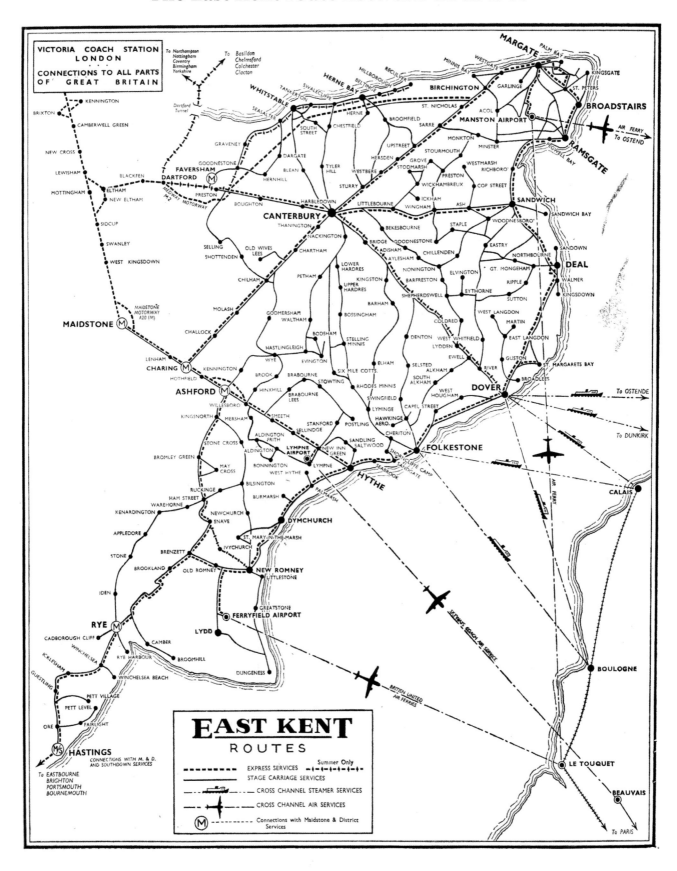

INTRODUCTION

The year 2016 sees the centenary of the founding of the East Kent Road Car Company, which, in various incarnations – including nationalization in 1969, a brief return to a local identity as a privatized concern in the 1980s/90s and finally takeover in 1993 by one of the new dominant players in the UK bus industry, the Stagecoach group – has served the people of east Kent well throughout those 100 years. This book takes the reader through those years and whilst it does not pretend to provide an exhaustive record of every facet of East Kent's operations, it is hoped that it gives a comprehensive account of the company's history as well as providing a brief insight into what it was like to work for East Kent.

For the author, the East Kent story started at the Light Railway Station at Hythe, terminus of the busy 103/A services from Folkestone. As a small boy attending infant school in the 1950s, I made the daily trip with my mother, around the corner to the bus stop, with its two quaint Greenly-designed wood and brick gabled bus shelters serving the buses but built by the RHDR; then boarding a smart burgundy and cream bus for the short journey of four stops to the eastern end of Hythe. Such a brief journey would seem odd to many people today familiar with the car-borne school run, but this was a different era and East Kent never let its passengers down.

At the start the regular vehicles were CJG-registered Leyland lowbridge PD1s but in 1956–7 a seismic change occurred with the arrival of the MFN-registered Guy Arab IVs with a well-proportioned Park Royal body. Even better, they offered an extremely good view of the driver's cab from the lower saloon — heaven-sent for a small boy of five years of age! The MFNs appeared to take over many of the 103/A services from then on but a move of schools brought these first East Kent journeys to an end until secondary school. Interest temporarily transferred to the sister Maidstone & District Company, coming into Hythe and Folkestone on the jointly worked service 10 from Maidstone. This was probably because of the rarity value and the fact that they were one of the early users of the futuristic rear-engined Leyland Atlantean, while East Kent stuck doggedly to traditional double-deckers until the late 1960s, being one of the last concerns to continue to receive the AEC Regent V chassis.

However, interest in East Kent returned, and a later need to pursue gainful employment led to an approach to the Company and a temporary position as a traffic clerk at the head office in Station Road West, Canterbury. A permanent position followed, then in later years moving to work as a conductor at Folkestone and a driver/conductor at Thanet. Little did that small boy of over a decade beforehand realize that he would be working on many of the vehicles that captured his interest in the late 1950s and early 1960s. While a longer-term diversion into the rail industry followed, East Kent always occupied a special position in the author's mind, not only through general interest but perhaps because the company was very much a social organization and friendships with old colleagues from the 1960s remain to this day. Even in retirement, East Kent is still there; the author is part-owner of an East Kent Regent V, PFN 874, which is rallied across Kent each year.

So while this work celebrates East Kent's centenary by recounting the history of the company over that time, it also reflects the author's experiences and personal recollections, with a focus on the pre-nationalization East Kent and particularly the post-war years. The more recent past is not forgotten though, and the success of the local Stagecoach management in developing an efficient network, meeting today's needs and at frequencies we could only have dreamed of in the 1960s and 1970s, is also recorded here. Finally, we should not forget the many groups and individuals who keep the memory of the traditional East Kent alive, particularly those who have preserved former East Kent vehicles, allowing the distinctive red and cream livery to be a regular sight still throughout the county. Welcome aboard!

Richard Wallace MA FCILT
Kenilworth, Warwickshire

Hythe Light Railway Station, where the author first became acquainted with East Kent, is the location of AJG 26, one of the last of the Leyland TD5s from 1939 remaining in service until the early 1950s. The smartly uniformed driver is of note. MDEK CLUB – C. HILLMER

PART I

THE FIRST THIRTY YEARS

CHAPTER ONE

COMPANY ORIGINS

FORMATION OF EAST KENT ROAD CAR COMPANY

Although the formal inception of East Kent as a registered company operating bus services was in August 1916, its origins go back further – to when a young entrepreneur, Mr Sidney Garcke CBE, stayed with friends in Kingsdown, near Deal, in 1906. While he was one of the few in possession of a primitive motor car, his attention was drawn to the fact that the majority of residents had to either cycle or walk to access the town of Deal; the only other option was a horse brake (small carriage), which ran three or four times a day. Although the railway was already established, the closest station of Walmer was some miles distant and there was no direct connection to Canterbury apart from a circuitous route via either Minster or Dover.

As fate had it, Garcke was already engaged in transport services, working for the Birmingham and Midland Motor Omnibus Company (BMMO), which was experimenting with early forms of petrol-driven buses as an alternative to the extensive, but limited in terms of range, tramway services in the Birmingham area. These Brush-built vehicles with Peter Brotherhood engines could not cope with the strenuous conditions of urban operation in Birmingham so a decision was taken to withdraw them. Garcke saw an opportunity for operation in the easier conditions of Deal, although whether he had considered their ability to cope with the hilly conditions surrounding the area

is not recorded. He gained approval to use six of the cars on experimental services around Deal and they were re-equipped with new bodies – five as single-deck buses with bodies by Birch of London and the remaining one with a double-deck body by Brush of Loughborough, recorded as an 'Olympia Show body'.

After earlier resistance by Deal town council to the issue of a licence, approval was gained, finally, for Deal & District Motor Services to commence operation and the vehicles were transferred from London to Deal, one driven by Garcke himself, although the time taken was excessive and arrival after dark resulted in a well-recorded prosecution for driving without lights. In April 1908 the services started, one between Kingsdown and Deal and the other, worked by the double-deck car, from Walmer to Deal. These are generally recognized as being the first regular, timetabled bus services in the United Kingdom.

Expansion followed and soon another service was run between Deal and St Margaret's Bay, albeit only twice a day. Each route took one car, according to Garcke's recollections in the East Kent Silver Jubilee brochure of 1941, with the other three needed as spares owing to poor reliability. Despite this, the venture was successful and by 1909 three more vehicles of Leyland manufacture were acquired, allowing the St Margaret's service to extend to Dover and a new service to Sandwich –and later Canterbury – to be introduced. At first Deal & District was a subsidiary of the midlands-based BMMO operation, provider

The first Deal & District cars were mostly Brush single-decker but one, O 1283 pictured here, carried a double-decker body. Behind can just be distinguished one of the single-deck cars. EAST KENT OMNIBUS

of the vehicles, but in 1910 the Deal undertaking passed to the British Automobile Development Company, which then became the British Automobile Traction Company (BAT) in 1912, which itself was part of the larger British Electric Traction Company (BET), which had tramway interests as well.

Meanwhile, in other areas of east Kent, omnibus and local coach services of various degrees were developing, some of which had commenced well before Garcke's enterprise, although perhaps not to the regularity introduced by the Deal concern. Records exist of services as early as 1899, while London & South Coast, Folkestone (later taken over by W.P. Allen) was reportedly operating by 1905. Wacher and Company, a coal merchant of Herne Bay, had taken over some early services there that may have been operated as early as 1905 or before; services in Margate were started by Walter French, whose company was eventually titled Margate, Canterbury and District Motor Services Ltd.

French also had an interest in the neighbouring Maidstone and District (M&D) concern operating in west Kent; the well-renowned Thomas Tilling had established services in the Folkestone area by 1914, while back in Thanet George Griggs set up Ramsgate and District Motor Coaches Ltd.

Thus the scene was set for what eventually became 'East Kent'. The advent of war in 1914 – with vehicles requisitioned, the consequent ban on supplies, the prospect of future competition and with three of the companies having a degree of common ownership in one way or another – led to negotiations to amalgamate the five concerns. Negotiations were complex and challenging but a successful conclusion was reached in 1916. The East Kent Road Car Co. Ltd was formally registered on 11 August 1916 with operations commencing on 1 September.

The constituent companies at the time of the formation of East Kent and their respective services (numbers based on East Kent numbering in 1937) were as shown in Table 1.

One of the reasons for lack of expansion in the populous areas of Thanet and Dover was the existence of tramways in those areas, which already served the densest traffic corridors of Ramsgate to Margate/Westbrook via Broadstairs at the former, and Harbour to River and Maxton at the latter. The Isle of Thanet Electric Supply Company (IoTES) also ended up operating a fairly extensive network of bus services in the local area before their takeover.

The war years were characterized by many demands on the emergent company; conductresses were employed to fill the gap created by many male employees either volunteering or being called up to fight, while the limitations on the availability of fuel saw some vehicles equipped with gas-filled bags on their roofs as an alternative means of engine propulsion. One oft-reported anecdote records that on one windy day, two cars operating the Dover–Folkestone route near Capel had their bags blown off and out to sea, never to be seen again! It is reported that in May 1918, 7,915 miles (12,997km) were operated by gas-equipped vehicles; this was probably less than 6 per cent of the normal monthly mileage but gave a saving of 1,584 gallons (7,201 litres) of petrol.

In terms of governance, Garcke became chairman, a role he was to undertake until 1946, remaining a director until his death in 1948, whilst the other directors joining him at the start were Messrs French, Grant, Griggs, Howley, Wacher, Wolsey and Wolsey Jnr, many names already recognizable from their interests in the aforementioned constituent companies. Alfred Baynton (awarded the OBE in 1945) became the company's first secretary and was to have a long association with East Kent, becoming joint general manager in 1926 and sole general manager from 1942 until

Table 1   East Kent Constituent Companies

Company	Routes	'East Kent' Service No. (1937 scheme)
Deal & District	Deal and Walmer/Kingsdown	79
	Deal and Folkestone via Dover and St Margaret's Bay	80, 90
	Deal and Eastry via Finglesham	13A
	Deal and Canterbury via Sandwich	13
	Dover and Canterbury	15
	Canterbury, Ashford and Hythe	1, 10
Ramsgate & District	Margate, Ramsgate and Canterbury	9, 52
Margate, Canterbury & District	Margate and Ramsgate	52
	Margate, Canterbury and Faversham	3, 8
Wacher & Co.	Herne Bay and Canterbury	6
	Whitstable and Canterbury	4
Tilling (Folkestone District)	Folkestone, Sandgate and Hythe	103
	Folkestone and Cheriton	106

retirement in 1948. In 1966 the company's Jubilee brochure records him as still attending company social functions at the ripe old age of eighty-four! While the first chief engineer was a Mr T. Clabburn, the key influence in engineering matters throughout these inaugural years was his successor, Major C. Murfitt OBE, who took over in 1919 and continued in the post until his resignation in 1942. In the intervening period he became joint general manager (with Alfred Baynton) in 1926. His positive direction in achieving a high degree of standardization on Leyland and Dennis chassis and the modern fleet that ensued should not be underestimated.

After one year, East Kent was recorded as having seventeen routes in operation, which, allowing for overlaps on some of those listed above, shows that the constraints of wartime had provided little opportunity for further development at this stage. The focus was on establishing the new company on a firm basis; one of the first actions was to set up their head office from 1917–18 in a property already owned and used as a depot by BAT in Station Road West, Canterbury, thus establishing East Kent at a location that became synonymous with their operations for more than sixty years. Nearby, a Central Works was established in Kirby's Lane from 1920, taking over the functions previously located at Deal (No. 2 shed) between 1918 and 1920. Prior to this, work was often farmed out to Tilling-Stevens at Maidstone and other concerns in London. The Central Works also carried out body work, transferred from Deal, before the coachworks as well as a new depot were established at St Stephen's in 1925–6.

EAST KENT'S LEGACY FLEET

The company inherited a mixed set of vehicles, as was to be expected. A total of seventy-two (excluding one not operated) came into stock. From Deal & District the Company acquired a varied set, totalling seventeen, of Daimler, Leyland, Burford, Straker-Squire and Brush chassis; the three Margate, Ramsgate and Wacher concerns likewise provided a mix of Sunbeam, Lacre, Daimler, Commer, Straker-Squire, Ensign, Karrier, Maltby and Albion chassis totalling twenty-seven whilst Folkestone District brought some degree of continuity with twenty-seven Tilling-Stevens TS3 petrol electrics plus a 24hp Tilling-Stevens. One of the Deal acquisitions, O 1284, had its origins with Garcke's original enterprise. Information published in the company's staff magazine, the *East Kent Omnibus*, in 1948, suggests a Thames chassis was also acquired but there is no evidence of this marque being acquired in the Maidstone & District and East Kent Bus Club's (hereafter recorded as MDEK Club) *Fleet History* of 1978. All were single-decks with a mixture of bus, charabanc and coach bodies from various builders; again continuity came from the Folkestone concern, with most bodies built by Tilling.

Table 2 East Kent Vehicles at Inception (1916)

Type	Chassis	Body	Registrations	Total	Date/Notes
Single-deck charabanc	Tilling-Stevens	Tilling 32-seat	LC 4197	1	1916 *Ex-Folkestone District*
	Leyland/Burford	?	FK 340/KT 6014	2	1912/15 *Ex-Deal & District*
	Lacre/Commer/Karrier	? 26- or 27-seat	D 8251/D 9578/ KT 6930/7090/629	5	1912/13/15/16 *Ex-Wacher Herne Bay*
	Straker-Squire/Albion	? 27- or 28-seat	KT 7779/LF 316/ 9976/82/90	5	1912/16 *Ex-Ramsgate Motor Coaches*
	Sunbeam/Lacre	?10- or 27-seat	BB 247/D 9412	2	19?/13 *Ex-Margate, Canterbury & Dist.*
	Daimler	?	KT 8752	1	1916/New
	Tilling-Stevens	?	LP 9300/694/LR 8008	3	1916/New
Single-deck coach	Lacre/Commer/Ensign	? 26- to 32-seat	FM 535/KT 3849/ 6149/352/458/ LN 9993	6	1911/14/15 *Ex-Margate, Canterbury & Dist.*
Single-deck bus	Brush	Brush	O 1284	1	1906 *Ex-Deal & District*
	Leyland/ Straker-Squire	?	D 8827/KT 1557/ KT 8013/117	4	1913/14/16 *Ex-Deal & District*
	Daimler/ Straker-Squire	? 28- to 31-seat	KT 384/2503/4487/ 6857/7228	5	1913/15 *Ex-Margate, Canterbury & Dist.*
	Commer/ Daimler	28-seat	KT 2152/6802	2	1914/15 *Ex-Wacher, Herne Bay*
	Tilling-Stevens TS3	Tilling 32-seat	LH 88xx/LH 9xxx/ LP 8249-51	26	1914 *Ex-Folkestone District*
	Straker-Squire/ Maltby/Daimler	?	KT 8166/8833/ 8934/8995	4	1916/New
Single deck, type unknown	Brush	?	O 1287/9/90	3	1906 *Ex-Deal & District*
	Commer	?	FH 903	1	? *Ex-Wacher, Herne Bay*
	Daimler/Burford	?	AC 29/30/36/ KT 7086/LH 8863/ M7741/2	7	1913/15 *Ex-Deal & District*
	Ensign	?	KT 6148	1	1915/chassis only *Ex-Margate, Canterbury & Dist.*
	Tilling-Stevens TS3	?	LC 5092	1	1916 (lorry body) *Ex-Folkestone District*

Source: MDEK Bus Club

Note: One ex-Wacher Daimler charabanc, KT 2153, was not operated and not recorded here although briefly taken into stock.

The Club's records also list a mix of eight new vehicles arriving in 1916 after the take-over, variously coming from Daimler, Straker-Squire, Maltby and Tilling-Stevens. These vehicles are believed to be the fulfilment of earlier orders from the acquired companies and again were all single-deck. A number of vehicles owned by the acquired companies were probably not taken into stock or not fit for service even if they were. Reports, again from the *Omnibus*, suggest that in the second full month of operation, October 1916, a maximum of thirty-six vehicles were in service with a total mileage for the month of 86,626 (142,243km).

VEHICLE LIVERY

The livery carried by the company's vehicles was a deep burgundy red, of various shades over the years but specially produced for East Kent, coupled with cream relief. The application changed over time but at the start, for single-decks (the whole fleet at this time) red covered the lower panels with cream above, being supplemented by black mudguards and lining out – yellow for coaches and black for buses. The lining was phased out from the mid-30s and the black mudguards reverted to red from 1948. To distinguish between coaches and buses, from around the mid-1930s the company introduced a predominantly red livery for the former with, depending on body design, a cream band below the windows and a cream flash above. Some vehicles had mulberry-red window surrounds, and later deliveries, probably from the Leyland TS8 coaches of 1937, introduced two shades of red applied to lower and upper panels respectively.

The company was quite forward-thinking in terms of paint application. Post-war anecdotes in the *Omnibus* record that East Kent had adopted a new synthetic paint process in 1921, at that time in its infancy. It is also recorded that prior to 1919 the company did not carry out its own painting; certainly an outside paint shop was recorded in use at Ringwould. The function was finally brought in-house, with

both paint and body work being carried out at Deal until around 1920. In this period the company employed only seven personnel in the body repair shop. These comprised three body makers, two panel beaters, one blacksmith and one trimmer. Once a premises at Dane Road, Margate was acquired with the Sayer's business in 1919, the paint and

One of the original acquisitions, AC 36 a Daimler of 1915 ex- Deal & District with a later East Kent charabanc body at Deal Pier with her crew, before South Street was brought into use for services. Note the conductor's Bell Punch machine. The 'ring numbers' either side of the dash were to do with licensing; the two different numbers were needed due to services crossing two local authority areas. MDEK CLUB – JESS WILSON

An unidentified car, probably one of the Daimlers with Birch bodies, stands at St Peter's Place, as evidenced by work on the new bus station, which opened in 1922. RICHARD ROSA COLLECTION

trimming shop was located there from 1920. At the time cars received twelve coats of paint and took three weeks to complete. By 1939, following the move to new premises at St. Stephen's, Canterbury, which took place in 1925/6, a more efficient process had reduced this to four coats, which took only five days to complete, resulting in an annual output of 388 cars. 'Cars' was always the term used by East Kent for its vehicles, deriving from the 'Road Car' element of their title and is used in this book where appropriate.

RENEWAL OF THE ORIGINAL FLEET

Upon cessation of hostilities, the company was at last able to purchase new vehicles; in 1919 thirty single-deckers arrived, comprising fourteen TS3s, twelve AEC/Daimler YCs, two Daimler Ys and two Thornycrofts. As far as is known, most were buses of 26- or 29-seat capacity, the most numerous being the Hora 26-seat bodies on the AECs with the rest being a mix of bodies by Tilling, Palmer and Birch.

The following year set the scene for the vehicle composition of the fleet in the 1920s with the arrival of thirty-nine Daimler Ys and one Daimler CD with Short, Palmer or Birch 29- or 30-seat bus bodies, although three Palmer 28-seat charabanc bodies were included in the order. Two TS3s also arrived, but one was the completion of the earlier 1919 order and the other is thought to be a re-registration of an earlier chassis already in stock. This demonstrated that

the focus was on expanding bus services rather than the excursion business, although there was nothing to prevent buses being used on excursions, as well as the vehicles originally acquired, and many actually would have been used as such in the summer season.

Most of the initial acquisitions were disposed of by the early twenties, the AECs only lasting until 1921; and only a number of the ex-Folkestone TS3s and a few other isolated vehicles survived to the early thirties. At this stage East Kent was embarking on a process of re-bodying or body transfer and a number of existing chassis had bodies either transferred from other chassis or were equipped with new bodies, a number built by East Kent themselves. The bodybuilding activity of the company commenced in 1922 and continued until 1934, mostly concerning their own vehicles although some were built for other concerns. They were all single-deck buses and coaches, mostly low-capacity vehicles of fourteen or twenty seats on Morris and later Dennis Ace chassis, although some 32-seat charabancs on Daimler chassis were manufactured in the earlier years.

In this period the company also took on major engineering modifications, rebuilding a number of War Department Daimler chassis to normal-control pattern and one, uniquely, to a three-axle design. The other aspect of vehicle intake was the use, again of War Department chassis, of lorry-type vehicles, placing seats on them and earning them the epithet 'lorribuses'. By 1927, the year when double-deck vehicles were first directly purchased, the fleet was largely of Tilling-Stevens or Daimler manufacture with the exception of vehicles acquired from absorbed

FN 4334 was a Daimler Y of 1920. The basic nature of chassis construction with solid tyres is evident, although the multi-doored charabanc body looks in pristine condition. MDEK CLUB COLLECTION

operators, although from 1925 an increasing number of low-capacity 14-seat Morrises had been taken into stock complemented by some Gilford 20-seaters from Aldershot & District in 1930, as operations began to be extended out to more rural areas; some of these were used for new 'one-man' services in towns as well.

The company generally favoured local bodybuilders such as Shorts of Rochester or Beadles of Dartford, although a fair number of Brush bodies were purchased in this period as well. They were a mix of bus, coach and charabanc bodies with capacity generally between twenty-nine and thirty-eight seats, mostly with rear entrances except for the 14-seat Morrises, which had front-entrance bodies to facilitate driver-only operation, and the charabancs. With the exception of two Thornycroft open-tops acquired with the Sayer's business in 1919, double-deck buses had not been taken into the formal operational stock up to this time; the only other one used had been that operated by the Deal & District Company at the start and this was not among the vehicles acquired by East Kent in 1916.

The Sayer's buses were soon disposed of, within a year, and probably remained in the Margate area during this time. There is photographic evidence of other companies in the area using double-deckers, for example on the Canterbury–Herne Bay route, but it is not thought that any of these were acquired by East Kent. However, in 1927 the company purchased three ex-London General open-top 46-seat bodies, which were, by then, fitted to Daimler Y chassis; the bodies were possibly from 'B' type vehicles but, if so, much-modified. They were purchased as an experiment to assess the viability of introducing double-deckers

FN 5006 was a Daimler, also from 1920, but with a bus body – pictured here on a Margate local service. It has pneumatic tyres, a later addition.
MDEK CLUB COLLECTION

to some routes; photographic evidence shows one employed on a Margate local service. As the rival IoTES concern also purchased open-toppers in 1928 and the Sayer's business had operated the type much earlier, it may indicate that the authorities there were more kindly disposed to the use of this type of vehicle.

All of East Kent's experimental batch were withdrawn by 1933, by which time nearly fifty new conventional double-deckers had entered service. The initial ten purchases also had open-top bodies but thereafter covered-top lowbridge buses comprised the normal intake.

The Sayer's and Isle of Thanet Motors (as distinct from IoTES) businesses were taken over in 1919 and 1925 respectively. These two scenes taken at Birchington Square, presumably prior to 1919, show Sayer's KN 2873, a Thornycroft new in 1919 which probably accounts for its being retained by East Kent, one of the first double-deckers operated. On the right, Isle of Thanet's D 9480 is a Straker-Squire charabanc of 1913, which was not operated. Note the competing horse-carriage, soon to be supplanted, while behind D 9480 is another competitor, one of the IoTES buses. RICHARD ROSA COLLECTION

CHAPTER TWO

TRAFFIC AND OPERATIONS – POST-FIRST WORLD WAR CONSOLIDATION

INITIAL OPERATIONS – COMPETITION AND NEW OPPORTUNITIES

After the First World War, the operations of the company were based around what were called stage carriage services (that is, bus services), a term dating from a legislative Act of 1832, and, of course, a good degree of private hire or local tours and excursions. Soon after the war, however, an additional business opportunity had emerged from an unexpected quarter. A rail strike in September 1919 saw large numbers of people stranded in the Kent coast resorts and East Kent stepped into the breach by providing special coaches to transport people to and from the coast. Having experimented with the concept by default, the company set about exploring options for limited-stop 'express' services to and from London and these commenced in 1921, albeit on a summer-only basis at first.

Competition was rife in these early years, an issue foreseen when the initial five companies were merged into the East Kent operation in 1916. However, these competitors did not have the combined resources and sustainability that the ever-growing East Kent had. Competing operations were generally based around individual services or coach

One operator acquired in 1927 was Wills of Folkestone. Car D 3913 was a Maltby charabanc from 1908, although it did not pass to East Kent, having probably already been withdrawn.

RICHARD ROSA COLLECTION

This early promotional tours leaflet dates from 1922 and shows a charabanc, probably a Daimler with Palmer body dating from 1921, in front of Kingsgate Castle. AUTHOR'S COLLECTION

tramway companies operating in Dover and Thanet, the latter with what eventually became an extensive network of local bus services. The other more substantial concerns, some of which were running both bus and coach businesses, included W.P. Allen and Silver Queen, based in both the Isle of Thanet and in Folkestone (acquired 1925 and 1926); Will's – 'Pullman Coaches' – of Cheriton (acquired 1927); Cambrian of London, who also ran a precursor of East Kent and Maidstone & District's service 10 but from Maidstone as far as Dover and perhaps Deal (acquired 1929 jointly with M&D); London & South Coast (acquired 1933); the Redbourn concern, based in the Isle of Thanet; and Auto Pilots, Folkestone (the last two both acquired 1935). The dates of acquisition shown here are either when vehicles were transferred into the East Kent fleet, or when long-standing arrangements were formalized – for example East Kent had had a long-term interest in London & South Coast many years before the final takeover.

Such interests stretched to inter-availability of tickets. The East Kent timetable of summer 1928 for the Folkestone services to Dover, Hythe and Shorncliffe Camp noted that tickets issued by East Kent, Silver Queen, Pullman and London & South Coast would be accepted on cars of any company. The earlier, April 1928, timetable only mentions inter-availability with Silver Queen – prior to London & South Coast's closer integration with the former – and only applied to the Dover and Hythe services.

Interestingly, vehicles of both the Silver Queen and Pullman concerns had been formally absorbed into East Kent some years beforehand, suggesting that the former brand-

tours, running one or two vehicles acquired from war disposals and based around the peak of summer operations. Many could not survive and made approaches to East Kent during this period, resulting in their acquisition. This certainly helped East Kent, as it could not work sensibly in a situation such as that recorded on the Dover–Folkestone route at one time, when there were eighteen departures by a multitude of operators in a period of 20 minutes.

There were some notable exceptions to the small operators in competition with East Kent – particularly the two

FN 5547 was a Tilling-Stevens TS3 from 1923 with Tilling bus body, although these could easily double up as private hires, as evidenced by this photograph, which appears to be on a bowls club outing at Folkestone Cheriton Road. Now equipped with pneumatic tyres, it also has the original style of fleet name, featuring a dot between the words. MDEK CLUB

ing of these two concerns was still being carried on some cars. Certainly Silver Queen branding existed on a number that were absorbed into the London & South Coast operation in 1928, a move which also accounts for the latter's subsequent inclusion in the list of companies whose tickets were accepted on the routes listed. MDEK Club publications show that all of the cars of the Silver Queen operation at Folkestone were withdrawn by 1927, and from this one may deduce that the reference was to Silver Queen cars operated by London & South Coast rather than by East Kent.

THE EAST KENT NETWORK DEVELOPS

From the limited set of inaugural services, and despite the trials of wartime years, by 1926 a proper network across eastern Kent had been established, assisted by the large influx of new vehicles earlier, although penetration to the more isolated villages off the main arteries between major towns had yet to occur.

By early 1926 a number of purpose-built depots had become established to service these operations, perhaps the most notable being the original Deal & District base in Albert Road, Deal, which started up in 1908 and survived to the very end of the twentieth century. Other major depots of the time were based at Canterbury (St. Stephen's Road), Dover (Russell Street), Folkestone (Kent Road), and Herne Bay (High Street); two of these, Folkestone and Herne Bay, dating from 1916 survived in 2015, although Herne Bay will be replaced by new premises in 2016. Dover

FN 6988 was one of the early Morris 14-seaters with East Kent body dating from 1925. The comprehensive destination boards for one of the newer, more rural routes are of note. These were carried prior to the use of roller blinds but are not thought to have lasted long. MDEK CLUB

and Canterbury were more recent, dating from 1923 and 1925 respectively. At this stage there were also a number of smaller sites supporting operations, most notably in the Isle of Thanet, Rye and Hastings, as well as minor outstations at country locations such as Ash and Wye. Ashford depot, in Station Road, opened in 1926, allowing expansion of local services in that area, and what was to become the major depot at Ramsgate – Westwood – opened in 1927.

New passenger facilities were also developed: a purpose-built bus station with offices and waiting facilities opened at St. Peter's Place, Canterbury in 1922; a smaller 'bus

Two pre-war views of 'St. Peter's Road Car Station'. The first (left) shows a variety of staff (and uniforms) in attendance. Note the driver's long summer dust coat and the inspector's white hat top. On the original photo a 'Dames' sign is just discernible on the Ladies – evidence of East Kent's focus on the French excursion market even at this early stage. The other view (right), taken from the Westgate Towers, shows a Tilling-Stevens single-deck following one of the first covered-top TS1s. The large sign reads 'ROAD CAR STATION FOR HERNE BAY, MARGATE, DEAL, FOLKESTONE AND ALL PARTS OF EAST KENT'. OMNIBUS SOCIETY – CHARLES KLAPPER

station', with just a shelter, was developed at Dymchurch in the same year; while the new Ashford depot featured an off-street bus stand and passenger shelter.

No service numbers were carried on the vehicle or identified in timetables at this stage; this would have to await further expansion and the acquisition of the Dover and Thanet tramway systems in early 1937, by which time the size of the network made a numbering scheme impera-tive. Some service numbers may have been carried in the early years and were certainly identified in early time-tables and on some Bell Punch tickets, but in the late-1920s the only services identified numerically were the limited set of town services operating in Ashford, Deal and Can-terbury, and for these the numbers used were duplicated across the three towns. Despite this, there is evidence of a numbering system being used internally within the

Table 3   Services in April 1926

1937 number	Route	Via
1 & 112	Canterbury–Rye	Ashford/Appledore
3	Canterbury–Faversham	Boughton
4	Whitstable–Canterbury	Blean
6	Herne Bay–Canterbury	Herne
7	Herne Bay–Canterbury	Broomfield
8	Margate–Canterbury	St Nicholas/Sarre
9	Ramsgate–Canterbury	Manston/Minster/Sarre
10	Folkestone–Ashford	Hythe
13/A	Deal–Canterbury	Sandwich
'' (part)	Deal–Sandwich	Walmer/Up. Deal/Eastry
15	Dover–Canterbury	Lydden/Bridge
16	Folkestone–Canterbury	Selsted/Denton
17	Folkestone–Canterbury	Elham
19	Hythe–Canterbury	Stone Street
35	Whitstable–Margate	Herne Bay and Upstreet
37	Faversham–Herne Bay	Whitstable/Graveney
42	Herne Bay Station–Hillborough	Betinge PO
43	Herne Bay–Westcliff	
50 (part)	Margate–Birchington Sq.	
51	Margate–Westgate	
52	Ramsgate–Margate	Westwood
53	Ramsgate–Margate	Broadstairs/St Peters
60	Margate–Deal	Sandwich
62	Margate–Hastings (Service suspended)	Folkestone
67 (part)	Canterbury–Charing	Chilham
79	Deal–Kingsdown Links	Walmer
80/90	Deal–Folkestone	Dover
87	Dover–Ramsgate	Eastry/Sandwich
88	Dover–Eythorne	Waldershare Park
99	Folkestone–Shorncliffe Camp	Cheriton
101	Folkestone–Newington	Cheriton
103/A	Folkestone, Wood Ave. or Junction–Hythe	Sandgate
104/105	Folkestone–Lydd	Dymchurch
112	Rye–Ashford	Wittersham/Appledore
113	Hastings–Rye	Winchelsea
119 (part)	Ashford–New Romney/Dymchurch (Service suspended)	

This early letter is interesting because of the list of company premises in the header. Whilst dated 1929, it is obviously of earlier stock, as the Ramsgate garage address is the earlier premises at Hereson Road acquired with the Isle of Thanet Motors concern in 1925, while Westwood was opened in 1927. The pencilled numbers are file references. AUTHOR'S COLLECTION

company before the 1937 scheme was introduced; the May 1933 edition of East Kent's *Fare Schedules and Instructions to Drivers & Conductors* has numbers allocated to each service, probably to assist the new licensing regime, although, apart from some limited examples (such as Service 1), there was little continuity with the scheme introduced later.

In tables 1 and 3 (beforehand) detailing services in 1916 and 1926, reference is made to the inaugural 1937 scheme, which, whilst it underwent some changes over time, was broadly recognizable up to the time National Bus Company (NBC) policy changes from 1971 onwards promoted considerable restructuring of services and their numbers, particularly for town services. *See* Appendix for a summary of the 1937 numbering scheme. Even today, after numerous changes of ownership, many of the 1937 route numbers remain or have been reinstated on their old corridors with necessary revisions to accommodate services to new developments.

At this time services did not start particularly early, generally between 8 and 9am, and finished around 9pm.

Exceptions to this were the small number of town services, particularly in Folkestone and Margate, where services started around 7am and operated until after 10pm, those in Folkestone probably stimulated by demand from the army garrisons in the area. On Sundays the normal first weekday start-up journeys did not run but afterwards services were little different from those operating in the week. Again, apart from the more intensive town services operating in Folkestone and Margate and the trunk routes such as between Canterbury and Herne Bay, Dover and Folkestone and Ashford and Folkestone, frequencies were irregular. Some routes operated hourly or two-hourly with infill journeys where demand was greater, such as the Dover–St Margaret's Bay section of the Dover–Deal service; others linked more rural locations such as Rye and Ashford or Hythe and Canterbury, running just a few journeys a day, often reflecting local markets.

Timetable booklets of the period carried summary details of some fares: for example, in 1926 the single fare from Deal to Canterbury cost 2/4d (12p), that from Deal to Eastry was 8d (3.5p), with a return at 1/2d (6p) giving a modest discount. Canterbury to Folkestone return was 3/6d (17.5p).

Season tickets had also begun to be issued from around this time, demonstrating that services were now rising to a level where they were attracting regular traffic rather than the leisure market. However, such tickets were only available quarterly or annually and, at first, only between a limited number of points such as Folkestone and Hythe or Canterbury and Herne Bay, where more frequent services

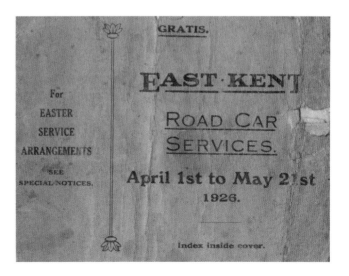

An early company timetable of 1926. At this stage they were issued free but were fairly small owing to the limited number of services then operated. AUTHOR'S COLLECTION

EAST·KENT
ROAD CAR COMPANY LIMITED.

Christmas Service Arrangements
1926.

FRIDAY, DECEMBER 24TH.
All Road Car Services will run as on SATURDAYS.

CHRISTMAS DAY.
All Road Car Services will SUSPENDED, except as follows:

Deal—Canterbury.
Leave Ash for Canterbury 8.15 a.m.
Leave Ash for Deal 8.30 a.m.
Leave Deal for Canterbury 8.40 a.m.,
    10.0 a.m., 11.55 a.m.
Leave Canterbury for Deal 9.45 a.m.,
    11.0 a.m., 12.30 p.m.
Leave Deal for Ash (via Eastry)
    2.0 p.m.
Leave Canterbury for Ash 2.0 p.m.

Canterbury—Faversham.
Leave Canterbury 9.0 a.m., 10.30 a.m.,
    11.15 a.m., 12.20 p.m.
Leave Faversham 9.0 a.m., 10.0 a.m.,
    11.30 a.m., 12.15 p.m.

Herne Bay—Canterbury (via Herne)
Leave Herne Bay 9.30 a.m. 11.35 a.m.,
    1.45 p.m., 3.55 p.m.
Leave Canterbury 10.40 a.m., 12.45
    p.m., 2.35 p.m. 4.45 p.m.

Margate—Canterbury.
Leave Margate 9.0 a.m., 10.30 a.m.,
    11.45 a.m.
Leave Canterbury 10.20 a.m., 12 noon
    2 p.m.

Canterbury—Whitstable.
Leave Canterbury 9.15 a.m., 10.25
    a.m., 12.15 a.m., 1.30 p.m.
Leave Whitstable 9.50 a.m., 11.10
    a.m., 12.50 p.m., 2.10 p.m.

Folkestone—Canterbury (via Elham).
Leave Folkestone 9.30 a.m. and
    11.15 a.m.
Leave Canterbury 11.20 a.m. and
    2.10 p.m.

Canterbury—Ashford.
Leave Canterbury 9.20 a.m. 11.0 a.m.
Leave Ashford 9.0 a.m. 11.0 a.m.

Deal, St. Margaret's Bay—Dover.
Leave Deal 9.20 a.m.
Leave Dover 10.30 a.m.

Dover—Folkestone.
Leave Dover 9.45 a.m., 10.30 a.m.,
    11.10 a.m., 11.55 a.m., 1.0 p.m.,
    1.45 p.m., 2.30 p.m., 3.10 p.m.
Leave Folkestone 9.45 a.m., 10.30
    a.m., 11.10 a.m., 11.55 a.m.,
    1.0 p.m., 1.45 p.m., 2.30 p.m.,
    3.10 p.m.

Rye—Hastings.
Leave Rye 10.15 a.m., 12.45 p.m.
Leave Hastings 11.30 a.m., 2.0 p.m.

Cheriton—Folkestone.
Reduced Service.

Folkestone—Hythe.
Reduced Service.

Dover—Lydden.
Leave Dover 9.45 a.m., 11.40 a.m.
Leave Lydden 10.30 a.m., 12.30 p.m.

SUNDAY, DECEMBER 26TH.
All Road Car Services will run as on SUNDAYS.

MONDAY, DECEMBER 27TH.
All Road Car Services will run as on SATURDAYS, except as under:

Rye—Hastings, **as on Sundays**
Herne Bay—Hillborough, service
    suspended
Herne Bay—Westcliff, service
    suspended
C'bury City Services, **as on Sundays.**
Ashford to Wye (via Brook) **as on
    Sundays**
A.M.
7.5 Folkestone to Ashford.
9.0 Ashford to Folkestone.
8.15 Herne Bay to Canterbury.
9.30 Canterbury to Herne Bay.
7.25, 7.45, 7.55, 8.40, 8.55, Canterbury
    to Whitstable.
7.20, 8.0, 8.20, 8.30, 9.25, Whitstable
    to Canterbury.

A.M.
8.0 Dover to St. Margaret's Bay.
8.35 St. Margaret's Bay to Dover.
8.5 and 8.55 Dover to Lydden.
8.30 and 9.20 Lydden to Dover.
7.55 and 9.10 Margate to Birchington.
8.35 and 9.40 Birchington to Margate.
7.45, 8.15, 8.40, 9.0, Margate to
    Westgate.
8.5, 8.25, 9.0, 9.20, Westgate to
    Margate.
8.40 and 9.20 Deal to Kingsdown.
9.0 and 9.40 Kingsdown to Deal.
9.15 Newington to Folkestone.
9.45 Folkestone to Newington.
8.30 Canterbury to Wickhambreaux.
9.0 Wickhambreaux to Canterbury.

Head Office: Station Road West, Canterbury.
6,000—11/12/26.

This early Christmas holiday arrangements leaflet shows that services were already operated on Christmas Day, an ongoing feature of the pre-Second World War years. AUTHOR'S COLLECTION

were operating. Surprisingly, the intensive route between Dover and Folkestone is not listed as having season tickets available, probably because of objections by the Southern Railway – which would be reconciled once inter-available facilities were introduced when the railway later took shares in East Kent.

Unaccompanied parcel facilities were offered at an early stage, while cooperation with the Royal Mail was to come later, in 1929, when post boxes were introduced on some cars. This developed further when the company also began to be engaged in the carrying of mail, the mailbags being secured by post office personnel at the point of loading and released upon arrival at the destination.

One problem facing all operators, and East Kent was no exception, was the complex licensing arrangements in place, which at this time were in the hands of local councils. A service proposal that may have been acceptable to one council would, for example, not be acceptable to another at the end of the proposed route. Another issue was double-deck operation. Many councils were opposed to double-decker buses on various grounds: one was modesty, as top-deck passengers were able to peer into people's bedrooms; another was the fear of such vehicles overturning on steep hills such as that at Sandgate. The unbridled competition, seemingly unrestrained by these local licensing arrangements, was another factor that was flagging up the need for change and better

Prior to the Road Traffic Act of 1930, licensing was in the hands of local authorities, as shown by this Folkestone and Hythe conductor's badge. AUTHOR'S COLLECTION

regulation. Eventually national concerns came to a head and the government of the day set about developing a structured approach to the licensing of services, vehicles and platform staff, which came onto the statute books as the Road Traffic Act (RTA) 1930 and which governed the industry in various incarnations up until the deregulation of the 1980s.

SERVICE EXPANSION IN THE LATE TWENTIES

By summer 1928, just twelve years after the Company's formation, the network had expanded and was approaching a form that remained in place throughout its existence until 1969 and is still recognizable today, although the operations have gone through differing forms of ownership.

In the two intervening years since 1926, East Kent's operations had expanded, incorporating a number of new routes that had begun to serve the more isolated communities off the main roads, while further local town networks had also become established. Local town services were, by now, also operating in Canterbury (four routes commenced earlier in 1927), Whitstable (one route introduced in 1928) and Ashford (three routes, two commencing earlier in 1927, with a further route introduced in summer 1928). The initial town or inter-urban services operating before in

Herne Bay, Deal, Folkestone, Ramsgate and Margate were supplemented by further routes expanding the company's presence in these areas.

Exceptionally, one in Ramsgate, the forerunner of what was to become service 71, was described as jointly worked with IoTES. Other routes, however, such as those from Margate to Ramsgate via both Westwood and St Peter's, are also believed to have featured a measure of joint operation although not described as such in the East Kent timetable. In the country areas new services in addition to those of 1926, listed in Table 3 above, now reached out to many areas and are summarized below (later, 1937 service numbers in brackets).

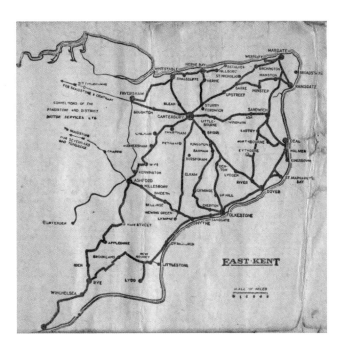

Network developments serving more rural areas in the two years between 1926 and 1928 are shown to good effect by comparing these maps from timetables of the period. AUTHOR'S COLLECTION

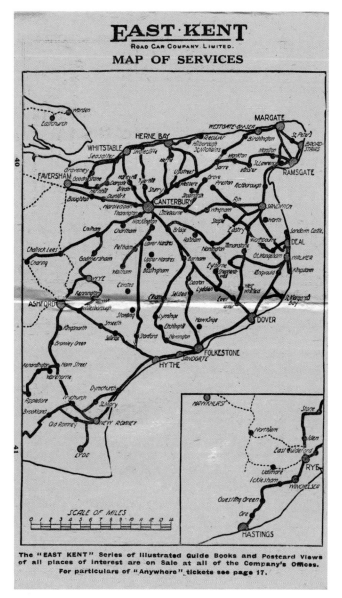

From Canterbury to:

    Hastings via Ashford, Brookland and Rye (2)

    Whitstable via Chestfield (5)

    Grove/Stodmarsh (11 and 12)

    Stelling Minnis (18)

    Hythe, extended to Dymchurch (19)

    Waltham (20)

    Dover via Adisham and Nonington (21 and 89)

From Faversham to Chilham (31)

From Herne Bay to:

    Faversham, now also running via Dargate (38)

    Reculver (39)

From Margate to Dover (61)

From Rye to Dymchurch via Brenzett, Ivychurch and St Mary-in-the-Marsh (62 part)

From Ramsgate/Sandwich to Dover via Nonington (68 and 89); terminus revised to Aylesham (68) by August 1928

From Sandwich to:

    Preston/Westmarsh via Ash (74)

    Sandwich Bay (75)

From Deal to:

    Staple (77)

    Barfreston (78)

From Dover to:

    Eythorne, now extended to Elvington (88)

    Guston/East Langdon (93)

From Folkestone to Aylesham (104 in the 1950s)

From Ashford to Wye via Brook (118)

In addition, the service between Canterbury and Whitstable/Tankerton had some through cars to/from Herne Bay, although these had been suspended by 1929 and the two trunk routes from Folkestone to Ashford and Deal respectively now featured through cars running between Ashford and Deal. Rural services to Preston changed soon after; by 1931 the service between Ash and Preston had been withdrawn. The Canterbury–Grove service was extended to Preston by 1929 and a Canterbury/Wingham–Margate route (later service 59) also now served the village although was only detailed in handbills that year. The Grove/Preston service had later been extended to Minster but was withdrawn from there by 1931. Further expansion in the same area saw a Canterbury/Wingham–Goodnestone service introduced on Saturdays, probably in 1929/30, while the Folkestone–Aylesham service was by then suspended.

    Interestingly, despite the major expansion from 1929 to the early 1930s, which saw rural and outlying locations such as Alkham, West Langdon, West Hougham, Saltwood, Stowting, Camber and Winchelsea Beach now being served by new routes, by 1937 some of the through links existing

The first double-deckers taken into East Kent stock were three Daimler Ys, FN 8092–4, in 1927, with ex-London General 'B' type bodies. They only lasted six years, so views of these cars are quite rare, but one is shown at Margate harbour on the Westgate service. EAST KENT OMNIBUS

in 1928 had ceased; some early on, possibly as a result of the recession at the time. For example, the services from Dover to Canterbury and Dover to Sandwich, both via Nonington, had both been split: the Sandwich service now ran from Ramsgate and diverted to Aylesham, while in the case of the Canterbury service, the link to Nonington had been withdrawn, the replacement service only running as far south as Adisham. The service across the Romney Marsh between Rye and Dymchurch via Brenzett, Ivychurch and St Mary-in-the-Marsh had meanwhile disappeared altogether. Possibly those isolated hamlets on Romney Marsh were abandoned by East Kent at this time to be served by local operators with lower overheads. In the post-war years a number of these services were re-established for a time, and that of the 21 and 89 runs today, albeit via the A2 to Aylesham, avoiding Adisham and operating under the latter number.

    Of particular interest in the 1928 timetables was the notice that 'passengers travelling on the upper deck of an omnibus are cautioned to keep to their seats whilst going under bridges and to beware of overhanging trees'. This notice was already in the April edition although the first new double-deckers on fleet strength actually arrived later that summer, the only others being the experimental 'B' types acquired in 1927, which were not thought to have been widely used. Complicit in the delay in introducing double-deck vehicles were the local authorities, who at this time held sway in terms of licensing vehicles, routes and operating staff and, as noted earlier, often had an inherent objection to double-deckers being used. Canterbury appeared to be one of the most vociferous in its opposition

FN 9096 is one of the original Leyland TS1s from 1928–30 with Short open-top bodies. These were the first large batch of double-deckers to enter service with East Kent. This view at Margate harbour is unusual as it is prior to takeover of the Isle of Thanet concern – here you can see one of their Thornycrofts with Vickers body (No. 27/ KP 418) on IoTES service 2 to Ramsgate (later East Kent 52). FN 9096 has a service number here although no such number was recorded in the timetable for the Westgate service.
OMNIBUS SOCIETY – R.T. WILSON

even though, prior to East Kent's operations, some local concerns had operated such vehicles into the city. All this was to change in 1931, when the role of local authorities in the area of licensing was replaced by a set of regionally based traffic commissioners once the new legislation governing bus and coach operations came into force.

Introduction of Joint Services with Maidstone & District

Despite concerns and impending changes in legislation, a long-discussed linking of two individual routes across Ashford to provide a through Folkestone to Maidstone service jointly worked by East Kent and M&D still had difficulties in gaining approval from the Folkestone authorities, according to Frank Woodworth in his book published to celebrate East Kent's seventy-fifth anniversary. Once M&D had purchased some local undertakings and thus gained the requisite vehicle licences the service commenced in March 1929. A link across Ashford had been in place for some time beforehand, at that time operated by the Cambrian concern that was taken over by East Kent and M&D in November of that year.

The joint service became an instant success, running twice an hour through most of the day until fairly late at night. This success saw a further joint service introduced across Charing, linking East Kent's established Canterbury–Charing service to Maidstone in November 1930. This was never to be the successful venture that the Folkestone service had been, however, and operations in

1931 saw only five journeys each way, one still involving a connection at Charing. By 1936 the service had improved to six journeys each way without any requirement to change buses. Despite this, the service would always be a Cinderella compared to the Folkestone route and it was

One of the Morris Commercial Imperial double-deckers from 1932. Rare vehicles indeed; most, if not all, were based at Folkestone, although Ashford may have operated a couple for a short time. JG 2907 is seen at Folkestone Harbour, on the joint service with M&D to Maidstone. Despite being numbered 10 by M&D, East Kent did not number its routes until 1937, dating this view to before then. MDEK CLUB

gradually reduced over the years, particularly in the 1960s and 70s, until its eventual withdrawal some years later.

Both jointly worked routes used the M&D numbering system already in existence – No. 10 for the Folkestone service and 67 for the Canterbury one. Despite this, East Kent studiously avoided using the numbers in any of their timetables prior to 1937. Bizarrely, the company's fare table of 1933 used the number 67 to identify the Folkestone–Maidstone route. The relationship of the two adjoining

Eleven of the Tilling-Stevens B10C2 buses from 1928 were re-bodied with Park Royal coach bodies in 1933–4. FN 9004 sports her new body and the pre-war coach livery. MDEK CLUB – JESS WILSON

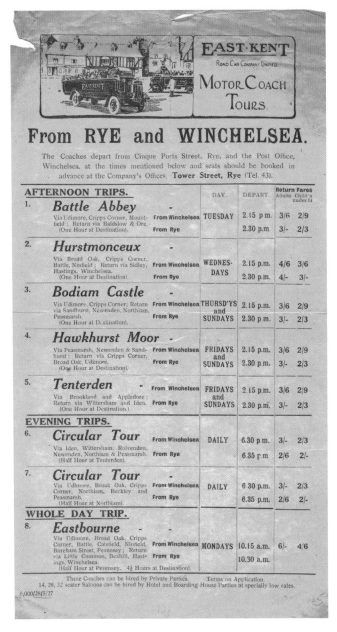

A Rye Tours leaflet of 1927 featuring images of the company's charabancs. AUTHOR'S COLLECTION

BET-owned companies was always close and agreement relating to their two spheres of operation had been reached at an early stage: East Kent's stage carriage operating area kept to the east of the notional line between Faversham, Ashford and Rye, including provision of the local services in the last two towns, where East Kent was the dominant operator, as well as projections from East Kent territory into the M&D area to both Maidstone and Hastings. Take-overs in the Hastings area in 1934 involving both companies saw East Kent venture a little further westward, details of which follow later.

1920s Tours and Express Services

The tours and excursion market had also grown. Not only were local tours offered, but in 1928 longer-distance itineraries to North and South Devon, the Wye Valley and Oxford and the Thames Valley were being promoted. The company was alive to the need to be forward-thinking, and in 1929 the tours programme was again expanded to offer other destinations, such as North Wales. Even in East Kent's westernmost outlying area of Rye, a comprehensive set of local tours was being offered: by 1927 excursions across into the bordering Maidstone and Southdown concerns' area to places such as Battle Abbey, Hawkhurst Moor and Eastbourne were being promoted, as well as more local excursions.

East Kent's location on the Channel coast meant that more innovative excursion options were also available by this stage. Special tickets allowing travel on both bus and steamers were being promoted for journeys to both Southend and Calais, as well as localized steamer and coach trips between Ramsgate and Margate, returning by 'Road Car', a term East Kent had always used and which is retained to this day on the legal lettering of Stagecoach's buses. A year later, in 1929, what was to become a significant business in post-war years, the Northern France day-tour market, was developing further, with day excursions to Boulogne and Dunkerque being offered plus longer, weekend trips across the border to Ostende in Belgium. East Kent's role was in promoting the excursions and then providing feeder cars to the boats; at this time no cars were transferred to the continent, and local French and Belgian carriers would have been used for any excursion operations across the Channel.

In 1928 the London express services were starting to expand. Some were still running summer only, but the network was well established with the following services:

London–Boughton–Canterbury–Margate–Broadstairs–Ramsgate
London–Chilham–Canterbury–Ash–Sandwich–Deal–St Margaret's Bay
London–Whitstable–Herne Bay
London–Ashford–Hythe–Folkestone–Dover–St Margaret's Bay

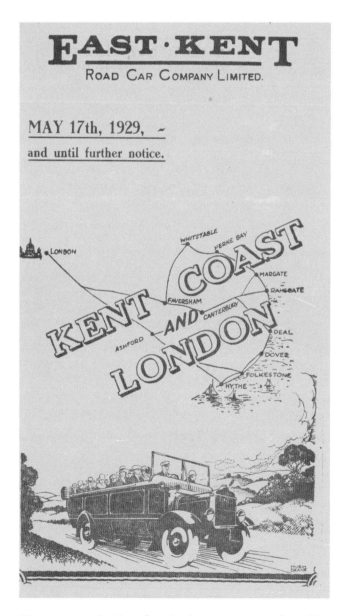

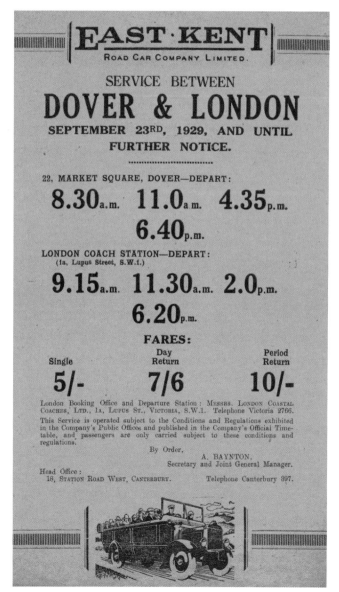

The company issued publicity for its London services in various forms. These views show the all-routes timetable and an individual handbill for the Dover service, both from 1929. AUTHOR'S COLLECTION

Surprisingly, the Ramsgate service remained suspended even into the Easter period but others were shown as operating by Easter, the Deal service apparently provided by an extension of the St Margaret's Bay/Dover service rather than by a separate car running via Canterbury. There was a degree of joint working: the Ramsgate service was operated jointly with Motor Coaches (London) Ltd, also known as MT, while the St Margaret's Bay service was worked with London & South Coast Motors (1915) Ltd, in which East Kent already had an interest. Both companies were to be absorbed into East Kent over the next few years. In the high summer there were generally three or four journeys each way, some of those to Whitstable and Herne Bay involving a change at Canterbury. One notable point is that in a spring 1929 leaflet the four express services were identified alphabetically as follows:

Service A – Margate/Ramsgate
Service B – Herne Bay
Service C – Dover/St Margaret's Bay
Service D – Deal

These identifiers were not set out in the company's main timetables nor were they repeated in handbills issued later in the year; a numbering system for express services would have to await the passing of the Second World War, only being introduced in 1950.

The terminal in London was, at the time, located at Lupus Street near to Victoria prior to the opening of Victoria coach station in 1932. For a period, in 1929, the company's services were extended to Schoolbreds department store near Tottenham Court Road, where passengers were invited to 'use Reading, Writing and Rest Rooms free of charge'. In summer 1928 there was some symmetry in London express fares, those to the outer terminals of all routes being 6/- (30p) single, 10/6d (52.5p) return. However, there appeared to be some idiosyncrasies in the fares policy at the time; the earlier Spring/Easter 1928 timetable, operating from 2 April, shows that single fares were considerably more expensive 6/6d (32.5p) to Herne Bay but the return was lower at 10/- (50p). By May 1929, a leaflet of the time shows that all four services were running and the single fare to the outer terminals had reduced to 5/6d (27.5p) with the return remaining at 10/- (50p), the 1928 off-season level,

with the following high summer fares increasing to the former 1928 high-season levels.

It is probable that the April 1928 single fares were actually misprints, it being more sensible to encourage traffic across the fringes of the main season through a lower fares policy. The company were alive to this as later handbills produced in September 1929 for the Dover service, now running in the winter, show even lower fares. This assumption on pricing is confirmed by a rider in the September 1936 timetable and fare table that states 'Reduced Winter Fares are now in operation'.

Another important development for express service operations, this time in 1929, was the introduction of the South Coast Express service, another joint operation, this time with Southdown Motor Services and M&D. It ran between Margate, Dover, Folkestone and Rye onward to Eastbourne, Brighton, Portsmouth and Bournemouth with other facilities through to Weymouth (though these were not operated by East Kent). By 1931 M&D's involvement had ceased and the service was shown as running only as far as Bournemouth. Further changes in 1932 saw the Bournemouth-based Elliot Brothers' 'Royal Blue' concern operating the service west of Portsmouth and from then on East Kent's literature up to the outbreak of war – and the service's suspension – showed it as a Margate–Portsmouth operation. Elliot's business was later taken over by Western National and the involvement of all three companies continued, with the exception of the wartime cessation between 1939 and 1946, until nationalization in 1969 and, more importantly, the near-total obliteration of individual company identities into the monolithic National Express combine in 1972.

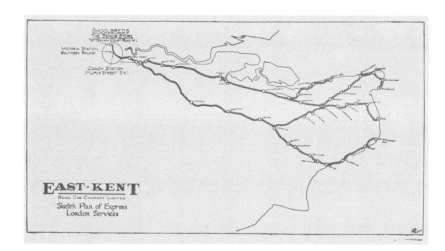

The route map for London services in the 1920s. Note the central London terminals of Lupus Street and also Schoolbreds, a short-lived extension. This would all change once Victoria coach station opened in 1932. AUTHOR'S COLLECTION

CHAPTER THREE

THE 1930s – TOWARDS A VIRTUAL EAST KENT MONOPOLY

FARES AND LOCAL TOURISM PRE-SECOND WORLD WAR

In the early 1930s stage carriage fares were largely unchanged from 1926, although, for example, the single fare from Deal to Canterbury quoted earlier for 1926 had actually reduced to 2/- (10p). From now until the outbreak of the Second World War, fares remained broadly the same, after having been reduced following the end of the First World War. Child fares were also now available, but only in the form of scholars' season tickets or scholars' privilege vouchers, the latter priced at 1/- (5p) per annum and allowing half fare on single or return journeys for bona-fide scholars up to sixteen years of age. Children under three were carried free, this concession limited to one child per adult. Freely available child fares were later introduced, probably after 1931, looking at regulations carried in timetables of the period, but certainly no later than 1933; the rate was generally half of the adult fare with the exception of the lowest fare values. The availability of season tickets had widened to encompass journeys between most main towns.

Recognizing the tourist appeal of the area, the company was now promoting a range of 'Anywhere' tickets available on all East Kent services, excluding London services and the Maidstone service west of Ashford, while 'Tourist' tickets for specific itineraries or round trips were also available. In 1929, the Anywhere tickets were priced at 7/6d (37.5p) per day or 38/- (£1.90) per week in the summer season, with reduced prices in winter. Prior to this, in 1928, there had been some variance in these charges and a mid-season rate was also available. The availability of these promotional tickets was short-lived – they ceased after 1931 and it was nearly forty years before the advent of the Wanderbus ticket in 1970 reinstated such a facility. One conjecture could be that the Southern Railway members on the board may have influenced this decision: circular tourist tickets were a routine feature on train services and East Kent's offer may have

been seen as unwanted competition. Party tickets for group travel were another short-lived promotion, advertised only in 1931; possibly further thought concluded that this could undermine East Kent's private hire market.

While a short summary of important fares was set against various services in the public timetables of the 1920s and early 1930s, for a period of time the full fare table was contained within the public timetable book, certainly for those published in 1936 and 1937. By summer 1938 the timetable had no reference to fares at all apart from in the Conditions. The company now advertised the publication of separate fare table books, however, also available to the public for purchase, price 2d (1p), the same price as the timetable. In the late 1920s the timetables had been priced at 1d (0.5p), and prior to that some had been provided free of charge.

The company published a number of different guides promoting local tourism. Shown here is one of a set of four area guides (left) and a more comprehensive guide (right), dating from the mid-30s, which continued to be produced until the early 1960s. AUTHOR'S COLLECTION

From copies in the author's possession it is known that the fares schedules were carried in a separate booklet for staff, certainly in 1933, when the fare tables and *Instructions to Drivers and Conductors* were combined in one volume, jointly numbered TS1505/6 in the company's internal system. As a separate *Rules and Instructions* booklet for staff was produced from March 1937, now TS 1505, it is likely that the combined timetable and fare table was discontinued shortly after. Thereafter, until public copies of fares schedules ceased to be made available, the company always published timetables and fare tables as separate booklets.

Indicating the comprehensive nature of East Kent's focus on local tourism, the company also produced a set of guide books for the area. Comprising four volumes, they covered Herne Bay and Whitstable; the Isle of Thanet; Deal, Sandwich and Dover; and Folkestone and Hythe. Each comprised a section on Canterbury, recognizing its historical importance and as a hub of the East Kent operating area. Later, after 1935, a complete guide for the company's whole area, including East Sussex, was published and this continued to be produced, with the exception of the wartime and early post-war years, into the early 1960s.

EAST KENT AND THE SOUTHERN RAILWAY

In 1928 the Southern Railway (Road Transport) Bill came before Parliament; once passed, it instigated a degree of cooperation between the railway and East Kent from then on. The aim of the Act was to: 'empower the railway companies to provide road vehicles in any district to which they had access and, by means of those road vehicles, to carry passengers and goods'. At first, it could be thought that this would cause the railway company to compete with or take over bus companies operating in its area, and while this occurred to a degree in some places, the Southern Railway chose to purchase shares in East Kent, which allowed them two seats on the East Kent board. Sidney Garcke, the founder of East Kent, was also instrumental in negotiating the coordination of road and rail services.

To the public this cooperation was visible in a number

Timetable covers of the late 1920s and 1930s. Note the reference to the association with the Southern Railway in the January 1937 edition, interestingly omitted from the special cover for the Coronation of King George VI in 1937. The top right image shows a typical advert of the time carried on back covers. Brewers George Beer & Rigden of Faversham (later taken over by Fremlins/Whitbread) produced 'Kent's Best' and promotion of this ale featured on most timetables until 1949, with the exception of the wartime editions. AUTHOR'S COLLECTION

of ways. Firstly, by 1931, bus timetables started to appear with 'in association with the Southern Railway Company' under the East Kent company logo on the cover. This rider continued, being replaced by the term 'British Railways' from 1948 until 1967, although it had been moved to the inner flyleaf in September 1962.

More importantly, summary details of rail services began to appear in the Company's timetable at this time and adverts were carried for season tickets for both road and rail. In 1932, probably due to the establishment of a Road/Rail Standing Committee dealing with common matters affecting traffic and operations, inter-available tickets were introduced, allowing the holders of return bus or train tickets to return on the alternative mode for a surcharge. At this time the facility was only available between Canterbury and Faversham and Dover, Deal, Sandwich, Walmer and Folkestone (and also London express services), but in later years was expanded to include many other routes. Strangely, for stage carriage services, in this period the return by road required a supplement equal to or more expensive than a return by rail, the reverse of which was the case, more logically, at the end of the scheme in the 1960s/70s which then required no supplements for most returns by road. On London services, it was normally always more expensive to return by rail, as one would expect, given the time advantage.

Another early indicator of cooperation was East Kent's replacement of the train service between Canterbury and Whitstable, the 'Crab and Winkle' line, when it closed to passengers on 1 January 1931. East Kent supplemented its existing service between the two points via Chestfield with further, direct, journeys via South Street, an early example of a rail replacement service. A further rail closure that affected East Kent was that of the Sandgate Branch of the Southern Railway, which actually terminated at Seabrook. The line was cut back to the Hythe station, situated remotely from the town on Cannongate Road, from 1 April 1931. A replacement bus service was apparently operated between Seabrook and Hythe between 1931 and 1933. There is no mention of it in East Kent timetables of the period but a Southern Railway poster announcing the closure clearly states that in connection with the closure, a 'Service of Omnibuses operated by the East Kent Road Car Co. Ltd. will be as shown'. The schedules shown on the poster are clearly extracts from East Kent's existing Hythe–Folkestone, Wood Avenue service, showing that from this time at least, certain journeys operated via Hythe station or Folkestone Central station, in both cases connecting with trains. The full frequent service, running direct between Hythe and Folkestone at 5-minute intervals, was not shown; only those journeys running via either station were portrayed. It should be noted that East Kent's timetable of the period only showed departure points at Hythe Red Lion Square, or Folkestone, Wood Avenue, Junction or Westcliff Gardens; there was no indication of any route variants. The 1933 fare table contains a Central Station fare stage for the route but nothing for Hythe station; the licence for the service to the latter point had already expired in June 1932 and was not renewed. However, it still displayed a stage for Sandgate station despite that fact that the railway had closed the station nearly two years previously. The service operating via Central Station ceased in March 1933 by common consent with the railway.

This Tilling-Stevens dating from 1930, JG 669, with its original bus body is now preserved. Pictured at Seabrook on the seventy-fifth anniversary rally in 1991, it has just passed the site of the overbridge leading to Sandgate station, the vacated land of which became an East Kent garage. Similar vehicles would have operated on the Hythe and Folkestone service (which became the 103) at the time of the Sandgate branch closure. AUTHOR

One further point was that the full bus service was shown in East Kent timetables as a joint operation with London & South Coast from 1930 although the Southern Railway poster makes no mention of this, suggesting that the cars operating via Hythe or Folkestone Central stations were always East Kent workings. From June 1931 the Sandgate station site was occupied by East Kent and a garage built on the land together with extensive open standing for vehicles on the old sidings, used mainly for scrapping until 1952/3 and latterly disposal of withdrawn cars. The garage was used for both bus and coach operations. Services 99 and 103/A were certainly partly resourced from this site; access to the former route was by extensions from the Shorncliffe Camp terminus and to the latter by short workings commencing or terminating at Seabrook Fountain. Bus operations ceased here in the mid-1950s.

VEHICLES IN THE 1920s & 1930s – PNEUMATIC TYRES AND DOUBLE-DECKERS

The MDEK Club's fleet history records that pneumatic-tyred vehicles were taken into stock from 1925 and with this and improvements to the roads, services became more comfortable, more reliable and faster. These changes also saw a large growth in passengers, prompting debate on how to cope with this increase in demand and the corresponding need to increase productivity, bearing in mind the capacity of most buses at this time was well under forty seats and most had a crew of two, driver and conductor. As detailed earlier, experiments with a trio of open-top double-deckers with second-hand London General 'B' type bodies took place from 1927, and the next year four Leyland TS1s, registered FN 9093–6, with open-top double-deck bodies and open-staircase rear entrances, were purchased. This order represented the first new Leyland chassis to be purchased by East Kent and was the start of an association with Leyland that was to last for twenty-five years. This quartet and the subsequent deliveries of another six TS1 chassis in 1929–30, registered FN 9544 and JG 651–5, all had similar open-top bodies, built by Short, with fifty-six seats, a massive increase from the limited capacity of the single-deckers purchased up to that stage. They were equipped with boards for destination screens but some were later modified with roller destinations and, from 1937, either number plates or blinds.

From 1930, probably as a result of forthcoming changes in legislation that would restrict the power of local authorities on such matters, buses with covered-top Leyland low-bridge 51-seat double-deck bodies on Leyland TD1 chassis entered the fleet, their capacity being slightly less than the open-top models. Ten cars, JG 977/8, 1057/8, 1411/2 and 1621–4, entered service between 1930 and 1931. The livery for double-deckers was, as for the single-deck cars, red panels below the windows and cream window surrounds, roof and upper panels with the between-deck panels painted red. In the early years of double-deck operation only Thanet and Dover were allocated the type but as further deliveries were made, notably the bulk order for TD4 chassis arriving from 1936, operation gradually spread to other depots, only Deal and Rye (including Hastings) remaining totally single-deck in 1938 according to MDEK Club records. One

JG 683, one of the 1930 Tilling-Stevens B10C2s with Brush bus body. It is shown at Folkestone's pre-war terminal at the harbour. The route to Dover via Alkham was one of the later additions to the company's network, being introduced on 1 August 1929. Numbered 91 under the 1937 scheme, JG 683 would not have much longer with the company, being requisitioned in 1940. MDEK CLUB – A. PORTER

Some of the Leyland open-top TS1s received roller blinds in place of their former destination boards, as shown by this pre-war view of JG 655 at Ramsgate harbour. This car, like a number of the batch, received Utility single-deck bodies by Burlingham during the war. MDEK CLUB

It was not long before covered-top double-deckers entered service. JG 1057 is a Leyland TD1 from 1930 and survived until 1947. This post-war view shows it still in its wartime livery on Minnis Bay service 46, still carrying a board for the route number introduced when services were numbered in 1937. MDEK CLUB – A.B. CROSS

reason for Deal remaining single-deck was the preponderance of low bridges in the area, even the trunk routes 13/A to Canterbury at this time running under one such bridge. At Rye, service 113, the depot's busiest route, at this time had to negotiate the Strand Gate Arch in Winchelsea, again mandating single-deck operation.

Meanwhile, on the single-deck front, East Kent's allegiance to local manufacturer Tilling-Stevens was maintained with bulk purchases of both buses and coaches, mostly on the improved B10C2 chassis and later the B49C2 up until 1931, which was the last year Tilling-Stevens chassis were purchased new. A further, solitary example was operated in 1933. JG 3705 was a demonstrator with Salerni transmission, but so unreliable it had gone after six weeks. East Kent now began to investigate the use of Leyland for the supply of single-deck chassis with an order for five Hoyal-bodied TS1 coaches to be delivered in 1931. However, these were diverted to Southdown Motor Services, now thought to be as part of the arrangements for the recently introduced South Coast Express service; they returned to East Kent a year later, having acquired Brighton registrations UF 7856–60 as a result.

The company's vehicle-buying policy now entered a period of further change when in 1932–3 they commenced procurement of a number of batches of Morris Commercial Imperials, most with attractive Park Royal lowbridge 55-seat double-deck bodies. In total thirty entered service with East Kent, one being a demonstrator with Short body; the company was the major purchaser of this model, the only other bus operator to show interest being Edinburgh Corporation. East Kent had also purchased some smaller-capacity Morris Commercial Viceroy/RP single-deckers from 1931 to expand services to smaller communities and it is likely that success with these vehicles influenced the decision to experiment with their double-deck chassis. The company did not need further double-deckers until 1936–7 when it then had to cover tramway replacement services following the takeover of Dover Tramways and IoTES, the latter operating both trams and buses. These orders for the Morris double-deckers were the only ones made therefore, and even the low-capacity single-deck market was eventually secured by Dennis in the future.

Fleet Standardization – Titans, Tigers, Aces and Lancets

When a major double-deck order was next required, Leyland dominated with their Titan TD4 chassis. No fewer than seventy TD4s were purchased at this time. The first twenty, JG 7010–29, arrived in 1936 with Brush 'piano-

front' bodies, which featured a new two-piece display; the smaller aperture, used for the service number from 1937, initially showed a single via point, the destination display being single-line at this time. The next fifty bodies, on JG 8201–50, were delivered in 1936–7, all coming from Park Royal with what was to become the conventional East Kent double-deck blind display that had a comprehensive single-piece destination and via point display and a separate number aperture. All were of rear-entrance, 53-seat low-bridge design. The earlier 'piano-front' build were rebuilt to the new standard destination display mostly before the war but one, JG 7016, retained its original style until 1948/9, when it was re-bodied.

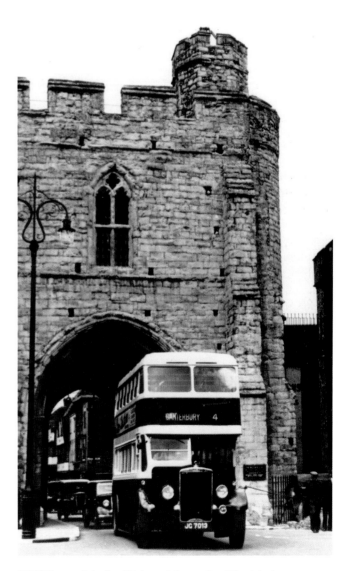

JG 7013, one of the first TD4s, with 'piano-front' Brush body, enters Canterbury through the Westgate Towers on the route from Whitstable in this pre-war view. MDEK CLUB – COMPANY ORIGINAL

Leyland TD4 JG 8241, still carrying its original body, is seen at Deal bus station next to a newly re-bodied TD4, JG 7029, with the Park Royal offering. JG 8241 later received an ex-AJG body, which dates this view to 1949–51. JG 7029 carries an early red roof livery experiment. MDEK CLUB

The Dennis Aces were mandatory for a number of restricted routes, mostly in the more rural areas. However, Ashford's 124 passed under a particularly low railway bridge, which limited the cars used on it. JG 4229, an Ace from 1934, sports an East Kent body, initially to coach specification but downgraded to a bus in 1936. She is seen in Ashford High Street; the early bus stop flag is of note. OMNIBUS SOCIETY – CHARLES KLAPPER

The single-deck market was not immune from change either. The relationship with Morris continued but another vehicle builder, Dennis, was about to capture major orders from East Kent. In 1934 twenty-six of the famous Dennis Ace buses with 20-seat bus bodies built by East Kent or Eastern Counties, another bus operator expanding into bodybuilding, entered service, followed by three the following year delivered with Park Royal 20-seat coach bodies. From now until the advent of the Second World War and a little after, the company's vehicle procurement policy generally specified Leyland chassis for single-deck coaches and double-deck buses, with Dennis the preferred supplier for standard and low-capacity single-deck buses on Lancet and Ace, later Falcon, chassis respectively. Many coach bodies of the pre-war period were equipped with side route boards for express services. These were mounted either above the roof cove on earlier models or flush with the body above the windows, particularly on the TS7/8 coaches.

Body procurement policy also entered a period of relative standardization, with Park Royal the normal combination Leyland while Dennis provided the bodies on their own chassis. Notable exceptions to this were the twenty double-deck Brush bodies on the first Leyland TD4s to enter service in 1936 mentioned above, with a further thirteen Brush-equipped TD5 chassis, JG 9919–31, arriving in 1938, part of an order for twenty-five TD5 double-deckers; the remainder, JG 9907–18, were bodied by Park Royal, who also bodied all of the further order for another forty TD5s, AJG 1–40, arriving in late 1938 and early 1939, the last double-deckers purchased by the company before the outbreak of the Second World War.

One of the handsome Leyland TS7 coaches, JG 5427 from 1935 is captured in the pre-war years on the Dover–London service, probably at Canterbury. MDEK CLUB – JESS WILSON

Similar Park Royal bodies to the TS7s were fitted to the later TS8s from 1937. Three survived as mobile offices; JG 9938 outlasted them all and was preserved for a time in the later coach livery. Seen here at Canterbury St Stephen's garage in December 1977, the road on the left led to the coachworks behind the garage. AUTHOR

On the single-deck front, over 100 Leyland TS7s and TS8s entered service between 1935 and 1938, mostly registered in the JG 54xx, 65xx and 99xx series, with similar Park Royal rear-entrance coach bodies of 32-seat capacity, with one exception. Meanwhile, the Dennis buses of Lancet, and later Lancet 2 specification, numbered seventy in total, delivered between 1936 and 1939, and were mostly bodied by Dennis with 35-seat rear-entrance bodies. These had various registrations, most of the first deliveries coming in the JG 68xx and 87xx series. Park Royal also bodied some Dennis chassis, notably the last three Aces to be purchased, mentioned above, and a handful of Lancet 2 vehicles; one, JG 9906, was an exhibit at the 1937 Commercial Motor Show while the other Park Royal bodies were on five of the batch of nineteen, registered AJG 41–59, delivered in 1939. Although many earlier coaches had roof luggage compartments, the Park Royal-bodied Lancets, AJG 41–5, had full-length wells on the roof for the carriage of band instruments, and a similar facility was incorporated on two re-bodied TS7s in 1941, JG 5431/3. They were then nicknamed 'Bandwagons'.

The early Dennis Lancets of 1936 were distinguished by their broad radiators; in 1949 ten were re-equipped with bodies of 1933–4 from Tilling-Stevens of the 1928 FN 9xxx batch – originally coaches but downgraded to bus specification. JG 6806 is pictured in Ashford garage with blinds for the 124 route. SOUTHDOWN ENTHUSIASTS CLUB – SURFLEET

Despite this large influx of vehicles and the expansion of the fleet, East Kent had not yet adopted a fleet numbering system, relying on identification through allocation, as far as possible, of unique registration numbers, a policy that sometimes saw the odd duplication but managed to survive until 1977. Despite the absence of fleet numbering, from around 1924 the company allocated unique body numbers to each vehicle. This system was probably introduced as a result of the tendency to swap bodies between chassis on a number of vehicles from the early years; this practice diminished somewhat in the late 1930s but saw a brief resurrection in respect of some vehicles in the late 1940s and early 1950s. The numbers were carried in the cab within a small brass holder but were later all plastic. The body numbering also, at one time, caused confusion in staff circles. Correspondence in the *Omnibus* around 1948 debated the rationale of not having a fleet numbering system, some writers alleging that there had been a fleet numbering system in place before the war. Fortunately, when they then went on to list a specific set of numbers, it became clear they were referring to the body numbers.

This publicity photograph of AJG 42, one of the 1939 Dennis Lancet 2s with Park Royal body clearly shows the layout of the 'bandbox' with which some cars were equipped. MDEK CLUB – COMPANY ORIGINAL

East Kent's body numbers were originally carried in the cab on brass plates with inserts. Here are two from BJG 339 (1224) and NFN 348 (1891). AUTHOR'S COLLECTION

All Dennis Lancet 2s were equipped with 'oil' engines from new. AJG 50, one of the 1939 batch with Dennis bus body, is pictured at Faversham on service 31, demonstrating that bigger buses operated this route as well as the smaller Aces and Falcons. This later Dennis body differs from the earlier style in the use of curved end windows, like the contemporary Park Royal product. MDEK CLUB COLLECTION

During this period, technological advances in the engineering field saw a move from petrol-engine vehicles to diesel (oil) engines. The Leyland TS7s delivered in 1935–6 and the first tranche of Dennis Lancets, JG 6800–20, delivered in 1936, were the last new vehicles to be equipped with petrol engines, and these were to be replaced by diesel equivalents relatively soon in some vehicles' lives. The Dennises were converted in 1938/9 although many of the Leylands had to wait until 1950/1 and the withdrawal of double-deck TD4/5s, from which their engines were sourced, before they were upgraded.

Complementing this massive new intake of stock in the late 1930s were the vehicles acquired through takeovers as a result of both East Kent's ever-dominant position and the fallout from the licensing regime of the RTA 1930, which eventually caused many competitors to throw in the towel and cease operations. Interesting acquisitions were the vehicles of Sims (Earlswood) of Westgate in 1935, which included two Dennis double-deckers, the only such cars operated by East Kent, and one, the Dennis Lance PL 3078, lasted until 1937.

The photographer may not have known that this postcard would be unique. In the centre is the only East Kent Dennis Lance double-deck, PL 3078, ex-Sims and probably bound for Westgate. On the right, behind the clock tower, is an ex-IoTES Daimler COG5, while to the left is a new Leyland TD4 on tram-replacement service 49. This all dates the view to 1937. SWEETMAN & SON/MICK WOODLAND COLLECTION

The IoTES concern saw the largest transfer, forty-nine vehicles, to East Kent. However, with the exception of the five relatively modern Daimler COG5 Weymann-bodied double-deckers (which had a comparatively long life with East Kent), the only vehicles operated were a handful of Hoyal-bodied Daimler CF6 single-deck buses, two of the Daimler CF6 open-top double decks and the only other covered-top Daimler double-deckers acquired, two early examples on CH6 chassis. The CF6 vehicles had all gone by the end of the year whilst the CH6s lasted a little longer, until 1938.

The COG5s had more interesting lives especially during the war; one, ADU 470, originally a demonstrator for Daimler, was converted into a tree-lopper in 1951 lasting until 1958. Its pre-selector gearbox, unusual in the East Kent fleet, earned it the sobriquet 'Leaping Lena' (although others called her 'Ada'). In 1948 she achieved a degree of stardom through correspondence in the *Omnibus*. A number of issues saw reference to her and through these one can judge that she was, by then, mostly employed on miners' services from Thanet, normally to Snowdown colliery, requiring significant cleaning to remove all the coal dust after such duties! Further anecdotes detail that, between layovers at Snowdown, she was often commandeered for relief duties at Dover. The writer humorously notes that one return to Dover, where ADU 470 was previously employed as a canteen during the war, was possibly of stress to her due to memories of the blitz! Due to this 'stress' she broke down and had to have repairs carried out, resulting in a Dover driver taking her back to Thanet. He corresponded with a fellow driver at Thanet after the experience:

> I had the pleasure of taking your car ADU 470 back to Westwood Depot last Saturday … Everything passed me on the way including a few bicycles, but I did manage to get by a steam roller. I found she was quite comfortable at 20 mph. Yours …
>
> (East Kent Omnibus, *September 1948*)

So this Daimler would not have won any awards for speed by all accounts; she also appears at one time to have been a regular on service 66 from Ramsgate to Deal, where she had a reputation as a 'boiler', probably unusually, given the level nature of the road.

The other takeovers in the period immediately preceding or following the RTA 1930 that saw significant numbers of vehicles being absorbed have already been described, but to recap, they included Cambrian in 1929; London & South Coast in 1933; and the Redbourn group and Auto Pilots in 1935. London & South Coast had effectively already

'Leaping Lena', ADU 470, the ex-Isle of Thanet Daimler COG5, spent some time as a mobile canteen during wartime; she is pictured here at Dover. Note the blast tape on the right-hand building windows behind the bus. MDEK CLUB – COMPANY ORIGINAL

been under East Kent control for some time, as many of the constituent Silver Queen operations had been absorbed since 1925, although even up to 1932 the Folkestone, Wood Avenue to Hythe, Red Lion Square stage carriage service and the London and St Margaret's Bay express service were still noted in the timetable as 'jointly operated with London & South Coast'.

In most cases these acquired vehicles were quickly disposed of, in a year or so, as new coaches entered the company fleet, although much of the Cambrian stock last-

East Kent's already well-appointed coach fleet was supplemented by five Leyland TS7s with Duple bodies acquired with the MT business in 1937. CYL 244, a 1936 example, is shown in this post-war view, by now on excursion duties. UNKNOWN – AUTHOR'S COLLECTION

Table 4   East Kent Vehicles in 1939 (includes cars withdrawn that year)

Type	Chassis	Body	Registrations	Total	Date/notes
Double-deck open-top	Leyland TS1	Short 56-seat	FN 9093–6/9544; JG 651–5	10	1928–30
Double-deck lowbridge	Leyland TD1	Leyland 51-seat	JG 977/8/1057/8; JG 1411/2/1621-4	10	1930
	Morris Commercial	Short or Park Royal 55-seat	HA 7639; JG 2601/2/4/6–11/4/5/2906–15; JG 3227–30	26	1931–3
	Leyland TD4	Brush or Park Royal 53-seat	JG 7010–29; JG 8201–50	70	1936–7
	Leyland TD5	Brush or Park Royal 53-seat	JG 9907-31; AJG 1–40	65	1938–9
Double-deck highbridge	Daimler COG5	Weymann 56-seat	ADU 470; CKP 876–9	5	1934/6 *Ex Isle of Thanet*
Single-deck coach	Tilling-Stevens B10C2	Short 32-seat	FN 9541–3; FN 9902–5; JG 706–21; FN 9949–50	25	1928–30 *FN 9949–50 B10D2 with 30-seat bodies*
	Tilling-Stevens B10C2	Park Royal 32-seat	FN 9001–11	11	1928 *Bodies 1933/4*
	Tilling-Stevens B10C2/B49C2	Brush 32-seat	JG 696–705; JG 1413–35	33	1930–1 *JG 1431 Park Royal 32-seat of 1934*
	Tilling-Stevens B49C2	Hoyal 32-seat	JG 1436–55	20	1931
	Morris Commercial Viceroy	Harrington 20-seat	JG 1456–71	16	1931
	Leyland TS1	Hoyal 30-seat	UF 7856–60	5	1931
	Morris Commercial Viceroy	Park Royal 20-seat	JG 4251/2	2	1934
	Dennis Ace	East Kent or E Counties 20-seat	JG 4225–50	26	1934; *Body of JG 4241 to BFN 176*
	Leyland TS7	Park Royal 32-seat	JG 5420–48; JG 6501–36; JG 6593–6600	70	1935–6 *JG 5436/9/41 not in stock*
	Dennis Ace	Park Royal 20-seat	JG 5449–51	3	1935
	Leyland TS8	Duple 33-seat	CYL 243–5; DXV 740–1	5	1936/7 *Ex MT Company*
	Leyland TS8	Park Royal 32-seat	JG 8979/9932–66	36	1937–8
Single-deck bus	Tilling-Stevens B10C2	Short or Brush 37-seat	FN 9920/2/42–4/6–8; JG 656-65/7–95	46	1929–30 *JG 668 35-seat JG 689 not in stock*
	Morris Commercial Viceroy	Beadle 20-seat	JG 1472–89	18	1931
	Morris Commercial RP	East Kent 14-seat	JG 3710	1	1933
	Dennis Lancet	Dennis 35-seat	JG 6800–22	23	1936
	Dennis Lancet 2	Dennis 35-seat	JG 6823/4/7808; JG 8702–25/9906; AJG 46–59	42	1936–7/9
	Dennis Lancet 2	Park Royal 35-seat	AJG 41–5	5	1939
	Leyland KPZ3	E Kent/E Counties 20-seat	AJG 607–11; BFN 176	6	1939 *Bodies 1933/4*

Source: MDEK Bus Club

ed longer and the small number of London & South Coast vehicles that had actually been purchased by East Kent under their arm's-length control arrangements were also retained although, as these were Tilling-Stevens or Morris chassis they fitted well with the existing fleet. All other vehicles acquired were in 'penny' numbers and generally were not operated. One notable exception was the acquisition of the MT (Motor Coach) Company in 1937, a coach firm operating out of New Cross that had a small fleet of Leyland TS7s with Duple coach bodies, two of which had yet to be delivered. These stylish machines complemented the East Kent fleet well and lasted until 1954. As described earlier, East Kent was working the Ramsgate–London express service joint with MT back in 1929.

OPERATIONS IN THE 1930s

As already noted, the most significant influence on East Kent, like many other well-established operators, was the Road Traffic Act passed in August 1930 and implemented in 1931. The combination of the development of the motor car and a need for greater control on both vehicles and drivers in the interests of safety had caused the government to regularize the situation by tabling this legislation before Parliament. It introduced licensing of drivers, control on types and sizes of vehicles including brakes and a requirement for third-party insurance. The term 'Public Service Vehicle' was formally identified in Part IV of the Act, and in this area the negative effects of unrestricted competition and the, perhaps myopic, attitude of some local councils in preventing the development of much-needed improvements to public transport were now addressed.

One important element of the Act for bus operators was the classification of operations into stage, express and contract carriages. This allowed a system of road service licensing primarily aimed at stage (bus) and express services. Licensing and other matters such as regulation of fares were now under the control of a newly formed set of traffic commissioners, that for East Kent being the South-Eastern Traffic Area. The commissioners' role replaced the former functions of the local authorities together with new powers. A key part of the service licensing arrangements saw the commissioners charged with, in terms of their decision-making in this area, the need to take account of:

- The suitability of routes
- The extent to which the proposed routes were already served
- The extent to which a proposed service was in the public interest

Operations to Hastings by East Kent were already established prior to the takeover of the services to Pett and Pett Level in 1933–4. The stage carriage service from Rye eventually became service 113 in 1937 and passed through the Strand Gate arch at Winchelsea, as evidenced by this post-war view of Dennis Lancet CFN 128. Use of larger vehicles eventually saw services diverted away to avoid the difficult manoeuvre. MDEK CLUB

Further controls were exercised over the level of fares, and a system of licensing vehicles, drivers and conductors was introduced. For East Kent, which had already developed a self-sufficient network together with the depots, administration and engineering resources to support safe, reliable operation, this was a godsend. While not wiping out the competition overnight, it obviously accelerated the demise of many smaller concerns, many of whom would not be granted a licence to operate where East Kent was the majority provider and thus the opportunity to cherry pick was now denied them. The result was that the sum total of East Kent's acquisitions up to 1941 was recorded as forty-one in the Company's Silver Jubilee commemorative brochure printed in *Bus & Coach*, including some major coach concerns and the significant fleet and service expansion through the takeover of the IoTES operation. If the takeover of operators where no vehicles were acquired is taken into account, the total is probably nearer fifty.

One notable acquisition was when M&D and East Kent took over the Hastings operations of Timpson's in March 1934. M&D acquired all the vehicles and the lion's share of services but, surprisingly, East Kent took over the service to Pett Level – perhaps because this headed east from Hastings and East Kent had already acquired a small operator, Morris, based in the village of Pett, some months earlier at the end of 1933. Some ex-Timpson vehicles then passed to East Kent from M&D and two Gilford coaches from this source were operated for a time, while a Leyland TA4 20-seat bus

Table 5 Christmas Day Services 1936

Number (1937 scheme)	Route	Notes
1	Canterbury–Chilham–Ashford	Two return journeys
3/8	Faversham–Canterbury–Margate	Four return journeys
4	Canterbury–Blean–Whitstable	Four return journeys
6	Canterbury–Herne–Herne Bay	Four return journeys
10	Folkestone–Ashford–Maidstone	Two return journeys
13A	Canterbury–Sandwich–Eastry–Deal	Two return journeys
15	Canterbury–Lydden–Dover	One return journey and one s/w Dover to Lydden
17	Canterbury–Elham–Folkestone	Two return journeys
37	Herne Bay–Graveney–Faversham	One return journey
38	Herne Bay–Dargate–Faversham	One return journey
51	Margate–Westgate	Frequent until early afternoon
52	Margate–Westwood–Ramsgate	Four return journeys plus s/w to/from Westwood garage
53	Margate–Broadstairs–Ramsgate	Three return journeys
62	Margate–Dover–Folkestone–Hastings	Two return journeys
80	Deal–St Margaret's Bay–Dover	Two return journeys
87	Ramsgate–Eastry–Dover	One return journey
88	Dover–Eythorne–Elvington	Nine return journeys until late evening
90	Dover–Capel–Folkestone	Frequent until late evening
99	Folkestone harbour–Shorncliffe Camp	Frequent until late evening
102	Folkestone–Hawkinge–Swingfield	Six return journeys, two extended to/from Denton
103/A	Folkestone Wood Ave.–Hythe	Frequent until late evening
105	Folkestone–Lydd Royal Oak	Two return journeys
113	Rye–Hastings	Five return journeys
Express	London–Canterbury–Ramsgate	Two return journeys
	London–Ashford–Folkestone–Dover	Two return journeys
	London–Canterbury–Dover	One single journey to Dover
	London–Herne Bay	One return journey by connecting at Canterbury
	London–Canterbury–Deal	Two return journeys

from Morris also passed to East Kent a couple of months earlier, in January 1934. This was to be the westernmost expansion of East Kent's stage carriage operations, with the exception of later extensions of service 10 to Sevenoaks and 711 to Brighton; these, however, were under the nationalized or Stagecoach regimes.

The 1930s saw express services now running throughout the year, and timetables from the period show that the company operated stage and express services on Christmas Day, a pre-war feature of operations even in rural Kent and which disappeared in the post-war period never to resume. Only a limited number of services operated, generally with a handful of journeys finishing by the early afternoon, although some operated more intensive

services. The table above details those scheduled for Christmas 1936.

Tramway Takeovers and Route Numbering

A route numbering system was finally introduced on 1 January 1937, long overdue as there were now more than one hundred and twenty services operating. The timetable issued on 23 September 1936, detailing the Christmas services listed above, was the last one without service numbers apart from the expanding local numbers being used to identify the town services at Canterbury (Nos. 1–7), Herne Bay (Nos. 1–3), Deal (Nos. 1–4) and Ashford (Nos. 1–5). Interestingly, by 1936 the numbers formerly used for

JG 1477, a 1931 Morris Commercial Viceroy with Beadle body, turns towards Grace Hill in Folkestone on 'Town Service No.1', evidencing the use of local service numbers prior to 1937. It also appears to be one-man operated, its front entrance and low capacity permitting such use. MDEK CLUB COLLECTION

a limited number of services at Folkestone and Hythe in 1931 had been removed despite a good number of town services operating in the area. The numbers used for the four services concerned did not last long – the Folkestone services 1 and 2 from Morehall to the Warren via Castle Hill Avenue or Cheriton Road respectively were no longer identified as such in the summer 1932 timetable, and while those at Hythe from Saltwood to Palmarsh estate (service 1) and West Hythe (service 2) were still identified as such in 1932, they are assumed to have been removed soon after.

The new numbering system saw some changes in the first year, notably as a result of the closure and replacement of the IoTES tram system in March 1937, and East Kent also taking over their bus interests three months after the numbering system was introduced. Services in Dover also expanded during 1937, once the company had been able to explore the serving of new areas previously inaccessible by the former corporation tramway system. This closed on 31 December 1936. It had only featured two routes, to Maxton and River, now replaced by East Kent buses. The corporation's former controls had probably prevented East Kent from introducing services to the many outlying areas of the town, often up steep hills, as they would have taken traffic away from the tramway routes, despite the trams being confined to the main road corridors. One example of the opportunity taken to divert from the constraints of the former tram routes was the introduction of service 97A to Elms Vale Road from 1 January 1938. This split from its parent tramway replacement service to Maxton, the 97, halfway along the Folkestone Road to serve this expanding area to the west of the town.

The numbering system was, with some exceptions, based on a logical progression radiating clockwise from Canterbury with a degree of future-proofing, which was to prove invaluable in the years to come. The scheme was fairly resilient and able to accommodate changes up until the 1960s/70s, when NBC plans dictated a modification in policy as town service networks underwent major restructuring. The full details of the numbering of services from January 1937 and their routes are detailed in the Appendix but the broad principles of the initial scheme are shown in Table 6 on page 42.

It is notable that London express services were still unnumbered, despite an earlier dalliance with route letters; it would be 1950 before a system of identifying numbers was introduced. From this time until the outbreak of the Second World War, East Kent saw a period of stability, apart from an expansion of both the local and national tours market, evident from the large number of handbills produced to advertise them to the public during this period, building on what had become a well-respected and reliable operation. Luxurious 'coach cruises' in 1938 now saw Cornwall, Derbyshire and Blackpool tours added to the destinations served as well as two weeks in Scotland, while local tours saw as many as twenty itineraries offered daily from various towns, covering whole-day, morning, afternoon and evening tours.

One interesting development on the tours front was the publication of leaflets in French advertising the attractions of Canterbury; the company obviously already had its eyes on the market across the Channel now accessible through the development of the 'Channel Packet' steamer services

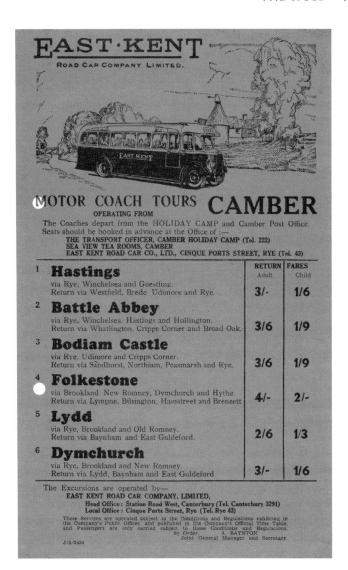

TOP: By 1938 the company had made an effort to standardize the format of tours leaflets although local handbills, as represented by the Camber item (left), still diverged from the form of the Hythe one (right), which was used for most towns in the area with minor variations.

By the 1930s East Kent was also focusing on the continental market, as shown by these two leaflets produced in French promoting Canterbury, the later one featuring one of the smart TS7 coaches from 1935.

Table 6   East Kent 1937 Route Numbering Scheme

Range	Service group
1–22	Canterbury area country routes, except No. 10, used at Folkestone/Ashford jointly with M&D
23–29	Canterbury City services (No. 30 spare)
31	Faversham area (No. 32 spare)
33	Whitstable area (No. 34 spare)
35–44	Herne Bay area (No. 45 spare)
46/47	Birchington area (No. 48 spare)
49–63	Margate area (No. 64 spare)
65–72	Ramsgate area (No. 73 spare), excepting No. 67, already used at Canterbury jointly with M&D
74	Sandwich area (No. 75 spare)
76–85	Deal area (No. 86 spare)
87–97	Dover area (No. 98 spare)
99–107	Folkestone area (No. 108 spare)
109–110	Hythe area (No. 111 spare)
112–116	Rye area (No. 117 spare)
118–125	Ashford area (No.126 spare)
127/128	Hastings area (No. 129 presumed spare)

between Dover/Folkestone and Calais/Boulogne. Even so, the initiative to encourage traffic from France as well as the obvious market for day traffic from England was a bold step.

The main trunk bus service operations saw little further change before the advent of hostilities. The only changes between 1937 and 1939 were generally localized; in Canterbury the 20 was extended onward from Waltham to Hastingleigh from 1 January 1939, albeit only for three journeys on Saturdays, while the 26 had been diverted to serve the newly opened Kent & Canterbury Hospital from 27 September 1937. Further south, at the end of Stone Street, two Saturday journeys on the 109 (one each way) were diverted to serve the hamlet of Postling on 18 March 1939.

At Ramsgate, from summer 1938 a new service, 73, appeared, running from Victoria (later Winterstoke) Crescent via Ramsgate Harbour and St Lawrence Bandstand (Westcliff) to Nethercourt Circus, a destination that was prefixed by the title 'Pegwell Bay'. Meanwhile, the earlier, but still current service 71, running from Broadstairs, Hare & Hounds, St Lawrence Church, the Derby Arms and King Street and serving the same terminus, used the description Ramsgate (Nethercourt Circus). Possibly the 73 was intended to serve the Coastguard cottages off Pegwell Road but was unable to reverse there. The 71 had recently been extended to run from Waldron Road in Broadstairs in February, while at the same time the 53 service was diverted to run via St Peter's Railway Bridge en route between Ramsgate/Broadstairs and St Peter's Church and from there to Margate. The 71 was later truncated to Broadstairs, Westcliff Road from 16 October 1939; it had retreated further to the Hare & Hounds by 8 March 1940 and had been completely suspended due to the war by November 1940.

From 26 September 1938 many Thanet services underwent fundamental change apart from the tramway replacement 49/A. Circular service 57 between Margate and Garlinge was withdrawn and the 54A diverted via All Saints Avenue in compensation, with the Westbrook garage route

This marvellous view of Tilling-Stevens JG 712, probably in summer 1939, shows her by Ramsgate's Royal Pavilion on town service 72 to the station, one of the many Thanet routes that did not resume post-war. Behind is the former Harbour station, by now an amusement park. The smartly dressed crew are of note, while the conductor has a new Setright roll ticket machine (later the Setright Speed); evidence that these were in use prior to the Second World War. MARK STANFORD

remaining the province of its companion, 54. The other Margate circular, the 63, was also revised to run to and from Westbrook garage rather than terminating at the station. The opportunity was also taken to revise the complex of services to Kingsgate, formerly numbered 55/A/B. Some service 51 journeys from Westgate were extended to Kingsgate (Percy Avenue) all year and were renumbered 50, also running via Cecil Square. The 51 still ran to Palm Bay in the summer, terminating at Margate Harbour in the winter as normal. Interestingly, the number 50 was origin-ally allocated to the former Palm Bay–Birchington service withdrawn from 25 March 1937, after which the local Cliftonville area was served by the town circular service 63 and in summer by the round-Island circular service 56, both of which lasted until September 1939. At Broadstairs only the 55 remained from Margate; services 55A/B were withdrawn and replaced by services 52/A running to and from Broadstairs from Kingsgate, the former via Lanthorne Road and the latter via Callis Court. The 52/A did not last long, however, and neither did the 63; both were withdrawn by the outbreak of war and were never recorded as temporarily suspended. Route 70, running across the back of the Island from Ramsgate to Minnis Bay, saw a winter revision with the introduction of a diversion via Pegwell and Minster, numbered 70A, partly replacing the long circular service 56, which ran

completely around the island and now became a summer-only operation.

In Dover, new service 98, from River to East Cliff, commenced on 1 June 1937 and the 86 from Monument to Tower Hamlets/Elms Vale from 31 July. In 1938 the 86 was cut back from Elms Vale to Tower Hamlets on 26 September; Elms Vale already now served by the direct 97A, the number that the 86 had first been registered under but never carried. Later, on 7 September 1939, the 97A was extended back to serve East Cliff, while the 98 was diverted to run from River to Elms Vale, serving the latter destination alternately with the 97A each every 20 minutes. In effect Elms Vale now had an improved 10-minute service, as the 97A originally ran every 12 minutes. At Folkestone, a link between Cheriton and Hythe via Horn Street, numbered 108 and running Wednesday and Saturday afternoons, was meant to start on 7 September 1939 but probably never ran, as it was omitted from the October timetable. In Ashford a new service had been introduced on 26 September 1938 from the High Street to serve the Hillyfields area in south Ashford on Friday and Saturday afternoons, numbered 126. However, storm clouds were gathering over Europe and events in September 1939 were to have a profound effect on East Kent's operations – arguably, with perhaps the exception of London, the company was going to be the UK bus undertaking most affected by the forthcoming hostilities.

AJG 32, one of the last double-deckers delivered before the war, in 1939, is shown when new in this view at Hythe Red Lion Square, the original terminus of services 103/A before they moved down to the light railway station in 1947. By now all deliveries had the standard destination display to accommodate the 1937 route numbers. Note the driver's summer dust coat, and, behind the bus, Keeler's sweet shop, a favourite of the author in his youth and which lasted until the late 60s.
LCC TRUST – J. BONNELL

CHAPTER FOUR

EAST KENT IN THE SECOND WORLD WAR — THE 'BUSMAN'S MALTA'

SERVICE REDUCTIONS — THE INTRODUCTION OF EMERGENCY TIMETABLES

With the outbreak of war on 3 September 1939 it was clear that the situation of East Kent meant that they would be in the forefront of military activity and most exposed to enemy action from across the Channel. One of the first changes was the early suspension of many of the summer services in the timetable introduced from 7 September 1939 – earlier than planned as the summer timetable should have run through to 24 September. This was obviously an emergency measure, as the revision came in on a Thursday, four days after Britain's declaration of hostilities; normally timetables changed over between Saturday and Monday, or in some cases at the beginning of the month.

The escalation of the war and the introduction of fuel rationing soon required further changes, and this hastily introduced timetable was quickly revised in a supplement from the same date, following which a new timetable operated from 16 October. This introduced fundamental changes across the network, with all journeys after 10pm being withdrawn. There were some exceptions on the trunk routes linking the major towns, either where the penultimate departure even at 9.30 would not see an arrival at the destination before 10; or to get crews back to home depots. The South Coast Express service was also suspended from this date, but the link across Romney Marsh was maintained by service 62. Later, by 23 June 1941, the 62 was truncated to run only between Folkestone and Hastings, an arrangement that continued throughout the war. London express services remained operational at this stage and hung on until October 1942, when they were also suspended.

This timetable still advertised the fact that a limited number of services, including London services, were intended to operate on Christmas Day. These were broadly similar to those operated in 1936, with a slightly earlier finish on the all-day services compared to earlier years. It is unclear what actually operated but the demands of the war effort would have probably necessitated some service.

On the publicity front, wartime saw the single system-wide timetable replaced in 1940 by a set of area booklets entitled 'emergency timetables', the first time a comprehensive set of area timetables had been produced; the only regional publications up to that time had been the set of tourist guides produced from the mid-1920s. The six areas were:

- Ashford, Rye and Hastings
- Folkestone
- Canterbury, Whitstable and Herne Bay
- Dover
- Deal and Sandwich
- Thanet

By June 1945 and the cessation of hostilities, the Dover and Deal areas were combined in one issue and in July 1945 a complete system timetable was again issued.

Scrutiny of these emergency timetables reveals the significance of the changes required by fuel rationing, and the lack of vehicles and crew due to the demands of war. In terms of frequency, many of the intensive town services such as the 49/A and 103/A were decimated, reducing from the 5-minute (49/A) and 4-minute (103/A) intervals operated pre-war on these routes to 20 and 15 minutes respectively. By comparison, some of the trunk routes

Wartime 'emergency' timetables were issued on an area basis with different-coloured covers for each one, while the fare table used a similar design. The reference to important notices on the Dover booklet concerns the introduction of fixed stopping places in the town.
AUTHOR'S COLLECTION

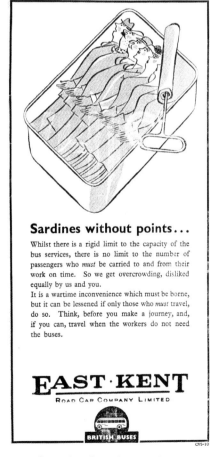

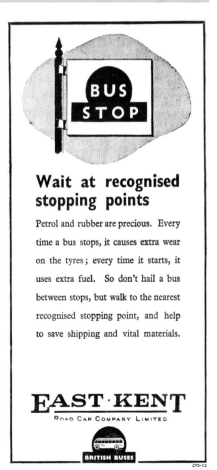

Two of a number of British Buses advertisements used throughout the nation during the war exhorting passengers to consider the need to travel. AUTHOR'S COLLECTION

connecting the main towns got off more lightly, probably because they covered for the town service reductions. For example, service 8 from Canterbury to Margate was reduced to hourly, supplemented on Friday, Saturday and Sunday afternoons by additional journeys bringing it back to its pre-war 30-minute headway, while the 10 between Folkestone and Maidstone still operated every 30 minutes at the height of the day. From October 1942 most services were also curtailed on Sunday mornings, not starting up before midday.

A number of services were withdrawn for the duration. More than forty were listed as suspended by 1942; those serving coastal areas that were formerly leisure destinations such as Reculver, Minnis Bay, Sandwich Bay, Winchelsea Beach and Camber were obvious candidates, but many town services, probably deemed as infill and serving points within easy reach of the remaining town or trunk routes, were also suspended. Places such as the Dane Valley and Garlinge in Margate (Services 54/A), Sandown in Deal (Service 85), Tower Hamlets and Elms Vale Road in Dover (Services 86, 97A and 98), and the East Cliff–Shorncliffe Crescent route in Folkestone (Services 107/A) were examples of areas and services affected. Ashford escaped such cuts, all of its town services remaining in operation, while in Canterbury, despite three of its city services being withdrawn, most areas of the town were still served by alternative routes.

It should be recognized that at this time the company was no longer master of its own destiny. The country was on a wartime footing and a Ministry of War Transport body had been established with a Road Transport Division that took responsibility for, and direction of, the country's bus undertakings. The name British Buses was used across the country in addition to the local undertaking's name, often in advertising, for example highlighting the need for passengers to use buses only when strictly necessary. The British Buses logo continued to be used in advertising material well after the war. The last known use by East Kent was in the summer 1948 timetable; possibly the recent changes in legislation, with the establishment of the British Transport Commission at the beginning of that year, rendered 'British Buses' redundant.

WAR DEMANDS ON THE EAST KENT FLEET

Ironically, at the start of war, East Kent had further demands placed on it as the locality became a reception area for evacuees from London. The impact on the fleet was soon felt. A number of the 1935 TS7 coaches were requisitioned by the War Department in 1940 for use as ambulances – the MDEK Club's fleet history records a total of thirty used, somewhat higher than quoted in earlier publications documenting this turbulent time. Some coaches were returned to service later in the year but a good number remained so converted until 1946, when they were reinstated to normal work; in the intervening period most had their petrol engines replaced by diesel units. Some of these coaches and most of the later 1936 batch of TS7s also requisitioned by the War Department in 1940 were never to return to East Kent. The fuel rationing imposed was reportedly draconian at first but later relaxed, the authorities possibly realizing the key part that East Kent's operations were playing in the conflict. One throwback to the First World War was a further experiment with gas during the mid-war years to reduce the reliance on diesel or petrol fuel. This time, gas producer trailers were fitted rather than the gas bags of the 1914–18 era. However, their use was not widespread. Only a limited number of vehicles were so equipped, believed to be all at Thanet, the lack of power being a distinct disadvantage.

What was first termed the 'Phoney War' soon turned into reality when the company was called upon to assist in the evacuation of British forces from Dunkirk in May and June 1940. It is recorded that at 4am one day in late May an instruction was received requiring 250 vehicles and drivers to be ready for urgent use. Such was the dedication of East Kent staff that by 6.45am the Company could report that they were all ready and standing by. The evacuation lasted many days; bus services were severely curtailed but East Kent soldiered on, many drivers working days with little relief. Even after the successful Dunkirk evacuation East Kent's involvement did not cease, and it is reported that fifty-five vehicles, together with their drivers, were stationed in Suffolk with the army for six months in order to provide a short-term replacement for army vehicles left in France.

Commercially, East Kent was also hit hard, as there was no longer the opportunity to bolster revenues through the summer holiday season, a key facet of East Kent's pre-war operations. A good number of vehicles and equipment were hired to other bus undertakings from 1940 to gain income, over 120 going to operators ranging from Scotland, Yorkshire, Lincolnshire and the Thames Valley to Sussex and Devon. They were mostly double-deckers, including all of the forty AJG Leyland TD5s, twenty of them going to Southdown with five passing on to Devon General, both companies painting them in their own liveries. Another sizeable loan was a batch of twenty Dennis Lancet single-deckers sent to Aldershot and District, an established Dennis operator, who also painted them in their own livery.

Vehicle shortages meant that all depots had to contribute to localized demands occasioned by war damage or other requirements. BFN 176, a Leyland Cub from 1939, leads a Tilling-Stevens and two TD5s all in wartime livery at Dover. However, BFN 176 is based at Canterbury, identified by the service 20 blind. These Cubs all received second-hand bodies from older vehicles, mostly Morris RPs, although BFN 176's is an Eastern Counties product of 1934 formerly carried by Dennis Ace JG 4241.
MDEK CLUB – COMPANY ORIGINAL

These numbers do not include the coaches requisitioned by the War Ministry, reckoned to total over forty Leyland TS7s and TS8s, mostly the former, with another thirty-five Tilling-Stevens B10C2s and forty-six B49C2s also being taken over. In total, it is reckoned that 132 vehicles were requisitioned from East Kent never to return, apart from one, JG 9948, in 1946. Some vehicles left the area temporarily, being stationed with their drivers near important wartime factories in the Midlands – Kidderminster being one location frequently mentioned, although their bases were subject to a good deal of flexibility. Others were used to support entertainment (ENSA) activities for the troops. Drivers were also loaned with vehicles to work on war contracts in London in 1941, according to a report in the *Omnibus*.

From the numbers recorded, a significant proportion of the East Kent fleet was either loaned or requisitioned, together with those converted to ambulances, from 1940 onwards. The loaned vehicles and ambulance conversions, as opposed to requisitioned vehicles, eventually made their way back to operate again for East Kent, although it took until 1946 before they all returned.

The wartime situation and centralized governmental control of vehicle supply meant that after the deliveries in early 1939 no new vehicles were taken into stock until 1943. The exception was BFN 797, a Leyland TS8 coach delivered in 1940 but with a redesigned Park Royal coach body, compared to those fitted to the pre-war TS7/8 chassis. It was meant to be the precursor of a new fleet of coaches but was to remain unique in the fleet. An outstanding 1940

order for ten new Leyland TD7 double-deckers with Park Royal lowbridge bodies similar to the pre-war deliveries was diverted by the Ministry of Supply to Crosville Motor Services in North Wales. They still carried Canterbury registrations, BFN 932–41, but never returned to Kent after the hostilities, remaining with Crosville until withdrawal. Vehicle availability was thus at a premium and two of the early TS1 open-top double-deckers, FN 9094 and JG 652, were re-bodied with what were termed 'utility' lowbridge bodies by Park Royal in 1942; in the case of the latter this was certainly as a result of wartime damage, and possibly for the former too, indicating a need to make the use of all available equipment. Later, in 1945, the remaining TS1 open-tops, FN 9095 and JG 651/3–5, were equipped with new utility Burlingham single-deck front-entrance bodies. Possibly the idea of operating open-top double-deckers on normal stage carriage services was by then seen as a rather outdated concept.

Eventually, East Kent was granted a supply of new vehicles, and from 1943 wartime Guy Arab chassis were taken into stock with double-deck utility bodies. Guy was one of the few approved manufacturers of chassis at this time and the utility bodies were of spartan, angular construction, initially with wooden slats for seats although by the end of 1944 matters had become more relaxed and later deliveries were equipped with upholstered seating. The Guy double-deck chassis was new to East Kent, although some single-decks had entered the fleet as a result of acquisitions before the war. Many had the smaller 5LW engines and care was taken not to place these at Dover due to the preponderance of steep hills. The first three, registered BJG 253–5, were of the Guy Arab I marque, with a further thirteen, BJG 281/2/301–4/339/53–6/461/2 arriving in 1943–5, all with Park Royal 56-seat highbridge bodies. The other 1944/5 deliveries were either of Weymann 56-seat highbridge (two examples, BJG 472/5) or 55-seat lowbridge construction (forty-seven examples, BJG 400–44/73/4). The highbridge vehicles were, apart from the ex-Sims Dennises and Isle of Thanet Daimlers, the first of this covered-top body type to be taken into stock and may have required careful allocation, given the number of low bridges in the company's area at the time.

These vehicles were delivered in a livery comprising grey roofs and side panels with the exception of red bands below the upper-deck windows and between-decks with red lower panels. Headlights were masked as a wartime precaution, with white edges painted on mudguards to aid visibility in the blackout. Over time, other vehicles in the fleet began to receive this livery, essential to reduce visibility of the buses and thus identification by prowling enemy aircraft. Other modifications concerned two of the Isle of Thanet Daimlers. CKP 877 was converted to a mobile office in 1942 following its strafing at Herne while working service 6, resulting in significant damage to the rear and a number of deaths. ADU 470 was converted to a mobile canteen in 1943. Both served at Dover, being allocated there to provide a flexible source of information and refreshment, particularly when services were prevented from accessing the town centre during shelling (see below). The vehicles resumed normal operations at the end of 1944, when they were converted back to buses.

WARTIME FARES

A further move to mitigate revenue loss as well as the loan of vehicles was to raise fares, by all accounts the first time

The Spartan lines of the Utility Guys are shown off well by Park Royal-bodied highbridge Guy Arab II, BJG 353, leaving Canterbury's Westgate Towers on the 25A in the early 1950s, before the newly introduced Spring Lane estate journeys were renumbered to 25. R.H.G. SIMPSON

The lowbridge Utility Guy Arabs are represented in this view of BJG 440 at Margate harbour on a short-working of the 58 to Manston. All lowbridge versions were bodied by Weymann, the later cars having sliding rather than half-drop windows. MDEK CLUB – BRIAN WEEDEN

in the company's history. In August 1940, 1d fares were increased to 1½d whilst the 1½d fares were increased to 2d. This still did not address the problem, and in November of the same year fares between 2d and 5½d were all increased by ½d, while other fares above that were all increased by a 1d in each 1/-. (Note: conversion to today's decimal values is not shown due to the low value; 1/- was comprised of 12d, which equals 5p in today's decimal system.) As the tide of war turned, the increases of November 1940 were rescinded in February 1944 but the other fares would have to wait until 1949 before they reverted to pre-war levels.

ON THE FRONT LINE

The war coincided, in 1941, with East Kent's Silver Jubilee, which was commemorated in a low-key way, although a special brochure was printed from articles in *Bus & Coach* by both Sidney Garcke and Alfred Baynton. On a more sombre note, East Kent's operations were not immune from being on the front line and thus targeted by enemy action. In 1942 the head office in Station Road West was hit, as were the depots at Dover, Deal and Canterbury, including the coachworks. St. Peter's depot near Broadstairs, the old

IoTES tramway depot, also suffered severe damage in 1943. Apart from the loss of some eight buses plus three staff cars at Canterbury, a number of employees lost their lives carrying out their duties. The raid at Dover in April 1942 saw ten staff killed, while a later raid near Canterbury in October saw two vehicles attacked: the driver of one and the conductress of the other, together with many passengers, lost their lives. The destruction of Dover depot saw a temporary move to the former tram depot at Buckland and other vehicles being stabled at River, allegedly leading to complaints from residents when buses were brought into service in the early morning.

As a result of the attacks and the loss of the head office through bombing, contingency plans were put in place. The secretarial department had already moved to Charing in 1940, but in 1942 the traffic and engineering staff moved to temporary accommodation at Alcroft Grange near Tyler Hill and the general manager and his staff to Tunbridge Wells. Traffic staff had earlier been housed in three double-deckers temporarily converted to offices. The coachworks staff, with the exception of the paint shop, which transferred to Margate, moved to the Faversham Cyprus Road garage and remained there until the end of the war and beyond. At a later stage, in early 1946, head-office functions moved to Odsal House, Harbledown, and remained there until the premises in Station Road West, Canterbury were rebuilt. The engineering side saw a change in management during the war in 1942, when S.H. Loxton became chief engineer, succeeding Major C.J. Murfitt upon his resignation.

The Dover area was particularly vulnerable to attack and here a policy of 'fixed omnibus stopping places' was brought in from 12 October 1942, together with the introduction of restricted fares on certain journeys in order to favour those making longer-distance journeys. When the town was being shelled, services stopped away from the town centre, reversing at the Engineer public house on the Folkestone Road and at Buckland for services coming down the London Road. In June 1943 the terminal point for Dover's country services was moved from the Market Square to Pencester Road, while at Folkestone services moved from the vulnerable Harbour terminus to Bouverie Square. Both termini would become permanent features

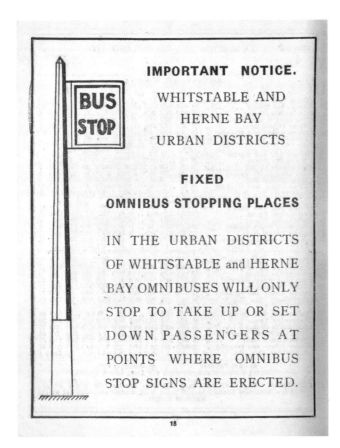

As the bus stop system was introduced across the company's network, a generic advert was introduced as shown by this example in the February 1945 Canterbury, Whitstable and Herne Bay timetable for its application in the latter urban districts. AUTHOR'S COLLECTION

after the war and remain to this day. Restricted fares were subsequently introduced on a number of journeys from the main towns across the company's operating area, with the exception of Ashford; while the fixed bus stop policy was later introduced in the Herne Bay, Whitstable, Margate, Ramsgate, Folkestone and Hythe areas, judging by adverts in the emergency timetables.

Some towns, such as Deal, may have been excluded from this policy at the time; Ashford had already introduced the concept earlier, by January 1939, and it may have also been applied at Canterbury during the war; certainly, it was in place in the city by 1946 and later references to fixed bus stops in 1949 state that the policy had been 'introduced during the war' so it can be assumed that it was eventually introduced in all major towns on the company's network during this period. As a result, introduction of formal bus stops eventually became the norm for all routes in the post-war period with some exceptions, generally on the more rural routes or on trunk roads where specific requests for bus stops had not been applied for formally by the local authority or the general public. The formalization was necessary as the fixed bus stop had to be recorded on the road service licence. As well as all these changes, legislation was passed in April 1942 requiring any more than six passengers waiting at a bus stop to form a queue.

Once the bus stop policy was formalized, East Kent adopted a degree of standardization. Fixed stops were red with cream or white lettering whilst request stops were white with black lettering. There were variations; some had service numbers affixed, while the appendage 'fare stage' was added to relevant stops.

One other interesting change was the introduction of special dedicated services to transport miners to the Kent coalfield pits at Chislet, Snowdown, Tilmanstone and Betteshanger. The need for these was probably due partly to the fact that many former miners had left to fight in the war and the new 'Bevin Boy' conscripts could not all be billeted in the former mining villages. Another factor was that East Kent took over two operators formerly providing miners' services in December 1942. Special miners' services expanded and continued until the late 1980s when the remaining pits were all closed and a valuable revenue source was lost forever, particularly affecting Thanet, Deal and Dover depots.

Given all the problems facing East Kent – the loss of vehicles, both planned and through enemy action, the logistical challenge of operations, both on the home patch and further afield, with staff subject to constant enemy attack – it is small wonder that it became known as the 'Busman's Malta' and their efforts were a credit to all involved.

PART II
THE POST-WAR ERA OF BET'S EAST KENT

CHAPTER FIVE

REBUILDING THE COMPANY

After the war's end, the company's focus changed from the demands of the war effort to reconstruction. This would be a long-term challenge, as for nearly six years the peacetime norms of regular maintenance and long-term service planning had gone by the board. The consequences of this had been building up, and by 1945, assets, both fixed and moving, were mostly in a poor state of repair. To ensure improved reliability, buses and maintenance facilities had to be brought back to something approaching pre-war standards. Staffing was also an issue; while women had filled the breach, making a valuable contribution to most aspects of operations during the war, there certainly were not the staff levels available yet to resume anything close to the services of the 1930s. Even if these matters could be quickly addressed, the erstwhile seasonal nature of East Kent's operations, based on the leisure market, would take many years to return to normal. This was in the company's interest, as it would have been impossible to meet pre-war seasonal demand levels at this stage; this breathing space allowed a measured approach to the recovery.

RETURNING TO NORMAL – THE ROAD TO RECOVERY

While hostilities in Europe ceased in June 1945, it was to be some time before operations would return to normal. Fuel shortages were still severe but by the autumn, serv-ice frequency started to improve. Sunday morning services had resumed and service 62 had been extended back to Margate, with more journeys as some compensation for the still-suspended South Coast Express Service. The weekday service on the 8 had also increased to every 30 minutes by October 1945 from the former hourly frequency operated during the war.

BJG 436, one of the earlier lowbridge Guy Arab IIs with drop windows, is pictured at Northdown Park Gardens entrance on the 53 before setting out for the Hare & Hounds. The latter point was the terminus before the route was diverted into Newington estate in 1954. The destination screen shows a full display before Thanet cars had the bottom section masked to accommodate smaller blinds. J. HIGHAM

Suspended services began to restart in 1945; in Thanet, both the 53 from Ramsgate to Margate and the 70A from Ramsgate to Minnis Bay resumed on 28 February, although the 53 reverted to its former direct route via St Peter's High Street rather than via Albion Road. Services to some of the more sensitive coastal areas suspended throughout the war also resumed at an early stage: Herne Bay's 39 to Reculver (18 July); Folkestone's 107A to the East Cliff Pavilion from Shorncliffe Crescent; and both Rye's 114 to Winchelsea Beach, routed via the Bridge Inn, and 116 to Camber (all 1 October) recommenced, albeit some with a limited number of journeys.

An opportunity was also taken to revise Folkestone's town services: service 106 was reintroduced on 1 June 1945, now running all year round, and diverted up Dover Road to serve Hill Road. In conjunction, the number 108 was then reintroduced on 18 July following its limited use, if used at all, on a service between Cheriton and Hythe in 1939. This new route ran from the Harbour and now served Hawkins Road, which had briefly been served by the 106 from 1 June. It was extended in summer to the Bathing Pool from 21 May 1947 and all year from 23 September 1951. These two services now provided a 10-minute frequency on their common route along Cheriton Road, while the former trunk route along this section, the 99 to Shorncliffe Camp, still operated at 5-minute intervals in the afternoons at this time although this enhancement was halved to the 99's by now normal 10-minute interval from 6 October 1948, no doubt due to the reducing demands of the garrison now that hostilities had ceased. These changes were long overdue, as connections from the developing estates up on Hill Road across town to Cheriton were very poor before the war; the company no doubt recognized that these housing areas would provide better revenue sources in the longer term.

Despite this gradual relaxation of constraints, twenty-two stage carriage services were still listed as suspended in October 1945, as well as the London Express services, while the seasonally based stage services around the Isle of Thanet had yet to return to pre-war levels despite the reintroduction of isolated seasonal services such as the 46 from Birchington to Minnis Bay in summer 1946. It was to take until summer 1947 before the major island routes 49/A could boast frequencies close to those operated in the 1930s, while the complex number of Thanet circular services operated before the war were never to return. One cosmetic change from 1 June 1945 was the renumbering of the Margate–Wingham service 59 via Acol and Minster to 58; this number was used pre-war for journeys terminating at Minster. At Canterbury, service 28 recommenced on 28 February 1945, now running from Hales Place to the Hospital (Rear Entrance) rather than Wincheap; 5 June 1946 saw the 25 (London Road/Golf Club) and a revised 29 (running Mandeville Road/Barton Estate) resume, while 2 July 1947 saw half of services 23/27 from Sturry Road/Thanington to Rough Common diverted to Blean and numbered 23A/27A, providing a 30-minute service to each terminal.

More minor changes occurred elsewhere. Service 78 had been extended from Eythorne in April 1944 to serve Shepherdswell station, and from 21 May 1947 further journeys on this service were extended to serve the expanding pit village of Elvington, demonstrating the increasing dependency of the more rural bus services in this area on the Kent coal industry.

An indication of the continued close liaison between East Kent and the Southern Railway was the introduction of what was effectively a rail replacement service, numbered 130, between Ashford and New Romney, operating by 10 May 1944 and initially only running on Sundays, when the train service between Appledore, Lydd and New Romney was suspended. While rail tickets were available on the service, holders of HM Forces leave tickets or warrant holders had to pay a small supplement. Even worse, passengers travelling to Lydd or Brookland had to decamp at New Romney or Ivychurch respectively with no further ticket availability on East Kent's normal services, 62 or 105, to enable them to reach their final destination. The service expanded to run all week from Wednesday 22 September 1948 but was then curtailed from 27 May 1950, only running every day in the high summer from 28 June (also a Wednesday, which seemed to be a regular change day for many service changes in this period); the winter service was now confined to Saturdays and Sundays only. Despite connections with service 105 to Lydd being displayed in later timetables, the seemingly perverse restrictions on inter-availability of rail tickets continued. While East Kent's association with this

JG 8229, one of the Leyland TD4s of 1937 re-bodied by ECW in 1948, is captured at New Romney Ship Inn on the 130 route. R.K. BLENCOWE

rail service across Romney Marsh would re-emerge in the 1960s, service 130 was withdrawn at the start of the summer 1958 timetable. Closure of the Hythe branch line on 1 December 1951 had resulted in some 105 journeys being extended to Folkestone Central Station to improve rail connections; these had actually commenced earlier, on 7 January 1951. The closure of the Elham Valley line from 16 June 1947 had seen no bus service changes, however – East Kent's parallel hourly service 17 was more than enough.

Express Services Return

London expresses resumed on 22 February 1946 while the South Coast Express Service recommenced in the summer of that year. Some journeys were projections of the enhancements to service 62 introduced in 1945, although for the time being they would operate only as far as Ports-mouth, joint with Southdown, with Royal Blue operating west thereof. Thus began a relationship between the two services that would continue until the latter's takeover by Maidstone & District in 1973, when East Kent's Rye operations were transferred, following which the service was later truncated to Dover/Folkestone from the south prior to its eventual replacement. A winter facility would have to wait until October 1948, when a limited service of one journey each way between Margate and Brighton would be operated.

The Herne Bay and Dover via Canterbury express services from London remained seasonal and were suspended during the winter. Later in the decade, in 1949, East Kent entered into an arrangement with sister BET Company 'Midland Red' with the introduction of a new summer-only

express service at weekends between the Thanet towns and Birmingham. The service initially interlinked with the times of the existing London services of both companies via Victoria coach station, but reportedly running through coaches to these schedules. However, as the northern section split into two services it is probable that some itineraries required a change of coach at London. Many years later, the through coaches were operated direct, not running via central London, numbered ME4. In addition to this new link, a service was also introduced between Oxford and Margate by the South Midland Company, although this was recorded as in connection with East Kent rather than as a joint operation.

RECOVERY GAINS PACE

The 25 September 1946 timetable was the last time a specific summary of suspended services, first introduced in

Soon after the resumption of express services in 1946 the first new cars arrived in the shape of the Leyland PS1/1 coaches. CFN 60 was taken out for publicity shots as seen in this view at Wingham Red Lion, although displaying boards for the Thanet service rather than Deal. The image may be black and white but the two-tone red livery is readily distinguishable.
MDEK CLUB – COMPANY

The first leaflets for the post-war resumption of London services featured an image of the earlier Park Royal-bodied TS7 coaches with roof luggage racks. AUTHOR'S COLLECTION

the wartime emergency timetables, was given. By now it was down to eighteen, comprising services 19, 36, 41, 44, 50, 56, 60, 61, 65, 70, 81, 94, 98, 100, 101, 104, 107 and 120, all listed with their pre-war routings (see Appendix). Some services had already resumed, as mentioned earlier, and from 25 March 1946 this would include the 21 (Canterbury/Nonington) and Ramsgate town service 71. The latter ran as a circular service from the station via Nethercourt Circus, Harbour and the Derby Arms but by 21 May 1947 would run as a normal end-to-end service from Gwyn Road on the Whitehall Estate via the Derby Arms and town centre to Nethercourt Circus. The 72 and 73 were not reinstated; both were based around Ramsgate's seasonal requirements as they existed before the war; while former service 104 was, sensibly, to be merged into an improved 105 route, which it had always duplicated from Folkestone to Dymchurch. A number of suspended services, such as the 50, 56, 94 and 98, would never resume in their previous form, although many numbers would be utilized for new services. Services 76 and 77, running from Deal to Betteshanger and Staple respectively, had already been combined as one service, 76, from 18 July 1945.

Dover's 95/96 services were revised from 25 March 1946; 'A' suffixes now identified Ropewalk diversions introduced in 1945 and the 96/A was extended to Kearsney. New routes 94/A from Marine Station/Ropewalk to Buckland Estate, Pilgrim's Way started by 1 October 1947 and new 98 from Pencester Road, also to Pilgrim's Way, ran from 12 May 1948.

Ashford's town services were improved when the 121 and 126 from Hunter Avenue/High Street to Stanhope School/Hillyfields had their earlier Friday and Saturday afternoon enhancements, applying from before the war, introduced throughout weekdays from 25 September 1946 (121) and 21 May 1947 (126) excepting Wednesday afternoon – early closing day. Looking back some journeys on Ashford's 122 had been extended to Chart Road (Ordnance Depot) *vice* nearby King's Avenue by or before March 1943, and from 2 July 1947 all King's Avenue journeys ran there. This destination would be revised to Cobbs Wood from 27 May 1950.

On 21 May 1947 Folkestone's service 100 was reintroduced as a circular service via Central Station, Cheriton, Shorncliffe and Sandgate thence to/from Folkestone via Sandgate Road. Pre-war it ran from the harbour via Junction station thence to Sandgate via Cheriton as a normal end-to-end service rather than a circular route.

Traffic levels had now begun to recover, and June, July and August 1947 were record months, exceeding the already exceptional levels of the same period in 1946 by 740,000 more miles (1.2 million km) operated and 2 million more passengers carried. Individual services were highlighted as performing well above normal: the 49/A group around the Isle of Thanet, for example, now operating at a 7½-minute frequency on weekdays in the summer, often had to be supplemented with all available vehicles commandeered for reliefs, including coaches from tours and London services. This was a logistical nightmare, as the London express services were themselves much in demand with bookings reportedly full weeks in advance during this period. Seasonal reinstatements continued with the summer-only service 61 from Margate to Dover resuming earlier on 5 June 1946, while its companion seasonal service 60 from Margate to Deal resumed two years later, on 30 June 1948. Both had been withdrawn since the war.

Down the coast on Romney Marsh, holiday traffic was also returning to pre-war levels; the 103/A services were extended from Red Lion Square to the Light Railway Station at Hythe, allowing connections with the little trains that had resumed the previous year, 1946. Probably commencing in July 1947 but certainly no later than 1 October, it avoided the difficult turning manoeuvre at Red Lion Square – especially important as road traffic was increasing and buses may have been running 'dead' via the station for some time before. Service 105, which ran across the Marsh from Folkestone to Lydd, had been enhanced in the high summer to a 30-minute frequency as far as Dymchurch and hourly beyond, well in excess of pre-war levels, but the *Omnibus* staff magazine records that many reliefs still had to be operated due to the popularity of Dymchurch sands and the nearby holiday camps.

Improvements in winter traffic levels were also evident, and from 1 October 1947 the company enhanced the low-season 49/A service to a 10-minute headway on weekdays, improved from the 12-minute headway the previous winter, while service 51 from Westgate was extended from Margate to Palm Bay throughout the year from the same date but only hourly in winter. Prior to this, Palm Bay was only a summer extension post-war; the change went some way to reinstate a pre-war winter facility to the area although this ran at a greater frequency then. The 51 had a complex history; in the war, from November 1940, it had run between Westgate and Cecil Square extending to Arlington Gardens (due to the suspension of service 54/A to Dane Valley) until the 54A resumed from 28 February 1945, followed by its companion service 54 by October. From June 1946 the 51 ran via the Harbour in the summer and terminating/via Cecil Square in the winter. Companion service 46 was reintroduced on 5 June 1946, first running as a Birchington/Minnis Bay shuttle thence from Margate Cecil Square via Garlinge Hussar from 25 September. This was then extended summer-only to/from Palm Bay via Dane Valley from 1 June 1949, while the shorter winter service was to remain until winter 1957–8, after which it was withdrawn in the low season, replaced to Minnis Bay by winter extensions to the 49/50 from 1958/9.

One short-lived experiment at this time was the extension of service 55 from Broadstairs to Relay House at Westwood via Rumfields from 1 October 1947, resulting in a widening of headways. By summer 1948 it had reverted to its original termini and an hourly headway. Later, from Wednesday, 22 December 1948, the service was extended again, this time locally in Broadstairs from the Broadway to Stanley Road near Callis Court, and this extension would be far longer-lived. Interestingly, a service to Westwood garage via Rumfields, this time numbered 56 and originating at Stanley Road, reappeared in May 1972; again, it was linked with revisions and later reductions to service 55, which it paralleled for a short section. At Deal, the winter 1947 timetable saw service 79 extended intermittently to Kingsdown Links from the Rising Sun, demonstrating that the improving popularity of the area was not confined to the major resorts; however, there was no increase in frequency. One minor rural improvement was on Ashford's service 109, also from 1 October 1947, when the Saturday service to Postling, requiring a double run to and from Stone Street, increased to two return journeys.

One overdue change from the wartime contingencies was the reinstatement of local fares on long-distance services from Dover on 1 October 1947, first introduced as a wartime measure to aid passengers genuinely needing those services for journeys out of the local area. The company stated that this relaxation would now avoid the requirement to provide additional relief cars on local services, adding that there was unlikely to be any detrimental impact on existing longer-distance passengers. The exact reverse of this policy was being carried out in Canterbury, where protective fares, in most cases prohibiting local journeys in both directions, had been gradually introduced from June 1946 or before, variously affecting services 4, 5, 6, 7, 8, 9, 11, 12, 13/A, 14/A, 18, 20 and 21. Some restrictions were introduced later, for example on services 5, 6 and 18. Protective fares would be a feature of some Canterbury country services over a long time, the 8 being one route that retained them into the 1970s.

The increase in post-war traffic was putting extreme demands on the engineering department, however; in June 1947 the company had a fleet of 440, over 100 cars fewer than in June 1939, with 214 double-deckers and 138 single-decks, of which 33 were the smaller cars and 88 coaches. The new traffic manager, Percy Dodge, recorded a year

Shortly after the war, in October 1948, service 70A was renumbered 70 just after CFN 159, one of the post-war batch of Lancet J3s, was delivered. It is shown here at Ramsgate harbour circa 1959–62, when the 70 was still crew-operated in the summer. MDEK CLUB COLLECTION

later, in the *Omnibus* of May 1948, that the supply of cars upon the summer timetable change of 12 May 1948 was fewer than they had budgeted for. These shortages would soon be alleviated by the arrival of the first batch of re-bodied pre-war Leyland Titans in June but the comment shows that the company was still facing a number of challenges as it emerged from the constraints of war.

This new blood for the fleet was very much needed as the company had been quite ambitious, implementing a significant number of frequency increases for the summer 1948 schedules. For example, services 3 (Canterbury–Faversham), 8 (Canterbury–Margate), 10 (Folkestone–Maidstone), 37/38 (Herne Bay–Faversham) and 113 (Rye–Hastings) all increased from the 30-minute frequencies operated in 1947 to 20 minutes in 1948 (high summer only for service 10). A precursor to the improvement on the 8 had seen additional hourly short-workings between Canterbury and Upstreet introduced for summer 1947, which, with the summer service on the 9 from Canterbury to Ramsgate becoming hourly, gave four buses per hour between Canterbury and Upstreet prior to the 8's short-working running through to Margate from 1948. The enhancement to the 9 was cut back fairly early on, however, and reduced to a 70-minute interval by summer 1950.

Services 4 (Canterbury–Whitstable), 53 (Margate–Ramsgate), 80 (Dover–Deal), 108 (Folkestone town service) all increased from 20-minute headways to 15 minutes, except the 108, which now went to a 10-minute frequency in the summer. This latter change gave seventeen buses per hour down the Cheriton Road on high summer mornings, when the complementary services 17, 99, 101 and 106 were taken into consideration. For this summer only, as the 99 service still operated an afternoon enhancement, an incredible twenty-three buses every hour operated on the common section, offering an interval of less than three minutes. However, the 99's afternoon enhancement would be withdrawn from the October 1948 timetable.

Although they already had intensive services operating, a number of routes in the Isle of Thanet and Folkestone, including the 49/A, 51, 54/A and 103/A, were improved to frequencies ranging from 6 to 9 minutes. Even the less-frequent routes 114/116, from Rye to Winchelsea Beach and Camber, saw their former 60-minute headways improved to 45 minutes in the summer, increasing to 30 minutes in the high season; these changes also saw the two routes linked as one service, numbered 114, at the same time. Also at Rye, rebuilding of the cinema following wartime damage was accompanied by later services operating Saturday nights from 3 July 1948 on all local services from Rye with the exception of the 112 to Appledore/Ashford and the 117 to Cadborough Cliff. Even the 2 featured a late short-working to Brenzett.

Another resumption of an earlier route with a new extension was the 101, which instead of starting at the Harbour, now ran from Folkestone, Wood Avenue, to its former terminus at Newington Star. This commenced on 12 May 1948; from 28 September 1949 it was extended from the Star to Beachborough Cross Roads, possibly to avoid a difficult turn on the busy A20. It would remain in this form until cut back from the Newington area to the bus station, nine years later, in September 1958, as service reductions took place. In the meantime, from 20 Septem-

East Kent's re-bodying programme also extended to some single-decks, and a number of the 1937 Dennis Lancet 2s were equipped with these smart Park Royal bodies in 1949. JG 8712 is pictured at Canterbury, St Peters, on the 14 to Goodnestone prior to the revisions in 1958 that saw it integrated with companion service 14A. MDEK CLUB

ber 1953, it was diverted via Downs Road Estate, providing a new service to this area.

Following a further review of operations, for the winter timetable issued on 6 October 1948, more improvements in the form of increased afternoon peak-hour frequencies were made to services 4 and 6, serving Whitstable and Herne Bay. Rural services 14/A from Canterbury were revised to both operate on Wednesdays and Saturdays; the 14A no longer ran on Fridays but was extended from Staple Three Tuns to the Black Pig. Whether this was to do with improved reversing arrangements is not known but the new terminus made the service more accessible to the villagers.

Timing revisions were also made in both Thanet and Folkestone to improve the coordination of services, while the 53 service in the former area was extended in Cliftonville from Leicester Avenue to Dalmeny Avenue, a precursor of its further extension eastwards as new housing was built. In Deal, the short-workings of the 83 to Upper Deal were renumbered 81, using the number vacated following the wartime withdrawal of the Sandwich Bay service. Two routes operating unnecessarily with 'A' suffixes, following the non-resumption of their pre-war 'parent' routes, became 70 and 107, thus regularizing the situation. Another number change was the revived identification of short-workings of service 16 from Folkestone to Swingfield as service 102, thus reverting to the pre-September 1946 situation.

Earlier, in Ashford, from 22 September 1948 the high-summer frequency improvements to service 10 recorded above were withdrawn, while the 121 would now operate on a 15-minute interval throughout from Hunter Avenue to Stanhope School (which was also re-titled back to Woodchurch Turning, its pre-March 1945 description), rather than just on its northern section. This applied on weekdays with the exception of Wednesday afternoons, early closing day in Ashford. One odd experiment was the introduction at the same time of a service from Ashford to Six Mile Cottages, Stone Street via Stowting, and Lymbridge Green on Tuesdays only, Ashford's market day. Numbered 109A, it did not survive long, being withdrawn from 1 June 1949. The area was still served, as service 19 from Canterbury to Stone Street Chequers was reintroduced on Mondays, Thursdays and Fridays from 3 January 1949. From the summer, it resumed its pre-war seasonal route through to Dymchurch daily although the limited journeys to the Chequers were retained, and these still ran in the winter. The 19 also had restrictive fares applied to it; local journeys within Canterbury were only permitted on inward journeys, complementing the arrangements already in force on services 18 and 20, which paralleled the 19 in the Canterbury area.

Sandwich Bay regained a summer service from 1 June 1949 but the former positioning journeys from Deal were no longer advertised – the new service described as operating from Sandwich town only. According to accounts, a special service on part of the route was operated in May of the previous year for a golf tournament. The service now took spare number 75; the former 81 number used before the war had been relinquished, more suitably, for a Deal town service. The service to Sandwich Bay, in its post-war incarnation, was at first not scheduled in the timetable, operating according to 'weather and traffic requirements'. In the 1930s seven return journeys had been scheduled all week, all except one operating in the afternoon, with outward and inward positioning journeys to/from Deal.

One interesting fact, derived from staff notices, was that by 1949 traffic had risen so much that auxiliary conductors were now employed on some double-deck vehicles at times of peak demand, all probably at Thanet. Increased services were not only required for seasonal demands: the pit village at Elvington, served from Dover by service 88, now had enough traffic to justify a 30-minute service on weekdays in the summer and Saturdays in winter, which was introduced on or by the 1 June 1949 summer timetable. Notwithstanding the problems in their ability to resource improved bus services, the *Omnibus* notes that the company were by now also able to operate a considerable number of hires for the Epsom Derby, although double-deckers were too much in demand to be spared for such work. This is unsurprising given the improvements listed beforehand. The comment on Derby Day operations also referred back to the earlier use of open-top double-deckers on such occasions before the war, but by now none existed, all such cars having been withdrawn or re-bodied.

The improving situation saw the company able to restore all its fares to the pre-war levels on 30 March 1949, thus removing all the earlier increases necessitated by the war. Canterbury's protective fares were also relaxed to only apply on outward journeys.

MANAGEMENT CHANGES

The immediate post-war period saw a number of changes in senior management. Mr R.P. Beddow CBE took over from Sidney Garcke CBE as chairman in 1946, while Alfred Baynton OBE was succeeded on retirement in 1947 by Mr R.G. James as general manager. The post of traffic manager, running under the title of senior traffic officer in the pre-war years, was taken up by Mr J. Chevallier in 1946 and then by Percy Dodge in 1948.

NORMALIZATION OF WORKSHOP ARRANGEMENTS

The coachworks, temporarily located at Faversham after the raids of 1942, returned to Canterbury St Stephen's in March 1948 but was relocated to the high-level site; service operations from the depot also fully resumed but were now carried out at the lower level – the reverse of the pre-war arrangements. Paint shop functions were still being carried out at Margate, Dane Road and moved back to Canterbury later, from April 1949. Whilst the MDEK Club's fleet history records that all functions moved to Faversham during the war, the chief engineer reported in the *Omnibus* of September 1947 that the painting function had first moved, presumably temporarily, to Broadstairs St. Peter's three separate times after repeated bombing. Presumably, once the need to abandon the site at St. Stephen's became clear, the paint team moved semi-permanently, splitting the bodywork and painting functions across the two sites of Faversham and Margate respectively. The temporary move of paint functions to Margate had a longer-term impact in that, despite the move back to Canterbury, many staff were now resident in the coastal town and a special 'paint shop car' to transport staff to and from Canterbury was operated at least until 1959–60, often using a car attending coachworks for minor remedial work. Some of these staff also worked as seasonal conductors or drivers at Thanet.

Another publicity shot of CFN 60, the first of the post-war Leyland PS1 coaches, sees it in Canterbury St. Dunstan's, with the iconic Westgate Towers as a background. This area seems to have escaped the worst of the bombing, although the company's head office, which had been destroyed, was only a few hundred yards away. Note the policeman on his cycle with his distinctive cape. MDEK CLUB – COMPANY ORIGINAL

RESUMPTION OF THE TOURING PROGRAMME

An important development in summer 1949 was the reintroduction of an extended tours programme, on a limited basis at first, with four itineraries being offered: Devon and Cornwall; the Wye Valley; North Wales; and the Lake District. A dedicated team of four drivers was selected for this work. Each tour operated on three dates in the summer with the exception of the shorter Wye Valley tour, which had four departures. They were priced at between 17 and 27 guineas depending on duration (1 guinea was £1-1s-0d, equal to £1.05 in today's decimal currency). The average national weekly wage at this time was around £9 per week so these tours were not for those of limited means. Despite this, these first tours were reported as enjoying 93 per cent load factors, with the last four fully booked. In the reverse direction a conducted tour was now offered from London to Canterbury, utilizing the express service and reinstating a programme that had been very successful in the pre-war period.

Only a year passed before the company expanded its tours horizons. In 1950, an extended coach tour to the French Riviera was run, the first time a passenger-carrying East Kent vehicle had operated on the continent with the exception of those on wartime service, according to company reports. The first tour departed on 17 June using new Dennis Lancet coach EFN 587. It had been conveyed over the day before on the Dover–Dunkirk ferry, passengers following the day after on the Dover–Calais Channel packet boat.

Henceforth, continental tours and, later, regular express services crossing the Channel by sea (and, later, air) would

become a constant and expanding part of the company's business. Only a year passed before the Dover–Calais route was tested for the conveyance of coaches by means of a drive on/drive off facility, and FFN 453 was pictured in the *Omnibus* undertaking preparatory trials on the Townsend car ferry boat *Haladale*, the port authorities at Calais having installed a new ramp to permit loading of larger vehicles. Prior to this, only cars were able to drive on and off and coaches had to be craned onto the ferry, and this was only on a limited number of sailings. It was to be several more years before coaches were regularly driving on and off the ferries; it is reported that coaches were still being craned on and off in 1953 as Dover's Eastern Docks was awaiting installation of a similar ramp. Meanwhile, the domestic tours programme expanded further in 1951, with additional destinations of Scotland, Blackpool illuminations and a further tour based in Devon, being offered in addition to those introduced in 1949.

POST-WAR FLEET INTAKE AND RE-BODYING

Despite immediate post-war restrictions on supply of new vehicles, particularly 'luxury' coaches, East Kent managed to order three batches of vehicles, albeit delivered over nearly three years. The Ministry of Supply was still exercising control over supply of vehicles for the domestic market; the ban on the building of 'luxury' coaches was to last until the beginning of 1949.

The first of East Kent's order to arrive, in late 1946, were the initial deliveries of a batch of fifty service coaches, registered CFN 60–109, based on the Leyland PS1 chassis, successor to the pre-war TS8, with Park Royal 32-seat rear-entrance bodywork continuing the basic design of earlier coaches but to an updated design. Next, in 1947, came the first of the single- and double-deck bus deliveries. As with the coaches, the pre-war choice of chassis manufacturer continued, Dennis Lancet J3s for the former, registered CFN 110–169/CJG 988–99; and Leyland Titan PD1As, registered CJG 938–86 for the latter. Both were replacement models of pre-war designs, although the Dennis Lancet J3s had some fundamental changes, having a 6-cylinder engine rather than the 4-cylinder of the pre-war Lancet 2s and a 5-speed gearbox rather than the pre-war 4-speed, although six of the JG 87xx Lancet 2s from 1937 had had similar gearboxes fitted; these changes were reportedly well received by drivers. However, the bodywork selection changed from the pre-war configuration. Park Royal rather than Dennis was chosen for the single-decks, with Ley-

One of the new Leyland Royal Tigers of 1951 is pictured during the loading trials at Calais the same year. MDEK CLUB – COMPANY ORIGINAL

The last Leyland double-decks for some years would be those of 1947/8. CJG 986 is pictured in Elham's High Street by the Rose & Crown on the 17; this was one of a number of these cars bodied by Salmesbury to Leyland's design.
OMNIBUS SOCIETY – C F KLAPPER

land's new lowbridge design for the double-decks, although some were bodied under subcontract to Salmesbury. The Leyland double-deck order was for fifty vehicles and the last one delivered, CJG 987, was to the PD2/1 specification with the 0600 engine rather than the E181 on the earlier PD1s. This car was always well liked due to its enhanced power and synchromesh gearbox, and spent most of its years at Folkestone.

Both single- and double-deckers continued the pre-war standards for seating capacity at thirty-five and fifty-three respectively and both had rear entrances. Delivery of the Leyland buses and coaches was completed in 1948, while the last of the Dennis buses arrived in mid-1949. Eleven cars (CFN 111–20/CJG 999) were upgraded to coach work between 1950 and 1954, which entailed their seating capacity being reduced to thirty-two during this time.

The ravages of war upon the existing fleet and the inherent difficulty in being able to secure sufficient new vehicles at this time led the company to initiate a programme of rebodying cars, starting with a number of the pre-war Leyland TD4 and TD5 double-deckers. Twenty-four received attractive Eastern Coachworks (ECW) 55-seat lowbridge bodies, which were completed and delivered in 1948.

Yet portents of change were in the air: the long-term association with Leyland was about to come to an abrupt end and no further double-deckers would be ordered from them until 1976. Dennis were still in favour at this time, however, and an order for fifteen low-capacity Falcons, EFN 556–70 with Park Royal 20-seat front-entrance bodies was delivered in 1949–50 for one-man operated routes replacing the Dennis Aces used on such services

The ECW version of the re-bodied TD4s/5s that arrived in 1948 was a very stylish product represented by the 1961 view of JG 8228 in Westcliff Road, Ramsgate on Thanet's 53A service prior to its renumbering in 1962.
MDEK CLUB – P.S.A. REDMOND

The Lancet coaches of 1950 sported a revised coach livery with a scroll fleet name, as illustrated by EFN 585 at the bowls club on Cheriton Road, Folkestone. Both the livery and fleet name style were short-lived. MDEK CLUB

hitherto. It should be pointed out that East Kent did not make broad use of the term 'one-man': all such cars and the rotas were generally referred to as 'D/C' – Driver/Conductor – within the company, although some bus running boards did refer to 'one-man operation'. Dennis was also successful in securing an order for twenty-five coaches, EFN 571–95, delivered in 1950. These were also on the Lancet J3 chassis used for the large number of buses delivered earlier but had a stylish, if not outdated, half-cab 32-seat body with a front entrance.

At the time these vehicles were ordered the company had decided to extend the re-bodying programme to encompass a further thirty-five double-deck vehicles, but this time Park Royal were to re-body the cars. By 1948 ECW were moving to a form of state ownership under the British Transport Commission (BTC) as a result of the Transport Act 1947, which meant they, together with the associated chassis manufacturer, Bristol, could now only supply companies of the Tilling group, also taken over as part of this process. BET-group companies such as East Kent did not come under the full control of BTC, as only the minority railway shareholding (36 per cent in East Kent's case) passed to BTC. BET's remaining majority share-holding meant that East Kent remained a private company, as it was not prepared to sell out at this stage. As a result it was denied the opportunity to purchase further ECW products from this time as well as Bristol chassis, although East Kent had never favoured the chassis builder. Thus Park Royal was chosen, and their 53-seat lowbridge bodies, to a more traditional design, were all delivered in 1949. There was also a more limited programme of re-bodying single-deck pre-war Dennis Lancet buses; thirteen of these, from the JG 87xx batch plus JG 9906, received new Park Royal 35-seat bus bodies with rear entrances in 1949, although for some the entry into service was delayed until 1950.

In addition to the supply of these new bodies, a number of cars underwent body-swaps; in 1949 ten pre-war Lancets of the JG 68xx batch had their Dennis bus bodies replaced by earlier bodies sourced from the 1928 Tilling-Stevens B10C2s of the FN 90xx series. These bodies were originally Park Royal coach products from 1933–4, downgraded to buses upon this programme, themselves replacing the original Beadle or Brush bodies first fitted to the Tilling-Stevens. This was part of a swap originally intended to involve a limited number of chassis from the newer CFN-registered cars but after one test change, involving CFN 110, it was decided to equip all the CFN chassis with new bodies.

Withdrawals in the 1945–9 period only totalled around 100 cars. This saw the remaining Tilling-Stevens marque and the early Leyland TS1 and TD1 double-deckers leaving the fleet, although JG 652 lasted until 1950 having been equipped with a utility body in 1942.

LATE 1940S LIVERY CHANGES

In the post-war period a number of experiments with, and (later) permanent changes to, the livery were undertaken. The pre-war fleet name style, featuring a large transfer with a dot separating 'East' and Kent', was gradually changed. In mid-1948 the dot disappeared and then, later, a slightly smaller fleet name, commencing with the 1950 EFN-series Guy deliveries, appeared. On coaches the two shades of red used pre-war were replaced by one shade from around 1948, thought to be slightly darker overall than either of the earlier colours, although the CFN coaches still sported the two shades when new. A major innovation was the use of a script fleet name and a large cream flash on the EFN Lancet coaches but this was not continued with; on repaint they received the predominantly red coach livery with cream relief around the windows.

The Park Royal re-bodying of the pre-war TD4s/5s was to a more dated style, shown by JG 8208 at Deal garage displaying blinds for a winter short-working of the 85. MDEK CLUB – P.S.A. REDMOND

CHAPTER SIX

THE 1950s – FROM INDIAN SUMMER TOWARDS A WINTER OF ECONOMY

As the company entered the 1950s, it seemed that the worst of the war privations were over; services were at near-normal levels compared to the thirties, while the tours programme was embarking on a major expansion on to the continent. Thus the 1950s were entered with optimism, but towards the end of the decade reducing revenues and higher costs became a constant feature, accentuated by a national strike for more pay in July 1957, which led to East Kent's passenger levels dropping by 6.3m (9 per cent) in that year. However, dividends were still being paid, one of 5 per cent being recorded for 1957. In January 1958 the chairman told shareholders that further cuts would have to be made to rural services although there was a political angle to this, as he was also lobbying for reductions in fuel tax to avoid the worst of such cuts. A fuel tax rebate for bus services would eventually emerge, but not until the next decade.

CONSOLIDATION

Emphasizing the return to normality in summer 1950 was the re-instatement of service 120, the high-season service from Ashford to Margate via Canterbury. This was one of the last of the seasonal services suspended since the war to resume. East Kent now started to consolidate its operations and it was to enter a period of relative stability that would last until the increasing need for economies forced change. However, the 120 was not long-lived – 1953 was its last summer of operation. The number later re-emerged on 8 September 1959 as a school service between Ashford, Essella Road and Wye via Evington Park Corner. Another change from May 1950 was a renumbering of the 49/A services, reverting to using 52 for the Margate–Ramsgate section via Westwood

used in 1937 prior to the tramway takeover, and retaining 49 for the service to Birchington via Reading Street but renumbering the 49A via Victoria Avenue to 50. The number 49A would re-emerge on 27 May 1967 for journeys via Dumpton Park Drive (as well as 50A), although these had been running since June 1966 with no suffix identifier.

One long-standing problem was finally rectified on 18 November 1951 when the 13 was diverted via Mill Road, away from a low bridge on the route near the Telegraph Inn at Deal; the 13A had been diverted earlier, via London Road, from 12 May 1948. The restriction removed, double-decks could now operate throughout, which must have relaxed matters for both traffic and engineering departments as prior to the route change, reliefs must have been a frequent occurrence on this trunk route.

Changing styles of the timetable covers of the early 1950s. The newer image of one of the modern Guy Arabs was introduced with the Coronation edition of May 1953, which featured a crown at the top centre. AUTHOR'S COLLECTION

On the publicity front, the timetable format changed from the summer 1950 edition to a larger size, 7¼in × 4¾in, which aided readability, but the number of pages remained broadly the same as in the former smaller 5¼in × 4¼in format. This also saw some tables moving to a landscape format; prior to this all were in portrait form.

The winter edition sported a stylized drawing of one of the new Leyland PD1As passing Dover Castle; this was not to be repeated and the next edition returned to the colour illustration of a pre-war Titan passing a Kentish oast house used from March 1946 but now in the larger format. The oast house was a reminder of the earlier demand for additional hop-pickers' services in the autumn, mostly sourced from Ashford and Canterbury, but changing lifestyles of the 1950s now saw this rapidly diminishing. Later, from the summer 1953 timetable, the Coronation edition, the pre-war Titan picture was replaced by one of the new FFN-series Guys at Ramsgate harbour, which itself was replaced from September 1957 by a rather more idyllic scene of an EFN Guy by Canterbury's Westgate Towers.

Over the decade, the use of different-coloured pages for services operating high-summer schedules or extended late-summer timings became prevalent, a practice which would continue into the 1960s. In winter 1954–5 a further 'mid-winter' subdivision of timetables was also introduced for a time, reflecting the lower demand in the period between November and Easter. Another addition to publications was the re-emergence of area timetables towards the end of the decade; their earlier use was during the wartime period up to 1945. Initially, the area coverage for some books could be quite small; in 1959, for example, Canterbury and Rye had dedicated books. In the end a more sensible division into six area books was adopted as follows:

- Ashford, Rye and Hastings
- Folkestone, Hythe and New Romney
- Canterbury, Herne Bay, Whitstable and Faversham
- Dover
- Deal and Sandwich
- Isle of Thanet (Margate, Broadstairs and Ramsgate)

Takeovers

The winter 1950 timetable proudly announced that it included 'services of other operators in the area'. This only seemed to extend to Sarjeant's journeys paralleling the 103 (incorrectly spelt Sargeant in the timetable), Carey's connecting services to Dungeness and Newman's service from Hythe to Ashford via Aldington, however. Potential users of Newman's other service to Sandling station were invited

One unusual feature was the use of boat racks on a small number of coaches for rowing clubs in the area. CFN 95 carried hers between 1958 and 1962 at the time when an experiment with cream roofs was trialled. Note also the smaller fleet name, compare with that carried on pre-war cars.
MDEK CLUB – P.S.A. REDMOND

to 'enquire at Newman's office', although their summer service to Imperial Hotel appeared later, other operators' services, such as Drew's serving Chartham and Carey Brothers' route from New Romney to Ashford, were omitted altogether. Drew's eventually made it into the timetable in June 1966, while Carey's services on Romney Marsh were taken over in August 1952, appearing as routes 132/133 in the September 1952 timetable. These ran from New Romney to Lydd via Dungeness and to Ashford via St. Mary's and Newchurch respectively, the latter running Tuesdays and Fridays only. By 23 May 1953 two short-workings from New Romney to Newchurch, running on Saturdays only, were advertised on the 133. This experiment was unsuccessful and they were withdrawn by the winter timetable change of 20 September, if they ever ran at all. Later, a further alteration to this service was an extension back to Greatstone, detailed in the winter timetable issued on 1 October 1961. This was more enduring and the route then remained largely unchanged through the 1960s.

Further takeovers continued in the early part of 1953 with the acquisition of the coach businesses of Saxby in Margate, also known under the 'Enterprise' name, and Sarjeant Brothers of Folkestone. In both cases the operators' fleets of Bedford coaches saw service with East Kent for a number of years despite their non-standard nature when compared with the rest of the fleet.

The floods of January and February 1953, which devastated the low lying eastern part of the country, brought another challenge for East Kent. The railway line from

Faversham to Birchington was breached in many places and the company was called upon to provide emergency replacement coaches. Fortunately, as this was the winter, plenty of de-licensed coaches were readily available, and these were taken out of store and pressed into service with the approval of the traffic commissioners. This drew parallels with the rail strike of 1919, when East Kent had also come to the rescue of stranded rail passengers.

Bus Stations and Depots

For East Kent in the 1950s, the process of consolidation of the company's operations was also marked by a programme of improving its property asset base, both for the travelling public and for its operational and engineering functions. By June 1950, a new bus station was brought into operation at Deal, South Street, enabling the country services to park off-street and assisting the queueing for these routes; town services continued to use the on-street arrangements. Four years later, on 13 January 1955, a new bus station was formally opened at Folkestone Bouverie Square, although the bays were already in use by or before the previous December. It replaced the previous arrangements where cars terminating in the town centre parked around the square. This had been in place since the war, when the previous arrangements, whereby most services terminated at the Harbour, were abandoned.

The next bus station to be opened was in Canterbury on 6 June 1956, with the first departure recorded as AEC Reliance KFN 211 on the L2 service. This had been a more complex project than the others as the company had been in dispute with the council and faced the prospect of hav-

The delightful enquiry office at Sandwich fitted well with the period nature of the town despite being built in 1922. Now disused, it is however still in place. This view shows it in better times when it was still manned and operated by the company. MDEK CLUB – JESS WILSON

ing to vacate the previous site at St Peter's Place without having a suitable, centrally located alternative ready. As the new site was at the other end of town, the changes were accompanied by timing and routing alterations to services, those from the west now negotiating St Peter's Street and the High Street whereas those from the south no longer ran through the town.

Although these sites were significant hubs of the company's activity, Pencester Road, Dover also enjoyed a small stand area in addition to the on-street stops, mostly for more rural services and off-peak parking, while the smallest 'bus station' was probably that at Dymchurch. In addition to the major bus stations, the company had a large number of their own enquiry offices in most towns; these included the wonderful timber-framed waiting room and office in Sandwich, dating from 1922, as well as the seasonal facility at Reculver provided by one of the retired Leyland TS8 coaches. The company offices were in addition to the numerous agents throughout the area, many of which acted as parcels offices.

At the end of the decade, the depot at Dover, Russell Street, having already been renovated by 1955, was modernized between 1958 and 1960, enabling it to accommodate highbridge double-deckers from June 1959. New depots at New Romney (outstation of Folkestone) and Hastings (outstation of Rye) were progressed at the same period and formally opened in 1960 and 1961 respectively. The remaining depots were at Rye, Ashford, Canterbury, Herne Bay (with an outstation at Faversham), Folkestone, Kent Road (with other outstations at Lydd and the, by now, coach base at Seabrook), the original, enlarged, depot at

This early 1960s company view of Folkestone's bus station shows, from left to right, the main office block bordering Bay A for express services and spare cars; Bay B with an MFN Guy on service 17; while Bay C is obscured by the CJG Leyland PD1 on service 99 heading for Bay D, its stand in those days. AUTHOR'S COLLECTION – COMPANY ORIGINAL

Deal and three sites at Thanet. These were Westwood, the largest company depot of all, which could accommodate around 180 cars, and two others used mainly for winter storage: the ex-IoTES depot at St Peter's and the ex-Sayer's site at Margate Dane Road, which was also used for off-peak parking. Westwood had a large outside hard-standing to accommodate the significant number of cars used for schools and works services, both key features of its operations until the 1970s/80s, and which would see lines of older cars stabled outside ready for such work.

Fare Increases

One key factor differentiating the post-war era from pre-war was the onslaught of rising costs and the need to raise fares on a regular basis. As early as January 1950, the chairman was recorded in the annual report as saying that 51 out of the 116 regular stage services were not covering their operating costs, although this was probably the situation in the winter months, as only a year earlier the former general manager, Alfred Baynton, had addressed the Omnibus Society and stated that only nine services were un-remunerative throughout the year. Baynton highlighted another point, which was the disproportionate utilization of vehicles. In 1949 all 540 vehicles were pressed into use during the summer months whereas by October over 200 cars were de-licensed. This heavily peaked demand had always been a feature of East Kent's operations but as costs rose and recruitment of staff in the summer months became more difficult, the ability of the company to lower vehicle utilization costs, balance the books and also deliver a reliable operation became an increasing challenge.

The increases in fares at this time were significant: for example, by October 1952 the fare between Deal and Dover had risen 25 per cent from the pre-war 1/3d (6½p) to 1/7d (8p). Taking into account that fares had reverted gradually to pre-war levels in 1948–9, the scale of increase is even more dramatic; against this, however, must be set the fact that inflation in both 1951 and 1952 was running at over 9 per cent per annum.

In an attempt to encourage off-peak traffic later in the decade, the company experimented with an offer of cheap half-day returns from 30 March 1958. These were offered from 1.45 in the afternoon but only on Sundays, Wednesdays and Thursdays. To aid assessment of the project, these return tickets were issued as 'Special' from the Setright Speed machines now in use across the company. When redeemed for the return journey the conductor cancelled and retained them, issuing a blue exchange ticket to the passenger. The cancelled returns were then placed in an envelope with the relevant service number and handed in with the conductor's waybill, machine and takings at the end of the duty. Normal full-fare returns were cancelled and handed back to the passenger. Unfortunately the experiment was not a success: passenger levels were recorded as dropping by more than 846,000 over three months compared with the previous year, and the offer was discontinued by the end of the summer.

A throwback to tramway days was the continued existence of 'early journey tickets', confined to routes 49/50 (previously 49/A) between Ramsgate and Garlinge, the former tramway mileage. These return tickets were available weekdays before 7.30am for outward journeys but holders could return any time of day; the company planned to remove these tickets in the fares increase of 1954 but as this was refused they had to wait until the fare changes of 1 May 1955 before they were abolished. At Dover another legacy of tramway days was the availability of workmen's tickets between Buckland, Marine Station and Maxton, also available before 7.30am (outward) but the return times were more restricted than Thanet, now being available only from 1pm to 5.30pm Mondays to Fridays, and 12pm to 1.15pm on Saturdays. The original plan for Dover in 1954 was to increase them from 4d (1.5p) to 6d (2.5p) but by 1955 they were also abolished. One interesting negotiation reported in 1956, also concerning former tramways, was the renewal of the agreement with Dover Corporation made when the tramways were taken over at the beginning of 1937. Up to this time the corporation were paid a proportion of receipts from the Dover town services. It is understood that following discussions the new agreement resulted in no more money changing hands thereafter.

SERVING THE NEW ESTATES

The fifties saw a notable increase in housing; the country was emerging from wartime restrictions and many were seeking to move out of London to the coast, while at the same time new estates were being built to accommodate the expanded workforce employed in the Kent coalfields and new light industrial developments, particularly around Thanet. Property developers also had an eye on proposals to electrify the Kentish railway lines, which would promote commuting and lead to greater demand for housing, and wartime prefabs also needed to be replaced.

The timetables commencing 3 June 1951 saw changes to Herne Bay town services, with a revised summer service group numbered 39/A and 43/A, improving the service offered from Studd Hill Estate to the Beltinge/Hillborough area across town. This resulted in the erstwhile service 42 from Greenhill to Hillborough only operating in the winter for a time, whilst the 39A/43A operated summer only, a confusing situation that was regularized in summer 1953 when a revised service group was introduced comprising the 39, 42 and 43 running all year with commensurate reductions in the winter season, plus the 39 seasonally withdrawn from the Studd Hill terminus. Although these changes were largely as a result of seasonal demand they heralded future changes to services in the area, which would cater for expanded housing in both Greenhill and the Beltinge/Hillborough areas. Later, in summer 1959, a limited summer-only 39A was reintroduced, running into the centre of the Greenhill Estate to and from Westminster Bank. Interestingly, the winter service variant saw the 39 running to Greenhill Estate rather than its summer Studd Hill terminus; it is unclear why the company chose to do this rather than retaining the 39A number through the winter. Further changes were made to these services from 20 May 1961, when a 42A variant was introduced serving the centre of Greenhill Estate, while the 39A was then consigned to some limited journeys serving Greenhill Road and, oddly, for high season Reculver/Railway Station journeys supplementing the Reculver/Studd Hill service 39. The area would have to await the middle of the 1960s before a major restructuring of all routes heralded a greater degree of consistency to Herne Bay's town services.

A small number of experimental services were introduced at the start of the decade; two of these were of relatively short mileage and most journeys were probably based on making good use of spare cars and crews at times of low demand. Service 30, running from Canterbury Bus Station to Highland Court Hospital, near Bridge, which had become an annex of the Kent and Canterbury Hospital, began on 17 October 1951 but only ran for visiting times on Wednesdays, Friday and Sundays. A further service, this time a replacement for an abortive earlier pre-war plan, was the 111, introduced on 5 November 1951, running on weekdays from Seabrook's Naildown Estate (described as Horn Street) to Hythe, Light Railway Station. Both of these services only operated a handful of journeys in any day and would never generate a long-term source of traffic, the 111 succumbing in September 1958 while the 30 lasted until the end of the summer 1966 timetable.

On 3 June 1951 service 53 was revised and new route 53A introduced to serve Quetta Road on Ramsgate's Newington Estate, diverting half of the former 53 service to the estate and providing a 24-minute summer/30-minute winter service over each leg with a combined 12- or 15-minute frequency on the common section from Newington Road to Northdown Park via Ramsgate, Broadstairs and Margate.

A lowbridge Guy of 1950, EFN 193 is pictured at the Hollands Avenue terminus of service 100. The prefab buildings behind were a notable feature of post-war Britain; later replaced by better quality housing, which also saw the 100 extended a little further up to Stanbury Crescent in 1970.
MDEK CLUB – B. WEEDEN

On 18 July 1954 the 53 was also diverted into the estate, running as far as the Centre, doubling the service thereat, while the 71 was extended the short distance from Gwyn Road to Allenby Road as partial compensation for the withdrawal of the 53 from its earlier Hare & Hounds terminus.

Round the coast at Dover, development of the Buckland Estate at Melbourne Avenue saw new services 131/A introduced to the area on 18 March 1951 in between timetable publication dates; these were effectively a diversion of half of the cars on service 96, allowing an hourly service to both destinations; Kearsney suffering a halving of frequency as a result. Much later, from 8 June 1957, further development across town at Aycliffe Estate saw new service 136 introduced from the town centre; eventually, on 14 June 1959, this was linked with services 98/A, which had also previously terminated in the centre, at Pencester Road, thus providing a cross-town service from Aycliffe to The Linces/Melbourne Avenue. These latter destinations had been served by the 98/A respectively since 11 November 1951, following a re-routing from the 98's post-war Buckland Estate terminus at Pilgrim's Way, leaving that destination the sole province of the 94/A group. The re-routing of the 98/A in Buckland Estate was due to increased demand and the success of the earlier inauguration of the 131/A services.

The linkage of the 98 to the 136 and replacement of the latter was, at first, marked by confusing publicity, both services still being (incorrectly) displayed in the late summer 1959 timetable with the revised cross-town service 98 only shown as operating in the high summer. Presumably this was an administrative error, as both the early/late summer timetables were normally the same and Supplement No. 1 from 6 September rectified the matter.

It should be noted that many alterations were introduced as soon as resources or access roads permitted. As a result they would only feature in subsequent issues of the timetable despite being introduced beforehand – the Dover changes of March 1951 being a case in point – although, undoubtedly, local handbills would have been issued at the time of the change. While efforts have been made to record accurate dates of introduction as far as possible, many changes only apparent from the introductory date of published timetables may have actually commenced before the stated date.

Aylesham now saw a trial of improved services following a number of requests for the company to provide more journey options for the expanding mining community, based there and largely employed in the nearby Snowdown colliery. Service 78 was extended to Aylesham from Barfreston twice a day on Saturdays from 28 July 1951, thereby providing a direct connection to Deal. A new service was introduced from Sunday 22 July 1951, numbered 104, running from Folkestone to Aylesham. Initially scheduled to run all week, demand was not as predicted and it was curtailed to run Saturdays and Sundays only from 2 December 1951; later, Sunday operation was confined to the summer with Saturday-only operation all year starting from 21 September 1952, which was more suited to the leisure opportunities offered. Neither experiment was a resounding success. From 19 September 1954 the 104 was suspended in the winter and was finally withdrawn in 1958, last running on 13 September. Likewise, the 78 was curtailed to run only as far as Eythorne/Elvington from 5 January 1958, with Shepherdswell now served on Wednesdays, Saturdays and Sundays only. In this case not only Aylesham lost its Deal connection but the long-standing pre-war service to Barfreston was also withdrawn, although it was still served by the 89 from Dover.

CONTINUED HOLIDAY DEMAND

Despite this, the seasonal nature of East Kent's services continued, which meant that most coastal resorts, stretching from Whitstable, Herne Bay to Margate and Ramsgate and also at Folkestone and Rye, still enjoyed significant enhancements to services in the summer months. Even Hythe's local service 110 from Saltwood to Palmarsh/West Hythe had enjoyed an improved service in the high summer in the early 1950s. From 23 May 1953 another minor improvement was the introduction of an all-year Saturday-only service from Hythe to Burmarsh, the 110A.

This tours brochure of the later 1950s incorporated continental and national tours as well as local excursions into the one booklet.
AUTHOR'S COLLECTION

In later years this service was generally resourced from Ashford by the 109 car when it was laid over at Hythe. Further across Romney Marsh, the 105 was supplemented by the introduction of summer service 105A to Littlestone on the same date, the takeover of the former local operator Carey's Brothers services in 1952 now permitting this. Earlier changes at Folkestone from 3 June 1951 had seen former circular 100 becoming a Hill Road–Cheriton via Sandgate service but later, from 6 February 1955, it was diverted from Hill Road to serve Hollands Avenue.

At Rye, the opportunity was taken from summer 1953 to split the 114 service running across town from Winchelsea Beach to Camber. Number 114 was retained for the eastern leg while 116 was used for Camber/Broomhill, thus returning to the pre-war numbering used up to May 1948. The Broomhill service was introduced on Saturdays only from 1 October 1950 with a high summer Sunday serv-

Rye's first double-decker is pictured at Rye harbour on service 115. JG 8225 was one of a number of pre-war Titans that received surplus bodies from the AJG-registered 1939 TD5s when their running units were used in new semi-chassisless coaches. MDEK CLUB

ice from 3 June 1951. In the low/winter season the two legs were reconnected to provide a cross-town service and reverted to using 114. In summer 1956 things turned full circle and the through service was maintained throughout the high season, retaining the number 114. A few years earlier, in 1952, Rye received its first double-deck, JG 8225, to meet summer demand but remaining that winter, while from 1953 three cars arrived for summer services, two of which worked mainly on the 116 with the other on services 115/117.

The exceptions to seasonal improvements on the coast were at Dover and Deal, which saw no increases to their town services with the exception of Deal's 79 to Kingsdown, which ran an enhanced service in the high summer. Despite the lack of enhancements to local services in these two towns, the trunk routes from Dover to Deal and Folkestone still operated at increased frequencies during the summer.

The inland centres at Canterbury and Ashford had no local enhancements either, apart from on some trunk routes serving the coastal areas. Conversely, some Ashford town services operated a reduced service on Wednesday afternoons, early closing day. Initially this only concerned the more-frequent 121/126 services from Hunter Avenue/High Street to Woodchurch Turning/Hillyfields, the latter first not running at all on Wednesdays. The 123 from Willesborough Lees to Beaver Green did not reduce. However, when the 121A/123A variants to Beaver Green and Woodchurch Turning respectively were introduced on 31 May 1952, neither of them ran on Wednesday afternoons, the pattern reverting to the earlier 121/123 combination.

At this time the 126 was also extended to run as part of the 121/123 group between Hunter Avenue and Beaver Green via Hillyfields, although this saw a halving of frequency to the latter point to hourly, although it did now run on Wednesday mornings. The less-frequent town services 122 (Cobbs Wood to South Willesborough) and 125 (Kennington to Kingsnorth/Bromley Green), running hourly, and 124 (High Street to Newtown), at 30-minute intervals, were unaffected. The 124 itself was suspended at this time, from 3 May to 25 August 1952, due to reconstruction of river bridges in Newtown Road.

At Canterbury, inbound services 6, 7, 8 and 9 and city service 24 turning from Guildhall Street into High Street had caused some concern, and in June 1957 the country services were diverted via Lower Bridge Street, leaving Guildhall Street the sole province of the 24 until service changes removed it. Pedestrianization gradually took all services out of the High Street as well. In May 1957 the company commissioned photographs to illustrate the problem at a public enquiry and two are shown here, with re-bodied TDs of both varieties on services 7 and 24. Note the workmen's handcart and the unattended cycles, a lasting statement to how things have changed. MDEK CLUB – COMPANY ORIGINAL

Further changes took place at Folkestone prompted by more housing developments. From 23 May 1953 a service to Shaftesbury Avenue in Cheriton, numbered 134, was provided by diverting one journey every hour off the 99 at Cheriton Library. At this time the 99 also ran a limited service to/from Folkestone's Pleasure Gardens Theatre; this had commenced post-war by October 1950 and remained until withdrawn from September 1958 upon closure of the theatre. Pre-war and certainly from 1927, cars on services to places as far afield as Dover, Hythe and Lydd would await the finish of theatre performances. On 28 May 1955 the 134 was extended up Shaftesbury Avenue to Biggins Wood Road, providing a better service to the estate. Later, from 14 September 1958, further changes to the west of Cheriton saw one journey every hour on the 108 extended to Horn Street, effectively replacing part of the 101, which was then withdrawn west of the bus station.

Referencing the earlier changes that removed the 'A' suffix descriptors from services 70 and 107, it was now the turn of the 25 in Canterbury to change. The expanding Spring Lane Estate had been served by variant 25A since summer 1951, alternate journeys running to the estate (25A) or golf club (25). By May 1953 the service focused on the estate and only a couple of isolated morning journeys ran to the golf club. It was thus anomalous to use a suffix descriptor for the main service and these were swapped in the timetable of 20 June 1954, with 25 used for the main London Road Estate–Spring Lane Estate service. Earlier, at the London Road end, from 20 September 1953, the service had also been extended from Mill Lane to the Square.

East Kent worked with local councils to promote the area, with a publicity bus touring the Midlands and the North from the 1950s. MFN 901, one of the smart Guy Arab IVs from 1956–7, worked as such from 1959 to 1962 and is pictured here at Canterbury garage before the tour. EAST KENT OMNIBUS

The Isle of Thanet Daimlers lasted until 1950 before being retired from service, a number gravitating to Herne Bay and Canterbury. CKP 877 is pictured heading for the golf club – at that time the 25's terminus, before the changes of 1954 – passing the Longmarket, where temporary buildings have replaced bomb-damaged structures. SEC – W.J. HAYNES

From 19 September 1954 the number range increased, with the addition of local service 135 serving The Citadel on Dover's Western Heights running Tuesdays and Saturdays only. With the takeover of the Carey's services earlier, numbered 132/133, new services 134, 135 and, later, the 136, the continuity of the original numbering system was starting to go awry, although ingenious re-numberings in later years and selective use of spare numbers would largely maintain the original 1937 scheme. Extending the range even further was service 140, introduced from 2 August 1957 running from Rye to Ferryfield via Camber on summer Saturdays and Sundays only. The recent opening of Ferryfield airport near Lydd had attracted limited coach services, but nothing like its near-neighbour Lympne, and the airport sightseeing trade for bus services was obviously negligible. From the high summer of 1960 it was revised to run in conjunction with the 132 to New Romney via Littlestone, a more logical leisure destination. It was also extended back to Hastings and ran on Wednesdays as well. Like many services across Romney Marsh it was never a resounding success and was withdrawn after the summer of 1962.

As the decade progressed, it was clear that Kent's popularity as a holiday destination accessed by public transport was waning, although the day-tripper market was still buoyant. This would, at first, particularly affect the low season and from September 1954 some of Thanet's evening services in the winter timetable were reduced.

Furthermore, the through service on the 2 from Canterbury to Hastings was curtailed from the same time to become a summer-only operation, with the winter service only running over the core section from Ashford to Rye. One initiative to promote holidays in the area was the operation of an annual publicity bus to the Midlands and the North involving conversion of a double-decker with display stands; it undertook a tour in January of each year from the 1950s to the mid-70s.

Later, other major routes succumbed to cuts; in summer 1959 the boosted 15-minute high-summer service formerly operated on the 80 between Deal and Dover was not brought in, and a 20-minute frequency ran in this period. However, this was still an enhancement, as the low season/winter service ran, as previously, at a 30-minute interval. Trunk route 10 from Folkestone to Maidstone was another service subject to rationalization, halving in frequency on winter Sundays to hourly from October 1959. Despite this, as the low season market changed, East Kent was ready to make the most of new opportunities: seasonal open-top services were introduced whilst the development of industrial estates had seen special works services emerge, commencing with the 57 introduced by May 1955, which ran on weekdays from Broadstairs station to the Margate Industrial Estate situated on the Ramsgate Road near Relay House/Corner. Some journeys on Ashford's 123/A were extended from Willesborough Lees to Batchelor's factory from 15 September 1957. Later, another works service, 59, was introduced in the summer timetable from June 1959, running from Margate harbour to Richborough, Petbow's factory, initially operating on Mondays to Fridays only, but extending to Saturdays between May 1960 and May 1965.

Towards the end of the 1950s, as more numbers were used up, the company took further stock of its route numbering and changes were made to free up some numbers. On 14 September 1958 the 11/12 services were modified, the erstwhile and less frequent 11 to Preston became 11A and the more frequent 12 to Stodmarsh took the number 11, while the 14 and 14A services were combined into one, the 14, running direct between Goodnestone and Staple, thus obviating the need for two different legs from Canterbury, saving a car in consequence.

EXPRESS SERVICES – NATIONAL AND CONTINENTAL EXPANSION

The express service operations were also entering their boom years and the London routes were finally formally numbered from May 1950 as follows:

L1   London–Canterbury–Margate–Broadstairs–Ramsgate
L2   London–Maidstone–Canterbury–Margate–Broadstairs–Ramsgate
L3   London–Ashford–Folkestone–Dover
L4   London–Charing–Canterbury–Dover
L5   London–Whitstable–Herne Bay
L6   London–Charing–Canterbury–Sandwich–Deal

The Birmingham and South Coast express services remained unnumbered at this stage. Although the traditional express market from London to the coast was expanding, new opportunities were also emerging, promoted by the development of ferry services to France and Belgium from the ports of Dover and Folkestone and by the entrepreneurial spirit of people interested in providing air services to the continent. As detailed earlier, the company had com-

Two London express service leaflets – on the left a stylish design and on the right one of the first portraying the recently introduced service numbers. The unusual East Kent logo is of note on the 1950 design although this was soon replaced with the standard style but with a similar format cover.
AUTHOR'S COLLECTION

Although withdrawn by the time this view was taken in 1968 at the former railway sidings at Seabrook garage, FFN 448 – one of the Leyland Royal Tigers from 1951 – displays blinds for the L4 service, which would cease in this form in 1957. AUTHOR

menced continental tours from 1950, and in 1952 were also operating on behalf of Global Tours in Europe. However, the improving prosperity of the population from both working- and middle-class backgrounds meant that there was a demand to explore new horizons beyond those of the Kent countryside but within a more affordable price range.

As early as 1951, a company handbill offered connections at Dover to and from boats to Dunkerque, Ostend or Calais using the existing L3 service. The more interesting development was the offer of dedicated coaches from London connecting to air services from Lympne to Le Touquet operated by Air Kruise (Kent) Ltd., trading under the name Trans-Channel Air Services. It is thought this operation was fairly limited, with initial arrangements to transfer to Lympne via Newingreen being mentioned in 1952. Air Kruise was eventually absorbed into Silver City Airways, by which time operations had transferred to Lydd (Ferryfield), certainly no later than 1955, due to problems with the heavier Bristol aircraft used. In the meantime another airline, Skyways, was more interested in Lympne, as they would operate Douglas Dakotas, more suitable for Lympne's grass runways. Key to their plans was the provision of dedicated coach services from London to Lympne and Beauvais to Paris, the former provided by East Kent, connecting with a short-hop flight across the Channel. The service was inaugurated on 21 September 1955 for dignitaries and the press, and two coaches, FFN 448/9, were photographed leaving Victoria coach station for Lympne.

The full service commenced the following summer and

was the start of a long relationship between East Kent and Skyways and the provision of coach/air services. Although FFN coaches operated the inaugural run, three of the more modern HJG-series coaches received Skyways branding, with a blue relief band, for operation on the services. They carried the livery from 1956 until 1957, and – until a Skyways livery briefly re-emerged in 1969 – Skyways journeys were then identified by the destination blinds and/or Skyways 'Coach/Air' slip boards, which could be placed over the East Kent fleet name on the service coaches delivered from the 1957 MJG-series until those of the OJG-F-series.

Meanwhile, down at Ferryfield, a coach/air service was offered from 1956 but it never expanded to the scale of Skyways. While a dedicated direct coach was operated, it appears never to have featured in East Kent's own publicity. Two of the HJG-series coaches received Silver City branding and silver relief in 1956 and 1957 to operate the dedicated Ferryfield service, which was marketed as 'Silver Arrow' in the airline's own publicity as it had a train connection to Paris from Etaples in France. A separate Lydd connection involved use of the normal L3 service to and from Ashford with a special express coach connection from Ashford to Ferryfield and return. This did feature in East Kent's leaflets and continued to appear in the 'London to the Continent' brochure up until at least 1967. It is unclear whether there was ever much demand, unlike for the competing and more successful Skyways operation.

The FFN Leyland Royal Tigers were soon displaced from the coach/air services by specially liveried Dennis Lancet LU2s of 1954, rare vehicles indeed – East Kent was the largest user. HJG 24 sits at London's Victoria coach station displaying Silver City's 'Silver Arrow' branding. This operation, based at Lydd Ferryfield, would never be as successful as the competing Skyways service. AUTHOR'S COLLECTION – UNKNOWN

Three of the 1957 Beadle-bodied AEC saloons were delivered in Europabus livery. MJG 286 is pictured at Canterbury in this publicity shot for the company. MDEK CLUB – COMPANY ORIGINAL

Meanwhile, East Kent developed further coach touring services to Western Europe by means of reciprocal arrangements with the Europabus network introduced in July 1953, such facilities using the ferry connections mentioned earlier. From 1957 onwards a number of MJG, WFN and FN East Kent service coaches would sport the blue and grey Europabus livery. The other development of continental operations was the offer of 'No Passport' day excursions, commencing in 1955 and running initially on Wednesdays, passengers transferring to the boat from Folkestone to Boulogne. In connection with this, Leyland Tigers JG 9937/8/55 were converted to mobile offices in 1957 and certainly JG 9937 was used to issue the 'No Passport' cards at Folkestone in the late 1950s. Although coaches connected to the ferry from Kent towns, a large number of foot passengers also took advantage of the arrangements. The next decade would see even further expansion of the continental market.

The London services also underwent development. New service L7 was introduced in the summer of 1957 although it only ran on Saturdays and Sundays in the summer from Canterbury to London. It was, in reality, a relief service to the L1, which it paralleled; it would not re-emerge in 1958 although the number would be reincarnated in the 1960s. A more successful introduction in the same year was the L8, providing a summer Saturday-only service between Folkestone and London via Hythe, Dymchurch, New Romney and Ashford. The summer of 1957 would also mark the last year of operation of the L4, running from Dover to London via Lydden and Canterbury, by now reduced to just one

journey each way. The route served and the number would both re-emerge in the 1970s but neither bearing any close resemblance to this service.

THE SUEZ CRISIS

The major issue of the decade was the Suez crisis of 1956; fuel rationing drove the company to reduce services, the greatest impact being on Sundays, where many services were reduced. One example was the 109, which was split for the period on Sundays, running Ashford–East Brabourne and Hythe–Stowting, leaving the intermediate section unserved on that day. There were also cuts on weekdays; services 33, Chestfield–Seasalter, and 41, Herne Bay–Seasalter, were withdrawn, although the latter only operated on Saturdays in the winter, while service 101 between Folkestone and Newington was also suspended (the 102 temporarily serving Downs Road). Express services were not immune either, all being reduced, while the L6 to Deal was curtailed to run Fridays, Saturdays and Sundays only and the South Coast Express was confined to one journey each way on Saturdays and Sundays only. The reductions were phased in, the first commencing in December 1956, with further cuts in February 1957. Fortunately, the crisis was short-lived and restrictions on the supply of diesel oil were removed by April 1957, when bus services could start to return to normal, with petrol restrictions affecting cars removed later, in May.

However, there were longer-term effects, and further economies were applied to the following summer timetable of 1957. A fundamental alteration concerned the 19; its summer-only extension to Dymchurch was withdrawn permanently, and the remaining Friday-only service to Stone Street was retained in its winter form but extended from the Chequers down to Six Mile Cottages. In compensation, by February 1957, one journey each way on service 18 was diverted via Six Mile Cottages to provide a limited service to the area. Other permanent or temporary economies in reaction to Suez were also evident – for example frequency reductions were applied to trunk services 3, 8 and 67 from Canterbury, Herne Bay's 37/38 to Faversham and local route 39, Thanet's heavily peaked 51 serving Margate, and the more rural 70 from Ramsgate to Birchington via Minster.

Hythe's local service 110 was reduced, as well as Folkestone's trunk route 90 to Dover in the mornings, while at Rye and Hastings the 113, 114 and 128 routes were also affected. Deal's 79 remained at its winter frequency, the 1957 summer enhancement limited to extending more journeys from Kingsdown, Rising Sun to Kingsdown Links.

LJG 306, from the second batch of AEC Reliance saloons delivered in 1956, is shown at the Stone Street, Six Mile Cottages terminus of the 19 in 1970 – the last year of the service's operation in this form. This was the southernmost terminus following the Suez cuts of 1957. AUTHOR

From 5 January 1958 it underwent a more fundamental revision to become a cross-town service combined with the 85, running from Kingsdown to Sandown, adopting the latter number, and which then saw the more frequent summer service resumed that year. Summer-only services 60/61 from Margate to Deal and Dover were completely suspended, although these had returned by summer 1958. A number of other services would also return to their 1956 summer levels in 1958. Exceptions were the 3, 8 and 37/38, which kept their reduced 30-minute weekday frequencies (all from the former 20-minute), the 67 now remaining at 90 minutes instead of its former hourly service and the 110 now running hourly throughout instead of enjoying its former 30-minute high-summer service.

A further outcome, possibly a combination of Suez and lower demand in the winter, was that the 8 would further reduce in frequency in the midday off-peak period on winter weekdays from 4 November 1957 to 29 March 1958. Only an hourly service was maintained to Margate, supplemented by hourly short-workings between Canterbury and Upstreet; this arrangement would gradually extend to operate throughout the winter period in future years. Another, later, reduction would see the 109's service east of East Brabourne reduced to a Tuesday, Saturday and Sunday operation from 14 September 1958, although the all-week service returned to Stowting from 14 June 1959 and resumed throughout from 26 June 1960. The winter 1958 timetable also saw the 49/50 extended to Minnis Bay from Birchington station, replacing the winter service on the 46, which was withdrawn. The 49/50 would for the time revert to terminating at Birchington station in the summer, when the 46 resumed.

The Leyland-Beadle rebuilds are illustrated by this view of two preserved examples at Herne Bay in 2009. FFN 446, one of the first batch, sports the cream roof livery adopted from 1953 onwards for these cars, while GFN 273, from the later tranche, carries the original livery. The Leyland marque is further represented by FFN 451, one of the 1951 Royal Tigers, carrying a replica of the board used on the introductory Skyways service operated by her companions FFN 448/9. AUTHOR

FFN 451 is pictured at Ramsgate harbour when it was still in service but by now relegated to local excursion duties. However, all cars of this batch retained the attractive two tones of red in their livery until the end.
MDEK CLUB – JESS WILSON

THE LAST LEYLANDS

The start of the 1950s, with delivery completed of the traditional Lancet coaches and Falcon bus orders, still saw some one-off or limited body changes on other cars – most notably five of the JG-registered Leyland TD4s from 1936–7 gained newer bodies from the 1939 AJG-series TD5s in 1951 when those chassis were reclaimed for use in new coaches. The running units of twenty-eight of these pre-war TD5s were utilized in 'new' semi-chassisless coaches built by Beadles. They were of a full-fronted, forward-entrance design to the newly permitted length of 30ft (9m) and width of 8ft (2.4m), and the changes involved lengthening the original chassis members and a new high-ratio differential to permit higher-speed running. The first batch, FFN 445–7, arrived in 1951, the balance following in 1952. The wider bodies on a 7ft 6in (2.3m)-wide chassis resulted in the driving position being angled to the left, disconcerting to some drivers. At this time the company also took the opportunity to move towards standardization on oil (diesel) engines, and during the winter of 1950–1 re-equipped twenty-five of the remaining petrol-engine TS7 coaches with oil engines from withdrawn Leyland TD double-deckers.

Despite the change away from Leyland, the company still purchased two small batches of their new underfloor-engine single-deck chassis, the Royal Tiger; these arrived in 1951 and 1953 respectively. The first batch, FFN 448–53, were equipped with distinctive central-entrance Park Royal bodies. FFN 448–50 initially seated thirty and were specifically intended for long-distance tours, while FFN 451–3 accommodated thirty-seven; all of these cars, however, were to undergo many seating changes in their later life, as did most tour cars of this era. Two notable features of these coaches were that they were the first 8ft-wide, 30ft-long (9m × 2.4m) vehicles in the fleet, the width factor precluding their use on express services until London's trams were abandoned in 1952, although they were allowed on specified routes in London for private hire purposes. They were also the first company vehicles to be equipped with heaters from new. Different in all aspects from earlier coaches, they became the company's flagship cars at the time and were the vehicle of choice on the newly introduced continental tours. The second and last batch of Leyland Royal Tigers, HFN 1/2, arrived two years later, in 1953, with Duple bodies to very different streamlined styling. These were also used for touring work from their date of delivery until 1963.

GUY DOUBLE-DECKERS AND DENNIS COACHES

For double-deck buses, Guy was now chosen – allegedly due to the long delivery times offered by Leyland but possibly because of positive experience with Guy's wartime chassis; certainly the company was exploring new pastures. If it was down to delivery times it was to no avail, as it took until 1951 before this order was completed, much of the delay attributed to the bodybuilders. Comprising eighty cars, the first forty were to the normal 53-seat lowbridge specification favoured by East Kent, bodied by Park

The final two Royal Tigers carried Duple bodies similar to the style on the later Dennis LU2s. However, unlike the Dennises, they first carried the predominantly red livery and, uniquely, the slanted fleet name shown in this view of HFN 2. Later, the fleet name reverted to the standard style and the cream roof livery was adopted. MDEK CLUB – COMPANY ORIGINAL

The highbridge FFN Guys were all first allocated to Thanet for the 49/50/52 group of services until supplanted by the PFN Regents in 1959. In February of that year FFN 382 is captured at Margate harbour displaying the slightly reduced blind display unique to Thanet. This car would later be converted to open-top in 1970. MDEK CLUB – P.S.A. REDMOND

Royal and registered EFN 170–209; they arrived in 1950. The next forty were a major departure from the earlier standard, however. Taking advantage of the delays and recent changes in legislation, FFN 360–99 were equipped with 8ft-wide (2.4m) 56-seat Park Royal highbridge bodies, which had some outline similarities to London Transport's RT/RTW class. Initially, they were all allocated to Thanet, commencing a long association with the 49/50/52 group of services until replacement by AEC Regent Vs in 1959.

Once the balance of the immediate post-war orders had been received, it was time for the company to assess its future needs, especially as a new range of underfloor-engine single-decks was entering the market and restrictions on vehicle size had been eased. However, the rebuilding programme of Leyland TD5 chassis into coaches was

One of East Kent's 'oddities', GFN 601 was one of two Bedford SBs with Duple Super Vega body. Originally delivered in the earlier red coach livery, they later gained cream roofs. It awaits local custom at the Margate clock tower stand. MDEK CLUB COLLECTION

The later Guy Arab IVs of 1952–3 were distinctively different from what passed before and were more widely distributed than the preceding FFN Guys. They enabled a number of longer-distance services to be upgraded, the platform doors being a welcome feature. Folkestone's GFN 924 is pictured at Dymchurch bus station on the 105A, one of the services originally graced with the new cars. MDEK CLUB – BRIAN WEEDEN

still under way and a further twenty-five, GFN 256–80, arrived in 1952 following on from the first three of the initial programme delivered in 1951. One minor order was odd, perhaps reflecting the delivery constraints of the time. Two Bedford SB/Duple coaches, GFN 600/1, arrived in 1952 to bolster the tours fleet; ostensibly for use on continental tours, according to the *Omnibus*, it is believed they were actually confined to local or national tours. East Kent was never a prolific Bedford user, but some OBs and one SB entered the fleet later, in 1953, through acquisitions of the Saxby and Sarjeant businesses and lasted longer than one would have expected, reflecting the boom years of the local tours business; the OBs were retired in 1957 while the acquired SB, OKE 470, lasted until 1963, when it and its East Kent-purchased companions, GFN 600/1, were withdrawn but the lightweight Bedford chassis, favoured by many coach businesses, was never a favourite of East Kent.

The company continued with Guy for its next two batches of double-deckers. Thirty of these, GFN 908–37, arrived in 1952–3, built to the Arab IV specification with the 'new look' tin front, first introduced on vehicles for Birmingham Corporation. All but the first car had 56-seat Park Royal bodies with rear platform doors, the first double-deckers in the fleet to be so equipped, but apart from these changes the body style was similar to the previous FFN batch. GFN 908, the first delivered, actually had a 1950 Guy body with an open platform, and was exhibited at the Commercial Motor Show in 1952; it retained the open platform until withdrawal. The next, and last, Guy order was for a further twenty-five, delivered in 1956–7 registered MFN 883–907, this time with a more attractively styled 61-seat Park Royal body, again with the new look

The last Guy Arabs from 1956–7 carried a far more elegantly proportioned body, even with the restricted blind display, as demonstrated by MFN 888 at Hythe Red Lion Square in 1968. Note the East Kent shelter fronting the Mackeson brewery in the background, both now long gone. Now preserved, MFN 888 spent most of its life at Folkestone depot. AUTHOR

These two views taken at Westwood's hard-standing in 1967 allow a comparison between the Park Royal-bodied lowbridge and highbridge Guy Arab IIIs of 1950 and 1951, with five- and four-bay construction respectively, and also show the restricted blind displays. By now both types were relegated mostly to relief duties, evidenced by FFN 379's Sevenscore destination, a schools service. AUTHOR

ABOVE: HJG 6, one of the original Dennis LU2 tours cars, displays the additional beading that they carried, pictured here in later years at Canterbury parked on the standing opposite the garage. AUTHOR

front and platform doors. Both the FFN and GFN batches were up-seated in 1958–9 from their original 56-seat configuration to 58 seats by the addition, at the rear upper saloon, of redundant seating from JG-registered Dennis Lancets upon their withdrawal.

While all double-deckers now had the traditional 'full' blind, with destination and via points, Thanet cars would now have the bottom of the aperture masked, the display being reduced in depth in order to accommodate the multitude of destinations covered by cars from that depot on one blind. This would presage a further change in the 1960s affecting

The modernistic Dennis LU2 'Spaceships' were later used in the forefront of the company's publicity, as shown by these two London service leaflets of 1955 and 1957 – seeing the earlier Leyland Royal Tigers being replaced by the Dennis on all such leaflets. AUTHOR'S COLLECTION

many depots when, due to the varied routing changes of the time, many of the earlier Leyland and Guy double-deckers would receive a single-line blind with the aperture masked top and bottom, thus removing any via point information. Some depots, such as Ashford, managed to retain full blinds, while for Canterbury the change allowed them to dispense with separate city and country blinds.

The most interesting order of the early 1950s was for thirty of the new Dennis underfloor-engine LU2 chassis with Duple central-entrance coach bodies. HJG 3–32 arrived in 1954 and were intended for both express and tours work. The first six, HJG 3–8, had additional beading when compared to the remaining order and were first used on tours work with a lower capacity, of thirty-two seats, than the others, which were delivered as 41-seaters. Two more, HJG 9/10, were converted to 32-seaters for touring work in 1956 but all eight were changed to forty-one seats at the end of the season, as the new MJG touring coaches described later would be in place for the 1957 programme. East Kent was the largest operator of the Dennis LU2 chassis. The body style, with its extensive use of quarter lights in the roof panels, gave rise to the nickname 'Spaceships'. This became a semi-official name – the author recalls noting a wheel at Folkestone Kent Road garage, intended for an HJG, with the code 'S/Ship' chalked on the tyre!

AEC ENTERS THE SCENE

The HJG LU2s were to be the last order with Dennis at this time, and the company broke with tradition again by placing orders for AEC chassis for its next single-deck requirements, commencing a relationship which was to last for nearly twenty years. The first cars were forty AEC Reliances to 30ft (9m) length; some initially had AH410 engines but these were replaced with the bigger AH470 in due course. Registered KFN 210–49 and equipped with workmanlike Weymann 41-seat dual-purpose bodies, making them suitable for infill on London coach work during the peak summer season, the order was followed by twenty-two similar cars, LJG 305–26. The KFNs were notable in that they introduced three-track number blinds to the fleet and were also the forerunners of large-scale driver-only (D/C) operation with cars KFN 240–9. East Kent were still not adverse to experimentation, and in 1955–6 took delivery of three Beadle-Commer integral vehicles, KFN 250–2, with bodies similar to those on the later AEC/Beadle orders of 1957. They were never downgraded to D/C work and remained on coach duties; one, KFN 250, wore the blue and yellow contract livery of Butlin's, Cliftonville, from 1965 to 1968 and was the last vehicle to be so adorned.

Expanding express and tours operations now saw further significant orders for AEC single-deckers following delivery of the first two batches of Weymann-bodied cars. Returning to local bodybuilder Beadles of Dartford, the company purchased a further two batches of dual-purpose front-entrance saloons, MJG 285–300 and NFN 327–49, totalling thirty-nine cars, while Beadles also bodied a further twelve, MJG 41–52, to luxury coach specification with central entrances and 32-seat capacity. All were delivered in 1957 and were on the Reliance 30ft (9m) AH470 chassis. Excepting those in Europabus colours, the saloons featured the all-over red coach livery with cream relief on delivery,

Rye will always be associated with the Weymann-bodied Reliances as they provided the mainstay of their operations throughout the 1960s. KFN 238 waits time at Rye Station Approach in 1968 before departing on its 8-minute journey to Cadborough Cliff, East Kent's shortest route at the time. AUTHOR

With their TS3 two-stroke engines, the trio of Beadle-Commers were an unusual purchase for a mainstream company like East Kent. Mainly confined to excursion and tours duties, as represented by this view of KFN 251, they were never converted to D/C. MDEK CLUB – JESS WILSON

Table 7   East Kent Vehicles in 1958 (including cars withdrawn that year)

Type	Chassis	Body	Registrations	Total	Date/Notes
Double-deck lowbridge	Leyland TD4/5	ECW 53-seat	JG 7011/5/7/8/22/4; JG 8201/2/4/26–31/8/ 40/3/4/8; JG 9917/22/8/9	24	1936–8 *Bodies – 1948*
	Leyland TD4/5	Park Royal 53-seat	JG 7012/6/20/1/8/9; JG 8207–9/11/2/4/8/21–4/ 8232–4/6/42/7; JG 9907/8/ 11/3/6/20/1/3–6/30	35	1936–8 *Bodies – 1949*
	Guy Arab II	Weymann 55-seat	BJG 400/5–7/9– 15/20/1/3/4/40–44/73/4	22	1944–5 *Utility bodies*
	Leyland PD1 or PD2/1	Leyland 53-seat	CJG 938–87	50	1947–8. *CJG 987 – PD2 Some cars bodied by Salmesbury*
	Guy Arab III	Park Royal 53-seat	EFN 170–209	40	1950
Double-deck highbridge	Guy Arab I/II	Park Royal 56-seat	BJG 253–5/81/2/301–4/39/ 53–6/461/2	16	1943–5. *Utility bodies BJG 253–5 Arab I*
	Guy Arab II	Weymann 56-seat	BJG 472/5	2	1945. *Utility bodies*
	Guy Arab III	Park Royal 56/58-seat	FFN 360–99	40	1951
	Guy Arab IV	Park Royal 56/58-seat	GFN 908–37	30	1952–3 *GFN 908 – Guy body*
	Guy Arab IV	Park Royal 61-seat	MFN 883–907	25	1956–7
Single-deck coach	Leyland TS7	Park Royal 32-seat	JG 5431/3	2	1935. *Bodies – 1941 Vehicles in reserve*
	Leyland TS8	Park Royal 32-seat	JG 9942	1	1938. *Butlin's livery*
	Leyland TS8	Park Royal 32-seat	BFN 797	1	1940. *Vehicle in reserve*
	Leyland PS1	Park Royal 32-seat	CFN 60–109	50	1946–8
	Dennis Lancet J3	Park Royal 32-seat	EFN 571–95	25	1950
	Beadle-Leyland TD5	Beadle 35-seat	FFN 445–7; GFN 256–80		1951–2. *From TD5 units of 1939*
	Leyland PSU1/15	Park Royal 32- or 37-seat	FFN 448–53	6	1951
	Bedford SB	Plaxton 33-seat	OKE 470	1	1951. *Ex-Saxby 1953*
	Bedford SB	Duple 33-seat	GFN 600/1	2	1952
	Leyland PSU/15	Duple 32-seat	HFN1/2	2	1953
	Dennis Lancet LU2	Duple 41-seat	HJG 3–32	30	1954
	AEC Reliance 470	Weymann 41-seat	KFN 210–49; LJG 305–26	62	1955–6. *Dual purpose. Used as D/C saloons. KFN 230–49 firstly Reliance 410*
	Beadle-Commer TS3	Beadle 41-seat	KFN 250–2	3	1955–6. *Dual purpose*
	AEC Reliance 470	Beadle 32-seat	MJG 41–52	12	1957. *Touring coaches*
	AEC Reliance 470	Beadle 37-seat	MJG 285–300	16	1957. *Dual purpose*
	AEC Reliance 470	Beadle 41-seat	NFN 327–49	23	1957. *Dual purpose*
Single-deck bus	Dennis Lancet J3	Park Royal 35-seat	CFN 110–40/2–69; CJG 988–99	71	1947–9
	Dennis Lancet J3	Park Royal 35-seat	CFN 141	1	1947. *Converted to front entrance D/C operation in 1956*
	Dennis Falcon	Dennis 25- or 29-seat	EFN 556–70	15	1949–50. *D/C operation*

Source: MDEK Bus Club

The individual tours leaflets for each town still incorporated attractive artwork. This example from 1958 featured one of the HJG cars and images of local destinations. AUTHOR'S COLLECTION

as did the MJG touring cars, but the latter's body design with extensive beading had an attractive if not, by this time, dated, appearance.

The MJG saloons were initially delivered as 37-seat cars while the NFNs were to 41-seat specification. The MJG saloons were modified to 41-seat capacity in 1964–5. The MJG touring cars vacillated between differing capacities to meet normal coach and temporary luxury touring duties in the 1960s, eventually ending up as 41-seaters with the exception of one car, MJG 42, which retained an intermediate capacity of thirty-four seats up to its withdrawal.

Always associated with Thanet, the PFN Regent Vs were equipped with attractive full-front Park Royal bodies. PFN 852 is captured opposite the Sportsman tavern at Pegwell Bay on a schools short-working of service 87 in April 1974; note the traditional bus stop, timetable case and the company-provided shelter, a style to be seen across the network. Although not a D/C car, 852 was being worked as such (illegally – according to the union!) by the author in preference to the allocated half-cab, the PFN's full cab easily lending itself to this. AUTHOR'S COLLECTION

Elegant is possibly the only way to describe the MJG tours cars delivered in 1957. By 1972 they had moved off the top-flight tours – MJG 48 is here awaiting custom at the stand opposite Margate Pier with a nice selection of East Kent's tour boards. AUTHOR'S COLLECTION

Although the last Beadle-bodied saloons of 1957 were to dual-purpose specification they all carried the red coach livery upon delivery. MJG 291 is at London's Victoria coach station on Skyways duties, although only the front slip board is carried. MDEK CLUB

In 1959 AEC secured their first double-deck order with the delivery of forty Regent Vs, PFN 843–82, with attractive full-front Park Royal bodies, front entrances and a revised three-piece blind display with separate destination and via apertures. The flexibility afforded meant that the Regents could always carry full displays, unlike the reduced displays on earlier cars. The PFNs were to the newly permitted length of 30ft (9m) and could seat seventy-two. They replaced the FFN Guys on the 49/50/52 group of routes and thus began a long association with Westwood depot, where the majority of the class were always based. Their greater capacity would eventually allow a gradual reduction in the overall frequency of many of the Thanet services, thus achieving much-needed economies.

The NFN Reliances were to be the last Beadle bodies purchased by the company; the next order, still on the 30ft (9m) Reliance AH470 chassis, was given to Park Royal, with which East Kent had had a long association. Delivered in 1960, TFN 400–39 were also specified with dual-purpose bodies, enabling use on a variety of duties from express work to local tours and later widespread utilization on stage carriage services following conversion to D/C operation. This continued a long-standing policy whereby East Kent routinely downgraded coaches to bus operation to cover peak demand. Examples in the early 1960s saw the Beadle conversions and EFN Lancets often used on relief or even service work, although these were of necessity crew-operated. One final surprise for the fleet was the delivery of a Ford Thames, TJG 440, with Harrington coach body in 1960.

1958 would be the last year of operation of the wartime Guys in covered-top format. BJG 475 (eventually converted to open-top) is pictured at Hythe, Red Lion Square in the mid-50s, the blind display 'Only Relief' was often seen on Folkestone cars due to the previous screen before 'Relief' being 'Cheriton Library Only', it was often accurate, if unintentional! Note the Mackeson brewery now replaced by housing MDEK CLUB – D. VINCENT

Vehicles leaving the fleet during this period were all of the wartime Guys, with the exception of those retained for conversion to open-top, the remaining pre-war Lancets, Aces – the last at Ashford in 1953 – and the TS7/8 coaches, while a start was made on removing the post-war PS1s from the fleet. Three TS8s, JG 9937/8/55, were retained for use as mobile offices; a move that saw JG 9938 retained into NBC days and eventual preservation. The author was privileged to drive it during 1974 when based at Westwood.

The remaining Isle of Thanet Daimlers all went at the start of the decade but one, ADU 470, was retained as a tree-lopper after conversion to open-top and remained with the company until 1958, when it was replaced by a converted wartime Guy, BJG 304. The re-bodied TD4/5s remained on strength but their days were now numbered.

LIVERY VARIANTS IN THE 1950s

The first of the underfloor-engine coach deliveries, the FFN Royal Tigers, still reflected aspects of the pre-war style but with a maroon relief band below the cream relief, which now surrounded the windows. The later HJG-registered Dennis coaches dispensed with the overall red style, with more cream surrounding

Many of the TFN saloons were converted to D/C at an early stage and in later years they lost some of their alloy beading. TFN 417 is pictured at Acol on the Birchington to Ramsgate service 70 in 1974. AUTHOR

the windows and across the roof, similar to the single-deck bus livery; this was later applied to the similar-looking Leyland Royal Tigers, HFN1/2. From 1953 the Beadle-Leyland integrals began to receive cream roofs while many of the CFN Leyland PS1s started to be similarly repainted from 1955, although this decision was later rescinded for these latter coaches and they reverted to the predominantly red livery. While the 1955 single-deck dual-purpose deliveries all sported the saloon livery of cream upper works and red below the windows, the overall red livery for coaches with cream relief below the windows was retained for both the later AEC dual-purpose saloons and coaches delivered in 1956–7. It even reappeared on 538 FN, one of the later 1962 delivery of modern 36ft (11m) AEC Reliance coaches, but it gradually disappeared, the last examples surviving to the late 1960s.

A number of experiments took place to develop a revised coach livery for the 1960 delivery of coaches, the TFN series. Three of the NFN-series Reliances were treated and a livery with more cream emerged, which suited the Beadle bodies on these cars quite well. When applied to the TFNs, however, it was clear that the more angular lines of the Park Royal product did not carry off the colour scheme quite as well, and more red was applied to the lower panels; this was then adopted as the standard coach livery for the next decade. Later, both NFN and MJG saloons carried a version of this new livery before eventually gaining saloon livery. As already mentioned, the 1950s saw a number of contract liveries carried on the single-deck coach fleet for Silver City, Skyways, Butlin's and Europabus.

On the double-deck side, two vehicles had red applied to the lower deck window surrounds in 1952. Later, in 1955, an experiment with red roofs was trialled on a number of cars but not adopted; photographic evidence now shows that this scheme was tested much earlier. More notable was the special livery applied to a double-deck car, first appearing on BJG 354 in 1952, for the Mayor of Canterbury's Christmas Gift Fund. Overall white with seasonal branding and posters, initially hand-drawn, later in vinyl, and, for some cars, coloured interior saloon lights, the vehicle chosen was normally a car in for repaint and received the special livery temporarily, operating on Canterbury city services up until 24 December. The Christmas Bus operated every December from 1952 until 1982, by which time single-decks were used. Another double-deck livery variation was that used for the new generation of open-top cars introduced in 1959, which bore a predominantly cream livery with red relief

ABOVE: One of the livery experiments applied prior to the arrival of the TFN Reliances was this version carried by NFN 334. MDEK CLUB – COMPANY ORIGINAL

The last vehicles to carry the Europabus livery were twelve of the first batch of 36ft (11m) Reliance coaches; 528 FN is pictured outside the rebuilt garage at Dover. AUTHOR'S COLLECTION – COMPANY ORIGINAL

The last double-deckers to carry the Canterbury Christmas bus livery were the AEC Regents. AFN 771B, with the standard, more angular body compared to the first batch, performed the duty in 1978 and is seen here at the bus station working the university service, by now renumbered 650 in line with the policy of the 1970s. AUTHOR

shoreline. The opportunity was taken to extend the life of a number of the utility Guy Arab IIs, now in the course of withdrawal. East Kent, unlike many other operators, had decided not to re-body these wartime chassis despite the fact that their construction was relatively robust, unlike their bodies. As a result, with work on the bodies, the company could rejuvenate a small number of cars and get many more years of revenue-earning service for a relatively small outlay. Four vehicles were converted for the 1959 season, BJG 353/4 with Park Royal bodies and BJG 472/5 with Weymann bodies. All were highbridge models, as the lowbridge version was not suitable for conversion. Later, in 1960, two more, BJG 339/461, both Park Royal versions held back as a contingency, were converted for service expansion and to cover for engineering requirements.

and 'Coastal Service' in a blue-coloured scroll script on the upper panels.

NEW OPEN-TOP SERVICES

On 14 June 1959 East Kent introduced two experimental open-top services, much to the delight of enthusiasts, as it resulted in the prolongation of the life of some older cars.

The aim was to explore a new revenue source from both the traditional holiday market but also the many day-trippers, who did not have time to take advantage of local coach excursions. These new services were first based on the Isle of Thanet and exploited the coastal roads, many offering fine views over the bays and beaches of the Thanet

BJG 475, one the Weymann-bodied conversions, is pictured at Ramsgate harbour, operating the later extension of the 69 into the countryside at Minster. AUTHOR'S COLLECTION – COMPANY ORIGINAL

The leaflet publicizing the introduction of open-top services in 1959 featured an image of one of the new conversions on the cover. Details of both services were carried in the leaflet. AUTHOR'S COLLECTION

Earlier, in 1958, another car, BJG 304, was converted to open-top for use as a tree-lopper, which involved the fitment of an additional crawler gearbox from a Leyland PD1. This vehicle replaced ADU 470 and in turn was itself replaced by BJG 461 in 1968.

Two services were introduced at first, although the concept was to expand significantly in the 1960s. These were the 56, from Palm Bay in Cliftonville to Minnis Bay near Birchington, and the 69 from Winterstoke Crescent near Dumpton to Cliffsend (Pegwell Bay) via Ramsgate. Both used former Thanet area numbers, which were now

Before the open-top service cars were dealt with, BJG 304 was converted for tree cutting duties, shown near the end of its life in 1968 in Canterbury Works. AUTHOR

The pre-war open-top cars, unlike their successors, were used on conventional services, sometimes on rural routes. This rare view of FN 9544, a 1929 TS1, at Minster is interesting, seasonal open-top service 69 also served the village between 1962 and 1965. The driver is Walter 'Chick' Perkins and the car displays the boards used before the introduction of roller blinds; the advert details fares for 'Daily London Services'.
COLLECTION: JOHN WATLER

available since the original routes carrying these numbers had been withdrawn either before or at the onset of World War II. At first they only ran Sundays to Fridays in the high season, from 14 June to 5 September 1959. Saturday was 'changeover' day for holidaymakers so was a flat day for the leisure trade and also allowed a rest day for crews. The services offered special return fares allowing a return trip from any point on the route, unlike a normal return ticket, which did not permit circular itineraries. The return fare for the introductory season was 2/6d (12.5p) on the 56 and 1/6d (7.5p) on the 69. At this time there were no 'all-day' system tickets available on East Kent, so taking the option of making a return trip for one fare from any point without having to rebook at the terminus was a wise move. Tickets issued on open-top services used green rolls rather than the standard old gold/buff colour used on normal services. East Kent was slower off the mark than its sister companies down the coast – both Southdown and M&D were already operating seasonal open-top services some years before. The venture was a resounding success and went from strength to strength in the late 1960s.

D/C (ONE-MAN) OPERATIONS

As noted earlier, East Kent always referred to their one-man operations as 'Driver/Conductor' (D/C), an idiosyncrasy of the company and, arguably one that would stand the test of time, as women drivers entered service in the 1970s. Another endearing quirk was the notice on the D/C tills that 'Season Tickets Must Be Shewn' – use of an archaic form of English that persisted into the 1970s.

Prior to 1955, with the exception of express services and tours, most cars were crew-operated apart from a sprinkling of services operated by low-capacity cars, the 20-seat Dennis Aces or Leyland Cubs and their replacements, the Dennis Falcons. Early post-war D/C services included:

Service	Route
31	Faversham–Chilham
55	Kingsgate–Broadstairs via Joss Bay
92	Dover–Capel via West Hougham
93A	Dover–West Langdon
109	Ashford–East Brabourne/Hythe
135	Dover, Pencester Road–The Citadel

Most of these services had restrictions on parts of the route, necessitating the use of smaller vehicles that were suitable for D/C operation. This summary should not be taken as an exhaustive list of early D/C services, however, as many other routes had had width restrictions, certainly in the

The Dennis Falcons replaced the similar capacity Dennis Aces on restricted routes, all being D/C operated. EFN 567 is pictured at the Broadstairs Callis Court terminus of the 55. MDEK CLUB – BRIAN WEEDEN

1930s. As road improvements occurred the restrictions were relaxed, allowing the use of larger, crew-operated single-decks. Service 31 was an oddity, as on Saturdays it used a crew-operated CFN Lancet due to heavy loadings. D/C working was as a result of an earlier width restriction at Selling and relatively low loadings on most days. Once the restriction was overcome, larger vehicles were permissible.

A further factor limiting the use of D/C operation was that, prior to 1955, regulations restricted such operations to vehicles with a capacity of no greater than twenty seats. Things were changing, however, and relaxation of these restrictions in 1955 to allow D/C operation of 45-seaters saw the last ten of the forty new Weymann-bodied dual-purpose AEC Reliances, KFN 240–9, purpose-built for D/C operations. These had a larger, squarer section internal cab surround (later modified), compared to the curved style on the remainder of the batch, KFN 210–39. These D/C cars were allocated to a small number of depots that

operated routes deemed suitable for the pilot conversions in autumn 1955, ushering in a new era that would see East Kent's operations eventually becoming totally D/C over a period of nearly twenty-seven years – in 1981, the final crew-operated routes, the Canterbury/Whitstable/Herne Bay circulars, by now numbered 604/6, were converted. The first routes and depots allocated with the new D/C cars are shown in Table 8 below.

This pilot programme was a success and the remaining KFN Reliances with the similar batch, LJG 305–26 from 1956, were all converted to D/C from 1957 onwards, although none had the modified cab fitted to the first cars. Later, their Beadle-bodied cousins MJG 285–300 and NFN 327–49 were also converted to D/C between 1958 and 1963 (NFNs) and 1966 to 1968 (MJGs) as they were downgraded from coach duties. However, conversion to D/C did not imply their prohibition from use on coach services and they would often reappear on express services at times of peak demand until late in their lives.

The company was also trying to eke out further capacity on those routes restricted to using the much smaller Dennis Falcons either due to road width or weight (capacity) restrictions. As legislation and union opposition were relaxed, the Falcons were up-seated between 1956 and 1959, firstly to twenty-five seats and then to a very cramped twenty-nine seats. The last routes thought to have been capacity-restricted to 25-seat cars until further relaxation after 1958 were the 55 (Thanet), 92 (Dover) and 109 (Ashford). Their original capacity of twenty seats had caused many headaches in preceding years when loadings increased on routes operated by these low-capacity cars. In July 1947 the company was recorded as having to schedule further short-workings on service 109 between Ashford and East Brabourne, as cars running beyond that point had

Table 8 Pilot D/C Conversion Programme with AEC 41-Seater Buses (KFN 240–9), 1955–6

Depot	Service	Route
Deal	76	Deal–Betteshanger–Staple
	78	Deal–Sutton–Elvington–Shepherdswell–Aylesham
Dover	89	Dover–Shepherdswell–Nonington
	93	Dover–Guston–East Langdon–Martin
Ashford	118/A	Ashford–Wye–Brook–Hastingleigh–Evington Pk Cnr
Rye*	2	Ashford–Brookland–Rye (summer Canterbury/Hastings)
	112	Ashford–Ham Street–Appledore–Iden–Rye
	114	Winchelsea Beach–Rye–Camber–Broomhill

Notes: * Rye routes are assumed conversions as no accurate records exist. The 2 and 114 were converted in autumn 1956; the 114 would have been D/C in the winter season only.

CFN 141 is pictured at Folkestone's East Cliff pavilion on service 107 while the pilot style of D/C conversion for these cars with a half-cab layout was tested. MDEK CLUB

to be Dennis Falcons or Aces due to the width restriction, and passengers on the busier Ashford section were being left behind. The hand-operated doors on the Falcons were all converted to air operation by 1957, much to the relief of drivers.

A more fundamental modification concerned the Dennis Lancet buses delivered between 1947 and 1949. Prior to the mid-fifties, these operated with conductors, owing to their rear-entrance configuration. However, with a 35-seat capacity it was clearly an economic absurdity to operate such cars while a number of 41-seat Reliances were now operating in the hands of one person. As the vehicles were not yet ten years old, the company looked for means of extending their lives while enabling necessary service economies to be made. As a result, in 1956, one car, CFN 141, was converted to D/C by opening up the cab, still to half-cab configuration, moving the entrance to the front and installing a two-leaf opening door under the control of the driver. In this form it underwent trials. Photographic records show it in use on service 107 at Folkestone, but the layout was unsatisfactory. Further changes were made in 1958, the cab being opened out completely with a full front to the bus, thus allowing an easier interface between driver and passenger. This was acceptable, and a further twenty-five of the post-war Lancet buses were

The revised form of D/C conversion for the Lancet buses is represented by CFN 117 in Ashford Station Road in 1968. Despite their tenacity, this was the last full year of operation of the type before being replaced by Bedford VAS1s. AUTHOR

converted to D/C during 1959, eventually operating across the company's network.

The conversions contributed to the longevity of the class, especially those at Ashford, which were mandatory on town service 124 due to a very low railway bridge on the Ashford–Rye line, which the 124 passed under on its way to Newtown. The flat roof profile of the CFNs allowed passage under the bridge whereas the later underfloor-engine single-deckers were too high. The CFNs hung on until 1969, even surviving a modification to Ashford services early in that year that saw the restricted southern portion of the route transferred to service 122.

With this new influx of D/C cars the company's programme of converting more routes to driver-only operation expanded, and gradually the less busy routes would be changed over to this form of operation. By early 1958 twenty-six services were recorded as D/C, and a report in *Commercial Motor* stated that this was to increase to forty-two from the September 1958 timetable change, affecting all crew depots and extending D/C operation to over 35 per cent of routes, although in terms of mileage and cars operated it would still represent a small amount of the company's stage operations. In January 1958 the services converted were the 11, 12, 18, 20, 33, 35, 39, 62, 74, 91, 119, 127, 128, 132 and 133, followed in the autumn by the 5, 7, 9, 14, 19, 37, 38, 58, 65, 70, 100, 102, 107, 115, 117 and 122.

Despite the D/C conversions, a good number of rural routes still saw double-deck operation, as shown by this view of CJG 976 at the quiet village of Minster on the 58 from Margate during the early 1960s. A. FOALES

Several services reverted to crew operation, some with double-deckers, in the summer. Herne Bay's 35, 37/38 and 39, Thanet's 9 and 70, Folkestone's 100 and 107 were cases in point for 1959, as was the earlier converted 114 at Rye, which, unlike the others, would continue seasonal crew operation until 1967. Progression of the programme would, at first, largely be achieved by continuing the downgrading of service coaches to D/C. The development of D/C operation in the 1960s would eventually see most country services converted by the end of the decade.

A later D/C conversion in winter was the former 41, prior to the large-scale changes of 1965, which saw it replaced by the 4/6 group of routes. In summer it reverted to crew operation albeit with single-decks, as represented by Lancet coach EFN 575 – here downgraded to bus work and pictured at Swalecliffe Plough bound for Seasalter Sportsman.
MDEK CLUB – B. WEEDEN

CHAPTER SEVEN

THE 1960s — THE ECONOMICS BITE

If the 1950s were entered with an aura of optimism, there was less in evidence upon the advent of the 1960s. From relative stability and a gradual process of enhancement, the company would now enter an era of retrenchment, striving for economies through further D/C conversions, service reductions, or both. There were high points though – the Northern France day tour market was expanding and improvements to the Eastern Docks at Dover and the opening of Ramsgate hoverport provided the opportunity for new, innovative services, both on stage carriage and express routes.

As a result of continuing economic constraints, in December 1958 the chairman reiterated his earlier message when he said that more service reductions and, consequentially, compulsory redundancies had been necessary. Seasonal employment had always been a feature of East Kent operations due to the high peak of services in summer; normally seasonal staff would, after a few years temporary service, be absorbed as permanent employees, although as a result of the situation in the late 50s and early 60s this became more difficult as permanent staff now had to be shed, particularly as D/C operation spread. This would change towards the end of the 1960s, as the improving economy of the time and the unsocial hours of bus work meant that East Kent would actually struggle to recruit staff, and wages had to rise to retain drivers in particular. Inevitably, more fare increases were in prospect and the cycle of higher fares, reduced patronage and the need for further economies would continue through the 1960s and 1970s.

CHANGES AND CELEBRATIONS — MANAGEMENT, HEAD OFFICE AND A GOLDEN JUBILEE

At the start of the decade, in 1960, the company was finally able to relocate from its 'temporary' head office at Odsal House, Harbledown to a modern, rebuilt office in Station Road West on the site of the former premises. This improved matters greatly for head office staff as, prior to the move,

complicated lunch arrangements were in place involving a bus or coach taking staff to and from Canterbury although later the return was made on a normal service car. This resulted in the staff being allocated an extra fifteen minutes to allow for travel but, surprisingly, the 75-minute lunch break remained after the move back to Station Road West and into the 1970s.

The year 1968 would be a pivotal one for the company's senior management. The long-standing chairman, Mr

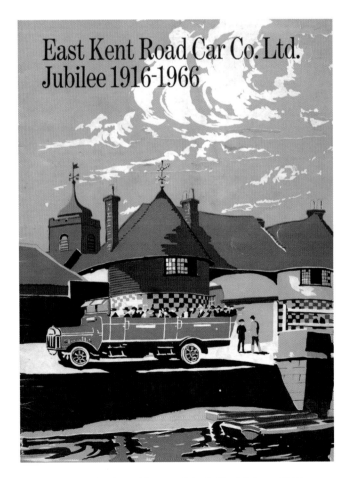

The brochure produced in celebration of the Golden Jubilee in 1966 featured an early poster design for the front cover. AUTHOR'S COLLECTION

EAST KENT ROAD CAR COMPANY LIMITED

1916 - 1966

JUBILEE
CELEBRATION LUNCHEON

Grand Hotel, Folkestone

❋

Tuesday, 4th October, 1966

The programme for the Jubilee luncheon at the Leas Cliff Hall, Folkestone.
AUTHOR'S COLLECTION

would take hold, East Kent being one of the constituents that attempted to retain elements of its individual identity to the bitter end.

A high point of the decade was the company's Golden Jubilee in 1966, and this was celebrated by the publication of a Jubilee brochure detailing East Kent's history up to that time. A special celebratory luncheon took place at the Grand Hotel, Folkestone on 4 October 1966, where superb wines such as Chassagne Montrachet and Nuits St. Georges were the order of the day, while the dessert was served with 1959-vintage Pol Roger Champagne – certainly an event to be savoured.

LAST OF THE RICH SUMMERS?

Notwithstanding the increasing problems of a reducing customer base, the company still had a significant seasonal market and, apart from the summer enhancements at the main holiday destinations such as Herne Bay, Thanet, Folkestone and Rye, a fair number of inland services radiating from Canterbury still saw high-summer timetables operating in the early 1960s. Services 2 to Rye/Hastings, 4 to Whitstable, 6 to Herne Bay, 13/A to Deal and the 67 to Maidstone all scheduled increases in their summer frequencies at this time. In the summer of 1961 a seasonal service from Herne Bay to Margate via the Thanet Way was introduced, numbered 36 and complementing the 35 route via Upstreet. This recreated the pre-war route via what was termed the Coastal Road at that time. Herne Bay was

Beddow, retired in February of that year and was replaced by Mr J. H. Richardson, whose tenure was short-lived, and Mr S. J. B. Skyrme took over the post later in the year. Mr R. G. James, who had been in place as general manager since the post-war period, was succeeded in April by Jim Gilbert, who would then hold the reins until 1972, seeing the company nationalized in 1969, following the Transport Act 1968 and the agreement of BET to sell its holding to the government-owned Transport Holding Company (THC). The THC already had bus interests as it controlled the former Tilling companies, having been in existence since 1963, when it took over the bus functions from the BTC, which was then abolished. However, it would take until the 1970s before the corporate philosophy of the National Bus Company (NBC)

The 35 and its companion 34 operated through very rural roads between Herne Bay and Upstreet en route to the Isle of Thanet, unlike the 36, which skated down the Thanet Way. KFN 215 is pictured at The Gate, Marshside in 1971. AUTHOR

the focus of another seasonal service to the Isle of Thanet holiday destination when the 34, running to Ramsgate, was introduced in summer 1963. Complementing the 35 through Chislet and Upstreet, it was not a success and its last summer of operation was 1965. The 36 lasted a little longer, until summer 1968, when it was withdrawn at the end of the season.

At Thanet, loadings were still sufficient to justify stand conductors at Margate and Ramsgate harbours. These conductors issued tickets from different-coloured rolls to distinguish them from the standard on-board issue, while auxiliary conductors were still employed, if resources permitted, to relieve very busy journeys. These arrangements were still evident in the summers of 1959 and 1960. On the other hand, the delivery of the high-capacity Regent cars in

One of the former dual-purpose Beadle-bodied AECs, now downgraded to D/C operation, awaits departure from Deal South Street bus station in July 1970 on the rural route 78 to Shepherdswell. AUTHOR

A trio of Bridgemasters arrived in 1962, necessary to bring new blood to operate Dover's service 129. YJG 809 is pictured when new negotiating the bridge en route to St. Radigund's. Note the blind disposition – after this time the destination and via screens were swapped to facilitate easier changes of blinds at termini. MDEK CLUB – B. WEEDEN

1959 then reduced the need for relief cars to be on standby at busy locations such as Margate harbour. Prior to their arrival it was a regular occurrence for such cars to cover the busiest sections, such as up to the hotels at Cliftonville.

Early in 1960, from 10 January, opportunity was taken to standardize the 78 service. Rather than offering a mix of destinations, the Elvington journeys were withdrawn and Shepherdswell became its western destination for all except one journey, reversing at Studdal. In Ramsgate the 53/A group was revised from 12 December 1960, when the 53 was diverted from Grange Road to provide a better service to the top of the town centre by running via Cannon Road. An earlier supplement indicated that this should have started on 2 October. Further changes to these services by 20 May 1962 saw the 53/A renumbered 63/64 respectively and later, by 25 April 1963, a diversion away from a low bridge on Ramsgate Road, Margate to run via Tivoli Road meant that mandatory operation of lowbridge cars on this route was no longer necessary; an essential change, as the service was to be operated by new highbridge Regents from the FN batch, about to enter service. This also saw the summer service reducing to an all-year 15-minute frequency rather than the 12-minute enhancement last operated in 1962. This was the penultimate busy double-deck route to require lowbridge cars; the last was the 129 at Dover serving St. Radigund's, and for this a small order of low-height AEC Bridgemasters had been delivered in 1962.

Works services in Thanet were expanded further by the addition of a route from Arlington Gardens, east of Margate, to Margate, industrial estate. Introduced on 24 July 1961 as service 63, it was quickly renumbered 72 in May 1962 when the 53/A services took the numbers 63/64. One oddity concerning works services at this time was the appearance, from 2 February 1961, of a special service from Lydd to the new nuclear power station at Dungeness, then under construction. This service never appeared in any timetable, and was only detailed in fare tables. Initially unnumbered, it then gained the number 105B in the fare table of 20 August 1961 and continued to be publicized in fare tables alone up to and including the 1962 edition, being omitted from the one published on 21 July 1963. Through fares were offered to Folkestone by interchanging at, presumably, Lydd Camp, judging by the fare stage number 21 used.

Experiments continued, and in consequence the number range expanded. A circular seasonal service at Dover, reusing number 136 and running from the East Cliff via the Castle and Connaught Park, was operated from 25 June 1961 but would only last one season. A link from Dover's Priory station to the Marine station, to cater for increasing

A 1970 scene in Folkestone's bus station with two of the author's colleagues, drivers Castle and Plummer with 6789 FN and YJG 821, both resident at Folkestone since new. Car 6789 shows a full blind for the erstwhile 101 service although it is unlikely that a Regent ever operated on it. Note the more relaxed uniform styles of the time! AUTHOR

continental foot-passenger traffic, was introduced in summer 1962, and numbered 137. It ran as a seasonal service, every day in the high season and Fridays, Saturdays and Sundays on the shoulders of the summer. Over time it was gradually run down, especially as the importance of the Western Docks reduced and the Eastern Docks correspondingly rose. It last ran in summer 1968. Another new service introduced in the summer of 1962, in June, was a further open-top route, the 44, at Herne Bay; while six years later, in 1968, another commenced between Folkestone and Dover. Fuller details of these are given later. At Thanet another short-lived experiment was the introduction of service 47, running from Broadstairs to Ramsgate station via Rumfields and Newington Estate. Operating hourly, all week, it lasted the season from 18 June to 29 September 1962, when it was withdrawn.

Summer 1962 also saw more revisions at Folkestone, again based around high-season requirements from 24 June. The group of services from Cheriton to Folkestone via Sandgate underwent a facelift: the summer pattern saw service 101 now running from Cheriton to Wood Avenue via Sandgate, the harbour, the former Junction station and Downs Road Estate, with new service 104 also running from Cheriton via Sandgate terminating at the Marine Pavilion while the 100, which normally ran from Cheriton, was consigned to a Bus Station to Hollands Avenue shuttle. The 101 had already commenced running via the harbour in summer 1961. The summer changes to the 100 reduced its summer service to Hollands Avenue by half, now run-ning hourly. In order to ensure the area was still adequately served, the 107 was extended from the East Cliff Pavilion to Hollands Avenue every half-hour, with one journey running to and from Wood Avenue, interworking with the 100 at Hollands Avenue and the 101 at Wood Avenue respectively. The spring, autumn and winter schedules entailed the 100 being restored to Cheriton and the 101 shuttling to Wood Avenue from the Bus Station, while the winter 107 service reverted to its earlier pattern, terminating at the East Cliff Pavilion.

In summer 1963, more economies were introduced; the summer service on the 9 was reduced to run every 140 minutes, partially compensated by new service 34 from Herne Bay, thus maintaining the 70-minute interval on the Ramsgate–Upstreet section. The 49/50/52 group and the 51 saw their summer service cut from the former 6-minute frequency to 7/8 minutes, while the 54/A services saw their former 9-minute summer frequency reduced to 12 minutes; the introduction of high-capacity double-deckers in 1959 easily permitted this reduction with little overcrowding. It could be questioned why this anomaly had lasted so long, given the chairman's statements of a few years earlier on the need for economies. Services 3 and 8 were joined from 30 June 1963, albeit first planned from 19 May 1963, providing a link across Canterbury between Faversham and Margate and recreating a through service, which had been part of East Kent's constituent operations.

One notable event in 1963 was the takeover from 6 May of the Newman's services based at Hythe. Previously

PFN 865, one of the first batch of AEC Regent Vs, had spent over twelve years working Thanet's 49/50/52 routes when photographed in July 1971; eventually converted to a towing car by M&D, she is now preserved in that condition. Descending Madeira Walk at Ramsgate, the blinds are already set for the 52, which was interlinked with the 49/50. The bend in the distance is where an IoTES tramcar ran away in 1905, ending up over the cliff! AUTHOR

Service 90 operated through to Deal from Folkestone in the mid-1960s. WFN 842, one of the 1961 AEC Regents, the first batch to the less attractive half-cab design, waits at the bus station in June 1968 bound for Deal. This was a Loadmeter-equipped car on exchange from Canterbury, its home depot. AUTHOR

unnumbered, the Hythe Stade Court–Ashford via Aldington route took number 111, while the local service from Stade Court to Sandling station, which had earlier run to Hythe station before closure of the branch line in 1951, was numbered 111A. Some 111 journeys also ran via Sandling. The Ashford terminus now changed from Vicarage Lane to the depot at Station Road. At the time this left just one independent stage carriage operator in East Kent's area – Drew's, which ran services from Canterbury to Chartham and Chartham Hatch. Later, from summer 1966, the Drew's services appeared in the East Kent timetable and a cordial relationship existed between the two operators until Drew's decided to finish and East Kent absorbed their operations in December 1974. In both cases no vehicles were absorbed as part of the takeover.

Another former link was re-established from 16 May 1964, when the 80 and 90 services were joined at Dover, providing a Deal–Folkestone through service now numbered 90, while the short-workings between Dover and Folkestone took number 90A. This link cost an extra car for the low-season service due to long layovers at Folkestone and Deal, although the frequency to Folkestone improved from the former 16-minute interval to 15 minutes; the interlinked, more frequent summer service saved one car. The two services inter-worked, alternating between 90 and 90A upon arrival at Folkestone. The Dover–Folkestone section still enjoyed an incremental rise in frequency on low-season Saturday afternoons due to the high demand at this time. However, Folkestone saw economies as the 103/A service was reduced that summer from the former seasonal 8-minute frequency to 10 minutes, although the winter 12-minute frequency remained unchanged. These changes also saw all journeys running to and from Crete-way Down, thus removing Wood Avenue as a terminus for these routes – a historic association that had been in place since the early days.

The opportunity was also taken to divert one 103A journey per hour via Downs Road Estate, replacing the former 101 shuttle; a single journey had operated this diversion since 20 June 1954. The number 101 was now reused for a new summer-only circular service, running in both directions to and from the Marine Pavilion, via the East Cliff, Hollands Avenue and Wood Avenue. Another short-lived experiment, like so many at this time, it did not reappear in 1965. This 1964 change also saw complementary revisions to the 100, remaining as a Cheriton–Hollands Avenue service all year, while the 107 would no longer run beyond Hollands Avenue to Wood Avenue. The summer-only 104 would be retained until summer 1965, its last year of operation. From 28 June 1964 Ashford's 125 was

Before the one-way system was introduced at Sandwich in 1964, the company took some views in July 1963. CJG 940, on summer-only service 60, negotiates the still two-way, but very narrow, Strand Street. COMPANY ORIGINAL

Sandwich's historic Barbican and toll bridge do not feature often in bus photographs. An MDEK Club excursion to bid farewell to Guy Arab II BJG 339 on 15 September 1968 allowed an unusual view of an open-topper passing under the arch and about to cross the bridge. On the right is the toll booth with the toll collector in his uniform just visible. AUTHOR

diverted to Arlington via Hillyfields from its former Kingsnorth/Bromley Green termini, with service 121 and odd journeys on 123A extended from Woodchurch Turning to Kingsnorth/Bromley Green in replacement. Some early journeys on 121 (and later 123A) had run here since 25 March 1946.

ONE-WAY SYSTEMS AND TOLLS

One feature of this decade was the introduction of several one-way systems as local councils sought to combat the effect of increasing car traffic. Folkestone introduced a system on 16 April 1961. The main impact was on services 100, 103/A and 107, which could no longer proceed directly eastbound down Sandgate Road and performed a loop around Bouverie Road East and Guildhall Street to rejoin their original route. The eastbound stop outside the well-known local department store, Bobby's, was replaced by one in Bouverie Place, adjacent to the bus station.

At Sandwich, problems in negotiating the narrow streets of this ancient Cinque Port were addressed in mid-1964, probably by 1 June, when a one-way clockwise loop system was introduced, with all buses calling at the Guildhall in a westbound-facing direction irrespective of destination. It seems amazing now that the narrow streets could ever have catered for two-way traffic, especially as many of the company's cars were now 8ft (2.4m) wide. Also at Sandwich, the existence of the ancient toll bridge on the Ramsgate Road required vehicles, including buses and coaches, to pay a charge for each crossing. Regular cars on services 62, 66, 68 and 87, which used the bridge several times a day, were allocated quarterly season tickets that were displayed in the windscreen. The requirement for a permit ceased

by June 1970 and was probably first replaced by a direct settlement and then waived altogether. Certainly, when permits were required the company was invoiced for cars crossing the bridge without the certification although in earlier days conductors had to pay the toll if their car was not certificated, deducting the cost from the waybill. Tolls were abolished for all vehicles in 1977.

In 1965 it was Ashford's turn: on 16 May the High Street became one-way eastbound only, making town services perform a clockwise loop while country services, such as

The introduction of the one-way system at Ashford required a change to town service blinds. Rather than adopt the single reduced display, Ashford chose to obscure redundant via points as shown by FFN 396 in Station Road, no longer serving High Street westbound on services 121/123, which has had the via point painted out. AUTHOR

the 1, 10 (westbound), 109 and 118/A, now headed out via Bank Street. Dover saw an experimental system introduced from 7 May 1967, with northbound services still routed via High Street and the London Road but those inbound from Canterbury, Ramsgate and the Buckland area routed via Maison Dieu Road.

TIMETABLES – LARGER BOOKS, REDUCED SERVICES

The published timetables underwent another change from May 1965, to a larger 5½in × 8½in size (14 × 22cm). This was as a result of a decision in 1964 by a joint committee

Whilst service 2 was cut back to run between Ashford and Rye from the end of summer 1965, connections were available from service 1. In April 1969 at Canterbury, GJG 734D displays the blind display advertising the Hastings connection. At its side KJG 576E carries the red domed livery; it has just been repaired following a major accident. AUTHOR

Possibly one of the best timetable covers issued by the company, the September 1968 issue was the last with the traditional logo.
AUTHOR'S COLLECTION

of the then Tilling and BET Groups to present timetables in a common format and presentation style. This was much better for readability, especially as all tables were now in landscape format. The cover picture had already changed in September 1963 to a side view of one of the WFN-series Regents at Canterbury with the cathedral and the newly developed Longmarket as a backdrop. This picture continued with the larger format for two editions, then in summer 1966 was replaced with a more general scene of Margate clock tower with East Kent vehicles in attendance; culminating in what was probably the best East Kent timetable cover, that for September 1968, which featured a magnificent view of one of the latest Regents, MFN 951F, heading out of Dover on the 80 with the castle as a backdrop. Unfortunately the 80 had already been converted to D/C so the picture remained a 'what might have been': instead of a view over Dover harbour 'from the top deck of a bus', as proclaimed in general terms in publicity of the time, the passengers were more than likely to be crammed into an overcrowded KFN or LJG Reliance with little opportunity to enjoy the sights.

Another important change in the summer 1965 timetable was that it introduced the 24-hour clock, and from now on this new format would be standard. Prior to this the pm times were shown in bold, but this did give rise to confusion and the change was generally welcomed once initial resistance abated. Running boards for cars (*see* Chapter 14 on working for East Kent) were amended to show 24-hour times from January 1965.

The quest for savings continued, and the summer of 1965 was to be the last year of operation of seasonal services such as the extension of the 2 to run between Canterbury and Hastings, the 34 from Herne Bay to Ramsgate and the other two Thanet seasonal routes, the 60 and 61 from Margate to Deal and Dover respectively. Even Sandwich lost its infrequent summer service 75 to Sandwich Bay after 1965, an odd route, which, for a time, did not even have a formal published schedule. The 75 would resume as a limited service to the nearby Sandown Lees Estate from 8 January 1967. In response to local requests, services 47 and 48 were introduced in summer 1965, radiating from Dane Valley Millmead Road to Cliftonville and East Margate Yoakley Square, running weekdays only from 17 May. Another failure, they had gone by the introduction of the winter timetable.

MAJOR CHANGES AT HERNE BAY AND WHITSTABLE

The winter timetable from 19 September 1965 saw significant revisions in the Herne Bay and Whitstable area. Services 4 and 6, running from Canterbury to Swalecliffe and Herne Bay respectively, were linked as a circular service, displaying the numbers 4/6 or 4A/6 for clockwise journeys and 6/4 or 6/4A anticlockwise. The 4A was now used to distinguish journeys running via Swalecliffe Court Drive. The changes also saw the introduction of peak-hour limited-stop services operating on each limb, numbered 4X, 4AX and 6X respectively. As these now linked Whitstable and Herne Bay, the former routes between these points, the 37/38 from Faversham, were curtailed to terminate at either Swalecliffe or Chestfield golf club, with 'A' suffixes used to distinguish journeys running via Whitstable station rather than Tankerton Circus. The former summer-only service 41 from Herne Bay to Seasalter was withdrawn, the number being used for a local service. Commensurate with these changes, Herne Bay town services were also revised, with new winter services running as follows:

Services 40/43: Westcliff Clifftown Gardens to Hillborough/Reculver, the 40 routed via the station and running on weekday evenings only
Services 41/42: Greenhill Estate (Post Office/The Grove) to Hillborough/Reculver and Broomfield respectively

In the summer season, from 1966, the 40 ran all day throughout the week and all three services, 40/41/43, ran on to Reculver, providing the normal seasonal uplift to the

Waiting at the attractive Hillborough terminus of service 43 in April 1969, GFN 909 displays full blinds for the route. Herne Bay was one of the last few depots to employ GFN Guys on regular service. AUTHOR

By the time GJG 762D, the last of the 1966 Regents, was photographed on Herne Bay High Street bound for Reculver on service 41 in May 1971, the Guys had all disappeared from normal service. Crew operation of Herne Bay's town services had not long to go either. AUTHOR

After five years the combined service numbering for the circular Whitstable and Herne Bay service was simplified, using singular numbers for the workings as displayed by 6795 FN at Whitstable Horsebridge in September 1971, displaying 4A for a clockwise working bound for Herne Bay. AUTHOR

site. Together with open-top service 44, four buses an hour still ran to Reculver in the summer but as a result of these changes the regular 20-minute frequency provided by the former 39/A services was replaced by one comprised of four different services to/from Reculver. Off-season, an intermittent service was provided to this terminus by service 41. From summer 1967 the 42 was diverted from Broomfield and extended to Mill Lane, a new estate above Herne Village. From 4 January 1970 the numbering of the 4/6 group was simplified, using simply 4 or 4A for clockwise journeys and 6 or 6A for anticlockwise workings rather than the combined numbers used beforehand.

SERVICES TO THE NEW UNIVERSITY OF KENT

Inland, at Canterbury, a precursor of the development of a major public transport hub was the introduction, in October 1965, of a route from Canterbury bus station to the newly opened University of Kent. Initially unnumbered, by April 1966 it became service 32 but was restricted to university staff and students only, with a single fare of 6d (2.5p). Infrequent at first, it gradually improved to something approximating hourly in term time by 1967 and a regular hourly service was in place by autumn 1968. From 10 October 1966 a fare table was published, intended for when the 6d flat fare was not in operation; it also showed a stage for Canterbury East station, but the published timetable did not display any journeys to or from this point. From 3 September 1967 multi-journey tickets were introduced for this service and the 6d flat fare was dispensed with. In 1969 a special canceller was fitted to 36ft (11m) Reliance KJG 578E to ease the workload of the driver/conductor, although this experiment was not pursued after the trial.

In April 1967 services to the university were expanded, with limited journeys to and from Herne Bay/Whitstable numbered 33 and 34 respectively, operating in the busy morning peak and in the late evening. From September 1967 the 33 operated via various routings in the Herne Bay area, which were then allocated A/B/C suffixes. The use of B suffixes was rare at the time, the only other operationally scheduled service being the 98B at Dover, introduced in May 1967. The use of a C suffix was even rarer. At first the 33A was not scheduled, creating the even odder situation of just the 33B and 33C being detailed. As the campus grew, university services were to expand, leading to today's intensive services, which now boast all-night workings.

FOLKESTONE – REDUCTIONS IN TOWN AND COUNTRY

At Folkestone in summer 1966 a further, and major, revision of the Cheriton Road services was implemented. These routes had remained largely unchanged since the 134's introduction in 1953 and the 108's Horn Street extension of 1958, although the 108's Bathing Pool service was withdrawn on 20 May 1961, being cut back to Marine Pavilion. The new pattern saw the 99 now running from Hill Road to Shorncliffe Camp; the 106 now terminated at the bus station but was extended from Cheriton Library to Horn Street while the 108 was diverted from its former Horn Street/Hawkins Road termini to run to Biggins Wood Road. The 134 was withdrawn. The three services ran at 20-minute intervals on weekdays over their complete routes and thus both Horn Street and Biggins Wood saw their services improved from the former hourly journeys provided by the 108 and 134. However, the overall impact was that the Cheriton Road lost three journeys per hour due to the 99/134's former 10-minute interval being halved. As with Thanet, the delivery of higher-capacity AEC Regents ameliorated the reduction. At the same time the 100 was rationalized, only serving Hollands Avenue on some journeys, while the seasonal 104 serving the Sandgate end of the same route was withdrawn. The 107 was also reduced in frequency from the previous summer weekday 15-minute interval to 20 minutes.

Staying in the Folkestone area, on 2 June 1968, just before the full commencement of the summer timetable, a

The last summer of full crew operation on services 105/A sees AFN 774B leaving Folkestone bus station in June 1968. The Littlestone display was changed on later blinds to read Greatstone, a more accurate description of the terminal. AUTHOR

set of revisions mostly affecting Hythe and Romney Marsh were introduced. The 103/A group was extended to serve Palmarsh Estate west of Hythe, while the local 110/A and former Newman's service 111A were completely revised. The 110 now ran hourly from Hythe to Sandling station, replacing the 111A, which had only run at a regular frequency in the high summer, while the westernmost part of the 110 route was separated and became 110A for both the West Hythe/Palmarsh and the Burmarsh legs, the latter of which had already carried that number. Earlier, on 29 January 1967, the 111A had been cut back from its former Stade Court terminus to the Light Railway station, while its fellow ex-Newman's service was also withdrawn from Stade Court at the same time, only to re-emerge for two weekday afternoon journeys from 3 September 1967. The 103/A also saw a short-lived diversion of some journeys via Central station but these were withdrawn at the advent of the winter timetable.

The 105/A was also prepared for D/C operation and, prior to conversion in 1968, a regular 30-minute summer service replaced the former three journeys per hour. This saved one car, and another advantage was that it meant that Lydd and Littlestone journeys operated at the same clockface time each hour, although the local council at New Romney laid an objection to the reduction before the traffic commissioners. As a result the company had to introduce an extra hourly shuttle service on the 105A between Hythe Red Lion Square and Littlestone throughout the summer. Similar shuttles had operated in the early and late season to supplement the lower winter frequencies for a number of years beforehand. The commissioners' hearing of the objection took place on Friday 20 September 1968 at Ashford, and the company was successful in having its original proposals approved. On the plus side for the area, a new seasonal service, 139, had been introduced between Ashford station and Littlestone Holiday Camp on 18 May, operating Saturdays only. A similar Saturday-only seasonal service, numbered 141, was introduced between Deal station and Kingsdown Holiday Camp for the summer of 1970 but only lasted the one season, while the 139 went on until the end of the summer 1971 season before being withdrawn.

The winter timetable from 8 September 1968 saw further changes at Folkestone; the 107 was extended from Brabourne Gardens to the new Golden Valley Estate, although this was soon revised. On 24 May 1970 the 100 and 107 were linked at Cheriton Library, the former now diverted via the Golden Valley and providing a much improved 30-minute weekday service over its entire route, which also saw it extended via East Cliff to Stanbury Crescent, near the former Hollands Avenue terminus, providing an easier

loop reversal. The remaining 107 service was reduced to a rump operating from Cheriton to the bus station along Shorncliffe Road, with some summer shuttles plus odd late and winter Sunday journeys extending to its former route to the East Cliff and also Stanbury Crescent. Later, from 30 May 1971, both services were linked to run direct via Golden Valley rather than diverting via Cheriton Library, except for a few garage journeys. From 25 May 1969 the 103/A route was seasonally extended to Dymchurch to further relieve the 105/A services; these were by now converted to D/C but suffering major overcrowding as often the scheduled 51/3-seat vehicles were unavailable and a 41-seater was substituted, which was completely inadequate for such a busy service.

The alterations at Golden Valley in May 1971 were accompanied by a major recast of Folkestone's other town services. The long-established 99 to Shorncliffe Camp was withdrawn, ending a route that had been in place from the very early days, but the barracks was now reduced to a shadow of its former self. To serve the nearby residential area, a new service 104 was introduced, which followed the former 99 from Hill Road but at Cheriton was linked with the 106 to perform a loop in the Horn Street area, thus easing D/C operation, avoiding the former reverse at Horn Street and complex number blind changes. Meanwhile, these changes saw the 108 diverted on winter evenings and partially on winter Sundays to serve Creteway Down rather than the Marine Pavilion, coming into effect from September. These journeys took the number 102, which had been vacated by numbering all journeys to Hawkinge as 16, a throwback to 1946–8 when the 102 route had, again, been briefly numbered 16.

ASHFORD EXPANSION

Ashford's development as an overspill town for London was now in full flow. Bockhanger was served by extending the 124, from 26 June 1966; and while a planned extension of services 121A/123/126 to Arlington, in south Ashford, was scheduled in the winter 1966 timetable, the roads needed improvement. The journeys reversed at Beaver Green, May Pits until at least 27 May 1967, being extended to Arlington by 25 June 1967. However, the 125 had continued to serve Arlington. Nearly two years year later, on 2 March 1969, further major changes to cater for the expanded housing development in nearby Stanhope were introduced: one journey per hour on the 121 was diverted from Woodchurch Turning into the new Stanhope estate and renumbered 134; alas, as with the earlier extension to Arlington, the roads were not ready and it took until 7 September before buses

Transition at Ashford. The building of new overspill housing at Stanhope in South Ashford saw the introduction of service 134 (top) in March 1969, although at first it was unable to access the estate as the roads were not ready, evidenced by GJG 743D in Station Road in August 1969 bound for Woodchurch Turning, the temporary terminus. The changes of 2 March also saw all Ashford town services on Sundays converted to D/C as shown by NFN 348 (bottom) at Kennington, bound for Arlington on the first day. The sucker board shows the 125 routing, compensating for the single destination screen. AUTHOR

could access the estate. In conjunction, the former 122 and 124 services would swap their southern termini; the 122 now running from Cobbs Wood to Newtown and the 124 taking the former 126 number and running from Bockhanger to South Willesborough. The route of the former 126 between Hunter Avenue and Arlington via Hillyfields had not disappeared, however, having been renumbered 136. The last part of the jigsaw was a set of improvements to services in north Ashford; the 125 from Kennington to Arlington was supplemented by an additional hourly service from Kennington to Woodchurch Turning, numbered 124/A. The A suffix was used for journeys via Penlee Point, the former route, either as 124A or 125A, while journeys on the new route via Bockhanger were numbered 124/125.

The author was heavily involved in producing these changes, and one innovative feature in the accompanying timetable supplement was a route map of the town services. This was possibly the first full town service map in the company's history, although a map of Dover's one-way system and a diagrammatic map for the 100/101/104/107 changes at Folkestone had appeared beforehand. Later, further services would be diverted into Stanhope, the former 123A workings being rerouted from Woodchurch Turning and renumbered 133 from the summer of 1970.

ACCELERATION AND DEVELOPMENT OF EXPRESS SERVICES – THE M2 MOTORWAY AND DARTFORD TUNNEL

A major change for express services was the opening of the M2 motorway in stages from September 1963. Journeys on what was first termed the 'Medway Motorway' reduced the Canterbury–London journey time from over 2½ hours to 1 hour 55 minutes. This also saw the introduction of service M2, which ran direct between Birchington and New Cross via the Thanet Way and the motorway, although some journeys on the L1 had already run direct via the Thanet Way for some time previously. The next year, 1964, saw the introduction of the L7, now enabling a faster journey to and from Deal via the motorway.

The next infrastructure change benefitting East Kent was the opening of the Dartford Tunnel in November 1963,

A busy scene at Canterbury in December 1967. No fewer than three of the Company's 36ft (11m) 49-seat coaches are operating a multiple set of departures on the L1 and L7, both via the motorway, plus a connecting L2/6 journey via Maidstone. Note the differing styles of radiator grille on the leading Reliances, both from the first batch. AUTHOR

allowing the development of fast through services from East Anglia, the Midlands and eventually beyond. These worked under the brand name 'Dartford Tunnel Coachways'. Prior to its opening, the only service to the north, that to Birmingham, had to run through central London. Two further services were introduced in summer 1964 – the MX8 from Northampton to Ramsgate, jointly operated with United Counties, and the X32/X34 from Clacton to Folkestone or Ramsgate respectively, jointly operated with Eastern National.

Two years later, in summer 1966, 'Yorkshire Services' were introduced, running from Keighley to Ramsgate and Halifax to Folkestone also via the Dartford Tunnel; these were numbered X20 and X21 in summer 1969. All these services ran at weekends only in the summer season on various days from Friday to Sunday, designed, as they were, for the holiday changeover traffic. From 1966 a direct Birmingham service appeared in the timetable, although a connecting service via London had operated for many years before; it now sported the number ME4. The other long-established service, the South Coast Express, was also numbered at this time as the X16 – but by summer 1968 it had been renumbered as the X26.

Another new service from summer 1966 was the X10 running from Manchester to Ramsgate, this time jointly operated with the North Western Road Car Company and Midland Red. It should be noted that some joint workings only involved vehicles from the northernmost companies, the X10 being a case in point, as the schedules were based on originating from Manchester and returning without any reciprocal working from Kent. East Kent's participation, if at all, would be confined to their drivers taking over the inward journey and crewing the first part of the return journey.

In 1968 East Kent experimented with a variation of the X26, with a diverted working from Ramsgate to Brighton via Canterbury numbered X28, introduced from 1 June; while from 22 June service X36 commenced running between Clacton and Rye. In 1969 new facilities to Cheltenham were planned from Ramsgate – service X65 – and later Deal – service X66 – running via Ashford and

Basingstoke and providing connections at Cheltenham to and from the range of departures offered there. These were a feature of the Associated Motorway operations at that time, who were named as joint operators, although East Kent cars were normally used throughout. The X65 should have commenced on 24 May 1969 but there was some doubt as to whether this did so on time as it was 'subject to Traffic

The London route from Dover and Folkestone, L3, did not have the benefit of fast motorway running before the M20 was built. An intermediate stop was normally made in the Maidstone area, which became Harrietsham Roebuck once the by-pass was built. Folkestone-based car 525 FN in the hands of driver Brian Mills, on the left, was captured there London-bound in May 1972. AUTHOR

The London service leaflets underwent a transformation in the 1960s and images of the company's express cars were eventually replaced by a more anonymous style as nationalization took hold. AUTHOR'S COLLECTION

The South Coast Express service was certainly slower than its London-bound partners, a situation not helped by slow roads and challenging pick-up points, as demonstrated by DJG 606C as she negotiates the access to Brighton's Steine Street coach station in July 1971. Note the display is SC62– a product of the inter-working of the two services. AUTHOR

Commissioners approval'; until that was granted it could not be publicized so was not shown in the timetable until 1970, although it probably started in summer 1969. The following summer, 1970, the X66 also commenced; both services ran Saturdays only and in most cases only one car operated onward from Ashford. The other new express service introduced in the decade was the X40, running from Manchester to Folkestone, starting in the summer of 1969 and also jointly worked with North Western and Midland Red like its sister service the X10.

CROSS-CHANNEL GROWTH – PLANES, BOATS AND HOVERCRAFT

Continental traffic was also booming. The introduction of roll-on roll-off ferries meant that East Kent could now operate through day tours from across Kent using the company's coaches throughout, and a varied range of tours was now offered with differing itineraries in the Boulogne, Le

East Kent's Continental leaflets held details of both boat and air crossings; interestingly the later 1963 publicity chose to focus on a picture of a boat with an MJG-tours car, although the earlier 1960 design featured both sea and air images. AUTHOR'S COLLECTION

This publicity shot shows one of the 1966 36ft (11m) coaches, the last batch with this style of body, adjacent to the apron at Lympne Airport with an Avro 748, which had begun to replace the earlier Dakotas. The informal nature of the surroundings and lack of security make a stark contrast to today's airline operations. MDEK CLUB – COMPANY ORIGINAL

The Duple-bodied AEC Reliance tours cars delivered in 1964 were to an intermediate 32ft (10m) length. July 1970 sees AFN 493B at Canterbury bus station about to board passengers bound for an Austria and Lake Achensee tour. AUTHOR

Touquet and Calais areas and extending into Belgium. This required a separate 'Northern France' section in the traffic office to coordinate matters. Longer-distance passengers were still offered connections with the boats, generally by the L3 service running through to Folkestone Harbour or Dover Marine, depending on the ferry service.

The Skyways coach-air service was also running at strength. A normal Monday in 1966, the busiest day of the week, could see at least twelve scheduled journeys to and from London with connecting flights offered not only to Paris but also Montpellier and Clermont-Ferrand. There was also a special local express service from Folkestone and Hythe to Lympne, offering flight connections to Beauvais and Paris. The opening of the Ramsgate hoverport on 2 April 1969 saw express coach services introduced offering connections via hovercraft to Paris and Ostende, whilst express services commencing or terminating at Ramsgate were now extended to the hoverport for pre-booked passengers. This facility also extended to the many Dartford Tunnel services, as well as East Kent's own London services.

East Kent's continental tours now offered a larger variety of destinations, although some were now based on air connections to be met by the 'East Kent' coach on the continent, thus avoiding a sometimes lengthy journey to the main destination. East Kent coaches still operated throughout on other popular itineraries, using the cross-channel ferries; for these tours the 1963 brochure offered destina-

tions such as Holland in the spring, Switzerland, the Italian Lakes, Venice and Western Austria.

On the excursion leaflets, progression through the 1960s saw the image of a TFN Reliance replaced by a number of differing images of town and country, as can be seen on this Broadstairs brochure. AUTHOR'S COLLECTION

CHAPTER EIGHT

TOWARDS THE 1970s AND NATIONALIZATION

CONTRACTION/M&D TRANSFERS

At Dover, from 7 May 1967, the 98B route variant running between the Linces and Marine station was introduced, one of the few East Kent services with a 'B' suffix. This saw the 98 group (Aycliffe/Buckland) combined in the 94/95/96/131 timetable. The latter group had seen certain evening Ropewalk journeys extended to Aycliffe from 19 September 1965 so it made sense to combine the services in one schedule although this made for a very complex timetable, with eleven different services in the title.

With the advent of the summer 1968 timetable on 30 June, D/C operation increased. To facilitate this, the linkage of four trunk routes implemented earlier was now reversed; service 3 from Faversham to Canterbury returned and the 8 from Margate reverted to its Canterbury terminus, while in the south the 80 and 90 were also split, reverting to their earlier Deal–Dover and Dover–Folkestone sections.

AFN 767B had been at Dover from delivery in 1964; this snowy November 1969 scene sees her coasting down Snargate Street on the 96A, bound for Ropewalk, a destination evocative of former sailing days. AUTHOR

Opinion at the time, both from the company and from union representatives, was that these shorter routes would be easier for D/C operation. Through fares across both Canterbury, between the 3 and 8, and at Dover, between the 80 and 90, were available for a time, but these facilities were withdrawn from 27 September 1968.

Further seasonal reductions continued this summer. At Herne Bay, service 43's regular hourly service to Reculver was withdrawn; most journeys now terminated at Hillborough, while 1968 would be the last season of operation of the 36 service to Margate via the Thanet Way, leaving the 35 to soldier on in future years as the sole link from Herne Bay to the Isle of Thanet.

At Margate, 1968 was also to be the last year of the long-standing seasonal service 46 operating via Dane Valley. This was interlinked with the 51; the mode of operation was that the 51 would reroute from Cecil Square to run via Margate harbour in the summer as normal to an improved frequency, while the service via Cecil Square would be hourly, provided by the 46. From 26 June 1966 the 46 had operated the hourly Warren Drive extension in summer with the winter service provided by the 51, all journeys operating via Cecil Square. The Warren Drive service had commenced, mainly as a 51 shuttle from Westgate, on 22 May 1960 and became part of the main service from that October. In 1961, the 51 would be extended in summer to Minnis Bay, complementing the summer-only 46 until summer 1966, when both the 46 and 51 were cut back to Westgate permanently and take the service pattern described above. A further consequence was that the 46 would now run via Westgate station. As a result, the 49/50 group would now provide an all-year service to Minnis Bay; another all-year extension in Birchington, to Sherwood Estate, had already been operating from 19 May 1963. Thus in 1969 the 46 would still operate in the summer but no longer via Dane Valley; this was to be the last year of its operation, as impending double-deck D/C conversion would completely change the structure and numbering of these routes.

The winter timetable from 8 September 1968 saw more reductions affecting Dover town services on the afternoons of early closing day, Wednesday. Kearsney journeys were withdrawn on Wednesday afternoons and a reduced frequency applied on other routes. Further changes in Dover from 4 January 1970 attempted to simplify the complexity of having a group of eleven services in one timetable and also to introduce savings. This was achieved by splitting the timetables for Buckland Estate (The Linces/Pilgrims Way)/Kearsney areas, service 94/A and 96 respectively, from those for River/Archers Court, service 95/A and 131/A respectively. The 98 group, which had led a somewhat duplicitous life by serving either The Linces (98/B) or Whitfield (98A) was removed from the Buckland and Aycliffe areas. These changes saw the service to River reduced on weekdays from a 15-minute frequency to every 20 minutes, allowing one more service per hour to Fulbert Road on the Archers Court leg whilst the Aycliffe service was also enhanced to every 20 minutes; the combined service across the centre was now every 10 minutes. The Pilgrims Way/Linces termini on the 94/A saw one less journey per hour, reducing to a 30-minute frequency, but as one Pilgrims Way journey now diverted via the Linces rather than terminating at the latter point, the earlier intervals to each former terminus were maintained. The 94/A/96 group would now be the only services to feature the reduced Wednesday afternoon service. These two groups would now provide nine journeys per hour on most weekdays between Buckland Mill and the Market Square, compared to ten journeys under the previous timetable.

As the changes saw the 98 group withdrawn from its former routes it allowed the number to be used for an extension of the Maxton/Elms Vale Road services to the new terminal building at the Eastern Docks, using 98 for Maxton to Eastern Docks and 98A for Elms Vale to Eastern Docks, the former 97/A services still terminating at the Market Square; a 20-minute weekday frequency operated to each terminal. Service 86, which formerly terminated at the East Cliff outside the port terminal, was reduced to running between Market Square and Tower Hamlets, still at a 30-minute frequency; it was renumbered 130 from 20 September 1970, permitting easier changing of numbers between similarly numbered services when inter-worked.

In the hinterland between Deal and Canterbury, 12 January 1969 saw the former 14 to Staple withdrawn and the mileage to Wingham covered by an extension of the Deal–Staple service 76, connecting there with the 13/A to Canterbury, which in turn would be renumbered 13 and 14 from 29 June. Service 68 would also be curtailed in January, with the main service now running from Sandwich to Aylesham only and the Ramsgate leg relying on connecting services apart from one afternoon peak journey. Changes from 2 March 1969 saw Deal's 82 diverted from Lydia Road to serve Walmer, performing a loop east of the station to avoid the low bridge, while its former terminus at Lydia Road was now served by an extension of the 84.

On the same date in March the 132/142 services were more closely integrated, the latter service being transferred from Folkestone to New Romney depot. A week later, on 10 March, a new works service, 140, was introduced, running from Folkestone, bus station to the new Park Farm industrial estate. At Lydd the outstation was eventually closed from 7 September 1969 and operations transferred to New Romney, as it was unable to accommodate the 36ft (11m) single-deckers now necessary for D/C operation on the 105. For a time the 'Long Dog' was secured with the garage doors partially open and a lock and chain! Other changes at

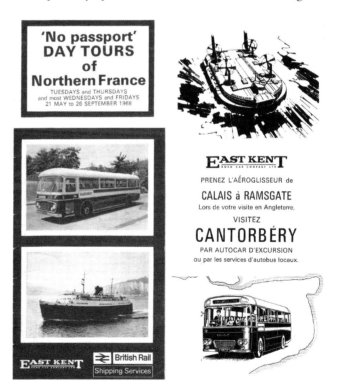

Northern France excursions from England were a lucrative business for the company but day tourism from France was also an opportunity, with the faster Hovercraft services. Two leaflets of the period are shown here – the French leaflet is reminiscent of those produced for visitors to Canterbury before the war. AUTHOR'S COLLECTION

this time saw ex-Carey's route 133 – from Ashford to New Romney and Greatstone via Stone Cross, Newchurch and St Mary's-in-the-Marsh – withdrawn and replaced by the 119 extended from Newchurch to New Romney. The 111 service from Hythe to Ashford also had some journeys diverted via Stone Cross in partial replacement of the 133 journeys via this location. In November 1970 the 119 was further extended to Lade in conjunction with the withdrawal of services 132/142.

When the new Pegwell Bay International Hoverport opened at Ramsgate on 2 April 1969, it acted as a new focus for stage and express services, seeing both dedicated services as well as diverting existing services 62, 66, 68, 70 and 87 via the terminal. New services introduced included the 60 from Cliftonville, Margate and Ramsgate for the summer, and the 61 from Margate via Cliftonville, Broadstairs and Ramsgate in the winter. The 69 open-top service was also extended to the hoverport from 25 May, as well as being linked to the 56 at Margate. Another, more minor change took place at Whitstable in May, with the 5 extended to the expanding Seasalter area while the opportunity was taken to distinguish journeys via Tankerton Circus by numbering them 5A.

The summer timetable of 1969, commencing 29 June, saw further cuts, with reductions at Thanet. The seasonal 7- to 8-minute frequency on the 49/50/52 group reduced to 10 minutes; the 51 service had a similar reduction, while the 54/A went from a 15-minute interval to 20 minutes, as well as being converted to double-deck D/C with new Daimler Fleetlines. The other new double-deck D/C operation, the 71, had to have its running time extended,

seeing the former 30-minute frequency protracted to 40 minutes. However, experience for the first season saw the running times reduced again, and the 30-minute service resumed from 7 September. Further Fleetline double-deck D/C conversions at Thanet, of services 63/64 from 4 January 1970, resulted in the former 15-minute through service reduced to 30 minutes on service 64 only; the 63 was split, short-workings still providing a 15-minute service jointly with the 64 between Newington and Dumpton at Ramsgate, but only one 63 per hour operating at the Margate end between Northdown Park and Margate Hospital via Northdown Park Avenue. The plan was for the Ramsgate-end 63s to serve Prestedge Avenue at Dumpton, but until suitable reversing arrangements for D/C operation could be agreed they reversed in the station forecourt. Even when extended, cars still displayed Dumpton station as there was no blind insert provided for the new terminal at that time.

At Rye, summer 1969 saw the number 116 reincarnated once again to separate out the high-season service to Camber. One reason for this was the transfer to Rye of two 36ft (11m) 'Long Dogs' from Folkestone, which were dedicated to the 116 to cater for the greater seasonal traffic. In 1969 NBC formally took over East Kent, and while there was no visible change at first, the rot started to set in from 7 September 1969, when the company's Hastings depot was closed and services 127/128 to Pett Chick Hill and Pett Level were transferred to M&D and renumbered 171 and 170 respectively.

Meanwhile, at Canterbury, the September 1969 timetable saw the beginning of major changes to the town services, following the opening of a new bridge over the

The last main routes to become double-deck D/C operated as part of the initial programme with the Daimler Fleetlines saw the 63/64 group converted. RFN 959G swings from Ramsgate's High Street into Cannon Road bound for Dumpton Prestedge Avenue on the Ramsgate section of the 63 in August 1975, still in original livery. AUTHOR

September 1969 saw East Kent's Hastings operations passing to M&D together with services 127 and 128, which had been part of their operations since 1933 and 1934 respectively. KFN 236 stands at Hastings Denmark Place on service 127 to Pett Chick Hill in the last summer of East Kent tenure. AUTHOR

Canterbury city services had remained virtually untouched by change until the end of the 1960s apart from Regents gradually replacing Guys. These two scenes from 1969 show PFN 880 bound for Blean on the 27A whilst the other view shows YJG 820 destined for the Sturry Road on the 23. Both display via blinds, which were rarely used by crews until the district superintendent of the time, Mr Elliot, cracked down and insisted they were displayed. These views are now history; pedestrianization has resulted in buses being banned – progress? AUTHOR

renumbered 165, leaving only one through journey each way to/from Canterbury on the alternative 65. The following summer, in 1970, a new high-season service, numbered 73, would run four times a day from Ramsgate to Canterbury via the hoverport and Sandwich in partial replacement for the former seasonal facility on the 9; it would only last two seasons, however, finishing at the end of summer 1971. From 24 May 1970 the former seasonal routing swaps concerning the 46 and 51 services were brought into line: the 51 remained routed via Cecil Square and journeys via the harbour would take number 151, the latter's summer service remaining crew-operated at this time while the 51 was now double-deck D/C. In March 1971 another Margate service, the 54A, became 154, continuing the policy of removing suffix letters, possibly on the grounds of legibility, or more likely, computerization.

Cuts were now gradually nibbling away at East Kent's more rural network; the 19, running Fridays only from Canterbury down to Six Mile Cottages on Stone Street, was withdrawn from 20 September 1970, covered in part by some diversions of service 20. Another casualty from 7 March 1971 included the 93A to West Langdon, covered by some extensions of the 93. Down at Rye, East Kent's shortest route, the 117 to Cadborough Cliff, was withdrawn from the same date except for some journeys on schooldays, a precursor of further cuts at Rye. From 9 May 1971 the 2 from Rye to Ashford via Brookland was totally withdrawn, while the 112 was decimated and ran on a varied set of routes, covering either Brookland and thence to Appledore (Tuesdays and Saturdays) or over part of its former route

railway, giving better access to the Hales Place area. Services 26/28/29 were completely revised and interlinked, giving rise to new services 30/A and 39. Later, different variants such as 29A and 30B would emerge. Canterbury city services had remained immune from major change for many years apart from the withdrawal of one hourly journey on the 23/A services from June 1969, which saw the link from St. Dunstan's to Sturry Road halved in its weekday frequency. The 27/A remained virtually unscathed but Blean saw its local service halved as a result.

Summer 1969 would be the last season of operation of the by now summer-only Ramsgate–Canterbury through service on route 9 via Manna Hutte and Sarre. On 4 January 1970 the remaining services to Manna Hutte would be

PFN 865 pulls away from Margate harbour in July 1970, displaying the newly adopted number 151 for this routing. Some journeys were now regularly scheduled to run as far as Westbrook rather than Westgate – further evidence of the drop in holiday traffic. AUTHOR

via Wittersham thence Appledore, Brenzett and Snave (Wednesdays and Fridays), both featuring only one return journey. Some short-workings were retained, running weekdays between Appledore and Rye via Brookland but the writing was on the wall for these services. One oddity linked to these changes was the brief emergence of new service 162 from 20 September 1970, running between Rye/Brookland and New Romney to provide a cross-Marsh link substituting for service 62 which was now withdrawn for the winter season excepting Christmas as was the X26. Always a limited service, its Sunday operation finished by 28 November. The later changes that withdrew the 2 and saw the 112 severely rationalized from 9 May 1971 also saw this service withdrawn.

FARES – INCREASES, BARGAINS AND IMPENDING DECIMALIZATION

Increased inflation as well as rising costs and falling revenues had forced the company to apply many fares increases in the intervening years since the big fares increases of 1952; by July 1970, the last fare table issued before decimalization in 1971, the fare from Deal to Dover had now risen from 1/7d (8p) to 2/10d (14p), an increase of 75 per cent. However, the company was alive to the need to encourage leisure traffic, and early in 1970 it introduced an all-day ticket, the Wanderbus, a name coined by one of the traffic office staff at the time, Vernon Bettison, after much humor-

ous debate in which the author also took part. The chief traffic clerk, Geoff Dodson, had suggested 'BusAbout' but this was summarily rejected by the traffic manager! The ticket cost 9/- (45p) and was initially only valid on Sundays and bank holidays; it excluded the university service 32 as well as the two jointly worked routes 10 and 67. It went on to be a major success with validity eventually relaxed and extending to M&D routes. It could be said to the precursor of today's Stagecoach Explorer ticket.

At 9/-, Wanderbus represented a real bargain as even a period return from Canterbury to Folkestone, which cost 3/6d (17.5p) in 1926, was now 7/- (35p). At the time there was a distinction between day and period return fares; the former had been introduced from the fares revision of 1 August 1967. Period returns valid for three months were now only generally valid for the main journeys such as that quoted above, and others such as Canterbury to Margate, but interestingly not from Canterbury to Faversham. With the advent of decimalization on 21 February 1971, all return fares became day returns only and from then on were only valid off-peak (9.15am–3.45pm) Mondays to Fridays; the Wanderbus availability was extended to Saturdays in replacement.

The pre-decimalization fare table of 1970 was the last to feature the traditional East Kent logo on the cover. The cover of the timetable had submitted to NBC corporate policy earlier, from summer 1969, although the internal flyleaf featured the traditional logo up to and including the May 1970 edition – perhaps the company managers thought NBC policy-makers would not look inside the front cover. This new style was standardized across the NBC; it featured a map of the local operating area on the cover, firstly with little detail then replaced in 1970 by one based on a more accurate representation with roads. Also published in 1970 was a network map in a separate folder mimicking the timetable cover, but in blue with the company name in a plain font as **East Kent**. The map had already been published in a separate folder circa 1967 and, interestingly, that also did not feature the traditional logo as it was part of a country-wide initiative, East Kent's being the last in the series, numbered 50. It was probably not much in demand as the map was still carried in the timetable. There was still local resistance to corporate policy, however – a handbill issued by Folkestone for amendments to services 104 and 106 in August 1971 proudly displayed the old East Kent logo in an extra-large font. Possibly this was a last-ditch act of defiance, as by now leaflets and internal documentation displayed **EAST KENT** in a plain block font rather than the characterful 'expanded Egyptienne' style used since the company's inception in 1916.

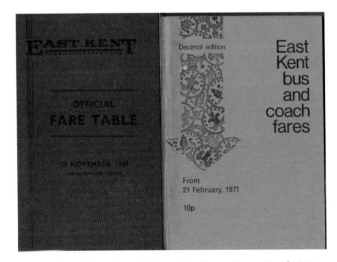

The last fare table issued in the former East Kent style was that of 1969, although this issue adopted a larger format rather than the smaller booklet beforehand. Next came the decimalization edition with a more nondescript format for the company name. AUTHOR'S COLLECTION

1960s RAILWAY CLOSURES – REPLACEMENTS AND PROPOSALS

On Romney Marsh, the Beeching cuts resulted in the train service between Appledore and New Romney being withdrawn from 6 March 1967; replacement service 142 was then operated from Lade via New Romney, Lydd and Brookland to Appledore in connection with the remaining services on the Ashford–Hastings line. The diversions to Lydd and Brookland made the 8-mile (13km) journey from New Romney take about 50 minutes, perhaps not an unfavourable comparison with around 30 minutes by train, but comparative comfort and lack of through-ticketing doomed the service. It was soon integrated more closely with the former Carey's service 132 from Lydd to New Romney but this could not save it, and it was last scheduled in the summer 1970 timetable. From 29 November 1970 service 119 was extended from New Romney to Lade in partial replacement as it provided a direct service from Ashford. While no details were provided in supplements, it is thought that this marked the end of the 142 and its companion 132, for the time ending services to Dungeness and to Appledore station. In the summer 1971 timetable, introduced on 30 May, all reference to them had gone.

This was to be the last passenger railway closure in East Kent's area, but in 1969 a number of further closure proposals were in the air. The author, working in East Kent's traffic office, prepared many of the proposed replacement bus timetables. The first, the proposed closure of Westenhanger station between Sandling and Ashford, led to detailed plans being prepared to divert the 109 between Ashford and Hythe via Sandling station rather than Pedlinge to connect with trains. Despite some minor improvements to the schedule, it did not seem to the author to be a viable plan.

A more fundamental closure planned was that from Ashford to Hastings via Rye which by 1969 had had ministerial consent. Again, the author worked on these plans, which involved an intensive set of services attempting to access the many isolated stations, few of which were on the main roads linking the major towns. Between Rye and Ashford an hourly service was planned off-peak and three route options would be offered: either via the existing 2 or 112 routes or a new one via the Royal Military Road, Appledore, Brenzett and Ham Street. Between Hastings and Rye the frequency would be half-hourly with a revised 113 service supplementing the through journeys to and from Ashford. Even with limited-stop services scheduled during the peaks, journey times were not far short of two hours compared with a rail journey of less than 45 minutes.

The other problem was the roads, limiting operations to East Kent's 30ft (9m)-long 41-seaters, perhaps leading to capacity problems or the need for multiple cars. The idea of bumping along the Marsh for nearly two hours in one of the Company's ubiquitous '41s' was not an appealing prospect! The services would have been operated jointly with M&D as by this time Hastings garage had closed. In the end, common sense prevailed and both closure plans were dropped, but it is an interesting conjecture as to what would have happened to East Kent's operations and indeed how it would have affected the future takeover of Rye by M&D in later years if the closure had been implemented.

RESTRICTIVE BRIDGES – AND FIRES

The company was affected by two major bridge restrictions in the late 1960s. At Deal, from September 1967, closure of the main bridge over the railway at London Road/Queen

The small depot at New Romney is the location of this view of 101 CUF, one of the ex-Southdown Leopards, in June 1974 about to work service 119. Despite being five years post-nationalization there is little evidence of the abhorred corporate identity. AUTHOR

The closure of the main railway bridge at Deal in 1967 now meant that every town service except the 85 became mandatory single-deck operation. It resulted in a number of transfers in of the new 36ft (11m) saloons, and the DJG-C batch became permanent features at Deal. DJG 356C is captured here at Deal South Street in August 1969 on the 82, by this time extended to Walmer from its former terminus at Lydia Road. Prior to the closure, the 82 was still single-deck, as it already crossed under another low bridge at Hamilton Road. AUTHOR

The WFN batch of Regent Vs would be associated with Deal after a mass transfer there during 1968 following the restriction on Black Mill Bridge, Sturry. WFN 827 is pictured on the 83 in July 1970 at South Street, displaying the 'lazy blind' used on most Deal town services – due, in part, to their short journey times. AUTHOR

Street entailed the diversion of town services 81/83/84 via Park Avenue, which was itself restricted by a 13ft (4m) height limit. As a result, 36ft (11m) single-deck saloons, albeit crew-operated, took over these services for a period lasting nearly two years, the repairs taking until May 1969.

Deal was affected again when a weight restriction imposed on the river bridge at Black Mill, Sturry required the transfer away from Canterbury and Herne Bay by March 1968 of most of the heavier, WFN-registered AEC Regents, which had been allocated to these depots from new. This was to avoid their use on the intensive 4/6 group of services. Most of the WFNs went to Deal, with their cars transferring in replacement. This transfer was also, inadvertently, to result in the early withdrawal of WFN 832, as a fire broke out in its upper deck, possibly as a result of a cigarette, while in Deal depot in August 1968. Luckily the fire was limited but 832 was deemed beyond repair and was scrapped, the first of the AEC Regents to go. Later, in 1971, another fire casualty was DJG 615C, which caught alight on the M2 motorway and was withdrawn and also scrapped. Other serious fires occurred later, in both the NBC and newly privatized era: a National, NFN 74M, had an engine fire that saw its front donated to accident-damaged EFN 175L in 1977; one of the new Bristol VRs had to be rebodied following a fire in 1982; and in 1989 a serious fire at the Pencester Road stabling site completely destroyed two of the Leyland Atlanteans from 1976.

OPEN-TOP SERVICES – NEW CARS, EXPANSION AND RETRENCHMENT

The success of the two Thanet open-top services caused the company to seek other opportunities, and in June 1962 a new service, 44, was introduced at Herne Bay; it ran hourly from the Western Esplanade to Reculver on Sundays to Fridays for its first season and daily thereafter, using one car. At first, BJG 339, spare at Thanet, was used but this was stretching resources a little, as Thanet now used all its cars and their services had been running all week from 1960. The 69 had been extended to run from Broadstairs in summer 1960 and was then extended at its southern end onward from Cliffsend to Minster in summer 1962, now requiring two cars, while its sister service at Margate, the 56, already required three cars. A further conversion was already in course though. FFN 380, a later Guy Arab III, had suffered a collision with a low bridge and was converted to open-top in June 1962; after a time at Thanet it later went on to become the regular Herne Bay car from 1964.

The extension of the 69 into the countryside to Minster was not a success, and from summer 1966 it reverted back to its former terminus at Cliffsend and with a widening of frequency now only required one car. Thanet again had two spares and a use was eventually found for the extra car. Once more BJG 339 was chosen to run a service from

A challenge for any vehicle, let alone a 5-cylinder Gardner-engined vehicle twenty-four years of age: BJG 339, in the hands of driver Keith Davidson and legendary conductor Bertie Wootton, reaches the summit of Castle Hill Road, Dover in summer 1968 before descending the even steeper Connaught Road, which would test its endurance in the other direction.
AUTHOR'S COLLECTION – COMPANY ORIGINAL

2 June 1968, numbered 101, running from Folkestone to Dover via the Old Road at Capel and Dover Castle, giving probably the most spectacular views of any of East Kent's open-top services. It was challenging for the drivers, however. BJG 339 had been equipped with a five-cylinder Gardner engine rather than a 6LW unit, which explained why Thanet was always keen to hive it off to other depots. The hills on the route were the most severe faced by any open-top service but 339 performed well throughout the summer season and celebrated its final withdrawal with a tour organized by the MDEK Club around East Kent's depots on 15 September 1968. Plans to operate low-season short-workings within Folkestone to the East Cliff after this were aborted, after minimal demand, on 8 September.

By 1968 the BJGs were becoming life-expired and, with one exception, 1968 was to be their last summer. Unfortunately, a crew shortage at Thanet towards the end of the summer of 1968 caused the premature withdrawal of all their open-top services. A programme of converting more FFN Guy Arabs was initiated, as these were now in the course of withdrawal from service. Eight more were converted between 1968 and 1970, followed by three of the later GFN-registered Arab IVs in 1970. This influx of new blood saw open-top horizons expand further. At Folkestone, the 101 was extended in 1969 from Folkestone

to Hythe with the addition of a Dover car. The next year, 1970, it was extended further, to St Mary's Bay, and alternate journeys, numbered 101A, terminated at Lympne, Ashford Airport. In common with all open-top services they were now operating all week. The next year, 1971, saw a contraction back to Dymchurch, first operating Sundays only on the shoulders of the high summer. The 101A also adopted an alternative routing via the Alkham Valley. This was to be the last year of operation of the 101/A in this form. Conversion of both Dover and Folkestone depots to complete D/C operation meant that such a service could

From 1969 more FFN-registered Guy Arab IIIs were converted to replace the wartime BJGs. Later conversions from 1970 were devoid of the 'Coastal Service' lettering, as shown by Dover's FFN 384 skirting Folkestone harbour in 1971 on the 101A. MIKE ANSELL

Herne Bay's regular car for many years, FFN 380 – the original FFN conversion and carrying 'Coastal Service' – is seen on a new venture at Herne Bay in September 1971. Service 45 ran from the station, supplementing the existing 44 to Reculver and replacing it in the early and late season. She emerges onto the seafront near the pier; note the company's office in the background, a feature of towns across the area. AUTHOR

The final Guy conversions in 1970 saw a small number of the GFN Arab IVs joining the Arab IIIs. In July 1971 GFN 920 descends Fort Hill, Margate near the harbour on the long service 69 from the Hoverport to Birchington, Minnis Bay. AUTHOR

not be resourced, and for 1972 and 1973 a seasonal 'Town Tour' numbered 121 operated at Folkestone, using former conductors taken on temporarily for the season.

In the north, at Herne Bay, the 44 was supplemented in the summer of 1971 by an additional hourly open-top service, numbered 45, from Herne Bay Station to Reculver. Although service 45 continued, open-top operation was not retained from 1972, and 1974 would be the last season of operation of Herne Bay's original service 44.

At Thanet things would fare a little better. The opening of Ramsgate's hoverport at Pegwell Bay in 1969 saw the introduction, on 25 May, of a now lengthy open-top service 69 running from Minnis Bay to Pegwell Bay, incorporating the former 56 and linking the two on new mileage from Palm Bay to Broadstairs. The 56 was retained at first, the combined services maintaining a 30-minute interval in the Margate area with an hourly journey to/from Pegwell Bay. As the new conversions were running behind schedule, Weymann-bodied BJG 472 enjoyed a further lease of life for this season. Intended for the 56, a discovery in Westwood depot one evening saw it with blinds for the full route; it is unclear whether it did perform such a major task. From 1970, a 30-minute interval on the 69 operated throughout and the 56 was withdrawn.

Later developments, which, for convenience, are dealt with here saw more conversions. From 1972 a selection of AEC Regents from the PFN batch were converted to open-top, seven being completed between 1972 and 1973. The

first three received traditional East Kent open-top livery; the others, dealt with at the end of the programme, succumbed to the NBC corporate white and red upon conversion but applied in similar fashion to the preceding livery. In 1973 the 69 was diverted to operate via Joss Bay, now that a width restriction near Kingsgate had been removed. Later years would see a gradual reduction in the service until final withdrawal, as detailed later. In 1972, at the instigation of Barry Robinson, assistant traffic manager of the time, a new side advert was produced for the cars used on the 69 with a map of the route proclaiming 'Thanet's 16-mile Open-Top Grandstand'. Allegedly, the initial idea was '69 – Have You Tried the Topless Ride', but this was thought to be an innuendo too far!

Another story pertaining to hoverport operations concerned the large number of French passengers in the early 1970s, most bound for Ramsgate on the 69 and without English currency. Geoff Dodson, district superintendent of the time, recalls that he devised a fare table in French francs covering the section between the Hoverport and Ramsgate; it is not entirely clear how the conductor sorted that on his or her waybill but the conversion rate was certainly in the company's favour.

One final point before leaving BET's East Kent open-top story is to detail some of the more adventurous parts of its operations. One was the annual venture to London for the Derby Day in June, which reminds one that in pre-war years the company's early open-top cars also made such a trip. Even more surprising was the use of five surplus East Kent FFN Guys on the Round London Sightseeing Tour in

Once crew operation ceased at many depots, open-top operation was concentrated at Thanet, using the later PFN Regent V conversions from 1972. PFN 853, one of the few to receive pre-NBC livery, sings her way out of Ramsgate Harbour in 1977 bound for the Hoverport on service 69. She features the approved advertising material for the route! AUTHOR

One of the surplus Guy Arab III open-tops seconded to Samuelson's for round London sightseeing operations is captured unloading at Piccadilly in September 1972. East Kent drivers were employed on the service, as evidenced by the company summer dust jacket worn by this driver. AUTHOR

double-decker was well past its sell-by date. The newer rear-engine designs of the Leyland Atlantean and Daimler Fleetline, both suitable for D/C operation, had already been adopted by most other bus companies, but East Kent held to a more traditional policy, somewhat like its sister company Southdown down the coast, and it was the last mainland English bus operator to purchase the Regent V. The body design of the Regents underwent cosmetic upgrades with each batch but they were very much recognizable as a product of the 1950s. East Kent loaned four of their Regents to sister company City of Oxford in winter 1968–9 to alleviate a severe vehicle shortage there.

1972 operated by Samuelsons of London, although the venture was not to be repeated. A number of the open-top Guys were retained for driver training after they were made surplus by the PFN conversions; the author spent a few happy weeks with FFN 375 on crash-box upgrade training on his return from London Transport in 1973. Their retention also saw them reappearing in service on the 69, particularly on Derby Day or in the event of failure, although 1974 was to be the last season of their cameo appearances.

FLEET – THE LAST OF BET EAST KENT'S DELIVERIES

For the fleet intake, the decade of the 1960s was characterized by the near-total domination by AEC. However, towards the end a more diverse approach was necessitated due to the non-availability of suitable AEC double-deck or low-capacity single-deck chassis. While the NBC had taken control from 1969 it would be a while – until 1972 – before the corporate body dictated the fleet intake. This section deals with the last new or acquired cars to be painted in traditional East Kent livery.

A further 121 AEC Regents were purchased during this period, making a total of 161 of the type taken into the fleet, although the subsequent deliveries after the PFNs had a more angular 'Orion'-style body and returned to a half-cab configuration. East Kent were to remain faithful to the AEC Regent V well beyond a sensible timescale and they were to take delivery of six different batches until 1967, by which time the concept of a front-engine, crew-operated

The years 1969–70 can be said to mark the swansong of regular operation of closed-top Guy Arabs in service. One surprising event in summer 1969 was the transfer to Canterbury from Thanet of three Guy Arab IIIs, which went on to be used on city services for a short while. Top, FFN 374 is seen on service 24 at Sturry Road, Vauxhall Road in June. Bottom, July 1970 sees a very smart GFN 932 departing Ramsgate harbour on a short-working of service 65. Its appearance contrasts with the weather-beaten condition of FFN 374. AUTHOR

All half-cab Regents were delivered with curved mudguards, but the offside was replaced with a squarer cover, reportedly to avoid mud being thrown up on the windscreen. MFN 949F, from the last batch of 1967, displays the more attractive original style working Folkestone's busy 99 route at the Central Station in 1969. MDEK CLUB

In 1962 East Kent also purchased three examples of the low-height AEC Bridgemaster, with integral construction but a body style similar to the majority of the Regent Vs. Intended for Dover's town service 129, which ran to St. Radigund's via a low bridge, they remained at this depot for most of their lives, apart from a short sojourn at Westwood in 1971–2 after the 129 had been converted to single-deck crew operation on 20 September 1970 and D/C operation in 1971 – crew operation finally being abolished at Dover.

Further AEC Reliances were taken into stock. VJG 500 and WFN 501–18, delivered in 1960–1, were to be the last of the 30ft (9m) 41-seat Park Royal-bodied saloons, and were similar to the TFNs but with body style differences. At first these also had the five-speed synchromesh gearboxes as fitted to the TFNs. The opening of the M2 motorway between 1963 and 1965 and the diversion of the company's Express services L1 and new M2 via the motorway required vehicles employed on these services, as well as tours cars, to be capable of maintaining a higher average speed over longer distances than was previously the case. Two cars, VJG 500 and WFN 518, were first fitted with an AEC six-speed gearbox in 1961, probably to test the concept. In order to accommodate the new gearbox these were of constant-mesh configuration, as the synchromesh six-speed option could not be accommodated within the 30ft (9m) chassis. The remainder of the batch were converted in 1963–4. This conversion saw them retained for express work far longer than their TFN cousins, and they only began to be converted to D/C operation from 1969. The six-speed 'crash' gearbox, although more difficult to

manage for an inexperienced driver, meant that these vehicles had a great turn of speed and, in the author's opinion, allowed a smoother and more positive change than the synchromesh box remaining on the TFNs. The gearbox change was also applied to the MJG tours cars, 41–52, in 1963 due to their regular use on the motorway. None of the other 30ft Reliances was so treated.

The relaxation of regulations on length of vehicles allowed East Kent to take delivery of 36ft (11m) length coaches from 1962. Bodied by Park Royal on AEC Reliance chassis with the larger AH590 engine and six-speed ZF synchromesh gearbox, they were of a smart but functional appearance. One car, 537 FN, had the AEC crash box as fitted to the VJG/WFN coaches – it is not known why. The first batch, 519–38 FN, was of 46-seat configuration, with a large rear luggage cage that was removed in 1963–4. The next delivery in 1963, 6539–48 FN, were of what became the standard 49-seat capacity for these cars. Both batches had manually operated front doors and opening windows, with the exception of 6548 FN, which had an experimental forced-air ventilation system, sealed windows and an air-operated door. The next three batches, delivered from 1964 to 1966, AFN 596–605B, DJG 606–31C and GJG 632–43D, all had the same ventilation and door operation as 6548 FN. A total of seventy-eight of these coaches was delivered, becoming the de facto standard car for the company's express services in the 1960s.

In terms of performance, they went like the wind; popular anecdote amongst drivers at Victoria Coach Station

The later WFN-registered dual-purpose saloons remained on mainstream London duties far longer than their TFN contemporaries due to being equipped with six-speed gearboxes. Hence Dover's WFN 517 is seen on the L3 at London Victoria coach station in April 1970. AUTHOR

A break with Park Royal as the preferred bodybuilder for coaches was made in 1968 with the delivery of these smart Willowbrook-bodied AEC Reliance 691s. Originally intended to be registered OFN 549–56F, a mistake by the licensing authorities resulted in them being changed to OJG 130–7F; this is OJG 135F at Westwood garage in the early 1970s after working an L2 service. Coach blinds of this era were white on red although other colours, such as blue backgrounds for Europabus workings, were also in place. AUTHOR

during this time has it that the only thing you saw of an East Kent coach was the rear-locker doors. The speedometer went to 80mph (130km/h) but it was fairly easy to take them 'off the clock', as the author can testify, and allegedly supported by police observations of the time; it was of course still legal then. Two cars, 520 FN and 6541 FN, had tachographs fitted and the author has in his possession one disc from 6541 FN that clearly shows speeds in excess of 80mph (130km/h). It will be left to the imagination what could be achieved unchecked if this was the speed reached when monitored. Much has been written about the speeds achieved by Midland Red's motorway coaches but these AECs could probably match them. The last batch of service coaches, as opposed to cars with a higher specification that came later, comprised eight AEC 691s with 49-seat Willowbrook bodies delivered in 1968, OJG 130–7F.

Another anecdote concerning the Park Royal coaches and paint-shop practice of the time relates to GJG 632D, which was allocated to Canterbury and the back-up car used for the annual directors' tours or for other dignitaries if a normal tours car was unavailable. On one occasion a tour took in the Rye area and made a stop at Dungeness to visit the former lighthouse, now open to the public. Apparently, upon ascending the 169 steps, the dignitaries looked down on the roof of the coach, only to see that the 632's recent immaculate repaint only extended to the top of the roof cove panels, visible from ground level. All too plainly in view from this lofty height was a very faded rectangle, by

now more a dirty off-white than a rich cream. Suitable comments made, it is unlikely that the mistake was repeated!

For tours work, the company took delivery of some intermediate-length AEC Reliance 470s, 32ft (10m) long, with smart 34-seat Duple bodies, in 1964, AFN 488–99B. They remained on tours until 1973–4, by which time a further batch of luxurious cars with 40-seat Duple Commander IV bodies on AEC Reliance 691 chassis delivered in 1970, UFN 480–7H, and a subsequent set of cars delivered to NBC standards, had replaced them.

For single-deck saloons, after a break of many years, in 1965 the company decided to purchase cars to proper

The next express coaches went even further in improvement, with stylish Plaxton bodies still on AEC Reliance chassis. VFN 40H, one of the 11m (36ft) versions, is at Canterbury bus station in the early 1970s with a smaller than normal fleet name, a result of diminishing stocks of the larger version and the impending NBC livery. MIKE ANSELL

The next tours cars, arriving in 1970, departed even further from the old standard, with modern Duple Commander IV bodies but still on AEC chassis. UFN 482H is seen at Dover Pencester Road in May 1971 on a private hire. Note the italicized fleet name, unique to these cars.
PAUL FURMINGER

bus – rather than dual-purpose – specification. These were DJG 355–8C on 36ft (11m) AEC Reliance 590 chassis with 51-seat Marshall bodies. Surprisingly, the chassis were to the same specification as the coaches, with six-speed ZF gearboxes. East Kent's sister company, M&D, chose similar vehicles, but with four-speed gearboxes, which were arguably better suited to bus operation. Interestingly, when these DJG-Cs were allocated to Deal for town work, the fifth and sixth speeds were blanked off. This had been removed when the author drove DJG 358C in 1973. These buses were followed by ten more, KJG 571–80E in 1967 and then a large batch of twenty-five, OFN 708–32F in 1968. This latter batch was to 53-seat capacity and equipped with the larger 691 engine. These cars were to usher in large-scale conversion of the company's trunk routes to D/C operation although many ran as crew-operated cars until 1968, when agreement was finally reached with the union to operate them as D/C cars to their full capacity.

Apart from the first batch, they were not equipped with opening windows and relied on a new forced-air heating and ventilation system. It did not work well, especially in hot weather, and soon some of the opening windows from the DJG-Cs were removed for use on the KJG-Es, while the larger windows on the OFN-Fs required new stock. They became known to crews as 'Long Dogs' and were often prone to overheating, especially those with the 691 engine. On hot days drivers would often arrive at a terminus with the vehicle sizzling and the temperature gauge at over 120°C. The usefulness of East Kent's wooden running boards then became obvious – they were ideal for knock-

At the other end of the scale were the 29-seat Bedford VAS1s, which arrived in 1967 to replace the Dennis Falcons on restricted routes. KJG 106E is captured in June 1974 on the back roads of West Hougham, bound for Capel. AUTHOR

ing off the clip to the – very hot – water filler cap. Thus released, a scalding plume of water erupted from the near-side of the bus. Given that this was regular practice at busy locations such as Canterbury and Folkestone bus stations, it is a wonder that passengers were not caught by the hot water. However, drivers were generally alert to the dangers and kept an eye out for the public; not so for the engine, as the radiator was immediately filled with cold water, which could not have done it much good.

At this time, the smaller-capacity cars, the Dennis Falcons and remaining Lancets, by now all D/C, had reached the end of their lifespan. In 1967 delivery was taken of ten Bedford VAS1s with 29-seat Marshall bodies for operation on the remaining width-restricted routes of the time, the 55, 92, 93A and 109. They also appeared on the 31, 110A and 135, although these routes were not restricted; a combination of difficult roads or inter-working meant that at first the Bedford cars were also the default allocation for these services. At Ashford, the intention was for them to replace the remaining Lancets used on the 124. As recorded earlier, Lancet operation was mandatory due to the low railway bridge on the entry to Newtown. Following changes at Ashford in March 1969 now linking the less-busy sections of Newtown and Cobbs Wood as service 122, with intended operation by Bedford VAS1s, problems arose when it was realized that even they would exceed the bridge height. As a result two CFNs hung on even after the service reorganization although shortly after, adjustments to the roadway permitted the Bedfords to operate. Mandatory use of the Bedfords on some services reduced quite soon due to a combination of relaxed restrictions and economies, and, following a suggestion in 1969 from Geoff Dodson,

Service 8 was a challenging schedule for D/C drivers. Speed was of the essence, which often caused the cars to boil, especially the 691-engined versions. One of these, OFN 709F, on the stand at Margate harbour in September 1972, awaits another run to Canterbury. Note the traditional East Kent bus stop and the 'Restricted Fares' board in the windscreen.
AUTHOR

The executive coach modernization of some of the Bedford VASIs with the interim coach livery suited them well. Unfortunately they did not see much demand. KJG 112E is seen at Canterbury in June 1974, surrounded by NBC-liveried cars. AUTHOR

chief traffic clerk, four were converted to an eighteen-seat executive coach configuration in 1971–2.

The Transport Act 1968 introduced a 25 per cent grant towards the purchase of new vehicles suitable for D/C operation, which from September 1968 would dictate a change in East Kent's double-deck policy. Twenty Daimler Fleetlines, RFN 953–72G, with attractive 72-seat Park Royal bodies, arrived in 1969 and spent some time as crew-operated cars at Thanet, Canterbury, Folkestone and Ashford depots before they all gravitated to Thanet, a depot

that was more open to the concept of double-deck D/C operation. This was to remain their home for life, although some were eventually transferred or loaned to M&D. They were all converted to D/C operation in 1969.

Rear-engine single-deck saloons would now be taken into stock: twenty-five AEC Swift 691s in two batches, RJG 200–9G and VJG 185–99J, arrived between 1969 and 1971 with Marshall 51-seat bodies to standard BET design but with detail differences between the two. Subsequently, a further twelve cars, YJG 581–92K, this time with Alexander 51-seat bodies, were delivered towards the end of 1971. These were the last new cars to be delivered in East Kent's traditional saloon livery. Although one was allocated to Herne Bay at an early stage, all were eventually allocated

The arrival of the AEC Swifts accelerated the D/C conversion programme, and eventually the long service 10 succumbed, as shown by VJG 199J at Folkestone Bus Station in late 1972. AUTHOR

Ten of the 1969 Daimler Fleetlines were first allocated to Ashford, Folkestone and Canterbury depots, all operating as crewed cars. Folkestone's RFN 969G is approaching Hythe Red Lion Square on service 10 in October 1969, the conductor visible in the front near side. Operating such vehicles as crew cars was clearly untenable, certainly judging by the low level of patronage on this journey. AUTHOR

Another departure from East Kent's normal body suppliers was a batch of Alexander-bodied Swifts. East Kent's old livery suited these cars extremely well, enhanced by the AEC badges. Normally confined to Dover's town routes in their early days, YJG 591K has escaped onto the longer 15 route and was captured at Canterbury in June 1974. AUTHOR

One of the 40ft (12m) Plaxton coaches delivered in 1971 with East Kent livery ascends Madeira Walk, Ramsgate on express service M2 in July 1971. AUTHOR'S COLLECTION

to Dover, which would become their host depot for life. All of these saloons were delivered suitable for D/C operation, while the earlier 36ft (11m) Reliance saloons were all converted after delivery.

An unusual acquisition in 1971 was thirty Leyland Leopards with Marshall bodies, 265–89 AUF and 100–4 CUF from Southdown Motor Services, by now also part of the NBC. Problems with gaining agreement on introducing double-deck D/C operation at several depots had resulted in this transfer. Originally to 45-seat capacity when work-

ing for Southdown, they were converted to 49-seaters, although some first operated with the lower capacity and in Southdown livery. All operated from Folkestone, and East Kent repainted them in traditional saloon livery between 1971 and 1972, just before NBC corporate colours were introduced, so these were effectively the last vehicles in normal service to receive traditional East Kent livery. As an interim measure, six Willowbrook-bodied Leyland Panthers loaned from M&D were operated at Folkestone in 1971 pending completion of the delivery of the Southdown Leopards.

Completing the pre-NBC livery fleet intake was a set of coaches delivered in 1970–1 with bodies by Plaxton and to a higher specification than earlier service coaches. Two configurations were delivered: twenty on 36ft (11m) AEC Reliance 691 chassis with 49-seat bodies, VFN 35–40H and WJG 138–51J; with a further set of ten AEC Reliance 691s VJG 474–9J and WJG 470–3J on 40ft (12m) chassis with 53-seat bodies. As four of the first batch were destined for dedicated Skyways coach/air services, however, three were delivered as shells and another, 477, with second-hand aircraft seats to fifty-seat capacity. One of the shell bodies, 476, was fitted with a bar to 48-seat capacity but by now the Skyways enterprise had collapsed and they eventually all emerged as 53-seaters. From 1972, a new era of vehicle procurement, dictated by the NBC, was to be ushered in. East Kent's fleet was really never to be the same again.

Table 9 East Kent Vehicles in 1971 (including cars withdrawn that year)

Type	Chassis	Body	Registrations	Total	Date/Notes
Double-deck open-top	Guy Arab III	Park Royal 58-seat	FFN 375–82/4	9	1951 *FFN 380 59-seat*
	Guy Arab IV	Park Royal 58-seat	GFN 920/3/8	3	1953
Double-deck low-height	AEC Bridgemaster	Park Royal 72-seat	YJG 807–9	3	1962
Double-deck highbridge	Guy Arab IV	Park Royal 58-seat	GFN 910/5–7/9/ 21/4–7/9/31/2/4/5	15	1953
	Guy Arab IV	Park Royal 61-seat	MFN 883–8/90–2/5–902/4–7	21	1956–7
	AEC Regent V	Park Royal 72-seat	PFN 843–9/51–60/2/4/5/7–77/79–81	34	1959. *Full-front*
	AEC Regent V	Park Royal 72-seat	PFN 850/61/3/6/78/82	6	1959. *Full-front converted to D/C*
	AEC Regent V	Park Royal 72-seat	WFN 827–31/33–42 YJG 810-26 6783-804 FN AFN 763–82B MFN 938–52F	90	1961–4/7
	AEC Regent V	Park Royal 72-seat	GJG 733–62D	30	1966 *Converted to D/C*

Single-deck	Daimler Fleetline	Park Royal 72-seat	RFN 953–72G	20	1969. D/C
	Dennis Lancet LU2	Duple 33-, 35- or 41-seat	HJG 9/12/5/6/9/24/31/2	8	1954
	AEC Reliance 470	Beadle 41-seat	MJG 41–52	12	1957 *MJG 41/2 34-seat*
	Ford 570E	Harrington 41-seat	TJG 440	1	1960
	AEC Reliance 470	Park Royal 41-seat	VJG 500 WFN 501–18	19	1960–1 *Dual-purpose WFN 504 D/C*
	AEC Reliance 590	Park Royal 49-seat	519–38 FN 6539–48 FN	30	1962/3
	AEC Reliance 470	Duple 34-seat	AFN 488–99B	12	1964 *Touring coaches*
	AEC Reliance 590	Park Royal 47- or 49-seat	AFN 596–605B	10	1964 *Converted to D/C*
	AEC Reliance 590	Park Royal 49-seat	DJG 606–31C GJG 632–43D	38	1965/6 *DJG 606–11C converted to D/C*
	Bedford VAS1	Marshall 18-seat	KJG 108E	1	1967. *Converted to coach 1971*
	AEC Reliance 691	Willowbrook 49-seat	OJG 130–7F	8	1968
	AEC Reliance 691	Duple 40-seat	UFN 480–7H	8	1970 *Touring coaches*
	AEC Reliance 691	Plaxton 49-seat	VFN 35–40H WJG 138–51J	20	1970–1
	AEC Reliance 691	Plaxton 53-seat	VJG 474–9J WJG 470–3J	10	1970–1
Single-deck bus (all D/C)	AEC Reliance 470	Weymann 41-seat	KFN 210–21/3–49 LJG 305–26	61	1955/6 *Originally dual-purpose*
	AEC Reliance 470	Beadle 41-seat	MJG 285–300 NFN 327–33/5–7/9/41–4/6/8/9	34	1957 *Originally dual-purpose*
	AEC Reliance 470	Park Royal 35-, 39- or 41-seat	TFN 400–39	40	1960 *Originally dual-purpose. Some cars not formally D/C*
	AEC Reliance 590	Marshall 51-seat	DJG 355–8C	4	1965
	Bedford VAS1	Marshall 29-seat	KJG 104–7/9–13E	9	1967
	AEC Reliance 590	Marshall 51-seat	KJG 571–80E	10	1967
	AEC Reliance 691	Marshall 53-seat	OFN 708–32F	25	1968
	AEC Swift 691	Marshall 51-seat	RJG 200–9G VJG 185–99J	25	1969–71
	AEC Swift 691	Alexander 51-seat	YJG 581–92K	12	1971
	Leyland Leopard PSU3	Marshall 45- or 49-seat	265–89 AUF 100–4 CUF	30	1963 *Ex-Southdown in 1971*

Source: MDEK Bus Club

EFN 588, one of the two Lancet coaches retained for snow plough duties, is shown at Deal garage, its base, equipped with plough and tyre chains. The other plough, EFN 587, was based at Canterbury. MDEK CLUB

1960s LIVERIES

As recorded earlier, the TFN Reliances ushered in a new express-coach livery with a greater degree of cream than had formerly been the case, and this style was carried through, with variations, up until the Plaxton-bodied coaches were received, the last in traditional livery albeit with more cream. Conversely, the two batches of touring cars delivered in this period carried a livery more akin to the saloons, although the larger windows of the two types of Duple Commander body meant that the cream upper works were carried off very well. The UFN-H batch featured an italicized fleet name, reminiscent of the scroll style carried on the EFN Lancet coaches of 1950. During the decade the dual-purpose Beadle-bodied Reliances gradually received the normal saloon livery of red lower panels and cream upper panels in place of the express-coach livery.

Most of the Lancet 'Spaceships' retained for Dover docks work sported the Seaspeed livery, as shown by HJG 31 at the Eastern Docks in August 1970. Only one, HJG 28, carried the Sealink colours. AUTHOR

Leaving the fleet in the 1960s would be the last of the Leyland marque in operational service. The pre-war, re-bodied Titans would finish in 1963, the PD1s and solitary PD2 by 1966, along with the FFN/GFN coach rebuilds, while the PS1 coaches went much earlier, by 1962, due to their outdated half-cab design. The more modern Royal Tigers lasted until 1967–8. Thus, with the exception of the remaining TS8, JG 9938, now used as a mobile office, East Kent's link with Leyland Motors, lasting nigh-on forty years, was temporarily severed.

The 1960s would also see the beginning of the end of another builder, Dennis. The half-cab buses and coaches from the CFN and EFN batches had gone by 1964, with the exception of EFN 587/8, which had been converted for use as snow-ploughs at Deal and Canterbury, undertaking these duties from winter 1962–3 until 1968–9 under contract with the county council. The Falcons went by 1967, the D/C Lancets by 1969; while, despite the high profile of such operations, five of the underfloor-engine HJGs had a temporary reprieve, being used on work at Dover Eastern Docks for Sealink boats and Seaspeed hovercrafts, and carrying specific liveries for that purpose. The last of these 'Spaceships' went in 1971. Inroads had also now been made into the traditional Guy double-deckers, and 1968 marked the year of withdrawal of the last of the EFN batch, which were the last of the company's vehicles to feature the low-bridge layout. The highbridge Guys would soon follow – with the exception of those converted to open-top, their last years of operation would be in 1970–1.

The earlier view of HJG 31 in Seaspeed livery contrasts with this view of HJG 19 at Folkestone harbour in fleet livery in August 1970. This was one of the cars equipped with boat racks, later fitted to TFN Reliances, the last cars to carry them. Contrast the beading on HJG 19 with that of tours car HJG 6 pictured earlier. MIKE ANSELL

A number of contract liveries appeared during this period. The Butlin's livery of blue and yellow was applied to four coaches, JG 9942, CFN 108, EFN 573 and KFN 250, between 1957 and 1968. New for this decade was the application of a special livery for Skyways operations. A scheme of blue, grey and white with red relief was applied to six of the GJG-D coaches from 1969; later four of the 40ft (12m) VJG-J coaches appeared in a similar livery but Skyways then collapsed, and by 1971 the cars had had the blue band repainted maroon and this ushered in a new, short-lived coach livery for East Kent before NBC corporate white took over. Two of the remaining GJG-D saloons had a modified livery applied, firstly as Skyways International and later with Dan-Air Skyways branding. The expansion of operations at Dover's Eastern Docks in 1969 saw two distinct liveries applied from 1970: that for Sealink was dark blue and white, while that for Seaspeed hovercraft operations was a lighter shade of blue.

D/C PROGRESSION

The 1960s was marked by important changes stimulated by the success, and necessity of progressing, D/C operation in order to cut costs; a programme that was accelerated in the latter part of the decade and carried through to virtual completion in the 1970s. After the first two batches of dual-purpose Reliances and the Lancet conversions were put into use on D/C operations, the NFN Reliances were next to be converted, most in 1963, though a small number were treated earlier, between 1958 and 1962. The 1960 delivery of 30ft (9m) AEC Reliances, TFN 400–39, succumbed at an early stage of their life, from 1963, although the programme was not completed until 1973–4. Their successors from 1960–1, VJG 500 and WFN 501–18, remained on coach work much longer, probably due to their suitability for motorway operation. With the exception of one early D/C conversion in 1969, WFN 504, these cars were only converted between 1972 and 1974. Strangely, the start of the programme on the TFNs preceded the MJG saloons, which hung on until 1966 but were then converted within two years.

The policy of using hand-me-downs downgraded from coach duties to expand D/C operation was to change in the mid-sixties. New 36ft (11m)-long single-deck buses were being taken into stock from 1965, and while these were crew-operated at first, the intention was to use them as D/C cars to achieve further economies by converting those routes with larger traffic volumes but not enough to justify continued crew operation. The company now encountered significant trade union resistance, due in part

to its reluctance to pay enhanced supplements for operating these larger cars, and in part to genuine concerns from staff about the ability of one driver to deal with in excess of fifty passengers and keep to time. An interim compromise was reached with the unions agreeing to operate these new cars as D/C but with a reduced capacity of 45, the earlier legally permitted limit, in which form a number entered service on routes such as the 17 from Canterbury to Folkestone via the Elham Valley and the 88 from Dover to Elvington. However, only a small proportion of the total number of 36ft (11m) saloons were so modified, as agreement was eventually reached with the unions in 1968 to operate them with their original capacity of fifty-one or fifty-three seats.

TFN 422 was the last of the 1960 dual-purpose Reliances to be converted to D/C, in 1974, the remainder having been completed in 1973; many, by now, with luggage pens and down-seated. As a result, it remained much longer on coach work, as seen in July 1969 at Folkestone, bound for London on the L3. AUTHOR

The first 36ft (11m) 'Long Dog' saloons were initially employed as crewed cars, like DJG 357C, seen here passing through Canterbury's Westgate Towers with the conductor just visible at the front near side. The first two batches, as well as the Bedford VAS1s, had red domes, which were later painted cream. MDEK CLUB

KJG 580E retained her red dome for a long period, as shown by this June 1969 view while loading at Canterbury bus station on the 16 to Folkestone. Originally fitted completely with fixed windows, she already has opening panes added, as the forced air ventilation system was inadequate. AUTHOR

Such protracted negotiations were typical at the time, even though regulations had been changed from 1966 to permit D/C operation of both large-capacity single-decks and double-deckers.

This agreement with staff ushered in further conversions so that, by the end of the 1960s, the greater number of the company's routes were D/C operated, the remaining crew operations retreating to the busier town services and a small number of trunk routes that required crew operations owing to route constraints or loadings. Examples of the remaining crew-operated trunk routes included service 1, which up until May 1969 had to negotiate a tricky reverse at Chilham, Woolpack; the busy 4/6 complex of services between Canterbury, Whitstable and Herne Bay; the also busy 8 between Canterbury and Margate, which would continue to alternate between periods of D/C and crew operation until nearly the end; the 10 between Folkestone and Maidstone, largely due to the inability to maintain a regular interval service within the increased running times necessary; the 13/14 between Deal and Canterbury; and the 105/A route between Folkestone and Lydd/Littlestone, the last of which, although converted to D/C in September 1968, would still see a good number of crew workings on the busier journeys until the cessation of permanent crew operation at Folkestone depot in 1971.

The first major depot to go completely D/C would be Rye, when summer-only crew operation of the 114 service ceased at the end of the summer timetable of 1967. There was now a policy to initiate gradual conversion of town services to D/C, firstly by converting services on Sundays only. At Ashford, the 122/124 services were already D/C but the major service changes there on 2 March 1969 saw all Sunday town services now converted to D/C. The *Omnibus* also records that town services 29/39 at Canterbury went over to all-week D/C operation on 7 September 1969, followed by Herne Bay's 43 and Dover's 86, 94/A and 96 on 4 January 1970. That date also saw Sunday D/C operation expanded, with the town services at both Dover and Folkestone being converted, while trunk routes 13 and 14 also went over on Sundays from the same time. Folkestone's Sunday services were now nearly completely D/C; the exceptions were service 10 and 106, due to the need for assisted reversing at Hothfield and Horn Street respectively. In fact the 106 was rostered for D/C operation on Sundays at this time having been part of the conversions carried out on 4 January, but contention over reversing and the fact that conductors were still needed for the 10 meant that they could be rostered with the D/C driver on the 106 at little extra cost.

One of the final set of conversions of service coaches to D/C in this era concerned sixteen of the 1964–5 36ft (11m) Park Royal coaches, AFN 596–605B and DJG 606–11C, between 1968 and 1971. The first conversions were intended to boost capacity on the 62 route, which, although only running two journeys each way, often enjoyed heavy loadings beyond the capacity of a 41-seater. This also mandated that the service could no longer run via the Strand Gate at Winchelsea and it was diverted via Ferry Hill. The single swing-door operation on these cars was a little risky as its inward swing could catch out unwary passengers, but for drivers these cars were excellent for making up lost time.

Crewed workings survived on the 105/A group for a number of years due to heavy peak loadings. The 1705 departures in summer from Folkestone featured a crewed journey to Lydd, worked here by GJG 755D in August 1969 and a D/C car to Littlestone, the rear of which is to the right of the picture. AUTHOR

Driving one, from recall DJG 608C, the author recovered a 35-minute late departure from Dover on an evening journey on service 87 to make an on-time arrival at Ramsgate, averaging well over 40mph (65km/h) point to point – quite remarkable considering the number of stops en route. Three others, DJG 618–20C, were later converted to D/C in 1973–4 but these were intended for specific use on Seaspeed services at Dover and underwent seating changes with additional luggage space being incorporated at the same time as did many of the earlier conversions.

From 1969, all buses received were capable of D/C operation although the Daimler Fleetlines were formally converted after delivery. These ushered in the first double-deck D/C operation, which commenced in June 1969 at Thanet on services 54/A and 71. It was also intended to convert the 66,

The first double-deck D/C conversions were two town services in Margate and Ramsgate respectively. RFN 958G is seen on a hoverport working of Ramsgate's 71 in May 1972. Adjacent is an early competitor, Eastonways, running a service to the station. AUTHOR

and an image of a Fleetline with the caption, 'new buses for service 66', appeared adjacent to the 66 timetable. However, after tests the Fleetlines were deemed too slow and they were confined to town services. The double-deck programme expanded during the winter timetable, seeing the conversion of the 51 on 21 September and culminating

One of the D/C conversions of 36ft (11m) coaches, first intended for the 62, rounds Margate clock tower on an inbound working of that service in July 1971. The Setright machine can just be discerned through the windscreen. AUTHOR

in the major change of 4 January 1970, when the 63/64 routes were converted, these now inter-working with the 51. The change also allowed works services 57, 59 and 72 to become double-deck D/C. With the exception of the conversion of some Rye routes in 1971, this would then represent the end of the introduction of double-deck D/C operations on all-day service until the mid-1970s. As a result the Fleetlines were permanently allocated to Thanet and spent most of their lives in the area.

Once agreement was concluded regarding the uplift paid for D/C work – finally agreed at 17.5 per cent for normal single-deck D/C operations and 22.5 per cent for double-deck (and, later, standee single-deck Leyland Nationals on town work) above the normal crew driver rate – the success of double-deck D/C with the Fleetlines caused the company to consider how to make use of their large fleet of AEC Regents, which, with the acceleration of D/C conversion could become redundant fairly quickly. PFN 863, one of the first batch, was thus converted to experimental D/C operation in late 1970, with periscope to view the upper deck, cab modifications and a motorized ticket drive to

PFN 866, one of the first batch of Regent D/C conversions, is seen at the remote Flete Farm near Manston on a special school working of service 65 in March 1974. AUTHOR

improve speed of issue of the Setright machines. Tested at Canterbury, Folkestone and Ashford depots with little success, it still did not prevent the company converting a total of six PFNs by early 1971. Faced with strong resistance across many depots, only Rye would accept their operation on all-day service, and services 114/116 went over to be operated by D/C PFNs in the summers of 1971 and 1972, with workings on service 115 as well.

Storm clouds are gathering as GJG 754D performs one of the minimal number of Folkestone D/C Regent workings at Hythe Palmarsh Estate while on a 105 short-working in May 1972. The driver is not using the electric ticket machine drive, preferring to issue tickets manually. The angle of mounting meant it was not easy to discern fare values on the machine – working a Regent D/C, the author once issued a number of '9p' tickets only to find the dial was set at 19p! There was no recompense.
AUTHOR

Despite this setback the company then converted all thirty of the 1966 batch of Regents, GJG 733–62D, and eleven of the final, 1967 batch, MFN 938–52F, to D/C operation in 1971–3. As these were of half-cab design the modifications to the cab were more substantial. In the event, use of these cars was limited mainly to Thanet depot, on schools services and some peak service workings, with Folkestone, Dover and Deal being reluctant users of them and then in very limited form. Canterbury refused to operate them as D/C cars to the very end. By April 1978 all remaining Regents, including the D/C conversions, were classified as crew-operated. However, this would not prohibit their working on contract services as these did not involve fare collection. A number of depots, such as Ashford, Dover and Deal, would make greater use of D/C Regents on such contracts; Thanet tended to use them on miners' contracts in the 1970s although that depot also had a more relaxed attitude to their use on peak-hour stage services, and the colliery shift changes worked well with such use.

Delivery of the AEC Swifts and ex-Southdown Leopards between 1969 and 1971 allowed further conversions, and the next two depots to be converted to complete D/C operation were Folkestone and Dover in September 1971, followed by Deal in March 1972. However, vehicle shortages at Folkestone in 1972 saw a number of crew workings reinstated in summer 1972 on the 103 and 104/106/108 group, using former conductors called back on a temporary basis. Folkestone's open-top 121 ran in the summer of 1973, and that was to be last instance of crew operation there. The last depots with crew operation – Ashford, Canterbury, Herne Bay and Thanet – would retain Regents well into the NBC era, and the conclusion is dealt with in that section.

PART III

THE NATIONALIZED YEARS

CHAPTER NINE

THE 1970s – NBC TAKES CONTROL

From the 1970s the pace and extent of change became greater, as the NBC attempted to control costs; in some cases revisions to town services made them unrecognizable from what passed before. Whether the multiplicity of changes introduced would have occurred under BET management is a matter for conjecture. Certainly, East Kent never stood still, but it may be argued that the frequency and scale of change in the 1970s, with repeated renumberings, was not necessarily in the best interests of the company or its passengers.

TOWN SERVICE RESTRUCTURING AND RENUMBERING

The 1970s were characterized by the NBC's corporate agenda dictating the detail of operations and influencing local policy on stage carriage services. One major change was the gradual restructuring of town services, affecting routes and their numbering, in order to differentiate between towns by introducing a separate number series. The first dealt with were those at Ashford, which were renumbered between 501 and 510 from 25 July 1971; this featured most routes starting and terminating in the town centre, thus removing cross-town facilities. This resulted in the routes to Stanhope and Arlington, now 501/502, and to Willesborough, now 505/506, becoming the last regular crew-operated services at Ashford. On 26 September it was Dover's turn, this time going totally D/C, with their services

renumbered 301–10 and introducing a complex system that resulted in several cross-town services originating from or running to different destinations on inward and outward journeys. The changes resulted in many problems, and further changes were introduced on 14 November to ease matters. Deal town services followed on 26 March 1972, when they were renumbered 381–5, introducing loop terminal and routing arrangements to facilitate D/C operation. At the same time the Deal–Canterbury services, 13/14, were rationalized from the earlier 40-minute frequency on weekdays to an hourly service on each route.

The Alexander-bodied Swifts were always part of the Dover scene. YJG 590K departs the High Street on the former Bridgemaster route to St. Radigund's, now renumbered 306. Note the bus stop, which is one of the more modern plastic versions but to traditional design, while the shelter is to a design common across the company's network. AUTHOR

The earlier Leyland Leopards acquired from Southdown in 1971 had a more curved rear dome than their later cousins from the CUF-registered batch. One of the former, 267 AUF waits at Folkestone bus station in August 1975 on service 101 to the harbour, by this time reduced to four journeys from the bus station. It still retains the former East Kent livery. AUTHOR

From 26 March 1972, a new one-way system at Folkestone saw the long-established 103A number disappear and all 103 journeys re-routed via Foord Road, its former route via the closed East station withdrawn and services running a clockwise loop via Creteway Down, Hill Road and Joyes Road. Other changes saw the 102 extended from Creteway Down to Hill Road, also returning via Joyes Road, and its sister service, the 108, no longer serving the Marine Pavilion, being replaced by a shuttle from Central Station to the new ferry terminal, numbered 101. Presumably Folkestone's 100-series numbers were deemed to be in order as no major renumbering took place. Another one-way system affecting services was that at Canterbury, introduced on 5 March 1972, which saw all eastbound services from the Westgate running via St. Peter's Place and the Rheims Way, with only westbound services using the High Street. This was the thin end of the wedge and eventually all bus services would be withdrawn from the High Street when it was pedestrianized.

EXPRESS AND TOURS SERVICES – 'NATIONAL' TAKES OVER

The final express service changes under East Kent auspices saw some L3 journeys serving Dover's Eastern Docks from May 1970 and taking the number L4; the L3 would serve the Marine station. The same summer saw special summer Saturday-only services introduced from London to the Maddicson's holiday camps at St. Margaret's Bay and Littlestone, numbered L17 and L18 respectively. The last full year that the company's Westcliff Coach Station at

Ramsgate would be used was 1970, and the council park at Cannon Road was used for a period thereafter. The Westcliff site originally housed the express service chart room before it moved to new accommodation at Westwood and which lasted in a much-expanded form under National Express management. One oddity was the cramped coach station at London New Cross, latterly used on outbound journeys only; it was really unsuitable for the longer 36ft (11m) coaches and was closed in the early 1970s.

A variation of the L4 introduced in May 1971 was the M4 running to and from Dover non-stop via the M2 motorway and later titled 'The Gateway Express' becoming summer-only from 1972. May 1971 saw new joint-worked service X11 from Manchester to Folkestone supplementing the X10 to Thanet but this date also saw the demise of the L6 and X66. In May 1972 short-workings of X32 from Basildon to Folkestone were numbered X22 whilst in May 1973 the X66 number was re-used for a new venture from Deal to Wood Green. East Kent's management of express services was soon to end, however – the National white livery had already started to appear and in September 1973 the winter express services were numbered into a national scheme as follows: M2 – 001; L1 – 002; L4 – 004; L5 – 005; L7 – 007; X26 – 026.

From May 1974 express service schedules were no longer published in the timetable, details being confined to a list of all express services in the area as they were now shown in separate leaflets published under the National Express brand. The remaining summer-only London services were renumbered as follows: L2 – 003; M4 – 006; L8 – 008; L17 – 011; L18 – 012.

The former jointly operated summer services from the Midlands and the North were also renumbered into the national scheme. Hereafter East Kent only acted as a partner

The earlier Reliance coaches were all re-bodied with more modern Plaxton bodies between 1972 and 1974. Car 528 FN, by this time in National white, is on the Gateway Express in April 1980, which has been renumbered to 007. AUTHOR

and later as subcontractor to National Express, and direct company management of express services ended. However, following the relaxation of express coach regulations in 1980, East Kent operated some experimental London commuter coach services; these included the 996 from Cheriton and the 997 from Herne Bay, both commencing 3 November 1980. The 996 finished by 4 January 1981 but the 997 survived until September 1990 with a localized variant, 998, running from 3 April 1983. This later ran via Canterbury, from 26 May 1985, and was renumbered E7 on 27 October that year before being withdrawn on 23 April 1986.

Express service schedules reappeared in the local area timetables from 1979 and in the loose-leaf timetables in 1981 – after that East Kent no longer published National Express service timetables. The company's coaches still operate London services for National Express. At the time of writing the main services were: 007 (Canterbury/Deal/Dover), 021 (Folkestone/Dover/Deal) and 022 (Canterbury/Margate/Ramsgate). East Kent involvement in the former South Coast Express service 026 ceased in 1983, shortly before its demise although sister service 025 (via Canterbury) lasted until 1991.

The long-distance tours also came under National Holidays management in the early 1970s, again with East Kent providing suitably branded coaches. This involvement diminished until it finished in the early 1990s. Local tours were still managed and operated by East Kent, however, generally on a day-tour basis, and these still included continental excursions to France, Belgium and Holland. Later they would be branded 'Daybreak Tours' and this continued with the newly privatized company from 1987.

EAST KENT AND M&D COOPERATION

One major impact of nationalization was the closer interlinking of East Kent and M&D's operations. On the administrative and engineering side the two companies rationalized functions, and by 1974 both traffic departments were integrated at Canterbury, with secretarial and financial functions moving to Maidstone. The long-established base at Station Road West was first leased, then eventually sold and between March and July 1979 the formal company address changed to the new premises in North Lane. During this period the close cooperation led to the possibility of the two organizations merging and being renamed 'Northdown'; fortunately this did not happen and as time passed, the two companies moved apart again. Interestingly, in 1977 the name Northdown was briefly

used to describe the Wanderbus ticket available from both companies.

On the management side, general manager Jim Gilbert, who oversaw the transition from BET to NBC, left in 1972 and the retitled post of manager/secretary was taken by Laurie Noble, former company secretary and a long-serving East Kent manager. On the engineering side, Mr Loxton, another long-serving East Kent man, retired and was succeeded by Ken Worrall. Len Higgins would assume overall control of both M&D and East Kent until 1977, when he moved on and was succeeded by Bill Jelpke.

Another key change was the transfer of operations at Rye to M&D following on from the earlier transfer of Hastings in 1969. The garage premises are recorded as transferring on 25 March 1973 but the M&D leaflet concerning the transfer of revised bus services in Rye is dated 6 May. Due to service licensing issues, for a time the services were badged as 'jointly operated with East Kent Road Car Co. Ltd', vehicles displaying 'on hire' labels. Some services were still shown in East Kent's timetable but by the time of their last complete network timetable, dated 26 May 1974, only the 62, 112 and 116 were shown, as they ran into the local area. In a reprint issued in August 1974, the 62, since May 1973 running only from Hastings to Dover, and 116, extended to Lydd also in 1973, had been numbered into the NBC's M&D Hastings area scheme as 426 and 416 respectively. From 15 June 1975 the Rye–Ashford 112 was renumbered 412 and operated solely by M&D, while East Kent would retain 112 for Ashford–Ham Street short-workings, shown with service 119 (Ashford–Lade).

In compensation for the Rye changes, M&D's local operations at Ashford changed hands on 6 May 1973, their workings on the 10 and services such as the 170 to Lenham

The last car to operate in service in East Kent livery was TFN 429 on the 518 in December 1976. Seen here in August of that year at the former M&D lower garage at Ashford, it displays blinds for the 170 to Lenham Heath, also transferred from M&D. TFN 429 has managed to retain its original beading – compare with the earlier view of TFN 417. AUTHOR

The first Swifts arriving in 1969 had a smaller cab window compared to the later batch, both bodied by Marshall. RJG 206G demonstrates the feature while standing at Whitstable, Harbour Street on a short-working of the former 38 in August 1975, by now renumbered into the M&D scheme as 638. AUTHOR

Heath moving to East Kent, while the 11 between Ashford and Faversham was badged as jointly operated. East Kent's Faversham interests moved to M&D on 30 December 1973, taking with it the former 31 service to Chilham, which later became the 661, and seeing joint operation on the Herne Bay/Whitstable–Faversham 37/A and 38/A (themselves renumbered 637/639 and 638/640 from 26 May 1974).

The closer cooperation resulting from both companies being under the NBC umbrella led to many inter-company vehicle transfers, the two fleets effectively being treated as one during this period. In 1971 six Leyland Panthers were loaned to Folkestone depot as described earlier, while the depot transfers resulted in a number of vehicle exchanges; some temporary, others – such as the four ex-M&D Leyland Atlantean double-deckers – becoming permanent. Daimler Fleetline single-decks unwanted by M&D were trialled on East Kent services before moving to Dover docks work. Moving the other way, a number of East Kent Regents went to M&D from 1972 onwards, mainly on a temporary basis, some as service cars but later many as driver-trainers. Eight were permanently acquired by M&D but a good number of East Kent's Regents spent shorter or longer periods with M&D up until 1983. In addition, a number of single-deck cars were loaned or acquired by M&D, as were several East Kent double-deck Fleetlines in the late 70s, with three eventually transferred permanently. On a historical note, East Kent was notable in retaining two venerable vehicles in the 1970s. One, JG 9938, was a Leyland TS8, first kept as a mobile office, while the other was Guy Arab IV MFN 888, last used as a towing vehicle. Both were renovated and kept in traditional livery but, unfortunately, they were later dispensed with; luckily both are still actively preserved.

FARES

For fares, NBC integration saw the Wanderbus ticket becoming available on both East Kent and M&D from 1972, priced at 50p, extending to Southdown in mid-1974 (now 60p). In 1977 the local ticket was then termed Northdown Wanderbus, priced at 99p with a new national Wanderbus ticket at £2 for a day; this was quickly and logically changed to a southern England availability while the local ticket was renamed Busranger in 1978. The national availability returned in mid-1978 but did not extend to the far north. In the privatization era the daily Busranger became the Explorer ticket and the Busranger was confined to a weekly ticket.

The 1970s saw numerous fares rises due to an automatic price-index trigger in force; 1976 may hold the record, with fare table books issued in March, August and November, all with increases. This year also saw the introduction of Freedom Tickets, valid on all buses within a specified area, which were far more flexible than the route-oriented season ticket. Folkestone and Hythe was the first area to have these, and the scheme extended to most major towns with the notable exception of Canterbury and Herne Bay, although a flat fare scheme was experimented with in Herne Bay from July 1981. Other offers, such as zonal fares on evenings and Sundays, were also trialled, for example at Canterbury and Dover, and would appear much later at Thanet to address competition under the privatized regime. Off-peak returns were trialled on service 3 in October 1977 and shopper returns, also off-peak, were introduced in January 1979. Other initiatives to reduce travel costs towards the end of the NBC era would see tickets such as Funfare for under-16s and Pricetrimmer for senior citizens, offering reduced-rate travel at off-peak times. Note that this was before the universal availability of senior citizens' passes.

Fare table booklets would be publicly available through the early part of the NBC era, the last-known example being the issue of 25 May 1980, priced at 50p. Thereafter loose-leaf fare tables linked by metal rings would be issued to staff up until the privatized era, together with smaller ring-bound ticket manuals, by which time the advent of electronic Wayfarer ticket machines would render paper-based fare tables redundant.

THE NEW NBC FLEET AND LIVERY – AND FLEET NUMBERING

In late 1972 NBC policy made a major impact on the fleet. Coaches began to be repainted into the anonymous white

THE 1970s – NBC TAKES CONTROL ■ 125

livery with National branding and the company's name, firstly in the form of small capitals underlined in red, later changed to a slightly larger form without underlining. Later still, an improved livery with National Express or National Holidays branding replaced National, but as responsibility for express services and the wider holiday programme had passed from East Kent they now acted increasingly as a subcontractor, their involvement gradually reducing to the handful of white coaches operated on behalf of National Express today. The National Holidays livery disappeared from the by-now privatized company coaches in 1990 although one coach featured Shearings coach livery that year.

One interim development applied between 1971–3 was a new coach livery, predominantly grey and maroon with

The Beadle-bodied touring coaches survived to receive the transitional coach livery of the early 1970s. MJG 52 shows the version with a white relief band at Canterbury in June 1974; other members of the batch had this band repainted red. AUTHOR

Thanet's Leyland Nationals were first employed on Margate's services 54/154 and 151, replacing Fleetlines. EFN 175L is captured at Palm Bay on a short-working of the 151 in summer 1973. The author was the driver, pictured to the right. MIKE ANSELL

white relief, an adaptation of the redundant Skyways livery. This form of livery, with variations, appeared on the former Skyways-liveried vehicles, the early Plaxton re-bodies, the Bedford VAS1 executive coaches and the MJG former touring cars. Some coaches received a local livery using NBC colours based on the earlier style or a dual-purpose application. Towards the end of the NBC tenure a new East Kent coach livery began to appear on cars not normally used on National operations; this had a broad, poppy-red band and red stripes above the front wheelarches.

East Kent's buses were now repainted into the corporate poppy-red and white with the fleet name in white capital letters with the skeletal 'double-N' symbol, later replaced by a red and blue symbol on a white square from the late 1970s. Many contract liveries were used at this time, particularly for Seaspeed and Sealink operations at Dover, which featured different shades of blue either predominantly or later as relief. Other contract operations, for example for Hoverlloyd or P&O ferries, were also in evidence on the cars dedicated to those operations. In 1973 an AEC Regent, GJG 751D, received an all-over advert livery for Rediffusion, the first such company vehicle to be treated and the precursor of many other advert designs, continuing to the present day.

The vehicle intake was now dictated by corporate policy. The first evidence of this was the ubiquitous Leyland National, which, for new orders, arrived between 1972 and 1977. Seventy-five of the 49-seat, 11m (36ft) version would be taken, registered EFN 159–84L, NFN 61–80M, JJG 883–902P and MFN 113–21R, with another nine of the dual-purpose 48-seat version, NFN 81–9R, sporting the NBC dual-purpose livery of poppy-red lower panels and white uppers. Thirty-five of the shorter 41-seat 10m (33ft) version, registered SJG 335–41N, GFN 541–53N, JJG 903–8P and PJJ 342–50S, were also taken into stock. All of these cars, like most larger single-deckers from this time, were built with standee allowances, which in many cases reduced the need for peak-hour duplication. By the start of the 1980s service reductions enabled the company to dispose of some surplus Nationals, while others, especially the shorter version, were stored for extended periods before returning to service. Six ex-M&D Nationals in use by East Kent when the companies separated in 1983, were formally transferred across, and in 1984 ten were acquired from London Country, of which six were converted to dual-doorway for Dover docks work to replace older stock, including Swifts RJG 201/3/7G, which had been converted to dual-doorway in 1979 for such work.

In the 1970s the other single-decks taken into stock were all oddities. In 1975 four Bristol LHSs, GFN 559–62N,

The shorter 10m (33ft) version of the National is represented here by JJG 905P from 1975, pictured at the sylvan terminus of Deal's 385 – just beyond Kingsdown Rising Sun – in August 1980. The overall red livery has now been relieved by the addition of a white band. AUTHOR

RJG 201G, one of the three AEC Swifts converted to dual-doorway for docks work, is pictured at Dover Eastern Docks in September 1981, sporting the current version of Sealink livery. AUTHOR

with ECW 35-seat special bodies to 7ft 6in (2.3m) width and 9ft 8in (2.9m) height were acquired for the remaining restricted routes – the 507 at Ashford and the 92 from Dover to Capel. In 1976–7 eleven Ford R1014s with Plaxton 43-seat bodies were delivered in two batches, registered KFN 328–34P and NFN 324–7R. Not popular vehicles, they were last used in 1981 and withdrawn by 1982. One special vehicle was a 23-seat Ford A series/Wadham-Stringer minibus, YKT 429V of 1979, intended for the new William Harvey Hospital's latterly unsuccessful rural services. The bus did not enter service until 1980 due to damage and was temporarily replaced by ex-Trent LHSs. It went on to be used on other rural services.

The first new double-deckers for seven years arrived in 1976 as resistance to the extension of double-deck D/C operation had finally been overcome. They were fifteen

Leyland Atlanteans, JJG 1–15P, with ECW 74-seat bodies. From then on, in NBC days, subsequent new double-decks were on Bristol VR chassis. The first six arriving in 1976 were highbridge examples, MFN 41–6R, with conventional ECW 74-seat bodies, but the next were twenty-eight angular Willowbrook-bodied 74-seat examples arriving in 1977/8 and registered PJJ 16–24S/RVB 973–8S and TFN 979–91T. The remaining thirty-six VRs had the normal low-height (13ft 8in) ECW bodies and arrived in 1980–1, registered XJJ 650–70V, BJG 671–5V, CJJ 676–9W and SKL 680–5X. At this time a number of Nationals, VRs and one Atlantean were equipped with fully automatic transmissions; all new VRs from XJJ 666V had this, starting an eventual transition to this form of gearing for all buses with the exception of the earlier minibuses.

The little Bristol LHS6Ls were primarily intended for restricted routes, such as Ashford's 507 to South Willesborough via the low bridge near Newtown. However, they often strayed onto other lower-density routes, such as the 511 to Watercress Farm estate, seen here at Ashford High Street in September 1978. AUTHOR

NFN 326R, one of the second tranche of Ford R1014s from 1977 heads along Deal's seafront in April 1979 inbound from Betteshanger on the 399, hotly pursued by one of the dual-purpose Leopards from 1978. AUTHOR

The Leyland Atlanteans arriving in 1976 would operate across the company's area, unlike their double-deck D/C predecessors. JJG 8P is seen at Tenterden in December 1981, by which time East Kent operation had extended to Hastings. AUTHOR

The service coaches with Duple Dominant bodies from 1973–5 could be distinguished from the tours cars by the destination display with a three-track number blind. The all-white livery did not do the coaches any favours, especially in winter weather conditions, as shown by HFN 32L bound for London on the 002 at Canterbury in December 1980. AUTHOR

Following the AEC/Plaxtons delivered in 1971, subsequent coaches would adhere more to the NBC standard. AECs were still favoured at first though: thirty-two Reliance 760s but with Duple Dominant bodies arrived in 1973–5; fifteen with 51-seat bodies, registered HFN 25–34L and PFN 790–4M; and five 12m (40ft) examples with 55-seat bodies, GFN 554–8N. The remaining twelve were to 42-seat touring specification, registered HFN 53–60L and PFN 785–8M. Later, Leyland Leopards, still with Duple bodies, would take over; the first five, PJG 794–8S, delivered in 1977–8, would have 47-seat coach bodies, but the following ten, PVB 799–808S would be to 49-seat dual-purpose specification and equipped for D/C operation. One reason for D/C-equipped coaches was that a bus grant was available for cars spending 50 per cent of their annual mileage on stage work, which saw them migrating to bus work during the winter. In 1979–80 further Leyland Leopard/Duples would arrive – three, VJG 809–11T, with 49-seat bodies, and four, XJG 812–5V, with 53-seat bodies. Eleven more dual-purpose coaches suitable for D/C operation came in 1982–3; UKE 827–31X and BKR 832–7Y were Leopards with ECW 49-seat B51 bodies first working on coach duties but later also migrating to bus work. The main coach fleet intake now saw more change, with five Leyland Tigers, FKK 838–42Y, with Plaxton Paramount 53-seat bodies, delivered in 1983, followed by a most unusual set of acquisitions. East Kent had been chosen to evaluate the new MCW Metroliner coach and took two batches with MCW 51-seat bodies in 1983–4. There were design differences between the two batches, totalling eleven vehicles, which were registered FKK 843–7Y, A848–9 OKK and B850–3 TKL. These would be the last new coaches delivered under NBC auspices.

After a spell of deliveries of dual-purpose Leopard coaches, 1983 saw five Leyland Tigers with Plaxton bodies arriving. Number 8842 (FKK 842Y) is seen on the fuel line at Westwood garage in December 1987 with an updated National Express livery. AUTHOR

The first Metroliners had a squarer body than the following examples. Car 8845 (FKK 845Y) exits Victoria coach station in April 1983 displaying the latest National Holidays livery, which was far more attractive than the plain scheme in place beforehand. AUTHOR

Table 10 East Kent Vehicles at June 1982

Type	Chassis	Body	Fleet Nos.	Total	Date/Notes
Double-deck open-top	Leyland Atlantean PDR1	Metro-Cammell 77-seat	0572	1	1961 *Ex-M&D 1974*
	Leyland Atlantean PDR1	Weymann 77-seat	0620	1	1963 *Ex-M&D 1982*
	Bristol VRT	Willowbrook 74-seat	0977	1	1978
Double-deck low-height	Bristol VRT	ECW 74-seat	7650–85	36	1980–1
Double-deck highbridge	Leyland Atlantean AN68	ECW 74-seat	7001–15	15	1976
	Bristol VRT	Willowbrook 74-seat	7016–24; 7973–6/8–91	27	1977–8
	Bristol VRT	ECW 74-seat	7041–46	6	1976
	Daimler Fleetline CRG6LX-33	Northern Counties 65- or 74-seat	7203–7/10–12	8	1969–70 *Ex-Southdown 1981 7210/2 dual-door – non-D/C; others single door D/C*
	Daimler Fleetline CRL6-33	Northern Counties 61-/65- or 74-seat	7313–6/8/9/20/2–6	12	1969–70 *Ex-Southdown 1981 7318–23 single-door D/C; others dual-door non-D/C*
	Leyland Atlantean PDR1	Metro-Cammell 77-seat	7571/5/85	3	1961 *Ex-M&D 1974*
	AEC Regent V	Park Royal 72-seat	7735/41–3/54/7/8; 7939–45/8–51	18	1966–7 *Non-D/C*
	Daimler Fleetline CRG6LX	Park Royal 72-seat	7953–72	20	1969
Single-deck coach	AEC Reliance 760	Duple 51-seat	8025–34; 8614/5; 8790/2/3	15	1973–4 *8026/9/30/4 D/C 8614/5 ex-National Travel (SE) 1976*
	AEC Reliance 691	Plaxton 49-seat	8035–40/138–47/50	17	1970–1
	AEC Reliance 760	Duple 44-seat	8053–60; 8785–8	12	1973–4 *Touring coaches*
	Leyland Leopard PSU3R	Plaxton 49-seat	8321	1	1971 *D/C Ex-Southdown 1976*
	Leyland Leopard PSU5C	Duple 57-seat	8424–6	3	1980 *Ex-Fox, Hayes 1982*
	AEC Reliance 691	Plaxton 53-seat	8470–9	10	1970–1
	AEC Reliance 691	Duple 40 or 46-seat	8480/4/5	3	1970 *Touring coaches*
	AEC Reliance 590	Plaxton 49-seat	8521/40/1	3	1962–3 *Bodies 1972/4*
	AEC Reliance 590	Plaxton 32-seat	8532	1	1962, *body 1972 Freedom coach with wheelchair lift*
	AEC Reliance 760	Duple 55-seat	8554–8	5	1975

	Leyland Leopard PSU3E	Duple 47-seat	8794–8	5	1977–8
	Leyland Leopard PSU3E	Duple 49-seat	8799–808	10	1978
					Dual-purpose – D/C
	Leyland Leopard PSU3E	Duple 49-seat	8809–11	3	1979
	Leyland Leopard PSU5C	Duple 53-seat	8812–5	4	1980
	Leyland Leopard PSU3G	ECW 49-seat	8827–31	5	1982
					Dual-purpose – D/C
Single-deck bus	Leyland-National 11351A	L-National 48-seat	1081–9	9	1977
					Dual-purpose
	Leyland-National 11351A	L-National 49-seat	1113–21; 1883–902	29	1976
	Leyland-National 1151	L-National 49-seat	1159–84	26	1972–3
	AEC Swift 691	Marshall 44-seat	1201/3/7	3	1969
					Converted to dual-door, non-D/C
	Ford R1014	Plaxton 43-seat	1324–7	4	1977
					All in store
	Leyland National 10351/A	L-National 41-seat	1339–50; 1903–8	18	1974/5/7
	Ford AO609	Wadham-Stringer 23-seat	1429	1	1979
	Bristol LHS6L	ECW 35-seat	1559–62	4	1975
					1560 not D/C
	AEC Swift 5P2R	Alexander 51-seat	1581–92	12	1971
	Daimler Fleetline SRG6LX	Marshall 25- or 41-seat	1805/14/7/8/20/2/4/6	8	1970
					1805/14/7 in store
					Dual-door non-D/C
					Ex-M&D 1976–7.
	Daimler Fleetline SRG6LX	Alexander 39-seat	1841/3/7/53/9	5	1970, *all in store*
					Dual-door non-D/C
					Ex-PMT 1978

Source: MDEK Bus Club

Notes: For clarity, cars are listed broadly in fleet number order within type rather than date new. All buses D/C unless noted. Some coaches carried Maidstone fleet names.

The most fundamental change in this period was the introduction of a fleet numbering scheme in May 1977, resulting in another East Kent idiosyncrasy disappearing. Single-decks were numbered in a 1xxx series, double-deckers 7xxx, with coaches in the 8xxx range, all prefixing the registration number. The scheme was designed to work with the existing M&D numbering but allow distinction between the two fleets. It was retained into the Stagecoach era but was eventually superseded by that organization's own scheme.

By the end of the NBC era most AECs had gone, but a few Regents, Swifts and modernized Reliance coaches hung on for a short while under privatized ownership although the buses were all withdrawn by then. The LHSs lasted to the end of the NBC, with two, GFN 560/2N, receiving Sealink livery at different times in the 1970s/80s.

SECOND-HAND ACQUISITIONS AND RE-BODYING

One throwback to former East Kent practice was the decision to re-body the first two series of AEC Reliance 36ft (11m) coaches with new Plaxton 49-seat coach bodies. Cars 519–38 FN were dealt with in 1972–3 and 6539–48 FN in 1974. This gave both batches a new lease of life with bodies far better equipped than the Park Royal examples formerly carried. They lasted until the early 1980s and one, 532 FN, was converted to a Freedom coach for the disabled by 1982, with wheelchair lift and a special yellow livery.

The closer working with M&D resulted in a number of temporary vehicle exchanges, as mentioned earlier, and in 1974 four Leyland Atlanteans from 1961, three on

loan since 1973 – 571/2/5/85 RKJ, equipped for D/C operation – were formally acquired, mostly operating from Ashford. In 1976–7 eight ex-M&D dual-doorway Marshall-bodied single-deck Daimler Fleetlines of 1970, registered SKO 805/14/7/8/20/2/4/6H, passed to East Kent. Some had already been on loan since 1974 and all ended up on Dover docks work, while five similar-vintage single-deck Fleetlines, this time with Alexander dual-doorway bodies and originating from Potteries, arrived in 1978. These, BEH 141/3/7/53/9H, also went to Dover, all for Sea-speed work.

Further Fleetlines, this time twenty double-deckers from Southdown with Northern Counties dual-doorway bodies, were acquired in 1981. Eight, PUF 203–7/10–12H, had Gardner engines but the remainder, VUF 313–6/18–20/2–6K, had Leyland units. Those intended for stage carriage operations were converted to single-doorway layout but many were used, unconverted, on Hoverspeed docks work at Dover. Six single-door conversions passed, without use by East Kent, to M&D in 1982. An unusual livery of light blue was carried by VUF 326K for the Canterbury City tour in 1985. All these acquired cars received appropriate fleet numbers in the 1xxx or 7xxx series.

The Leyland National acquisitions in the 1980s have already been described, but on the coach side a number of vehicles changed hands; two Reliance/Duple coaches were exchanged with National Travel in 1976 following the Hoverlloyd contract passing to National and the East Kent cars carrying their red livery with it. Later a number of Leyland Leopard coaches

Ex-M&D single-deck Fleetlines were acquired in 1976–7, some having been on loan since 1974. Some were first used on stage carriage services although they did not find favour and all ended up on docks work at Dover. Car 1820 (SKO 820H) in Sealink livery, applied in 1977, is about to enter the approach road for Dover Priory station in autumn 1978. AUTHOR

from Southdown, Fox of Hayes and M&D passed to East Kent in 1976, 1982 and 1983 respectively; all had Duple bodies except for the Southdown example, which had a Plaxton body. Some vehicles went to M&D when the fleets split in May 1983.

East Kent's penchant for re-bodying coaches persisted and ten from the two HFN-L batches received new 49-seat Berkhof bodies in 1983–4 being re-registered A197 PPU and A198–206 TAR. During this period East Kent also transferred many cherished older registrations to their coaches, the fleet number now becoming the clearest way to identify vehicles.

DOCK AND HOVERPORT SERVICES

One feature of East Kent's operations from the 1970s was the provision of courtesy services both within Dover docks and connecting to rail services at Dover Priory station on behalf of the ferry, hovercraft and Seacat operators. These first commenced in 1970 using some of the HJG-registered Dennis coaches but went on to see a number of differing vehicles adapted for the services, many with extra luggage space and thus reduced seating. This first included TFN and DJG-C registered Reliances, GJG-D Regents and the single-deck Fleetlines obtained from M&D/PMT. Later, converted RJG-G Swifts, second-hand Leyland Nationals and the ex-Southdown Fleetlines, all to dual-doorway layout, joined the fleet of dedicated vehicles on these services. At Folkestone a connecting link to the harbour from the station on behalf of Sealink, later the Hoverspeed Seacat, was operated from 1975, using firstly a Bedford VAS1, KJG 109E, then Bristol LHSs, GFN 560/2N, and subsequently a National, GFN 552N, all with special Sealink or Hoverspeed liveries.

Contract liveries, many based on white with differing relief colours, were carried by the vehicles, featuring various brands including Seaspeed, Sealink, Hoverspeed and P&O, while some were left all-white to act as spare for use on any service. Hoverlloyd operations at Ramsgate also saw a number of special liveried vehicles in dark red and white; four DJG-C Reliances were treated followed by two Duple-bodied Reliances, PFN 791/4M, in 1976. The latter were soon transferred to National Travel, when they took responsibility for the contract in the same year. Another of this batch, PFN 790M, by now numbered 8790, received a livery for Townsend Thoresen ferries in 1978.

Most of the ex-Southdown Fleetlines acquired in 1981 ended up on docks work, as shown by 7210 (PUF 210H), carrying Hoverspeed livery (the successor to Seaspeed), captured at the Pencester Road parking area, Dover in December 1982. AUTHOR

The ex-Potteries single-deck Fleetlines all carried the Seaspeed livery sported by 1847 (BEH 147H) as it speeds up Pencester Road, Dover, heading towards Priory station in December 1980. AUTHOR

The Hoverlloyd livery applied from 1972 suited East Kent's coaches quite well and made a welcome change from National white. DJG 617C is pictured at Ramsgate Hoverport in the early summer of 1974. AUTHOR

CHAPTER TEN

STAGE SERVICES OF THE 1970s

LIMITED-STOP SERVICES AND CANTERBURY MARKET

In the 1970s Canterbury's market on Wednesdays had become a major attraction and required many reliefs to accommodate the extra demand. By May 1971 special limited-stop journeys on the 16 from Folkestone on Wednesdays were introduced, numbered 16X. Later a market-day service from Deal, numbered 13X, was introduced from 29 March 1972, as well as one from Seabrook, Hythe and Sellindge via Stone Street from 31 May 1972, numbered 19X. The 1 from Ashford also featured limited-stop journeys from September 1971, numbered 1X, avoiding Wye and Chilham. However, these ran every weekday and were not for market demand but to permit the return of an hourly service in the day, which had ceased upon conversion to D/C. In October 1976 the 1X journeys took the number 2 and, while keeping to the main road, now observed all stops. The 19X led a varied existence, becoming plain 19 in 1976 and 799 when extended to Folkestone in December

1977, the 13X and 16X lasted through the decade, the latter running both in the summer and sometimes in the run-up to Christmas. By May 1978 they had been renumbered 713 and 716 and in the mid-1980s they were withdrawn.

THE 1970s – A CHANGEABLE DECADE

The quest for savings continued; one notable change from Christmas 1974 was the final withdrawal of Boxing Day stage services, apart from a special service at Dover, which was not repeated. These had run on a limited basis for some time based on a Sunday service for those routes operated; it would take until 2012 before a regular Boxing Day service – rather than a contractual service such as the 598 (now D-line) to the Ashford Designer Outlet – would reappear, firstly on the Thanet loop but from 2015 also on the 4X, 6X, 8 and 16 routes. Withdrawal of New Year's Day services would follow later, with effect from the 1983–4

Nine of the Leyland Nationals delivered in 1977 were diverted from M&D and were to dual-purpose specification in the NBC livery for such vehicles. They were intended to be dedicated to a scheme of service improvements that never took place. NFN 86R is pictured at Canterbury bus station, in December 1977 on the direct service to Ashford, renumbered from 1X to 2 – a reminder of that section of the former link to Hastings. AUTHOR

Some of the dual-purpose Leopards from 1978 carried dual-purpose livery, as seen here on 8801 (PVB 801S) at Folkestone bus station in June 1980. However, use on National Express work would see it later painted all white. AUTHOR

Christmas season, but these would also resume from 1 January 1991, when service 300 (Ashford–Hastings) operated under contract. At present (2014–15) a number of New Year's Day contracted services operate, predominantly in the Canterbury and Ashford areas, but oddly not the Loop, a commercial service.

Sunday services in towns would be severely curtailed in this period, and country services in the week were also pruned. From 30 May 1971 the 68 was further revised to run between Richborough and Aylesham only, while the winter timetable of 26 September 1971 wrought more country cutbacks. The Ramsgate–Deal service 66 ceased as a through service in winter, while service 76 now ran from Deal to Eastry only, with the Staple journeys first covered by an extension of service 58 from Wingham. The Herne Bay to Upstreet (for Margate) service 35 was withdrawn, and to replace it, some journeys on the 7 were diverted via Marshside whilst short-workings on the 8 to Upstreet were extended to Marshside. By 23 April 1972 these were numbered 9, and the diversions on the 7 were withdrawn.

In Herne Bay itself the opportunity was taken from 30 May 1971 to revise town services in conjunction with the introduction of the new open-top summer service 45. Numbers 40 and 43 would go and new services via the station, the 46 from Greenhill to Hillborough via Mickleburgh Hill, and the 47 from Clifftown Gardens to Mill Lane via Beltinge Road, would run on weekdays whilst the 42 would now only run on Sundays. The 41 was largely unchanged except for the withdrawal of most Reculver journeys, which were served by the 44/45 in the summer; the limited winter service to Reculver would be withdrawn except for schoolday journeys.

On 26 September 1971 service 109 was withdrawn east of Stowting and the 110A West Hythe and Burmarsh routes were withdrawn completely. In compensation for the changes at Hythe, the 110 had some journeys extended to Stanford, while the 111, although reduced, saw some journeys routed via West Hythe between Hythe and Lympne on weekdays, involving ascent of the steep Lympne Hill. The 10 had some journeys diverted via Lympne in compensation for the 111 reductions. Four Sunday afternoon journeys between Hythe and West Hythe were maintained on the 111. The 111 had had journeys extended to Folkestone from 7 March 1971, which saw the last Stade Court journeys at Hythe withdrawn. By 28 May 1972 the 109 was further curtailed to East Brabourne and the 110's Stanford journeys were withdrawn. The Sunday West Hythe journeys on the 111 went by 27 May 1973.

From 28 May 1972, the former 11 service was renumbered 33/34/35, distinguishing between the various routes

July 1971 saw MJG 287 at Margate's Clock Tower bound for Wingham on the rural 58 route before it was curtailed to Minster. AUTHOR

out to Wickhambreaux, Stodmarsh and Stourmouth, while the 58 was cut back from Wingham to run between Margate and Minster only, with its Staple service, removed since 26 March, provided by diverted journeys on the 13. At the same time a reincarnation of the former seasonal service 36 commenced, this time from Faversham to Margate via Herne Bay and the Thanet Way, partly to compensate for the loss of the 35. Prior to its withdrawal in September 1971, the 35 had operated from Seasalter to Margate in the summer, being split into two sections, Seasalter–Herne Bay and Herne Bay–Upstreet, in the low season of 1970–1. However, the link from Herne Bay to Upstreet was reinstated in a limited form from 27 May 1973, this time numbered 48, although it would eventually disappear by February 1976, when it was replaced by a further diversion of service 7. Another change in May 1972 affected the long-established interchange at Sarre, diverting the Ramsgate service 65 to St Nicholas to facilitate simpler connections. The 65 had already served St Nicholas since March 1971 with some journeys running via Sarre, so this change removed any confusion.

Later, from 1 October 1972, the 8 was enhanced to run every 30 minutes to/from Margate by extending Upstreet short-workings on weekdays, while a local improvement at Ramsgate saw the 71 now extended to the Hoverport, at first on an irregular basis except on Sundays, when an hourly service was operated. Other routes to the Hoverport at first, such as the 70 and 87, were infrequent at these times and the open-top service did not operate in the winter. The next year saw another link via the Hoverport introduced, with the 65X running from Ramsgate to Canterbury on summer weekdays from May 1973. Supplementary limited-stop journeys on the 10 operated by M&D were also introduced in the summer as 10X.

The 27 May 1973 timetable now advertised the availability of area timetables prominently on the introductory

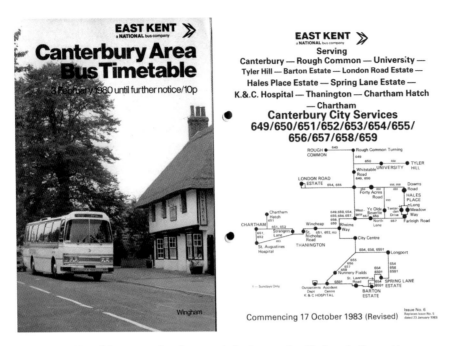

The area booklets of the NBC era lasted six years before being replaced by loose-leaf timetables with route diagrams (right), first in folders. Some of the last examples had attractive images on the cover rather than the plain map used at first. However, why the Canterbury edition of 1980 (left) featured a dual-purpose Leopard in National coach livery rather than a bus defies explanation.
AUTHOR'S COLLECTION

page – a portent of things to come, as the network timetable would only last another year. A tidying-up of boundaries with M&D had reduced area books to four: Ashford, Folkestone and New Romney; Canterbury and Herne Bay; Deal and Dover; Ramsgate, Broadstairs and Margate (Thanet).

The penchant for adding 100 to numbers rather than suffix letters continued on 30 September 1973, with service 13 journeys via Staple numbered 130 and some 64 journeys on Sundays running via Dumpton Park Drive numbered 164, although these had gone by 1975. The 164 would reappear in May 1977 for service 64 journeys diverted via former service 63 mileage along Northdown Park Road.

The 26 May 1974 timetable was the last of the old network-wide format; from 15 June 1975 only area booklets were provided, which were eventually replaced by individual leaflets, albeit first contained in area folders, from 1981 onwards. This last timetable also, for the first time, featured town maps on the reverse of the system map, a useful addition. The book was reprinted in August 1974 and that was the last edition: another final milestone in East Kent's history had been reached. The area booklets published between 1975 and 1980 were numbered into a system common with M&D, East Kent taking area numbers 5 to 9, comprising Canterbury and Herne Bay; Thanet;

Dover and Deal; Shepway (Folkestone); and Ashford respectively. Moving the other way, a joint map showing all services of M&D and East Kent was published in the mid-70s but later replaced in the early 1980s by area maps corresponding to the area booklets, which, ironically, had by then been superseded by loose-leaf timetables.

In 1974 a further attempt was made to revitalize the link from Ramsgate to Deal with the introduction of a new summer-only service 66X, running from Margate to Dover via the two towns. The author worked the first journey from Margate on this service on 26 May 1974 with car TFN 413.

Another milestone was reached in December 1974 when the final independent operator at the time, Drew's at Canterbury, threw in the towel and East Kent took over, first numbering the services 122–124, then later 651–653.

At the end of 1973 female drivers were trained and subsequently appointed on a permanent basis, the first being former conductresses. Women had played an important operational role on East Kent in both wars; in the First World War conductresses were in place but for the duration only, while in the Second World War both women drivers and conductors were employed; at the cessation of hostilities women had to cede their driving positions to men returning from the war. However, things were

The author at Dover Pencester Road on 26 May 1974 with inspector Bill Ratcliffe upon arrival of the first 66X journey from Margate. Despite the NBC livery, TFN 413 looks well turned out. AUTHOR'S COLLECTION – P. DELAMERE

changing and this time women could, and did, remain as conductresses after the war, many going on to give lengthy service to the company. One long-serving conductress was Beatty Macdonald. Starting at Folkestone in 1941, she continued after the war and, following a short break in service in the late 1950s, she returned, moving temporarily to Canterbury as there were no vacancies at Folkestone. She recounted that when first at Folkestone she was only allowed to work town services but it is unclear whether the bar was to do with her youth, being under 21, or policy for junior road staff, as was certainly evident elsewhere. After a few years she returned to Folkestone and worked there until the end of crew operation in 1971, returning in 1972 to assist with the short-term reinstatement of some crew journeys and open-top service 121. After retirement she was a regular attendee at East Kent rallies, attired suitably in her old uniform, maintained in pristine condition. She passed away in 2013 and is sadly missed.

Beatty Macdonald had a career with East Kent spanning over thirty years. Even in retirement she acted as a conductor as seen here near Walmer in September 2000 at a FotEK rally based at Deal. She was conducting on GFN 273, one of the 1952 Beadle-Leyland coaches. Beatty is assisted by former drivers, Ted Hood (left, ex-Dover depot) and Ted Blanche (right, ex-Deal depot). AUTHOR

On 27 October 1975 new services were introduced in the Folkestone area (now called Shepway following local authority changes), with the 121 to Lynwood and 131 to Holywell, albeit with only limited journeys. Later, on 1 December, local services in Hythe were revamped and improved with a new 30-minute shuttle to Saltwood, service 113, which also served Stade Court, reinstating parts of the old Newman's route last operated as a 111 in 1971. However, this also resulted in the former hourly service 110 to Sandling station being reduced to a peak-hour operation. A little later, in February 1976, further innovations were introduced at Deal, with new services 387/388 to Redsull Avenue and Birdwood Avenue but running Fridays and Saturdays only.

More economies were put in place in 1976. At Thanet, from 1 February, the 49/50/52 group was reduced from a 10-minute to a 15-minute frequency. The 63/64 group, meanwhile, saw the 63 journeys removed from Dumpton and at Margate, with only hourly 63 shuttles from Ramsgate harbour to Newington, while the 64 still ran throughout the route at 30-minute intervals weekdays. Later, in May, service 163 commenced running from Ramsgate harbour to Dumpton, Prestedge Avenue to replace the former 63 journeys, while to the west of the town a service to Nethercourt Farm was operated as a variant of the 71, numbered

171. Some 71 journeys also served Manna Hutte from 15 June 1975, replacing the withdrawn 165.

From 22 February 1976 the former 105/A services on Romney Marsh were renumbered, becoming 94/95 (the latter upon seasonal introduction from 30 May). One reason for this was to clarify validity of the newly introduced Freedom Tickets from 25 February (on 100-series services), while the new Atlanteans did not have the facility

The six highbridge Bristol VRs with ECW bodywork were all first allocated to Folkestone. MFN 43R accelerates out of Dymchurch in March 1980 on a short-working of the 95 to New Romney. AUTHOR

One of the fifteen Atlanteans from 1976, JJG 12P, was painted silver to commemorate the Queen's Silver Jubilee and ran across the company's area. This was sponsored by Riceman's, a store which was a feature of Canterbury in the post-war years before more recent development. It is in Ashford High Street on the 501 to Arlington – still, at that time, crew operated. AUTHOR

to display three-digit numbers with a further suffix letter, unlike the blinds on older East Kent cars. In August further changes took place in the area, with, once again, journeys to Densole being identified separately, now as 16A, while the main town services were reduced to a regular 10-minute service along Cheriton Road with a new link to the harbour following withdrawal of the 101 shuttle. The former 102/104/106/108 group were now renumbered 106/108/116/117/118, with 116/118 serving the harbour. Golden Valley services were also revised; the 100 (Hill Road via Sandgate) withdrawn and 107 to Stanbury Crescent halved to an hourly interval supplemented by new service 127 to Downs Road/Holywell Avenue. A new town service to Linksway took the recently vacated number 111. At the same time the 19X along Stone Street was numbered 19/A to run all year, with the 19A service planned to run via Stanford. In the event the 19A did not operate, perhaps indicating the uncertainty of service planning and support at the time. On summer Saturdays a limited-stop service 96 was trialled between Folkestone and Greatstone. Meanwhile, the developing estates to the west of Hythe saw an offshoot of the 103 running to Grebe Crescent at Palmarsh and numbered 133. In October 1976 the Canterbury–Charing services 67/A became 667/668 and the 11 from Faversham to Ashford became 665/666, assimilating into the M&D scheme.

The Queen's Silver Jubilee of 1977 saw the timetables of that year carrying the Jubilee logo, while one of the company's latest Atlanteans, JJG 12P, was repainted silver and toured various depots throughout the year. The start of the year also saw the rural route 92, from Dover to Capel via

West Hougham, summarily withdrawn from 31 January and taken over by Allen's Taxis of Folkestone. By now a schooldays-only operation with Bristol LHSs, the withdrawal was allegedly occasioned by the discovery of a long-standing restriction that banned their operation. The last service ran at the end of term on 21 December 1976.

May 1977 saw further changes to Ramsgate local services involving routes 163 and new numbers 172/173, while July saw further experiments over former 66 mileage with new high-summer service 779 running from Ramsgate to Deal, extending to Dover on Saturdays and Sundays. The fixation with renumbering continued and in December 1977 the 19 was numbered 799 and extended to Folkestone, whilst the 16A to Densole was in January 1978 renumbered again, to 98 and the 16X to 716. In May 1978 the former 36 to Margate was renumbered 736 and the 10X became 710, the 7xx series now used for limited-stop or special seasonal services.

The next major changes concerned what were called 'New Look' services for Dover and Deal, introduced on 8 January 1978. Dover services were renumbered, the former town services 301–7/310 now replaced by 560–9/574; country services 87/88 to Ramsgate/Elvington became 587/588 (both running to Ramsgate but omitting the Hoverport); the 89 to Nonington, 589; the 90 and 91 to Folkestone becoming 590/591; West Langdon's service 93 now 593; the 80 to Deal became 594/595; but Deal town buses retained their 38x series. Elsewhere the 68 to Aylesham became 398 and service 78 to Studdal and Whitfield became 395, both later to be renumbered again by 1981 to 571/570 respectively, while the former 74/76 mileage to Westmarsh became 399. Service 75 to Sandown Lees had already gone, from 17 October 1976, by which time it had been a schooldays-only operation. However, the trunk route to Canterbury, the 15 and now extended to the Eastern Docks, remained unchanged at this time; in May it would become 615.

On 7 May 1978 all Canterbury services were renumbered into the 600 series, e.g. 3 (Faversham) to 603, 8 (Margate) to 608, etc. The 32 (University) became 650 and was now part of a through service to Thanington. The former town services to Blean and Sturry Road were partly replaced by diversions of the former 4/6 services, now the 604–7 group with new service 649 serving Rough Common. The former 25 from London Road to Spring Lane became 654/655, while the Hales Place area was served by routes 656–9, both groups providing links to the Kent & Canterbury Hospital and Spring Lane. Out of the city, Herne Bay town routes 41/42/45/47 were replaced by new services, all from Greenhill, the terminus which was cut back from the post office to Herne Drive. New 645/646 would run to Hillborough/Reculver and the 647 to Mill Lane. The section to Clifftown Gardens formerly undertaken by the 47 was withdrawn; Mickleburgh Hill gained a better, 30-minute service on weekdays with the 646, while the Beltinge Road was now only served hourly with the 647. At the same time the 637–640 routes from Faversham now terminated at Whitstable and East Kent operation ceased.

As can be judged by this and future changes there was no real consistency; the idea of individual groups of numbers by town, allegedly part of a nationwide NBC plan, had gone out of the window and numbering seemed now to be a random process with little awareness of historical precedents. The timetable introducing these changes would be the last one with a map on both sides of the cover – from now on a more artistic line was followed, with either a picture or sketch on the front corresponding to the local area, with the map consigned to the rear. The first of the new design was Thanet's of May 1978 with a picture of the Viking ship at Pegwell. A little later, on 11 June 1978, there were further changes in Dover, the 563 was extended to Elvington with services 566/568 now providing a new service to Dover Hoverport.

There now seemed to be a lull in changes, probably as a new planning process was under development, although there were still minor modifications such as at Canterbury, where in the summer of 1979 the town routes were revised to remove some of the circular operations at termini.

LOCAL AUTHORITIES ATTEMPT TO CURB THE CUTS

The 1970s saw greater involvement of local authorities in the provision, or financial support, of loss-making but socially necessary services due to changes in legislation. One manifestation was the issue of concessionary passes for senior citizens, enabling reduced-rate travel, while some authorities introduced special free town services such as Ashford's services 181–7 for pensioners. Kent County Council (KCC) started to subsidize unremunerative services that would otherwise be withdrawn. Romney Marsh, however, saw heavily-subsized services rationalized in August 1976; the former 112/119 routes now became services 512/513, running as far as New Romney only, while journeys to Lade were replaced by all-year extensions of the 95 to Lydd-on-Sea. A complex series of irregular day-specific routes were introduced, criss-crossing the Marsh and serving isolated hamlets such as Brookland (817) and Dungeness (818) from New Romney. Longer routes were the 813 (Ham Street–Burmarsh–Folkestone) and 814 (New

Romney–Appledore–Tenterden). They were later consolidated and rationalized from 12 February 1978, using the range 813–7 – Dungeness's 818 was withdrawn.

Romney Marsh services had always been an odd and costly operation for the company, and their presence had been somewhat reduced when the Kent Education Committee took to running their own school services in 1972. Prior to that time, Folkestone-based cars, many crew-operated, would run to the New Romney area to provide schools services to the local Southlands school or to convey children from the Marsh to secondary schools in the Folkestone area, involving much dead mileage. Other changes bordering Romney Marsh took place from 3 October 1976, related to mileage covered by the former 109 and 111 services. Earlier, in April, the 111 had been numbered 99 and was now further renumbered 524–6, when it was curtailed to run between Ashford and Newingreen with limited extensions to Folkestone via West Hythe. North of the main road, new service variations 10A/B were diverted to run daily via Brabourne Lees. The remaining 109 journeys to East Brabourne were renumbered 519, while the 118 to Hastingleigh was also renumbered – to 518.

Due to the sparse population of the surrounding areas, Ashford seemed to see a good number of supported services in this era, but none were very successful. Another failed experiment was a group of services introduced 2 July 1979 to serve the William Harvey Hospital. The hospital, near Ashford, replaced local facilities, hence the need for better access from rural areas; but the services, numbered 801–5, using a specially purchased Ford minibus and serving the Lydd, New Romney and Aldington areas, were not well patronized and were replaced by two more limited services, 801/802, from 5 November 1979.

Car 572 RKJ, one of the Leyland Atlanteans transferred from M&D due to the changes in operating areas in the early 1970s, departs Folkestone bus station on a direct routing of the 10 rather than diverting to serve local villages, as became the case after 1976. MIKE ANSELL

CHAPTER ELEVEN

THE EARLY 1980s — A NEW DAWN?

MARKET ANALYSIS — TOWARDS A PLANNED FUTURE

If the 1970s were characterized by a rather disjointed approach to service planning, the 1980s were to introduce the concept of the NBC's new Market Analysis Project (MAP), which involved a far more analytical approach to assessing current and potential demand flows and which would also see the final demise of crew operation.

The fixed assets of depots were also reviewed. The depot at Deal, the original site of the company's operations, closed, officially ceasing operations when the timetables changed on 26 July 1981 but used for fuelling until August, when alternative arrangements were finalized. Deal, South Street was then brought into use as an outstation for overnight parking only. At Ashford the new site at Cobbs Wood, which had opened in 1976, closed on 9 August 1981, and operations moved back to the Station Road premises. This encompassed both the East Kent and M&D garages, which had been jointly owned as Ashford Properties Ltd since the early 1960s and operationally treated as one depot since 1971. The former coach depot at Seabrook was sold, having

latterly been used in a non-operational role from 1980 until 1982. The old tramway depot at Broadstairs, St Peter's had been disposed of earlier, circa 1978, having been used as a store for many years.

East Kent and M&D were now moving apart after a period of closer working in the 1970s. The companies were reorganized and split in 1983 with a separate engineering facility set up, Kent Engineering Ltd. This resulted in the Canterbury works and coachworks sites coming under this new concern as well as M&D's remaining works at Hawkhurst; following financial problems both Canterbury premises were closed in the early 1990s. The resultant changes in the 1980s saw East Kent's sphere of operation extending into M&D territory. In February 1980 the 333/603 services based on Faversham were linked, seeing East Kent now running through to Maidstone via Sittingbourne and Detling.

On 7 September 1980 there were major MAP revisions to Shepway and Ashford area routes. Services 590 (Dover–Folkestone) and 94 (Folkestone–Lydd) were linked and extended and became services 550–2, depending on routing, running between Dover and Hastings; the 550/551 were jointly worked with M&D, thus seeing East Kent running back to Hastings over part of its old 62 and 113 routes. The former, under M&D operation from 1973, had latterly been running between Dover and Hastings as route 426 but, as a possible throwback to its antecedents, had been renumbered 762 from 21 May 1978 as a Folkestone–Rye service (but may have carried 462 for a short time). The associated route 95 to Lydd-on-Sea now became 553–5 and also ran through from Dover in conjunction with the 550–2 services. M&D's establishment of a separate marketing identity, Hastings and District, on 14 December 1980 saw this name appearing on the 550 group, a precursor of its eventual separation as a stand-alone company.

These new services also absorbed the old 103/133 routes, the Grebe Crescent terminus now being served by new service 558, while the former service along Stone Street became a Dover–Canterbury itinerary via Hythe, Saltwood and Stanford, numbered

A few of the ex-Southdown Fleetlines were used on stage carriage workings in a converted single-door format. 7320 (VUF320K) is at Hythe, Red Lion Square in April 1984 bound for Lydd via the coastal route, by now numbered 554. AUTHOR

559 and absorbing Hythe's 110/113 services. In conjunction with these changes, all Folkestone's town services were revised and became routes 541–4 for the Creteway Down–Cheriton (Horn Street/Shaftesbury Avenue) corridor; the 98 to Densole became 546 now running from Horn Street; and the Stanbury Crescent–Golden Valley route 107 via East Cliff became 547. The remaining less-frequent services to Holywell and Lynwood were renumbered 548/549, while the Linksway service 111 was withdrawn.

Towards Ashford, the 10/A/B variants were rationalized at the same time with a standardized routing via Lympne and Brabourne Lees all numbered 10, while alternate limited-stop 710 journeys were provided, giving a basic hourly service on the Folkestone–Maidstone route. There were indicators of last-minute changes, probably consequent upon local authority support not being forthcoming. Services 518 and 519 from Ashford to Hastingleigh and East Brabourne were shown in the timetable booklet but an addendum records them as withdrawn; the MAP cuts would have reduced them anyway to run Tuesdays, Wednesdays and Fridays only with two journeys each way on a loop route. The 519 had had a brief resurgence with a Friday-only extension back to Hythe from 23 July 1978. Ashford's 512/513 to New Romney via Bilsington were reduced to two journeys on weekdays only with a return journey on new route 523 running via Brookland, this being the only replacement for part of services 813–7, which were all withdrawn. Services 524–6 were cut back to Aldington from Newingreen, with one journey to Folkestone remaining as new service 539 and route 529 now running as a daily afternoon loop via Aldington, Bilsington and Ham Street. The Ashford town services underwent change, including removal of crew operation and extensive new cross-town facilities, most all-day services were numbered 503/504 and 533–6 although former numbers also remained for limited workings and the 507 to South Willesborough was relatively unchanged. These caused a number of problems and were further revised in November back to a pattern more akin to the former services by terminating in the town centre.

The two booklets for Shepway and Ashford detailing these changes would be the last under the NBC area schemes; from 1981 onwards services were publicized in individual leaflets or booklets detailing specific service groups, although at first folder covers for some areas containing all relevant leaflets were issued. These last books and some subsequent area folders also incorporated express services, despite these being under the National Express umbrella, as had been the case since 1972.

From 1981 MAP changes came fast and furious. The next major revision, from 3 May, concerned Thanet, mak-

Twenty-eight of the angular Willowbrook-bodied Bristol VRs entered service with East Kent between 1977 and 1978. Number 7977 (RVB 977S) is pictured at Margate Cecil Square on the 154 to Garlinge in July 1979, before MAP-based changes would completely revise the structure of services across the area. This bus would later be converted to open-top in 1981 following a collision with a low bridge. AUTHOR

ing significant changes to the 49/50/52 group, which had seen little major change apart from reductions in frequency since 1937, a legacy of forty-five years. Crew operation finished and the new weekday timetable saw the 49 running from Newington via Ramsgate/Broadstairs and Cecil Square to Margate Hospital, removing it from Birchington. The former 52 was extended to Northdown Park, while the 50 ran via Westgate, replacing the former 51/151 routes. Ramsgate town service 71 was partially replaced by new service 53, running every 30 minutes from Ramsgate to Birchington via St. Luke's Avenue, Allenby Road and Margate. The 172 from Prestedge Avenue to Nethercourt Farm remained as an hourly service. These combined routes would still provide a basic 15-minute frequency on the main corridors but with new links.

Associated changes saw the former 64/164 services rationalized to a KCC-supported infrequent route from Broadstairs to Margate Hospital, while at Margate the 54/154 routes now served Westgate, Warren Drive, replacing the 51, with the 151 reduced to an hourly summer service between Northdown Park and Westgate, a shadow of the 7/8-minute service operated on this corridor in the 1960s. Service 56 was also revised to run from Cecil Square to Westwood via Palm Bay and Broadstairs, but by 1982 it had reverted to a Westwood–Broadstairs route, with service 57 running from Palm Bay via Margate and St Peter's to Broadstairs, Stanley Road and the infrequent 64 now largely replaced, with the exception of some journeys on evenings and Sundays from Ramsgate to Margate Hospital. These changes demonstrated the increasing reliance on local authority support. For example, service 70, the country link from Ramsgate to Birchington via Minster, was announced as being withdrawn but last-minute intervention saw it retained. The other Minster link, the 610, reverted to its former number, 65, although 610 was retained for the remaining two journeys to/from Canterbury.

Further MAP-related changes on 26 July 1981 concerned Canterbury's 604 group of routes; crew operation finished, the last in the company, and the routes now served local areas in Herne Bay with diversions via Beltinge (taking the numbers 685/687) or Westcliff, enabling the rationalization of the remaining town services there. On evenings and Sundays, variants 684/686 served Canterbury's London Road Estate in conjunction with city service revisions. One unusual operation at Canterbury in 1981 was service 611, running to the Civic Centre. It only ran a limited number of journeys and did not last long, the number later being used for a new Ramsgate–Deal service in 1986. Despite the continued need for economies, the sparsely populated area west of Deal and Dover saw the 570 to Studall/Whitfield and 589 to Nonington still hanging on, while the concept of diverting longer-distance routes to serve local areas, as implemented in Herne Bay, also saw, from 26 July, some of the 593–6 group run via Mill Hill at Deal as well as the village of East Langdon. The remaining town services to Mill Hill, the 581/583, ran hourly, as did the 585 from Sandown to Kingsdown, although this was split at South Street.

The southwest of the company's operations at Ashford saw further expansion and coordination with M&D from 9 August 1981. East Kent now served Maidstone on services 13/404/424, which headed west from Ashford through the Pluckley area as well as operating other rural services, such as the 407 to Tenterden and the Village Link for senior citizens. They also reached Hastings via Tenterden on the 400, which now ran from Canterbury, replacing the former 1 and 2 services. Another extension towards the end of 1981 resulted in the 10 running on to Sevenoaks; apart from the later extension of 711 to Brighton, it was one of the furthest west of any regular East Kent stage carriage operations, excluding limited-stop express operations.

On 5 May 1982 a new seasonal limited-stop service 718 was launched jointly with Southdown and ventured further into the Weald, running from Canterbury to Brighton via Hawkhurst and extended to winter operation from 1983–4. East Kent ceased involvement from 17 April 1985. Many of these operations west of Ashford or Maidstone would cease with deregulation. On 7 December 1982 another experimental service, the 560 to Horn Street, Naildown Estate from Hythe, was trialled, running Tuesdays and Thursdays only with one journey each way supported by Hythe town council. Sadly, the experience of past decades in attempting to serve this area had been forgotten, and like the others it was a failure. Another new venture, launched on 12 January 1983, was service 759, linking Lydd, Hythe and Canterbury Market on Wednesdays only; while another shopping-oriented service, the 733, running from Canterbury and Faversham to the Hempstead Valley SavaCentre near the Medway Towns was introduced on 3 November 1983, but only ran to 4 February 1984. The summer of 1984 saw the by-now regular publication of a leaflet detailing seasonal services, showing open-top 69; the 736, which now ran from Reculver to Margate on limited days on the fringes of the season, extending to operate Sundays to Fridays in the high summer; with new service 787 running from Margate/Ramsgate to Dover and Folkestone summer Sundays only. Storm clouds were gathering, however, and legislation published in 1985 would mark the end of nationalized bus operations and the secure environment of service licensing dating back to 1931.

THE END OF CREW OPERATION

From April 1972 the last depots retaining an element of crew operation were Ashford, Canterbury, Herne Bay and Thanet. Ashford's 505/506 would go from 1 October 1972, leaving them with the 501/502; East Kent's remaining Regents at Canterbury and Herne Bay operated the 4/6 services (later as the 604 group), while Thanet's were employed on the 49/50/52 group. In their final years,

In 1981 the 10 would be extended to Sevenoaks, previously the province of M&D and London Transport's country area. BJG 674V is well into its marathon route as it loads in Maidstone in October 1981. AUTHOR

The penultimate crew route to be converted was the 49/50/52 group at Thanet. Number 7778 (AFN 778B) has less than a year to go as she loads at Ramsgate harbour on a cold July in 1980; despite this a good crowd is boarding. The bus sports a 'Unibus' advertising display. Note the LT Routemaster behind on a staff tour to the seaside. AUTHOR

however, a number of other workings, radiating from Canterbury, saw regular Regent operation – particularly on the 608 to Margate, the 612 group, mainly on short-workings (to Wingham/Sandwich), and the 650 to the University. The last year of crew operation was 1981. Ashford had gone earlier, with their MAP changes from 7 September 1980, and Thanet's 49/50/52 group went on 3 May 1981, those routes seeing a mix of cars in the final years – Regents mingling with crew-operated Fleetlines and VRs. Canterbury and Herne Bay's 604–7 group would be the last, 25 July marking the conclusion of crew operation. But was it? When Regent MFN 943F was about to be repainted into former East Kent livery as a heritage vehicle, it made a foray from Dover onto the 558 on 3 February 1983, presumably using two drivers, an interesting postscript to East Kent's crew operations. It would not mark the end of the Regents, however; a number were retained for contract work until 1986, while those used as service vehicles (tree loppers/ trainers) would last until 1991. Even today Stagecoach retain one, MFN 946F, resplendent in East Kent red and cream, replacing the role first undertaken by MFN 943F.

OPEN-TOP SERVICES – THE LAST GASP

By 1975 East Kent's remaining open-top service, 69, was in the hands of recently converted members of the PFN

Regents but reduced to an hourly frequency; the 1974 season had seen a halving in frequency from August due to staff shortages. All the Guy Arab conversions had been withdrawn and the reduction in frequency also allowed three PFNs to be stood down. In 1981 Saturday operation ceased. The service had already seen its operating period contracting from 1976, generally running from July to September, although between 1980 and 1983 a May or June start-up operated.

In 1981 the service became D/C-operated, facilitated through two ex-M&D Atlanteans – 572 RKJ and 620 UKM – and Bristol VR RVB 977S, a lowbridge victim, all being converted to open-top. They carried fleet numbers 0572, 0620 and 0977 and a revised livery of white with a map of the route on a fawn background, and names 'Viking

The conversion of the 69 service to D/C operation in 1981 was facilitated by two vintage ex-M&D Atlanteans and a more modern VR. One of the former, 0572 (XKO 72A, re-registered from 572 RKJ) is seen climbing Madeira Walk at Ramsgate (top), while 0977 (RVB 977S) rounds the Paragon on the other side of Ramsgate's harbour. Both views were taken in August 1987. AUTHOR

Open Top Seaside Special

Minnis Bay
Westgate
Margate
Kingsgate
Broadstairs
Ramsgate

23 JULY until
3 SEPT 1989 (incl)

Service 69
New Low Fares

EK EAST KENT BUSES   in association with THANET DISTRICT COUNCIL

Glory', 'Spirit of Kent' and 'Pride of Thanet' respectively. The Atlanteans were re-registered in 1984. In 1991 three convertible ECW-bodied Bristol VRs were acquired from Southdown, numbered 7613/6/22; these replaced the Atlanteans and the older VR and operated the service until its withdrawal. They all carried the privatized East Kent livery.

The closure of the hoverport in 1982 saw the 69 termin-ating at the Chilton Tavern the following year, and from 1984 it ran from Minnis Bay to Ramsgate, Westcliff, which would be the final route apart from 1986, when it ran between Westgate and Broadstairs only. From 1987 Thanet District Council supported the service, which allowed it to revert to its earlier 1985 terminals until the financial assist-ance ceased. It survived into the newly privatized era and the final season of operation was 1992. As these last open-tops were convertible it allowed their retention for normal double-deck operations after service 69 ceased and one, 7613, visited the Derby in 1993, the last year an East Kent open-top attended; it also ran on a Folkestone local tour in 1994 in conjunction with the Shepway Festival, marking the formal end of East Kent's open-top operations.

LEFT: *Thanet District Council's support for the 69 was demonstrated by their logo on the timetable leaflet. By this time, summer 1989, the new privatized logo for East Kent Buses was evident.* AUTHOR'S COLLECTION

One of the ex-Southdown convertible Bristol VRs climbs out of Broadstairs, Joss Bay, in 1991 — its first year on this service.
MIKE ANSELL

PART IV

DEREGULATION AND PRIVATIZATION

The year 1986 was to be a time of substantial change: the Transport Act of 1985 paved the way for deregulation of bus services, overturning a system that had been in place for fifty-five years, since the inception of the 1930 RTA in 1931. Changes in 1980 had already seen coach operations freed from the earlier licensing constraints. In the meantime, the Conservative government was preparing the NBC for eventual privatization and was hiving off parts of this mammoth corporate institution into more manageable units suitable for sale.

CHAPTER TWELVE

THE NEW 'EAST KENT'

From 1983 East Kent had again been running as a stand-alone unit, separate from M&D, and from 1986 it began to carve out a new identity, stimulated by the local management preparing to make a bid for the company. This saw East Kent adopting a new identity 'East Kent Buses' and logo featuring an italicized *EK* by April 1986. A new livery appeared, with a throwback to the former East Kent colours, featuring burgundy red lower panels and cream upper works. The five districts had already been given a greater degree of autonomy from 1985 with devolution of previously centralized administrative work, and this was now reflected in individually styled leaflets from 1986, depending on the area. The NBC double 'N' symbol disappeared. Dover and Deal used a block capitalized 'EAST KENT ROAD CAR CO.' style by March, while by May Folkestone were using the new logo, which became common on all leaflets issued from October although with different designs. The Thanet booklets used an outline of the area surrounded by light blue representing the sea, whereas Dover persevered with the former style but adapted an

earlier image of a VR double-decker with the new livery. Canterbury used a completely revamped design, most featuring red and cream colours, the new livery, but apart from the 604 group the leaflets were folded to half A5 size.

The new Minilink leaflets were in yellow with black and red relief, mimicking the livery used on the minibuses operating these services. Folkestone was unique in producing an area booklet for all services, firstly a completely non-standard A4 design, then reverting to A5; they also produced a route map and information leaflet of the area, which would run to a number of editions. Ashford eventually produced a separate booklet containing all their town services titled 'Ashford Local'. In parallel, the KCC produced a map of bus services across the county, first termed a 'Local Bus Guide', which has been produced in various forms, occasionally for local areas, to the present day.

The management buyout with a team led by John Berkshire was successful, despite heavy competition from a French-led consortium, and the new East Kent was privatized on 5 March 1987. Following a notice to quit, the

Services
56   56A
57   57A
58

Broadstairs
Westwood
Margate
Palm Bay

Margate   Palm Bay

Westwood

Broadstairs

Commencing 26 OCTOBER 1986

EK EAST KENT BUSES   Westwood Garage, Margate Road, Ramsgate

400/401/
652/653
Canterbury – Chartham
– Chilham
667/668/669
Canterbury – Chartham
– Chilham – Charing

Thanington   Canterbury

Old
Wives
Lees   Chartham
            Hatch

Charing Challock Molash Chartham   Chartham
                            Turning

                    Chilham

A great deal
for Canterbury

EK Minilink

C2
LONDON ROAD ESTATE
Priest Av.   Westgate/   Bexonsfield Rd./
        Knight Av. St. Dunstans Mandeville Rd.

Merchants Way   Downs Rd./
            Nunnery Fields   Marwood Av.
            Hospital   St. Martins Sussex Av.
                        Church
            GRAVEL WALK

C4   Spring Lane
KENT & CANTERBURY
HOSPITAL

C1
HALES PLACE
Long Meadow Way

Tenterden Drive

Hampshire Rd.

C3
SPRING LANE ESTATE

STARTS OCTOBER 27th 1986

The new era ushered in some diverse styles of timetable leaflets. Shown here, from top to bottom: Thanet's coastal theme; Canterbury's focus on the new fleet colours of red and gold but in a small-format leaflet; the same size Minilink leaflet but with the minibus colours of yellow, red and black.
AUTHOR'S COLLECTION

Although by now separated out from the previously nationalized umbrella, East Kent continued to provide cars for the London express services and still does so today. VJG 811T, one of the Duple-bodied Leopards from 1979 in the improved National Express livery, exits London via Elizabeth Bridge on a Folkestone journey of the 008 in August 1987. AUTHOR

depot at Canterbury was closed in May 1989, having seen a significant reduction in its allocation in 1984. Herne Bay now serviced Canterbury routes using overnight parking at the Garth, the hard-standing opposite the former depot. A plan to compensate for the closure by using outstations at remote sites such as Wingham, reminiscent of earlier 'dormy' sheds, was soon scrapped.

Competition was rife as a result of deregulation, but despite some challenging times and a good number of competing operators emerging, East Kent was resilient and many of the rogue competitors eventually disappeared, while the more reliable operators were routinely successful in KCC tenders and still are to this day. One early competitor, Marinair, was bought by East Kent in November 1987 and was used as a stand-alone operation to ward off some competitors but by 1991 it had been absorbed into the mainstream operation. The period of East Kent's new independence would be brief, however, lasting just over six years.

THE PRIVATIZED EK FLEET, 1986–93

The fleet intake of the new company was characterized by a large influx of minibuses to support the new Minilink services, although these, as with some of the second-hand acquisitions, arrived prior to privatization. The new red/cream livery had emerged even before the formal purchase, with the new *EK* logo bordered by horizontal stripes on the lower panels for double-deckers and on the cove panels for single-decks. Minibuses carried a yellow livery with red and black lining and were numbered in a new two or three-digit series. East Kent coach livery was cream with a broad red mid-band and red stripes to the fore and 'EAST KENT' in cream letters. This was later simplified in 1992 with the omission of the stripes, the red band carried round and the revised insignia 'EAST KENT COACHES'. Vehicles normally used on National Express work, such as 8901–10, carried their white livery. Advertising and contract liveries continued, especially for docks work, but one innovation was the livery used for the new Canterbury Park & Ride service, which was grey with a dark blue skirt and appropriate branding.

In 1986–7 forty-six Dormobile-bodied sixteen-seat minibuses arrived: fleet numbers 1–27/79 were Ford Transits whilst 28–45 were Freight Rover Sherpas. Number 79 was diverted from South Midland following a terminal accident with one of the Sherpas. To support the major changes in operations, a large number of second-hand double-deckers were acquired. Twelve Leyland Atlanteans,

The new Minibus intake first saw Fords arriving, such as these two examples, 7 and 16 (C 707/16FKE), at Dover Castle on the D77 in September 1988. The striking new livery was also reflected in publicity for Minilink services. These minibuses featured body conversions by local firm, Dormobile. MIKE ANSELL

allocated numbers between 7097 to 7893, with Park Royal 77-seat bodies, came from Northern General in 1986, while a further sixteen Atlanteans with Northern Counties 75-seat bodies came from Greater Manchester in 1987, numbered 7112–845 and 7500–95. An interim solution, they had short lives and the last were disposed of in 1991. A low-height ECW-bodied VR, 7570, came from Devon General in 1986, while the three convertible VR open-top acquisitions of 1991 have already been described. Later, in 1988, four more Leyland Nationals were taken into stock;

The new livery for 'big buses' was a modern interpretation of the former BET colours. It suited these vehicles very well, as can be seen by its application here to one of the second-hand Northern Counties-bodied Atlanteans acquired in 1987 from Greater Manchester, 7844 (HNB 44N), and one of the original Willowbrook-bodied Bristol VRs, 7020 (PJJ 20S), seen at Canterbury in August 1987. AUTHOR

three from Bristol Cityline and one oddity, a National 2, the only one operated, from Dunlop, Coventry. In 1991 two further Nationals, 1024/7, came from Robson of Thornaby. These Nationals were all dual-door and used on docks work, carrying Hoverspeed or Sealink Stena Line livery.

New big buses came on the scene in 1988–9, with fifteen 77-seat MCW Metrobus 2 double-deckers, numbered 7746–55 and 7771–5, while a further seven delivered in 1989, 7761–7, had 70-seat bodies with high-backed seats. Scania were also represented by two double-deckers with 80-seat Alexander bodies, 7781/2, delivered in 1989 to replace fire-damaged Atlanteans. New large single-deck buses were rare deliveries to the privatized company; only three arrived, in 1991 and these were DAFs, 1401–3, with Optare 49-seat bodies intended for the Canterbury Park & Ride contract.

Two Scanias arrived to replace vehicles lost in a fire. One, 7781 (F781 KKP), is captured heading out of Cliftonville towards Ramsgate on the revised group of routes from Canterbury in September 1989. MIKE ANSELL

The later Metroliner coaches had a more curvaceous frontal arrangement, as shown by 8855 (E855 UKR), waiting at Dover Eastern Docks in July 1988 on a mini-break tour. MIKE ANSELL

New single-deck coaches were first represented in 1987 by a Scania with Berkhof 41-seat body, 8211, as the new Freedom Coach for the Disabled, while two more new 51-seat Metroliner coaches, 8854/5, arrived in 1988. Three second-hand Metroliners, 8244–6, dating from 1985, came from Premier Travel; an earlier 1984 model, 8192, kitted out as an executive coach, came from the same source, all in 1988. A further model, this time a Metroliner demonstrator, 8399, was acquired from MCW also in 1988. Two further acquisitions were in the formal transfer of two ex-Marinair Bovas, both with Bova 49-seat bodies in 1991. All of these acquired coaches had toilets, the Metroliners at first varying in capacity from forty-five to forty-nine seats. New arrivals in 1989 for National Express work were eight Volvo B10Ms, 8901–8, with Plaxton Paramount Expressliner 49-seat bodies, also with toilets, while three further examples, 8243 and 8909/10, arrived in 1992–3. Of these, 8243 was a 1991 example and acquired from Park of Hamilton in 1993, whilst 8910 had a Première body.

One further Scania coach, 8856, was delivered in 1992, also with the Plaxton Paramount 49-seat body with toilet.

More minibuses in the shape of Ivecos with larger-capacity bodies were delivered between 1987 and 1990. The 23-seat examples were bodied by Robin Hood, numbered 51–75; Carlyle, numbered 46/7/91–4; and Phoenix, numbered 95–8/101–4. Eight others, 80–7, had 19-seat Robin Hood bodies. The company acquired some second-hand minibuses in 1989–90 with three smaller Freight Rover Sherpa/Dormobiles from Eastern Counties, 663/4/8, swapped with Transits 25–7, and three larger Iveco/Robin Hoods from Brighton and Hove numbered 226/30/1. The last minibuses to arrive under East Kent's tenancy were ten Ivecos, 112–21, delivered in 1991. All should have had 23-seat bodies by Carlyle but the firm went into administration and they only completed three; the remaining seven were bodied by Dormobile.

The minibuses' sphere of operation was not necessarily confined to town routes. In the early 1990s, service 15 from Dover to Canterbury saw Dover's minibuses operating to Canterbury in the evenings, while the 90, between Dover and Deal, was also operated by minibuses on evenings and Sundays. At Folkestone the evening service to Densole had already been covered by minibuses, as Minilink F9, since early 1991.

Possibly the most spectacular new buses acquired by East Kent were ten long-wheelbase Leyland Olympians with Northern Counties 85-seat bodies, numbered 7801–10. They arrived in 1990 and were followed by four smaller 77-seat examples in 1992, numbered 7811–4, and later a further ten, 7821–30, in 1993. Only the first five carried the privatized East Kent livery; the remaining five received the first, rather utilitarian, Stagecoach white livery with red, blue and orange stripes. Five of the first batch carried names such as 'Thomas Beckett', following a competition involving local schoolchildren.

Five of the long-wheelbase Olympians delivered in 1990 received names; 7807 (H807 BKK) was named 'Enterprise' and is seen at Canterbury on the 604 circular route out to Whitstable in June 1992. AUTHOR

Table 11   East Kent Vehicles at July 1992

Type	Chassis	Body	Fleet Nos.	Total	Date/Notes
Double-deck convertible open-top	Bristol VRT	ECW 74-seat	7613/6/22	3	1977–8 Ex-Southdown 1991
Double-deck low-height	Bristol VRT	ECW 74-seat	7650–85	36	1980–1 7655 re-bodied 1983
Double-deck highbridge	Bristol VRT	Willowbrook 74-seat	7016/21–4; 7973–6/8/9/82/5–91	19	1977–8
	Bristol VRT	ECW 74-seat	7041–3/5/6	5	1976
	MCW Metrobus 2	MCW 77-seat	7746–55; 7771–5	15	1988–9
	MCW Metrobus 2	MCW 70-seat	7761–7	7	1989 Coach seats

	Scania N113	Alexander 80-seat	7781/2	2	1989
	Leyland Olympian	Northern Counties 85-seat	7801–10	10	1990
	Leyland Olympian	Northern Counties 77-seat	7811–4	4	1992
Single-deck coach	MCW Metroliner	MCW 49-seat	8192; 8244–6; 8399	5	1983–5 *Fitted with toilet Ex-Premier Travel or MCW (8399) 1988*
	Scania K112CR	Berkhof 41-seat	8211	1	1987 *Freedom Coach with toilet and wheelchair lift*
	Bova FHD12	Bova 49-seat	8513; 8996	2	1984/6 *Fitted with toilet Ex-Marinair 1991*
	Leyland Leopard PSU3G	ECW 47 or 49-seat	8828/31/2/4–7	7	1982 *D/C cars Dual-purpose 8828 to bus standard*
	Leyland Tiger TRCTL11	Plaxton 53-seat	8838–42	5	1983 *Dual-purpose*
	MCW Metroliner CR126	MCW 51-seat	8843/4/6–53	10	1983–4
	MCW Metroliner HR131	MCW 51-seat	8854–5	2	1988
	Scania K93	Plaxton 49-seat	8856	1	1992 *Fitted with toilet*
	Volvo B10M	Plaxton 49-seat	8901–9	9	1989–92 *Fitted with toilet*
Single-deck bus	Leyland-National 11351	L-National 30-seat	1024/7	2	1974 *Dual-door Ex Robson 1991*
	Leyland-National 1151	L-National 30-seat	1060/7; 1145/53/6/9	6	1973 *Dual-door Ex LCBS 1984*
	Leyland-National 11351A	L-National 48-seat	1081–4/6–9	8	1977 *Dual-purpose*
	Leyland-National 11351A	L-National 49-seat	1115/7/8; 1890/2/3/5/8/900	9	1976
	Leyland National 2	L-National 30-seat	1255	1	1981 *Dual-door Ex-Dunlop 1988*
	Leyland-National 11351/A	L-National 30-seat	1300; 1559; 1851	3	1974–6 *Dual-door Ex-Bristol 1988*
	Leyland-National 10351/A	L-National 37-, 40- or 41-seat	1344–6; 1546/52	5	1975–7 *1546/52 reinstated 1983*
	DAF SB220	Optare 49-seat	1401–3	3	1991 *Park & Ride service*
Minibuses	Ford Transit	Dormobile 16-seat	1/4/12	3	1986
	Freight Rover Sherpa	Dormobile 16-seat	28/35/6/41–4; 664/8	9	1986 *664/8 Ex-Eastern Counties 1989*
	Iveco Daily	Carlyle 23-seat	46/7; 91–4; 112–4	9	1990–1
	Iveco Daily	Robin Hood 23-seat	51–75	25	1987–9
	Iveco Daily	Robin Hood 19-seat	80–7	8	1987
	Iveco Daily	Phoenix 23-seat	95–8; 101–4	8	1990–1
	Iveco Daily	Dormobile 23-seat	115–21	7	1991
	Iveco Daily	Robin Hood 21-seat	226/30/1	3	1986 *Ex-Brighton & Hove 1990*

Source: MDEK Bus Club

Notes: For clarity, cars are listed broadly in fleet number order within type rather than date new. All buses D/C except dual-door cars, which were used on docks work.

DEREGULATION OF BUS SERVICES

From 'deregulation day', 26 October 1986, the British bus network was opened up for competition – the former system, whereby operators had to be granted a licence for each route by the traffic commissioners and consideration was given to abstraction from existing operators, was abolished. Now bus companies, providing they had an operator's licence, merely had to register their intended routes of operation. For this first round, operators had to have registered the routes they intended to operate commercially at least six months beforehand in order for local authorities to have time to consider the implications for services they needed to support and for a competitive tendering process to be initiated.

For East Kent it was the opportunity to remove some of the earlier nonsensical renumbering and revert to more traditional numbers. However, those routes that were supported by KCC generally retained their existing numbers. For example, the former 590 and 594/595 returned as a commercial operation, now running between Deal/Martin Mill and Folkestone as service 90/A, while the service from Dover to Folkestone via Alkham was supported by KCC and remained numbered 591, although the tender was won by East Kent. The 90 service later (February 1988) underwent some radical reorganization, with a new link from Folkestone to Elvington running on Sundays, numbered 94, with

the Dover–Deal section running as a separate service on Sundays. Routes radiating south from Canterbury such as the 615, 616 and 617 also reverted to their former 15, 16 and 17 identities. Across Romney Marsh from Folkestone to New Romney and Rye the services were now split from their former Dover leg consequent upon the reintroduction of the 90 group and took numbers 11 and 12, while journeys to Hythe, Grebe Crescent or Saltwood were numbered 18 or 19 respectively with Hythe–Saltwood short-workings as 19A. Grebe Crescent was also served by a local service to Naildown Estate or Sandling Station, numbered 28/A. This group of numbers were all formerly based around Canterbury. Later, by May 1987 the Rye route was extended back to Hastings, while March 1988 saw it reach Eastbourne.

The major revisions of deregulation now saw the 608 from Canterbury to Margate renumbered 8/A and linked to the former 49/50 group to provide a round-island link to Canterbury. This service group also incorporated the numbers 9/A/B, which diverted at Birchington to serve Minnis Bay. A complex number of itineraries saw the group providing a 10-minute weekday frequency around the island with diversions to serve the Newington and Westgate areas, as well as maintaining a service that linked back to the former 49/A tram replacement service of 1937. However, on weekday evenings and Sundays the services were KCC-supported and ran as the 49/50. A number of other Thanet town services were also supported, including the 51/A and 52/A linking Northdown Park and Margate, Cecil Square

One of the MCW Metrobuses of 1988 received traditional East Kent livery in celebration of the company's seventy-fifth anniversary in 1991. Here 7755 (E755 UKR) is seen at Folkestone bus station in March of that year on the 94, which by now extended to Sandwich. Changes to the road layout in Folkestone's town centre means that some services now enter the bus station from the northeast – a contraflow when compared to its original design. AUTHOR

The post-deregulation revisions in the Isle of Thanet introduced a number of new links as shown by 7412 (OTY 412M) on service 9 at Stirling Way, Newington, bound for Margate via Westwood in August 1987. Number 7412 is one of the first batch of second-hand Atlanteans acquired in 1986 from Northern General with Park Royal bodies. MIKE ANSELL

The Leyland Nationals survived into the newly privatized East Kent era and the new livery enhanced their appearance. JJG 893P, now numbered 1893, one of the longer versions, passes Vale Square, Ramsgate in May 1988, displaying the 'lazy' blind with both terminals (Nethercourt Estate/Prestedge Avenue) for service 172. AUTHOR

to Ramsgate via Allenby Road or Margate Road; the 56/A and 57/A from Broadstairs, Callis Court to Westwood or Margate; and the small number of journeys on service 58 from Palm Bay down to Margate. The Dane Valley and Garlinge services remained commercial operations in the day on weekdays, terminating at Margate Station or Cecil Square respectively, numbered 54 or 154 with a restricted service to Westgate, Warren Drive, provided by new service 153/A. At night and on Sundays another supported service, the 61A, ran from Northdown Park via Dane Valley to Margate, also successfully gained by East Kent. At Ramsgate a weekday commercial service to the Nethercourt Farm estate was maintained as services 68 or 172.

On the rural fringes of the Isle of Thanet most services were KCC-supported, not being commercially registered. East Kent was successful with the routes from Ramsgate out to Minster and St. Nicholas, now numbered either 65 or 71, but the rump of the 70, running from Birchington to St. Nicholas via Acol and Minster, was won by the then independent operator Marinair Coaches. Over at Canterbury the 604 group was restructured, now serving the University with, on weekdays, a 30-minute 'full loop' service, but with the other half of the 15-minute service terminating at Greenhill from the Herne direction (607) or Hillborough/Reculver from the Whitstable direction (605). The tendered Sunday service, running hourly and numbered 684/685, was gained by Regent Coaches, probably to the surprise of East Kent, although they regained

it by July 1987. Regent Coaches also provided most of the local Herne Bay services – 645/646 – between Greenhill and Hillborough/Reculver.

From Ramsgate to Dover a number of journeys on the 587/588 were also KCC-supported, accounting for their former numbers being retained, but won by East Kent; while a new commercial venture, service 611, was launched by the company trying again to revitalize the Ramsgate–Deal connection. At Deal, the town services to St. Nicholas and Mill Hill became 81–83 again, with the Deal–Sandown service reverting to its former 85 identity, although Deal–Kingsdown took the erstwhile Dover number 86 while former Folkestone number 99 was used for a Mill Hill circular. A number of journeys on these services were also KCC-supported. Several minor country routes put out to tender were lost by East Kent to smaller operators; the 589 from Dover to Aylesham/Goodnestone, operating on Saturdays only, was gained by Star Coaches, but East Kent retained the connection to Canterbury on the 621, as well as the Thursday-only service 571 from Sandwich to Aylesham.

In the towns of Dover, Folkestone, Ashford and Canterbury, new commercial Minilink services were introduced, offering more frequent operations by small-capacity minibuses. At Dover the D3/5/7/9, serving St. Radigund's, Elms Vale and River, ran every 10 or 20 minutes, with the D6 to Pilgrims Way/The Lines every 7–8 minutes. The remaining services to Aycliffe/Buckland/Whitfield were provided mainly by 'big buses' on the 562/564, and between Eastern Docks and Tower Hamlets by the 568, the 564 serving the Docks on Sunday. At Folkestone the F1–6 Minilink services

Following the delivery of the initial minibus fleet, more substantial Ivecos arrived; 67 (E167 UKR) is one of the Robin Hood-bodied versions of 1987 seen here at Folkestone bus station on the F2 to Hollands Avenue in June 1992. She carries the seventy-fifth anniversary logo but looks in need of a repaint judging from the worn red band. AUTHOR

replaced the former 54x series of 'big bus' services across the town, now running a combined frequency of every 3–4 minutes along the Cheriton Road. The F7 provided the former 547 Stanbury Crescent/Golden Valley service with F8/9 the limited operations to Holywell Avenue/Lynwood and Broadmead. At Canterbury, Minilink services C1–4 (and later C5) were provided to the Hales Place/London Road estate/Spring Lane estate/Kent and Canterbury Hospital terminals; the services to Hales Place ran every 6 minutes and this, plus the introduction of a zonal fares system with the ability to transfer between services, made the new services far more flexible for passengers. Ashford was the only town not to renumber their new Minilink services and, surprisingly, used existing numbers 503/505 for the new minibuses operating from Kennington to the Harvey Hospital every 10 minutes; and the 507 to South Willesborough, running every 15 minutes. Services to South Ashford, again retaining their 501/502 group numbers, remained 'big bus' although Farmers gained supported Sunday cross-town variant 531.

On the country routes running through or from Ashford, the 10 to Maidstone and Folkestone was now split at Ashford on weekdays, with the Folkestone leg mostly commercial and run by East Kent, and the Maidstone leg supported by KCC and jointly operated with Boro'line Maidstone, the successors of Maidstone Borough Transport, rather than M&D. On Sundays it ran through as a completely subsidized operation. Deregulation had seen the Maidstone area scheme abolished. East Kent was successful in retaining a number of tendered services based around Ashford, including the 424/524 out to Smarden and Pluckley, the 517 hourly town service to Godinton Park, the 518 to Hastingleigh/East Brabourne and the 521 to Westwell, as well as the 511–3 group out to New Romney and Lydd.

The trunk route 400/401 from Canterbury now saw East Kent operations terminating at Tenterden or Rolvenden instead of Hastings, again with some journeys supported by KCC.

East Kent were also successful, with the exception of the Sunday 604 group mentioned beforehand, in gaining tendered operations on full or partially supported routes in and around Canterbury, including the 612 group to Deal, the 622/623 to Plucks Gutter, the 625 to Whitstable/Seasalter and the 626/629 to Herne Bay via Broomfield, Hoath or Marshside. The company also returned to operate the 638 between Faversham and Tankerton. Through-workings to Maidstone from Canterbury ceased as only the 603 to Faversham remained with East Kent, with the exception of the 333, which continued on Sundays as it became a KCC-supported operation (and was renumbered 833 in January 1988).

AFTER DEREGULATION – THE DUST SETTLES

Once the major upheaval of deregulation was overcome, further Minilink service conversions took place. In January 1988 a number of services at Thanet were reorganized in the Broadstairs, Northdown Park, Dane Valley Garlinge and Westgate areas, providing more frequent commercial services; confusingly, the new numbers ranged from 12 to 18, duplicating several service numbers in the Folkestone area. There was still an element of KCC support in the Dane Valley and Northdown Park area on evenings and Sundays, running as services 61/A. At Deal, 1 February 1988 saw Minilink town services introduced taking numbers D80–2 and D86/96/97, while another new service, numbered 84, served Sholden from 16 January 1989. The 84 only lasted until April 1990 and revisions to the Minilink services at the same time saw most of the hourly D81/82 circulars via St Nicholas Close replaced by improvements to other services.

At Ashford in March 1988 Minilink buses were introduced on the 502 to Stanhope with increased weekday services of every 7–8 minutes, while the 'big bus' 501 to Arlington and Singleton was improved to a 15-minute frequency. From 29 March 1988 Folkestone's 19 and 26 services were joined to provide an hourly through link between Saltwood and Hawkinge/Densole, taking the former

Contemporary minibuses with the Fords were Freight Rover Sherpas, evidenced in this trio, numbers 35, 39 and 44, on Canterbury Minilink services in August 1987. AUTHOR

One of the 1989 Metrobuses with high-backed seats, 7761 (F761 EKM), awaits custom at Sandling station on the 558 in May 1992, a route by now back in the hands of East Kent. AUTHOR

By March 1992, when this view was taken, the dual-purpose ECW-bodied 'B51' Leyland Leopards of 1982 had largely gravitated to stage work, most wearing this attractive version of the East Kent livery, which had its origins in the later NBC style. 8836 (BKR 836Y) enters Lenham's picturesque square heading for Ashford on the 10, which had been split into two sections. AUTHOR

number although 26 was retained for the KCC-supported Folkestone to Densole journeys on Sundays.

KCC were now settling in regarding tendering, and as matters progressed East Kent saw a good number of mainly rural services passing to other smaller operators as a result of the competitive process. For example, in 1988 Town & Around gained the 558/559 service from Hythe to Canterbury, Kent Coach Tours (Farmer) the Ashford to Faversham 666 (and town service 517), Seabrook Coach Company ran the 591 from Dover to Folkestone via Alkham and Leisure Motors operated most of the Dover to Guston/Martin service, 593. On Romney Marsh, services 511–3 had been won from East Kent by Hastings & District in 1988 although by April 1990 it would pass to Westbus, who also gained the main service on the 558 with the evening journeys to Sandling station captured by East Kent, a sign of the dynamics of the tender process. At Canterbury, Poynters had now become firmly established on the former East Kent 620 to Waltham, Hastingleigh and Bodsham and the 667 group to Charing gaining both on 1 February 1988. On the other hand, the Sunday operation on the 10 from Folkestone through to Maidstone was regained by East Kent in April 1990 following a period of operation by Town & Around and Allways.

In response to persistent competition from an operator 'cherry picking' in Herne Bay, the company had been operating a competing service 647 from April 1990; on 31 July it was relaunched as the HY-TEK minibus running from Greenhill to Herne together with service 657 to Canterbury, while the 607 provided an improved Sunday service in response to the competition. In Canterbury itself the university service was enhanced by new route 601 to Darwin College, branded the Beagle, introduced from 23 July and running every 15 minutes. Over at Thanet, Chisholm

(Thanet Bus) had been a persistent thorn in the side of East Kent but in 1990 a measure of accommodation had been reached that saw Chisholm operating the 172 at Ramsgate and East Kent withdrawing some of their own local competing Marinair-branded services. For a time Chisholm's competition would see Thanet's Sunday operations cease completely in 1991, although Stagecoach's reaction was a different matter and Chisholm threw in the towel in 1995. Another competitor running local services in the area was the Eastonways concern, which would prove more long-lived than Chisholm, eventually succumbing in 2013 after a fire in their depot that saw Stagecoach East Kent stepping into the breach to operate their KCC-contracted services.

A successful venture at Canterbury was the 921, a limited-stop service to Aylesham introduced in 1989, which by September 1990 was also running on Saturdays. It

Ramsgate harbour in May 1991 sees 8513 (XSU 913), one of the stylish Bova coaches absorbed with the Marinair business in 1991, loading on National Express service 001 for London. The coach dated from 1984 and was re-registered from A513 HBC in 1990. AUTHOR

largely replaced the 621, although this retained a Saturday-only operation. A more tenuous service was the 611 from Ramsgate to Deal, which from 2 April 1990 ran through to Kingsdown, with some journeys running via Worth rather than Eastry and numbered 631. This resulted in Deal's local service 86 to Kingsdown being withdrawn. Later the 611 would be cut back to Sandwich, no longer serving Ramsgate, and the link would have to await a new initiative from Stagecoach. From 1 April 1990 Folkestone's Minilink services were extensively revised, with the Cheriton Road weekday frequency widened to 6 minutes; this was mainly because of changes to routes in the East Cliff area, with the trunk F1 from Creteway Down to Cheriton maintained at a 15-minute frequency.

Meanwhile the new Eurotunnel exhibition centre at Folkestone saw seasonal service 17A running to the site from the bus station on Tuesdays to Saturdays from May to September 1990. The following year it became Minilink F6 running from the harbour; on Sundays an extension of F1 covered the route. In September 1991 most weekday Folkestone-Hawkinge extensions on the 19 were withdrawn; Millfields/Aerodrome now served by diversions of through workings on services 16/A. Minilink changes at Dover also occurred from 1 April 1990 and larger-capacity minibuses replaced the 'big buses' on the Whitfield service together with some economies. These larger-capacity minibuses also allowed Ashford's remaining 'big bus' town service 501 to become a Minilink operation from 20 May 1990. From 28 October 1990 East Kent was running back to Hastings from the Weald on services 400/401 while also working the 300 tendered variant on Sundays from Ashford jointly with Coastal Coaches.

FROM THE SEVENTY-FIFTH ANNIVERSARY TO TAKEOVER

The year 1991 marked seventy-five years of East Kent and a diamond logo with '75' was featured on vehicles and publicity. A special brochure was produced, reminiscent of that published in 1966 but on a much smaller scale. Metrobus 7755 was painted in the traditional pre-1971 livery. The festivities culminated in a celebratory rally held at Folkestone's Eurotunnel Exhibition site on Saturday 7 September. The event featured a road run of a wide range of preserved and operational East Kent vehicles and a static display at which the company stall had commemorative material on sale, such as mugs and old photographs. The display vehicles ranged from a superbly restored Tilling-Stevens of 1930 to one of the latest long-wheelbase Leyland Olympi-

The seventy-fifth anniversary was marked by the issue of this brochure summarizing the changes to the company over the years. AUTHOR'S COLLECTION

ans. One unusual postscript was that open-top VR 0977, made redundant by the arrival of the convertible cars from Southdown, operated service F6 to the site and the following week was used on a number of services in conjunction with the Shepway Festival, venturing as far afield as Lydd. On the administration side, responsibility for Dover passed to Folkestone in October while Thanet took over at Deal, allowing economies in the overall managerial structure.

The persistent competition at Herne Bay caused more activity in reaction: the 604 group reverted to a 15-minute circular service from 3 February 1991, all running via Greenhill, while new service 635 was introduced to run from Grand Drive to Hillborough via the hospital, with services 647/657 being withdrawn. Further response to the competition was the introduction of a 30-minute service on weekday mornings on the 625 from Seasalter to Whitstable by means of extra short-workings between these points, supplementing the Canterbury service, which underwent a slight reduction as a result. Meanwhile at Canterbury the recently introduced 601 to the University was reduced to a 30-minute frequency. Eventually, in April, the competition at Herne Bay collapsed and some of East Kent's earlier responses, such as the additional journeys on the 625, ceased.

At Dover, from 24 February, the hourly 90A weekday workings from Folkestone to St Margaret's Bay were withdrawn and replaced by diverting them to Elvington and Sandwich as 94s, maintaining a 30-minute frequency between Folkestone and Dover. This change replaced the former 561, which had previously operated from Dover to Sandwich.

Minilink services were reorganized many times in 1991; losses of tenders at Thanet from 31 March allowed a reorganization removing the duplication of service numbers with Folkestone routes and saw the withdrawal of evening and Sunday operations. The renumbering included the 31/32 serving Garlinge–Dane Valley/hospital; the 34/35 serving Birchington Sherwood Estate–Newington/Ramsgate/Broadstairs or Northdown Park; with services 36/37 running from Northdown Park to Newington/Ramsgate/Broadstairs. The Newington and Northdown Park areas were supplemented by local services 33 and 39 running from Ramsgate and Margate respectively. At Folkestone and Dover, their changes from 2 April saw, at the former, a further widening of intervals down the Cheriton Road to 7–8 minutes, largely through a reduction of services to the East Cliff area; while at Dover, services to Maxton and St Radigund's were also reduced to 30- and 15-minute intervals respectively. The Minilink services at Canterbury and Deal were also rationalized in October, while Dover was reorganized again with the more frequent routes reduced to a 15-minute frequency. This saw a large reduction in the number of minibuses required at Dover, although the service reductions in both April and October were ameliorated slightly by the operation of larger 23-seaters. Thanet was not immune either, and the new services of March were also revised, seeing the withdrawal of the 31 at Margate and curtailment of the routes 34/36, removing the former south of Margate Hospital and both from serving Broadstairs. A more general revision at this time saw Saturday afternoon headways thinned out on many Minilink routes, reflecting lower demand.

Thanet's big buses were also changed in March 1991 consequent upon the KCC tender losses temporarily removing all Sunday operation, with weekday frequencies reduced. East Kent's main competitor, Chisholm, had gained tenders involving services 8B and 9B from Margate/Ramsgate/Broadstairs to Canterbury and Minnis Bay on Sundays as well as the weekday evening service on 9B. Later, in October, the 833 tender would also be lost, ending the workings to Maidstone from Canterbury. Yet earlier, in March, East Kent gained the contract for new service 21 from Lyddon-Sea and New Romney to Ashford via Ham

One of the later Ivecos from 1990, 95 (G95 SKR) with Phoenix body, runs along Margate's seafront in June 1995 on service 32 to Garlinge, which had been introduced in the changes of 1991. Despite the Stagecoach takeover in 1993 it is still carrying the old East Kent colours. MIKE ANSELL

East Kent took the opportunity of the special road run at the seventy-fifth anniversary rally in September 1991 to display some of the latest entrants to the fleet shown by Optare 1401 (J401 LKO) at Seabrook in the new Park & Ride livery, hotly pursued by an Olympian and Metrobus 7755. AUTHOR

The days of docks services were numbered by the time this photograph was taken of Folkestone's shuttle in March 1993, now numbered 151 but originally carrying code number 133 in 1975, thence duplicating and finally replacing stage service 101. 1552 (GFN 552N) one of the short Nationals reinstated in 1982/3 is crossing the harbour branch line; both it and Seacat services from Folkestone are now long gone. MIKE ANSELL

Street. This was let by the Employment Service at first, later transferring to KCC, while later in the year, in December, East Kent registered the Boro'line services on route 10, taking over all their journeys and removing the joint operation.

One major event in September 1991 was the introduction of the new Park & Ride scheme from a specially designed site at Canterbury, Sturry Road, following the success of the earlier schemes in place for some years, the latest being located at Kingsmead. The dedicated DAF/Optare Deltas were used for the Sturry Road site and it would be the fore-runner of the major future expansion of the concept.

The following year started a little better for East Kent. They gained some KCC tenders in Ashford from 30 March involving services 523/524 to Smarden/Pluckley (the 523 being the former 424) and 525/526 to Aldington; the company had already decided to operate all the weekday services on the 10 commercially thus avoiding any risk of loss through tendering. The 525/526 were later exchanged with Farmer in November 1992 for their workings on the 401/402. The lesson of the disappointing results of tenders in 1991 had not been lost on the company and in May East Kent registered a number of commercial services based at Thanet. On Sundays the 8B was operated commercially to/

Even with unibus advertising, the East Kent livery was still very attractive and would be sadly missed when Stagecoach took over. Car 7658 (XJJ 658V) runs along Ashford Road at Chartham in May 1991 on the 652 to Chilham via Chartham, a route that had its origins in the Drew's services taken over in 1974. AUTHOR

from Canterbury, while a further competing service with Chisholm's operations, the 7, from Birchington to Ramsgate via Margate/Broadstairs, was introduced firstly on Mondays to Fridays in June. In conjunction with this a system of zonal fares in Thanet was introduced to offer better value on East Kent's services in the area. As a result, KCC then withdrew their relevant tendered services, compromising the viability of Chisholm's operations. However, East Kent lost the 'Kent Karrier' Margate to Westgate, Warren Drive, service 51, from June to Easton of Ramsgate. Further positive developments were seen at Herne Bay when from 23 May 1992 the 635 was revised to provide a regular scrvice to Reculver, extending eastwards from Hillborough, the service running from the Westcliff/Grand Drive end of town. One interesting venture from November was service 410, linking Canterbury with Maidstone but via Ashford, one journey each way on weekdays.

East Kent's provision of courtesy services to Dover docks, dating back to early NBC days, was now reducing. Following the Stagecoach takeover it would gradually fall off, largely as a result of changing requirements – the Channel Tunnel would open in 1994. Shortly afterwards involvement in this docks work would cease. Despite traditional areas of work now retracting, the opening of new superstores in this era was already providing a useful stream of new services, some under contract, although many of them would turn out to be of short duration. Examples included service 34 operat-

ing from Birchington to Sainsbury's at Westwood from 4 December 1990, while contract code 101 would also operate at Thanet serving stores at the Westwood site from outlying areas. In 1992 more new Sainsbury's stores opened at Folkestone, Ashford and Chestfield, also with special services and with vehicles painted in Sainsbury's colours (one Iveco and two Nationals) to operate them. Later, in the Stagecoach era, the Ashford store would be served from Tenterden and Pluckley between October 1993 and March 1994 by routes S6/S7. Another new business venture in 1992 would be a service from Canterbury to Howlett's Zoo near Bekesbourne from June to September, numbered 177, which had operated in the later NBC days (1984–6) as service 600. The service was reincarnated under Stagecoach in 2014, now numbered 200.

However, despite – or probably because of – better success in tendering and the fact that East Kent's operations were returning an annual operating profit of more than £1m, predators were gathering. In 1993 Stagecoach made a bid of £4.3m for the company (formally known as the East Kent Travel Group), which was accepted. East Kent had survived nationalization and, for a brief period, undergone a resurgence that, with the new livery, reminded one of the former company. The end was now in sight and on 7 September 1993 the all-enveloping Stagecoach would take over and the outward identity of the 'old East Kent' would finally, to all intents and purposes, be lost.

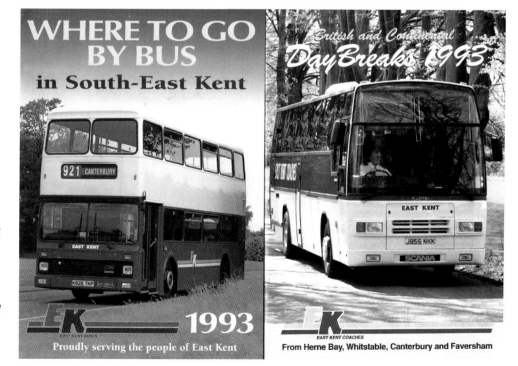

In the last year of independent operation under the East Kent Travel brand, the company produced some attractive brochures, as shown by these two examples promoting bus travel and coach tours, the former featuring one of the shorter Olympians, while the latter featured 8856 (J856 NKK), the smart Scania with Plaxton body acquired in 1992. AUTHOR'S COLLECTION

CHAPTER THIRTEEN

THE STAGECOACH ERA

NEW STRUCTURE AND DEPOT CHANGES

The takeover by Stagecoach was viewed with sadness by many employees and enthusiasts and, it must be said, that the youthful organization of the time went through a number of teething pains. However, in the longer term, 'Stagecoach in East Kent' has acquitted itself well, both in terms of services to passengers and in supporting the memory of the former East Kent through assistance to enthusiasts. It restored AEC Regent V MFN 946F in the old livery as well as repainting Olympians 14808, 14821 and 16246 into that livery from 2002 onwards to celebrate various landmarks in the former East Kent history, including the ninetieth anniversary in 2006. Concerning fares, Stagecoach's corporate policy saw the Megarider or Dayrider name adopted for area-based tickets, while the Explorer was retained for the system-wide tickets. Special tickets for the University of Kent at Canterbury are entitled Unirider.

Management of the unit was first from Stagecoach South at Lewes, although the local office at North Lane, Canterbury was initially maintained for a time before being disposed of; the remaining staff moved, via temporary accommodation at the former Coach & Horses pub, to the reconstructed bus station and new offices at the opposite end from the previous block in 2000–1. In 1999 management functions returned to Canterbury from Lewes although the legal address was first shown as the Stagecoach London base at Ilford, the Canterbury, St Georges Lane address being used from November 2002, bringing the Hastings and later, in 2008, Eastbourne management within its remit. Following internal debate, from June 2014 both Eastbourne and Hastings came under East Kent's operating licence; the origin of this was that the legal lettering 'East Kent Road Car Co. Ltd.' remained on vehicles in the former East Kent area – one proposal would have seen it change. Therefore the centenary year will be ushered in with the East Kent Road Car name still carried on vehicles, an apt commemoration

The local Stagecoach management have held the history of East Kent in high regard, repainting three modern vehicles in the old livery to celebrate anniversaries in 2005–6. One of the Olympians from the East Kent travel era in 1993 displays the colours at the celebration of fifty years of Folkestone's bus station in March 2005. AUTHOR

At first Stagecoach retained a number of coaches for tours work in an adaptation of the former livery, now as East Kent Coaches, shown on Plaxton-bodied Volvo, 8405 (M405 BFG) in Boulogne in October 1997. Contemporary as well as earlier Volvo coaches carried National Express white for use on their London services. MIKE ANSELL

of 100 years of service. East Kent remains the dominant operator in the area although small competitors, such as Regent Coaches, coexist, albeit running mainly KCC-tendered services. One interesting takeover, in 2003 by mutual agreement, was the Town & Around concern based at Folkestone, which had been operating a mix of services since NBC days; this involved one Dennis Dart being taken into stock. East Kent also stepped in in 2013 when Easton-ways failed, as recorded earlier.

Then and now at Hythe, Red Lion Square. The view of Reliance coach DJG 621C in September 1969 contrasts with the modern image of 8902 (S902 CCD), one of the 1999 Volvo B10Ms with Jonckheere body in National Express 'Shuttle' branding in August 2001, both bound for Dover. 8902 is on service 021 in the more anonymous national scheme – it was previously numbered L3 with East Kent as shown by the earlier view. The period bus shelter, for long a feature at Hythe, the brewery and bus stop with guard rails have all gone. Only the brewery perimeter wall remains. AUTHOR/MIKE ANSELL

Under Stagecoach there have been some further changes at depots and outstations. At Ashford a volte-face saw the Station Road premises closing for good in 1995 and operations moving back to the reacquired Cobbs Wood site. The Deal outstation at South Street finally closed on 15 May 1999. The bus station function had already ceased at the site from 28 May 1994, while the old premises in the centre of Dover, at Russell Street, closed on 24 February 2008, operations moving up to a new site above the town near Whitfield. On Romney Marsh the former small East Kent depot at New Romney was closed in September 2000, but changing circumstances saw a new outstation opened at Old Romney in 2012. More recently, the hardstanding at Canterbury, The Garth closed in July 2015 whilst Herne Bay's depot is planned to be replaced by new premises at Eddington Lane in 2016 after many years' delay.

The conclusion of the centenary story, moving to 'Stage-coach East Kent', will, of necessity, be more limited; the corporate ethos and scale of operations, for example, in terms of vehicle transfers between fleets across England and Scotland, would be an impossible task to record in depth here.

THE STAGECOACH FLEET

One disappointing fact was the replacement of the priva-tised East Kent livery by Stagecoach's corporate livery of white with red, blue and orange stripes. Fortunately, at the inception Stagecoach retained the coach tour operations

Stagecoach began to make its mark with the introduction of the 'Compass' group of services, with additional branding applied to the corporate Stagecoach livery. Number 660 (K790 DAO), a 1993 Volvo B10M, one of the numerous examples with Alexander 'PS' body, this one transferred from the Stagecoach Cumberland operation in 1994, loads at Dover Eastern Docks on anticlockwise service 100 in July 1997. MIKE ANSELL

Mercedes Benz 709Ds with Alexander Sprint bodywork replaced the old guard of minibuses from 1995–6. Bus 968 (N968 NAP) seems to have a struggle worthy of a Himalayan mountaineer as she ascends Maxton Road on Dover's D5 service in May 2001. MIKE ANSELL

The low-floor 'Easy Access' Dennis Dart SLFs of 1998 with Alexander bodies were transferred from Thanet to Ashford, as shown by 21 (R821 DCD) on service 1 at Arlington. MIKE ANSELL

under the 'Daybreak' brand and with it, the former East Kent Coaches red and cream colours. Eventually, Stagecoach decided to move out of the local tour market and by 2000 the former coach livery had gone; the remaining coaches operated would be those provided under subcontract to National Express and in their livery, which was changed to Express Shuttle in 1997. One exception was Volvo 8410, which carried Stagecoach livery and branding for the Duo Line service to Boulogne until this ceased in 2001.

Stagecoach ownership has seen many transfers between their various fleets. Initially, more Iveco minibuses appeared while new and transferred-in big bus deliveries first saw Volvo B10M/Alexander PS single-deckers to 48-seat dual-purpose specification arriving from 1994, as well as some transferred Leyland Olympians later, followed by a large number of new Volvo Olympian/Alexander double-deckers from 1995. By 1996 the former minibus fleet had been replaced in its entirety by Mercedes Benz/Alexander 23- or 25-seaters, with some second-hand examples from 1990. A quintet of Dennis Lances, 1404–8, with Berkhof fully accessible bodies, came in 1994, largely replacing the DAF/Optares on the Canterbury Park & Ride for which they also had the special livery; while further Dennises in the shape of a trio of Javelins, 1105/6/8, with Plaxton dual-purpose bodies, arrived from Sussex Coastline in 1995 for the Dickensian X64 service. The mainstream coach fleet had an injection of new blood in 1994–5 with a number of Volvo B10M chassis with Plaxton Premiere bodies; eight 49-seaters with toilets for National Express work, 8911–8; and seven 53-seaters, 8404–10, for local coach work. Three earlier Volvos, two with Van Hool bodies and one,

8618, with a Plaxton body, 8503/5, arrived in 1995 as a result of another internal Stagecoach transfer. The express fleet saw nine more Volvo B10Ms, 8901–9, this time with Jonckheere Mistral 50 bodies, arriving in 1998–9 carrying fleet numbers from now-withdrawn Plaxton-bodied examples. At this time a number of coaches received individual 'Spirit of' names reflecting their home area, such as 'Spirit of Folkestone'.

The bus fleet now gained a varied number of new and transferred vehicles. Dennis Darts included some new low-floor SLFs with Alexander 200 bodies (these six,

The Leyland Titans sourced from Stagecoach's London operations are represented by 7208 (OHV 688Y) on a Herne Bay local service in front of the backdrop of Reculver Towers in 1997. Most had gone by 2003. The first Stagecoach livery, exhibited here, can best be described as unflattering, particularly on double-deckers. MARTIN SMITH

18/9, 21–4, arriving in 1998, were East Kent's first low-floor buses for stage work, initially used at Thanet; they were branded as 'Easy Access Bus', subsequently gaining 'Buggy Bus' lettering when transferred to South Ashford town services in 1999). Others had Alexander Dash high-floor bodies. More new Olympian double-deckers with Alexander bodies arrived as well as second-hand examples, a number with Northern Counties or ECW bodies. An interesting transfer saw over twenty 1980–4 vintage Leyland Titans from Stagecoach London arriving from 1997; all were converted to single-door layout, numbered in the 72xx series, some with Park Royal bodies, the majority featuring the Leyland offer; they would only last until the early 2000s. A further five new Volvo B10M single-deck buses, 676–80, this time with an attractive Plaxton body, arrived in 1998 (two leaving after a year), but many other transfers in and out occurred involving the more common Alexander PS-bodied version.

Entering the 2000s, the Leyland Nationals would bow out, the last remaining being some late transfers into the fleet, and the VRs and the remaining local touring coaches would also go. Further transfers, from East London in 2000–2 saw more Scania double-decks dating from 1991/2 joining the two indigenous examples, 7781/2 with Alexander bodies, although these versions had Northern Counties bodies on the over forty vehicles transferred in and first numbered in the 77xx series. These enabled the withdrawal of the last MCW Metrobuses. Some Dennis Lance single-decks arrived from Selkent in 2000 but were quickly removed, accompanied by the Park & Ride batch once new vehicles arrived. Three Dennis Darts with high-floor Wright midibus bodies arrived from Hastings in 2002, but by now the majority of the fleet was comprised of double-deckers, a change from the bias towards single-

The later Stagecoach livery, shown here on Plaxton-bodied Volvo B10M 20679 (R679 HCD) of 1998 at Sandwich in August 2013, is a far more attractive product. To the left the former East Kent enquiry office still stands; the name remains engraved in the door lintel. AUTHOR

Most of the high-floor Dennis Darts used for rural services in the early 2000s had Alexander bodies. 32311 (N311 AMC) had arrived from the East Sussex operation in 2002. It is seen at Burmarsh Shepherd & Crook in July 2004. Service 813 had its origins in the NBC changes of the 1970s and later KCC cuts would see it disappear. MIKE ANSELL

Two styles of Northern Counties bodywork on the Volvo Olympians are shown here. Left is 16021 (P821 GMU) at Sandwich in August 2013 on the 13A, displaying the Countybus Palatine 1 style, while the right-hand image is of 16187 (S957 URJ) at Ramsgate Granville Theatre on 9 in October 2014 with the later Palatine 2 version. Judging by the nearside dome damage, both have suffered from low overhanging trees! AUTHOR

decks that had resulted from NBC policy in the 1970s/80s. New single-decks did arrive, however. MAN/Alexanders entered the fleet in 2000–1: although the first three, 1001–3, in a yellow livery for the Designer Village service at Ashford, were transfers and dated from 1999 but a further six, 1004–9, were new to East Kent and were for the Canterbury Park & Ride service. This service also gained double-deckers at the same time with the arrival of three fully accessible Dennis Tridents with Alexander ALX400 bodies, numbered 7001–3.

By 2002 the new Stagecoach 'group standard' livery would be introduced, still based on white but featuring a blue skirt and greater upswept areas of red, blue and orange relief. Various applications of the fleet branding have seen 'Stagecoach East Kent' or 'Stagecoach in East Kent' used as the fleet name. The original numbering system was now going awry as transfers from other Stagecoach companies occurred, and in 2003 a new standard Stagecoach scheme was introduced generally using the 1xxxx series for double-deckers, 2xxxx for large and 3xxxx for midi single-deck buses, 4xxxx for the smaller minibus vehicles and 5xxxx for coaches.

Through the first decade of the twenty-first century the Stagecoach East Kent fleet would undergo substantial changes as older vehicles were transferred in, including Volvo B10Ms with Plaxton bodies from Thames Transit in 2008; Alexander-bodied Dennis Dart SLFs from Hastings in 2009 (formerly from East London in 2003–4); Plaxton-bodied SLFs from Cavendish the same year; and numerous Volvo Olympian double-deckers from various sources. The new intake would also be prominent in enabling the removal of Leyland-produced Olympians and the early Scanias towards the end of the decade. Alexander/Dennis Trident double-deckers came in large numbers from 2004

Alexander Dennis E40Ds rather than Scanias were chosen for the double-deck Enviro400s used on the newly regained Park & Ride services at Canterbury in 2013. Bus 10065 (SN63 NCE) loads at Canterbury in March 2015, displaying the livery used on both single- and double-deckers employed on these services. AUTHOR

some new, others transfers, until superseded by the Scania product, still with Alexander Dennis bodies (now termed Enviro400), from 2009.

For single-decks, the Alexander Dennis Dart was the favoured product – twenty-two SLFs, 34645–62/844–7, with Alexander Pointer 2 bodies arrived in 2004–6 with Loop branding, while the Enviro300 body was carried by eight 12.5m (41ft) Darts, 27516–23, delivered in 2006 for the Diamond network, also suitably branded. Minibuses were completely replaced, the old Ivecos giving way to the far more advanced Optare Solo delivered between 2004 and 2008, of which forty were maintaining the bulk of town services at the end of the decade; these would be further strengthened by internal transfers to East Kent from within the Stagecoach East Kent and East Sussex parent. Two other larger Optares, 25242–3, this time Versas and first branded for Ashford's E-line route, arrived in 2009. Stagecoach East Kent's contribution to the National Express services continued to be updated on a regular basis; earlier Volvo B10M/Plaxtons were replaced in 2002 by ten B12Ms, 53001–10, also with Plaxton bodies. In 2005 eleven Volvo B12Ms from 2003 with Transbus Paragon Expressliner bodies, numbered 53011–21, transferred in, followed in 2010 by fifteen Scanias, 59201–15, with Caetano bodies dating from 2006–7, although these were replaced by 2013 with thirteen Volvo B9Rs with Plaxton Elite bodies dating from 2010, numbered 53701–13 reflecting a reduced express requirement.

On the bus side, aside from second-hand transfers, four new Darts, 36122-5, with Enviro200 bodies appeared in 2010 whilst more recently thirty-four new Alexander Dennis E20Ds with Enviro200 bodies, 36855–81/91–7, arrived in 2013, twenty-four with Loop branding, three

Stagecoach's contribution to the National Express network in early 2015 was Volvo B9Rs with Plaxton bodies. Number 53708 (AE10 JTU) runs through the village of Sarre on the 022 in March 2015. In East Kent days this was the L1 service. AUTHOR

Table 12   Summary of the Stagecoach East Kent Fleet at November 2014

Type	Chassis	Body	Fleet Nos.	Total	Date/Notes
Heritage Double-deck	AEC Regent V	Park Royal 72-seat	19946	1	1967
Double-deck	Alexander Dennis E40D	Alexander Dennis Enviro400	10063–6	4	2013 *For P&R service*
	Scania N230UD	Alexander Dennis Enviro400	15180–9; 15440–3; 15475–506 (range); 15538–62; 15701–5; 15903/4; 15914–9	77	2008/9/10/14 *15914–9 are bio-fuel for Unibus 15180–9 to Gold specification*
	Volvo Olympian	Northern Counties Countybus	16012–26 (range); 16187/8	11	1996/9
	Volvo Olympian	Alexander RH	16130/9	2	1998
	Volvo Olympian	Alexander RL	16270–99 (range); 16315; 16356–90 (range); 16501–9 (range); 16592/3; 16739–92 (range)	34	1995–8 *16315 and some of 16356–90 have dual-purpose seating*
	Volvo Olympian	East Lancs	16804	1	1996
	Alexander/Dennis Trident	Alexander ALX 400	17402; 17689/90; 18160–7/9–71; 18331	15	1999–2001/4–6
	Dennis Trident	Plaxton President	17691/3; 18292	3	2000/1
	Alexander Dennis Trident	Alexander Dennis Enviro400	19005–59/19659 (range)	15	2006/10
Single-deck coach	Volvo B9R	Plaxton	53701–13	13	2010
Single-deck bus	Volvo B10M	Plaxton Countybus	20007–8/10/1/20654/79	6	1998
	Volvo B10M	Alexander PS	20312; 20638–59 (range)	5	1993/5 *Dual-purpose seats*
	Volvo B10M	Alexander PS	20832/955/6	3	1996/7
	MAN 18.220	Alexander or Transbus ALX 300	22004–9; 22057; 22192/4; 22943/4	11	1999/2000/1/3
	Optare V1040	Optare Versa	25242/3	2	2009
	Alexander Dennis Dart	Alexander Dennis Enviro300	27516–23	8	2006
	Alexander Dennis E30D	Alexander Dennis Enviro300	27891/919–24	7	2013 *All except 27891 are branded for Park & Ride*
	Dennis Dart SLF	Alexander ALX200	33022; 34064/71	3	1998
	Dennis Dart SLF	Plaxton Pointer	33385	1	2001
	Transbus Dart SLF	Transbus Pointer 2	34482/3/8	3	2004
	Dennis Dart SLF	Alexander Pointer 2	34647/8/50; 34651–60/2; 34778; 34844	16	2004/6
	Alexander Dennis Dart/E20D	Alexander Dennis Enviro200	36122–5; 36855–97	38	2010/13
Midibuses	Optare M	Optare Solo	47112–20/63–6; 47173–7; 47369–79; 47461; 47477/8; 47660–9; 47676–88	55	2004–9
	Optare M	Optare Solo	47560/1	2	2009 *ex-Eastonways 2011*
	Optare M	Optare Solo	47874	1	2013 *Park & Ride*

Source: MDEK Bus Club

Notes: For clarity, cars listed broadly in fleet number order within type rather than date new. Excludes reserve and withdrawn cars. All buses D/C. Seat capacities not recorded due to varied configurations. Fleet numbers and totals approximate, due to the high degree of movement between Stagecoach fleets in the southeast area.

others badged for the Diamond network. Five Scania/Alexander Dennis Enviro400 double-deckers, 15914–9, entering service in September 2013 were to bio-fuel specification for Unibus services with an appropriate green livery and 'bio' branding. The regaining of the Canterbury Park & Ride services in 2013 saw four Alexander Dennis E40D/ Enviro400 double-deckers, 10063–6, and six E30D/ Enviro300 single-decks, 27919–24, arriving in September, the latter joining standard-liveried E30D 27891 which arrived in August, with another Optare Solo, 47874, for the P5 service.

Ten new high-specification Scania double-deckers, 15180–9, arrived in October 2014 for the Gold upgrading of service 16, while around twenty Transbus Darts with Pointer 2 bodies transferred in at the turn of the year, joining others acquired earlier, to enable the replacement of non-DDA-compliant vehicles. Some of the latter Darts have gone to the fleets at Hastings and Eastbourne, which now come under the East Kent operating licence. Other second-hand vehicles from Stagecoach London, in the form of Dennis Trident/Alexander ALX 400 double-deckers modified to single-door format and DDA-compliant specification, were arriving in early 2015, with further cascaded Darts and Tridents expected over the year. This will see the remaining older non-compliant vehicles gradually disappearing – quite a change, as East Kent had latterly become the major user of B10M single-decks and Olympian double-deckers in the Stagecoach group, holding sixty-four Olympians and twenty-three B10Ms in February 2014.

Ending this analysis of the Stagecoach East Kent fleet as it moves towards the centenary, the bus fleet composition has settled down to a degree of standardization, mostly on Scania and Alexander/Dennis products with Optares for the smaller vehicle requirements. Further cascades from within the Stagecoach group are likely in 2016, and thirty of the new, more fuel-efficient and environmentally friendly Enviro400 MMC (major model change) double-deckers on Scania chassis are expected by the beginning of 2016 to upgrade and increase the 4 and 6 group of services. The fleet certainly now presents a modern image to the passenger, and the recent upgrades, for example to Gold concept, and the new Enviro400 MMC due to arrive by the centenary can only enhance this view.

STAGECOACH – A NEW GENERATION OF SERVICES

Stagecoach's tenure can be characterized by innovation and expansion, although some early developments arose

as a robust response to competitors, particularly Thanet Bus. The introduction of the hourly 'Pickwick Express', X81, from Broadstairs/Ramsgate to Canterbury on 2 April 1994, with the similarly branded X80 from Ramsgate and Margate to Canterbury following in May, with a full service from 4 July, were the first examples. Later innovations, from 24 October 1994, were the rebranding of the former 921 from Canterbury to Aylesham as X90, the 'Aylesham Collier', with a half-hourly frequency and a new service from Margate/Ramsgate (from Birchington in April 1995) to Sandwich with connections to Deal – the X70 'Sandwich Express'; this had started in August as short-workings of X80 between Margate and Ramsgate. On 31 October 1994 an hourly X63 from Davington/Faversham to Canterbury also commenced. 'Pickwick Express' branding was also intended to apply to express services X11/12 between Canterbury and Deal, but apart from display on one leaflet it never materialized.

In 1995 ventures into former M&D territory first saw a Minster–Canterbury service, X65, running from 22 January (on college days for students), then the 'Dickensian', service X64, running from 5 May (weekdays) between Canterbury and Chatham/Rochester. The X64 was later extended to Strood from 8 October 1995 and the X65 to Leysdown on 27 October 1996. Eventually, on 5 July 1998, the X81 took over the route to Strood and on 5 January 2000 its short-workings running as far as Canterbury were renumbered X82 to permit operation under domestic rules for bus services rather than the more restrictive EU legislation (required for services over 50km); it also enabled

A number of transferred-in Scanias joined the two already in stock, although these had Northern Counties bodywork as shown on 15339 (J139 HMT) at Cliftonville Foreland Avenue on the X82 in July 2004. This was a short-working of the X81 'Pickwick Express', subsequently changing in 2004 when the more appropriately numbered 9 was introduced for the Broadstairs/Ramsgate link to Canterbury. MIKE ANSELL

passengers to distinguish between journeys bound for the Medway towns and those for Canterbury alone. The longer X81 ceased on 28 October 2001, with the X82 strengthened to compensate for its withdrawal. When the Thanet Loop was introduced in October 2004 (*see* below) the X82 was also withdrawn and new service 9 was introduced between Broadstairs/ Ramsgate and Canterbury, recreating, in part, the original service 9. Prior to this the number had been used for a local Thanet service. It is interesting to note that the two main services to Canterbury from Thanet now run under their 1937 numbers, the 8 from Margate and the 9 from Ramsgate. These are of course just two of a number of the current Stagecoach East Kent services using their original numbers; other former links, such as from Minster to Wingham and Canterbury, once service 58, now runs as new service 11, while even the 36 now runs regularly between Margate and Herne Bay once again following on from the Kent Compass innovations described below.

One of the Alexander-bodied Volvo Olympians from 1995, 368 (N368 LPN), is captured at Dover Pencester Road on the Clipper service 111 to Deal in June 2000. MIKE ANSELL

The real foundation of today's busy Stagecoach East Kent network can arguably be traced back to the decision to introduce an adventurous concept called Kent Compass from 1 April 1997. This loop network ran both anticlockwise (services 100/101) and clockwise (services 200/201) between Dover, Deal, Ramsgate, Margate, Herne Bay, Whitstable, Canterbury and back to Dover. It reintroduced the link between Margate and Herne Bay on the former 36 route, abandoned for many years. On weekdays it ran at 30-minute intervals on the northern section between Canterbury, Herne Bay and Ramsgate and hourly on the remaining southern section.

This was then followed by the 'Kent Clipper' loop from 16 May 1999, linking Canterbury, Folkestone, Dover, Deal and back direct to Canterbury, numbered 111 (anticlockwise) and 211 (clockwise). Both Compass and Clipper had specific branding applied to vehicles and both interworked with, or partly replaced, pre-existing routes; for example, the former was part of a 10-minute local service across Thanet with the 8/9/88/99 and also replaced the 15 in the day between Canterbury and Dover, while the latter replaced the 13 and 16 services between Canterbury,

Deal or Folkestone in the day. Both Compass and Clipper also largely replaced the Deal–Dover–Folkestone service 90 over all or part of the route, while service 711 'Coastliner' from Dover to Hastings/Eastbourne provided, with the Clipper, a 30-minute service between Dover and Folkestone and then went on to inter-work with the services across Romney Marsh. East Kent commenced operation on 711 from 7 May 1995, with companion 714 via Lewes, both running from Folkestone to Brighton. The 714 ceased by 26 May 1996 while the 711 would start back from Dover from 30 March 1997. At the time, Stagecoach was consolidating its interests westwards; this also saw the 400 from Canterbury extending for a time to Eastbourne, from 25 May 1997, under the Wayfarer brand, later cut back to Hastings on 31 October 1999, as was the 711.

Following experience, in 2001 it was decided to revert to more localized services as delays and unreliability caused by 'losing' buses for four hours from their home base (the full running time of the Compass service) were unsustainable; but the impact that improving services to frequencies undreamt of only a few years previously would have on ridership levels and revenues was not lost on Stagecoach East Kent. The publicity format also changed. Prior to this, the former East Kent Buses leaflet format with the initial

The earlier timetable leaflets (left) were broadly in the style of the earlier products but with Stagecoach branding until replaced by the revised corporate style as illustrated on the right. AUTHOR'S COLLECTION

the assistance of the government's Kickstart funding programme, running every 10 minutes between Margate and Ramsgate either via Westwood or Broadstairs with clockwise and anticlockwise loops, largely following the former tramway-replacement service 50 and its linked 52 route (both originally numbered 49A). It would later run at a 7- to 8-minute frequency on weekdays, an interval last experienced in the early 1960s. On 16 July 2006 the circular 'Diamond' brand, linking Canterbury, Deal and Dover, was introduced, another joint initiative to reduce car use, also involving Kickstart funding. Diamond was also a circular service but unlike the Compass and Clipper concept, part of which mileage it ran over, it featured more traditional numbers – 13/14 between Canterbury and Deal and 15 between Sandown/Deal and Canterbury via Dover. Another part of the Kickstart programme saw improvements to Aylesham, with the 89 group now providing a 30-minute weekday service to Canterbury and hourly to Dover superseding the earlier Aylesham Collier initiative.

The next improvement was the 'Link' from 1 June 2007 for services 16/17 between Canterbury and Folkestone,

style of Stagecoach branding had been used, but numerous other variations had appeared, for example for the Compass services. Now the publicity would mainly be in the 21mm × 10mm pocket-size format using the new house colours of white with blue and orange relief, which is still in place in 2015.

At Sandwich, the Richborough area, which had always been a source of special services to the many factories in early days, underwent a transformation in the late 1990s with expansion of the Pfizer concern. Many contract services were run to/from the Thanet and Deal/Dover areas at this time, stimulating the issue of a special timetable booklet as well as a revitalization of the Dover–Whitfield–Sandwich–Ramsgate link in 2000 as service 94. Pfizer's decision to close their site in 2011 would end the long association of factory services with the area whilst bus service 94 would revert to its former identity as 88/A by or before 2006 (and later as 87/88/A).

Further new brands were introduced from 2004. On 6 September the 4/6 group between Canterbury, Whitstable and Herne Bay received 'Triangle' branding, while on 24 October 2004 the Thanet Loop service was launched with

The Scania product with Alexander Dennis Enviro400 body is shown by Triangle-branded 15559 (GN59 EXK), entering Canterbury bus station in March 2014 about to return to Herne Bay on the 6. The company office block is to the left, replacing the facilities at the other end, which were demolished when the bus station was rebuilt. AUTHOR

The long Alexander Dennis Dart 4s employed on the Diamond routes are challenging to manoeuvre around the turning circle at St Margaret's Bay, Bay Hill. Bus 27518 (GX06 DYY), with later Diamond branding, demonstrates this to good effect in October 2014 as it makes its way to Deal. AUTHOR

The Alexander Dennis E20Ds with Enviro200 bodies replaced Dennis Dart SLFs on Loop services in 2013. Bus 36874 (GN13 EYJ) loads at Dumpton Racing Greyhound in October 2014. The red relief is a nice concession to the former East Kent colours. AUTHOR

with 'Direct' describing the 16 and 'Scenic' for the 17, via the picturesque Elham Valley. From 5 April 2009 'Wave' branding was applied to routes 100/101/102 running across Romney Marsh from Folkestone, extending to Hastings (these were formally numbered 11/12 or 711/712); a month later, on 3 May, 'Breeze' was applied to the Thanet–Canterbury trunk route 8/8A/8X. On 5 November 2012 it was Faversham's turn, with the route from Canterbury, the 3 service group, branded as the 'Hop', reflecting the brewing industry of the area. Many of these trunk services have seen major increases in frequencies compared with the 1980s/90s; at the time of writing the Triangle runs every 10 minutes (shortly to increase), Breeze and Link Direct (now Gold) every 15 minutes, Diamond from Canterbury to Dover every 15 minutes and to Sandwich every 20 minutes, while the Wave provides a bus every 15 minutes to New Romney. More recently the Link 16 was, from 2 November 2014, rebranded as Stagecoach Gold, with upgraded vehicles featuring leather seats and free Wi-Fi.

Branding is now being discontinued but has also been applied to town services. 'Stars' was used at Thanet, 'City Arrows' at Canterbury, while 'Heart' was used at Dover and Folkestone, on services mostly operated by the Optare Solos that replaced the former minibuses on town routes, although Alexander/Dennis Darts also feature. These town services have also changed their identity from the former letter-prefixed minibus numbers; Canterbury has regained numbers in the 20 series while Dover's services are now in the 60 series with Folkestone's in the 70 series. Thanet's minibus services never carried the letter prefix. Before their current use as town service numbers, Canterbury had, by 2000, reclaimed 25/A for the Seasalter via Tyler Hill service and 26/29 for those to Herne Bay via Hoath/

Closure of Canterbury's Westgate Towers to buses in 2012/2013 resulted in a number of revisions to services. One product of this was the 26 running to the university and Hales Place, a number that was used for services to Hales Place in the 1960s. Bus 34658 (GX54 DXJ), one of the Dennis Dart SLFs from 2004, passes time at Canterbury West station in April 2014. AUTHOR

Optare Solos replaced earlier minibuses. Number 47173 (YJ05 XNG) is at Millmead Road, Cliftonville in June 2005, displaying the 'Stars' branding used at the time for these local services. MIKE ANSELL

Chislet; these services would eventually adopt their historic identities, as 5 and 7/A respectively. Over at Ashford, the former route numbering was gradually replaced by letter-branded services; A line to Stanhope was introduced on 26 November 2006, followed, much later, by B line to Park Farm and C line between Kennington and the William Harvey Hospital from 8 February 2009, with subsequent changes continuing the letter branding.

East Kent's forward-looking policy saw the Unibus services at Canterbury expand further, in line with the development at the campus, and, at the time of writing, services were running every 7–8 minutes on weekdays during term time, with a new venture 'Unibus Nite', introduced on 21 September 2014, running past 4am. Such a facility is a far cry from the limited services running in the mid-1960s. On the down side, in March 2012 the Westgate Towers in Canterbury closed to all traffic experimentally. When it was decided to reopen the Towers from April 2013 a combination of circumstances meant that buses were unable to resume operating through them and another iconic view of bus operation in East Kent was lost.

One welcome return was the success in regaining the Canterbury Park & Ride contract from October 2013, which had been lost to Kent Top Temps in mid-2008. The routes are currently numbered P1 (Sturry Road), P2 (Wincheap) and P3 (Dover Road); the vehicles for this are now resourced from the new Dover depot. As an adjunct to this, a further Park & Ride service, P5, ran from the New Dover Road site to the Kent & Canterbury Hospital using an Optare Solo, but was withdrawn from 1 January 2016. This positive note is an appropriate juncture to conclude the review of the development of East Kent's services under the Stagecoach concern as it enters its centennial year.

The new image of Stagecoach in East Kent is a fitting credit to the company as it enters its centenary year. This is demonstrated by the latest Scanias with Alexander Dennis Enviro400 bodies. Left is 15914, one of the bio-fuelled versions for university services and captured on the Campus in March 2014; while on the right, 15184 at Folkestone Manor Road is in the spectacular livery of the Gold service 16 introduced in 2014 and seen in November of that year.
AUTHOR (LEFT), MIKE ANSELL (RIGHT)

PART V

AN INSIDE VIEW – EMPLOYMENT AND TICKETING SYSTEMS

CHAPTER FOURTEEN

WORKING ON BET's EAST KENT

As a moderately sized company with, in the 1960s, over 600 vehicles and over 100 stage carriage services, the organization of East Kent in its final days of BET ownership was still labour-intensive and diverse. The following account is a snapshot of the situation in the 1968–74 period in order to give an insight into some of the backroom functions and how the service to passengers was delivered with the bus 'on the road'.

ADMINISTRATIVE AND MANAGEMENT FUNCTIONS

The central administrative functions were based at Canterbury at the head office in Station Road West, while Kirby's Lane catered for the engineering and coachwork overall management and administrative services, such as the drawing office. The head office covered five floors, with the ground floor set slightly below the main carriageway of Station Road West but level with Kirby's Lane, which it backed on to. This floor housed the main accounting and audit departments and also became the location for the first computer-based systems, introduced in the late 1960s. On the first floor, where the public access was via a flight of steps, was located the reception, the publicity office and the central tours and private hire functions. The second floor housed the secretarial department and the general manager's office. Above, the remaining floors housed the

EAST KENT
ROAD CAR COMPANY LTD

HEAD OFFICE
STATION ROAD WEST · CANTERBURY · KENT
TELEPHONE 66151 · 9

OUR REF. JMB/CAM
PE.1.   YOUR REF.

18th September, 1968.

Dear Mr. Wallace,

Referring to my letter of the 24th July and to Mr. Bodger's subsequent discussions with you, I confirm that we are now prepared to employ you on a permanent basis and that this appointment was effective from week commencing Sunday, 1st September.

The terms and conditions of the permanent appointment remain as set out in my letter of the 24th July and its enclosures.

Yours sincerely,

(P. W. Dodge)
Traffic Manager.

Mr. R. Wallace,
c/o Traffic Department,
East Kent Road Car Co. Ltd.

Where it all started! The formal letter of permanent employment for the author in September 1968 after a period when he was a temporary traffic clerk. AUTHOR'S COLLECTION

Mobile inspector Harry Nutt checks loadings on PFN 858 in August 1968 at St. Peter's while it is working the 49A, which ran via Dumpton Park Drive to Ramsgate. These intensive checks supervised by the mobiles resulted in the following summer's service frequency on the 49/50/52 group reducing to 10 minutes from the 7–8 minutes operated in 1968. AUTHOR

operational functions, the third floor the Traffic department, including licensing functions, with the fourth floor having the schedules office and a conference room.

In those days, service schedules were first prepared in isolation of allocation of crew duties. Only after the timetables were planned were they passed up to Schedules for preparation of duties. Traffic and Schedules clerks were allocated individual depots; the author commenced in the Traffic office with Rye and Hastings and went on to cover Ashford, with a brief dalliance with Folkestone, before moving to the operations side. Once the duties were prepared they were then subject to scrutiny by the union officials from the depot concerned – a critical part of the process. Often one or two duties were rejected and intense negotiation took place, in those days often at a local hostelry. One story concerns rejection of the second half of a turn that was deemed too long, albeit within legal hours. The Schedules Officer of the time was Mr Williams, a well-respected individual and a canny negotiator, having been a conductor in his first years with the Company in the 1940s. At lunchtime, he took the union representatives out for refreshment but, prior to departure, took the schedules clerk to one side and issued his instructions. On return, the officials made straight for the offending duty only to see the second half was now far more acceptable and agreed to the proposals. What they had overlooked was that the second part of the turn had not been altered; it had just been swapped with another duty!

In earlier days the duty schedules function was carried out locally, at depots, only moving to become a centralized head office function in 1946. Duties cast and timetables prepared, the former, together with individual running boards for each car – these prepared by the traffic office – were sent out to the depots. Timetable books and area posters were prepared centrally by the Traffic office, as were individual typewritten posters for specific locations, such as Ramsgate, Cannon Road, for the coach station there. This office also carried out licensing functions, for example, preparing submissions to the traffic commissioners for approval of increases in fares or service changes, requiring, in those days before deregulation, the completion of either form PSV 8 for new services or PSV 89 for changes to existing services.

The depots had a degree of autonomy in some administrative functions, however. The larger ones, such as at Thanet, Dover and Folkestone, had their own private hire managers, for example. District Superintendents were in place at Canterbury, Thanet, Dover (with Deal covered by Dover's assistant superintendent), Folkestone and Ashford – the latter covering Rye and Hastings, although at one time those two depots had been managed as a unit separate from Ashford. Depot engineers were also in place, overseeing local day-to-day maintenance and in some cases carrying out major works if necessary, although this was normally carried out at Kirby's Lane (central works) or St Stephen's (coachworks). Recruitment of operational staff was also undertaken on a local basis; conductor-training facilities were at the larger depots, as were driving instructors. Uniform issue was a centrally based function located at the former tramway depot at St Peter's, Broadstairs. Even London boasted its own local organization and had a chief inspector based at Victoria coach station who oversaw operations there, as they had their own allocation of inspectors and express service drivers.

Inspectors were also based locally although there was a cadre of mobile inspectors based at the head office who toured the whole area, on a rota basis, using two cars allocated for the purpose; in 1968 they were Morris Minors. Generally working with a special driver, or later in pairs, a 'mobile' would pop up in the middle of nowhere – owing to the flexibility of having their own car – and often catching out an unwary crew. They also assisted or oversaw operational matters such as loading checks for major changes. One amusing anecdote concerning the comparative performance of a 'Long Dog' and the mobile inspectors' Morris Minor is worth recounting. OFN 714F was one of the best cars at Folkestone at the time and a stint on the 90 saw this car Dover-bound taking full advantage of the long dash down from Capel with no boarding or alighting passengers and a straight road. A slow-moving Minor was passed with due aplomb, the bus driver foolishly not recognizing either the registration or the occupants. Efforts by the mobiles to catch 714 were in vain – they could not match its speed. Unfortunately for the driver, they did catch up with him at Pencester Road, though it is not recorded what disciplinary action was taken!

Upon the advent of NBC changes, closer cooperation between M&D and East Kent saw many functions merge; as noted earlier Station Road West was vacated by 1979 and the remaining functions moved to new premises in North Lane, Canterbury. Eventually these were also relinquished and a number of functions then passed to depots; but later, under Stagecoach management, most local administration is again carried out centrally, but from the bus station at Canterbury, a far cry from the extensive organization of BET days.

ON THE ROAD – CONDUCTING

On recruitment 'off the street', a trainee conductor would spend one week in the conducting school. That at Folke-

All crews had to carry a rule book and display their PSV badge. Here is the last East Kent BET version with conductor's and driver's PSV badges, both from the South Eastern traffic area as denoted by the 'KK' prefix. In place since the Road Traffic Act 1930, changes in later years would result in the requirement to be issued with and display PSV badges ceasing.
AUTHOR'S COLLECTION

stone was based at the depot at Kent Road. The week was spent getting familiar with the Setright machine and with waybill preparation but it also allowed a buffer time for application for one's PSV conductor's licence and for the badge and licence to arrive from the South Eastern traffic commissioners, who were based at Ivy House, Eastbourne. In those days the conductor would also have to deal with parcels, specialist transfer tickets or warrants, which all required different treatment and thus training in how to issue them. Some of the varieties of tickets issued by East Kent and the machines used are described later.

After initial training, a day had to be spent travelling to St Peter's to obtain a uniform; thereafter a further week was spent under supervision with a conductor-trainer. All being well, you were now on your own, and allocated a clock number, which was key for knowing your rostered work. Duty schedules were displayed in glass cases on two types of charts in the drivers'/conductors' booking-on rooms adjacent to the detail office. The first schedule showed what duties were allocated to each clock number in a particular week; they were basically a set of numbers, one for each day on a single line. These alternated between a set of early turns and a set of late turns. The clock numbers were on two separate pieces of paper and moved each week – drivers went 'down' and conductors went 'up'. This meant that conductors were allocated a different driver every week, unlike some companies that 'paired' crews permanently. The working week ran from Sunday to Saturday.

On the duty rota shown overleaf, odd numbers were used for early turns and even numbers for late turns. 'R' shows a rest day. '27A' was an amended duty changed after

Specimen Duty Rota Schedule – Crew, Folkestone Garage, 1970

Clock No.	Sun	Mon	Tue	Wed	Thu	Fri	Sat
↑	R	33	67	R	23	15	401
266	R	32	R	6	4	65	418
				C.3			
↑	R	509	9	27A	63	25	R

Duty 32 – Folkestone Garage, worked on 7 September 1970

Duty start	Takeover	Service/car	Handover	Car	Finish
1621 Bus Station	1631 Bouverie Road East	108/Car 1	1837 Bouverie Road East	GJG 756D/AFN 775B change-over	
	1910 Bus Station	10/Car 1	2321 Garage	AFN 779B	2331 Garage

Call-out 3 and Duty 6 – Folkestone Garage, worked on 9 September 1970

Duty start	Takeover	Service/car	Handover	Car	Finish
0740 C.3	0750 Garage	Spare 141	0910 Garage	MFN 885	
1330 Bus Station	1340 Bus Station	99/Car 2	1717 Bouverie Road East	YJG 822	
	1900 Post Office	103/Car 5	2035 Post Office	GJG 753D	2045 Bus Station

The crew of Canterbury-based 6798 FN are obviously coming off for a break or end of duty, judging by the speed she is entering the approach to the bus station on service 13 in June 1969. The conductor can be seen through the nearside window, probably picking up his ticket box; he has already changed the blind for the return working to Deal. AUTHOR

the original rotas were posted. The 4xx numbers were at this time used for Saturday work, while 3xx numbers were used for Sunday turns, although the number series were often revised when duty schedules changed. Duty 509 was an August Bank Holiday duty and on that week a special rota plus duties would be posted. Lastly, C.3 was a 'call out'. This was rostered overtime, which in this case started before the duty.

The content of the duties themselves were displayed on separate sheets for Monday to Friday, Saturdays and Sundays. Separate sheets were displayed for school holiday schedules and bank holidays. At this time there was still a large amount of crew operation at Folkestone and the author's records allow the reader to have an insight into what some duties involved and the cars worked on.

East Kent used the 'Spare' designation for cars that worked either schools/contract services or reliefs to normal services. There was no consistency to this nomenclature; many reliefs on the 105 service were at the time allocated car numbers in that group, for example 105 car 9, but other 105 reliefs carried the 'Spare' number designation.

When booking on, the conductor received a ticket machine, different each day, with a waybill that had the start numbers already recorded by the detail clerk for ticket numbers, shillings and pence indicators (later converted to 10p units and 1p units). In later days at some depots, such as Thanet, there was a system of double-sided cabinets; staff were allocated one with their own key and when booking on retrieved a by-now permanently allocated machine from the cabinet and at sign-off replaced it there. This probably became the standard arrangement once more modern locker rooms were in place at depots. At other depots, depending on arrangements, the machine was replaced in either a set of secure cabinets for that purpose or handed back to the detailer if he was on duty. During the duty the conductor (or D/C) would record the machine's ticket and monetary entries on the reverse of the waybill at takeover, at each terminus and at handover of the car worked on. When changing crews mid-journey a local service transfer sheet had to be filled in and handed to the next conductor, detailing opening and closing ticket numbers so an inspector could verify tickets issued by the first conductor.

On finish of a duty, as well as handing in the machine, the waybill was completed with final numbers of tickets and their total value, also recording details of warrants and other special tickets issued, such as emergency tickets in the event of a machine failure. This was then placed in a linen bag together with the cash, and any tickets in lieu of cash, such as warrants, and deposited in a safe to be counted when the cashiers were on duty. Each week a 'shorts and overs'

list was published where either the cash did not match the waybill or a conductor's maths were at odds with what was recorded. This money was then recouped or paid out on payday. In those days non-salaried employees were paid in cash by means of a 'see-through' envelope which allowed you to count the notes and view coins before opening; no bank transfers in those days. Payday was on Thursdays for the previous week and included all overtime as well as the rostered week's pay. This day was marked by a greater participation by staff in the 'card schools', which were a way of life in some canteens, especially at Folkestone, Canterbury and Westwood. Many wanted to enhance their earnings but it was a sad fact that a number came out with a lot less money than was in their original pay packet.

Some of the essential items carried by a conductor in his/her ticket box. Seen here (top to bottom): 'ready-reckoner' and Thanet service fare cards; fare table; book of transfer sheets; emergency tickets; cash bag (with 'T-key' for unlocking blind displays and so on); back plate for ticket machine; later Setright machine; spare ticket rolls and rule book. AUTHOR'S COLLECTION

T.S. 1422

EAST KENT ROAD CAR COMPANY LTD

Conductor's Name _WALLACE_

LOCKER NUMBER _266_

Depot _FOLKESTONE_   Date: Day _9_ of _APRIL_ 19_70_   Ticket Machine No. _537_

CLASS OF TICKET	LAST NUMBER	CLOSING NUMBER	OPENING NUMBER	TOTAL TICKETS	CLASS OF TICKET		LAST NUMBER	CLOSING NUMBER	STARTING NUMBER	TICKETS SOLD		£	s.	d.
					EMERGENCY		4499	4421	4401	20		2	5	0
EXCHANGES	7599	7501	7501	—	PARCEL	3d.	1199	1162	1154	8			2	0
					PARCEL	1/-						2	7	0
TRANSFER BOOKS	33349	33328	33327	1	PARCEL	1/3								

CONDUCTOR'S REPORT ON TICKET MACHINES, ALSO LOST JOURNEYS

MACHINE JAMMED AT COPEL STREET EMERGENCY TICKETS ISSUED.

MACHINE COUNTER SUMMARY

	TOTAL TICKETS	RETURNS	PARCELS	STAT COUNTER	HALF-PENCE			SHILLINGS				
					£	s.	d.	£	s.	£	s.	d.
CLOSING No.	17540	81401			27	3	10	872	6			
OPENING No.	17249	81342	—	—	20	14	5	859	8			
TOTAL	291	59	—	—	6	9	5	12	18	19	7	5

IN ALL CASES WHERE DEDUCTIONS ARE MADE FOR TICKETS PRINTED IN ERROR FORM E.K. 219 MUST BE COMPLETED AND HANDED IN TOGETHER WITH WAY-BILL

NO. EXCHANGE TICKETS HANDED IN

WARRANTS AND VOUCHERS ACCEPTED IN LIEU OF CASH   1 P.O. WARRANT 9d

TOTAL 21 14 5

LESS:— TICKETS PRINTED IN ERROR   2 8

SUMMARY OF ROUTES OPERATED   FOR OFFICE USE ONLY

TOTAL 21 11 9

ROUTE	CAR NO.	JOURNEY	PASSENGER	£	s.	d.		£	s.	d.	SUMMARY OF CASH:	NOTES £	16	0	0
156	885	½	32		15	8					NO. OF RAILWAY TICKETS HANDED IN	„ 10/-	3	0	0
90	885/779	2	200	14	6	11						SILVER	2	2	0
108	822	1	38		19	8						COPPER		6	9
102	918	1	98	5	7	6						3d. PIECES		3	0
		PARCELS			2	0					IN LIEU OF CASH:	WARRANTS AND VOUCHERS			9
		TOTAL	368	21	11	9						TOTAL	21	11	9

CONDUCTOR'S SIGNATURE _P.S. Wallace_   DRIVER'S NAME   WAYBILL CHECKED BY   CASHIER'S SIGNATURE

TS 830 **EAST KENT** ROAD CAR COMPANY LTD   S   67285

LOCAL SERVICE TRANSFER SHEET

DATE _23/10/70_   SERVICE NO. _103A_

TIME OF JOURNEY _2035 Mythe Ex_   POINT OF TRANSFER _Bts Sta - 2055_

TICKET MACHINE NO. _504_

	Opening Nos.	Closing Nos.
TICKET NUMBERS ...	JA 504 31 670	JA 504 9 673

Conductor's Signature

A specimen waybill front page from the late 1960s (above) and a local service transfer sheet (below). The waybills underwent format changes over the years. On the transfer sheet the conductor (the author) has used the machine cancellation stamp, which shows the next ticket number to be issued. AUTHOR'S COLLECTION

Conductors and D/C drivers also had their personal 'box', which was used to store spare ticket rolls, emergency tickets, exchange tickets and other items such as a cash bag, back plate and strap for the ticket machine, fare table and rule book. The early boxes were quite small but later ones were bigger and could accommodate a Setright machine. The issue of personal boxes also caused some logistical problems where there were two signing-on and-off points, for example at Folkestone, which had both the depot at Kent Road and the bus station. This resulted in use of the 'box car', which conveyed conductors' and D/Cs' boxes between the two sites so that those on early turn who had booked off at the bus station had their boxes at Kent Road for the next morning's start and vice versa. Crew conductors and drivers were given 10 minutes to book on and off whereas D/C drivers had an extra allowance and were given 15 minutes to commence and finish their duties.

While conductors were issued with a full fare table, at Thanet an extract of fare schedules for the busiest Island routes was also issued on a folded two-page card sheet, probably due to the intensity of use and the high number of seasonal staff who needed to have quick reference to many unfamiliar fares. The last known issue of this extract of fare tables was in 1969 and covered services 46/51, 49/50/52 group and the 63/64. A separate company-wide issue was that of the conductor's 'ready-reckoner' on a single card, printed on both sides with details of child and privilege fares, which were reductions on the normal standard fares. It is appropriate to record here the benefits staff gained as employees. Privilege ticket cards allowed quarter-rate travel on stage carriage services for staff, spouses and two children under fourteen, while on express services a 25 per cent discount was given. For travel to and from work a separate Home & Duty pass was issued, allowing free travel between two points nominated.

ON THE ROAD – DRIVING

In terms of paperwork a driver had it easy compared with a conductor. At one time each vehicle carried a 'Driver's Running Sheet', which was filled in by the driver with duty number, journeys run and opening and closing speedometer readings. In later days these were rarely filled in properly and they gradually fell into disuse by the mid-1970s as more sophisticated logging systems were introduced.

Running boards were carried on each car. These detailed the trips to be worked plus any relevant notes – for example, connecting journeys or special arrangements. They were picked up by the first driver at the start and remained on the car until the final duty. These were produced at the Traffic office and sent out to the depots, who then varnished the paper copy onto plywood boards, which made them more durable in use. In order to find the car allocated, a large board with all service running numbers was in place adjacent to the booking-on point at the depot and the car numbers were chalked onto the relevant space by the engineers.

At the end of the duty the driver would log any faults with the vehicle on a sheet provided for the purpose. If the duty was a finish at the end of the day, the driver would have to take his vehicle into the fuel bay, where engineering staff would refill the tank with diesel fuel and then the driver would run it through the wash before parking in a space advised by the engineers.

As well as separate rotas for crew and/or D/C operations most depots had various other rotas or 'boards' for drivers. Thanet's other separate 'boards' in the early 1970s were:

- South Coast Express/62 – which also had some D/C work
- London Express – which also covered miners' contracts normally on alternate days
- Miners'/contract services
- Coaching – which covered excursions, private hires and some Miners' services
- Tours – an elite set of drivers covering longer tours both nationally and on the continent, normally starting at Canterbury, where the luxury tour cars were allocated

A driver's running sheet from September 1970. The lack of information was typical at this stage, and these had gone by 1973. AUTHOR'S COLLECTION

```
16.4.68 AER/VW                    ST KENT ROAD CAR CO. LTD.
                                  BUS RUNNING SCHEDULE
WEEKDAYS AND SUNDAYS                                        SERVICE 105/105A    CAR NO. 2
FOLKESTONE AND LYDD/LITTLESTONE                             COMMENCING: 30th June, 1968
```

		C	D	A	C		
		SMFH	SuMFTO				
Folkestone Central Station	dep.	0830	..	1055	1330	1555	1830
Folkestone Bus Station		0836	..	1100	1336	1600	1836
Sandgate Post Office		0843	..	1107	1343	1607	1843
Seabrook, Fountain		0847	0847	1111	1347	1611	1847
Hythe, Red Lion Square		0855	0855	1119	1355	1619	1855
Palmarsh Estate		0902	0902	1126	1402	1626	1902
Dymchurch Bus Station		0913	0913	1137	1413	1637	1913
St. Mary's Bay Post Office		0918	0918	1142	1418	1642	1918
New Romney, Station Road		..	..	1149	..	1649	..
New Romney, Ship		0925	0925	..	1425	..	1925
Littlestone Holiday Camp		..	..	1159	..	1659	..
Lydd, Airport Turning		0934	0934	..	1434	..	1934
Lydd Camp	arr.	0939	0939	..	1439	..	1939
							D
Lydd Camp	dep.	0944	0944	..	1444	..	1944
Lydd, Airport Turning		0949	0949	..	1449	..	1949
Littlestone Holiday Camp		..	..	1212	..	1712	..
New Romney, Ship		0958	0958	..	1458	..	1958
New Romney, Station Road		..	..	1222	..	1722	..
St. Mary's Bay Post Office		1005	1005	1229	1505	1729	2005
Dymchurch Bus Station		1010	1010	1234	1510	1734	2010
Palmarsh Estate		1021	1021	1245	1521	1745	2021
Hythe, Red Lion Square		1028	1028	1252	1528	1752	2028
Seabrook, Fountain		1036	1036	1300	1536	1800	2036
Sandgate Post Office		1040	1040	1304	1540	1804	2040
Folkestone Bus Station		1047	1047	1311	1547	1811	2047
Folkestone Central Station	arr.	1050	1050	1314☼	1550	1814☼	2050☼

```
A - on Mondays to Fridays
    School Terms Only -
    operates the following
    journey:-

99. Cheriton Library   dep.  0802
    Hollands Avenue     arr.  0820

    Hollands Avenue     dep.  0821
    East Station              0825
    Westcliff Gardens         0828
    Bus Station               0830
    Central Station           0832
    Cheriton Library    arr.  0838
    Cheriton Library    dep.  0840
    to Seabrook Fountain to pick
    up Service 105 at 0847

C - Connect at New Romney, Ship, with
    Service 133 at 0925 on Tuesdays &
    Fridays only.

D - Runs DEAD from or to Garage.
```

☼ - To be operated beyond Bus Station to Central Station only when required
    for passengers already on the bus on arrival at Bus Station.

SMFH - Saturdays, Mondays to Fridays School Holidays.   SuMFTO - Sundays & Mondays to Fridays School Terms only.

A running board for 105/A car 2 operating the summer 1968 timetable. This was relatively simple; some spare cars had timings on both sides of the board due to the variety of services worked. AUTHOR'S COLLECTION

In earlier years some depots operated separate rotas for town and country routes. Generally junior staff, both conductors and drivers, started on the town services and moved up with experience. Canterbury and Thanet were two depots where this was practised, but it may not have been company-wide policy as a Dover driver does not recall such a system in operation there in the 1950s. This policy also allowed separate allocation of machines to routes, which was invaluable when the company had both short-range and long-range Setright ticket machines, which are described later. By the mid-1960s, if not before, the practice had ceased.

Drivers' training differed from conductors' both in the duration and the fact that a stringent test had to be taken, involving a test drive of 30–45 minutes with an oral test afterwards. Instructors were taken from the cadre of senior drivers and were given the necessary training. They were based at the major depots. Normally the examiners were external, Ministry of Transport staff, but for periods in the

1960s and 1970s certainly, East Kent was allowed to conduct its own examinations by suitably qualified staff.

The author rejoined East Kent at Thanet depot in 1973. While he held a PSV driver's licence, this was badged 'automatic or semi-automatic transmission only' as he had been trained at London Transport's Chiswick Driving School on RTs and RMLs and this was a normal stipulation at the time. Thus the licence had to be 'upgraded' to drive manual gearbox vehicles, which still involved a full test. Therefore, a near-normal period of training taking almost three weeks had to be undertaken; having passed, there was then a need to carry out vehicle familiarization. As was normal with bus companies, training was carried out on the oldest vehicles; at the time East Kent's open-top Guys were used for the purpose. The author's steed was FFN 375 with instructor George Templeman and a number of other trainees. The bus, like many of the Guys, had a very forgiving gearbox, so they were extremely suitable for training. Familiarization was then carried on the main different types operated,

On return to East Kent the author first worked on one of the remaining crew-operated routes, the 49/50/52 complex at Thanet (Westwood). The complete circuit took 3 hours, which fitted nicely with the half of a duty and made crew scheduling fairly simple. In July 1971, a smart 6799 FN runs through Birchington, Station Road on service 50 at the start of its 90-minute run to Margate Harbour via Ramsgate, the point where it will change to service number 52. AUTHOR

which at the time included an AEC Regent, a 'Long Dog' 36ft (11m) coach with six-speed gearbox and a Fleetline with semi-automatic gears. This took a further two days.

The trained driver was now ready for the road, apart from the need to learn routes and, most importantly, await confirmation from the traffic commissioners that the paperwork was in order and a suitably endorsed licence had been sent out. In the author's case it took only one day out with another crew before confirmation was received and he was in the cab and soon on the crew drivers' sheet at Westwood. Experience on this sheet was to be short-lived, thankfully, as by now crew operation was limited and being confined to the 49/50/52 group could be boring. After only five weeks' crew work, he was rostered on the D/C sheet immediately after applying for the post – earlier conduct-

ing experience and thus needing only a short period route learning with another D/C driver probably being a factor.

Below is an example of a D/C duty worked at Thanet by the author in 1974 showing the more complex nature of this work as crew operations contracted. By this time Thanet's crew operations only covered the 49/50/52 group, with some additional reliefs, for example on route 8 and the 69 open-top service in the summer, for which a separate rota operated.

Note that this duty required the driver to travel from Margate to Westwood Garage to pick up 66 Car 1. The need for D/C drivers to travel to or from Margate or Ramsgate for either the start or finish of their duty was normal, as the only signing-on/off point was at Westwood and few D/C routes passed by or near the garage, with the exception

Duty 141 and Call-out 20 – Westwood (Thanet) Garage, worked on 26 February 1974

Duty start	Takeover	Service/car	Handover	Car	Finish
0720 Garage	0735 Garage	64/Car 5	1001 Margate Cecil Square	RFN 954G	
	1044 Margate Harbour	151/Car 1	1344 Margate Harbour	EFN 176L	
	1410 Garage	66/Car 1 (Service 55)	1525 Garage	TFN 416	1540 Garage
1545 Garage	1600 Garage	Spare 27 (B/strs	1655 Garage	GJG 733D	
C.20		Schools – Birchington)		(D/C)	1710 Garage

The 36ft (11m) saloons ushered in D/C operations in a big way on trunk routes in the late 1960s. DJG 357C, top, is at Ashford in August 1969, displaying the onward connecting facility to Hastings between service 1 and 2. To the right of the vehicle console, below the steering wheel, can just be seen the rectangular holder for the fare board. On this car, and on RJG 208G on service 105 at Folkestone in June 1970, can also just be seen the single unit for the ticket machine and till, which was mounted on the half-height cab door. AUTHOR

of the 55, 56 and 71 routes. In this case the travel would be by service 52, departing the harbour at 1352 and arriving at 1404. The timing would seem tight but the takeover of 66 Car 1 allowed 10 minutes before departure at 1420, a normal interim allowance made where possible. For example a takeover of service 8 at Margate Harbour, a terminus, would be on its arrival, although takeovers on the road in the middle of a journey had no such leeway.

Inter-working of cars is evident, as the journey on the 55 to Kingsgate via Broadstairs and Joss Bay was covered by a car that also worked on the Ramsgate–Deal service 66, which by this time had a very sparse winter service – the Thanet car only performing one journey from Ramsgate to Sandwich. Finally, a call-out was also posted on this duty

and involved D/C working of one of the converted AEC Regents for a service from the Charles Dickens and Dane Court schools complex at Broadstairs, which saw a significant number of such workings to all parts of Thanet, by now covered mainly by D/C Regents.

To ease fare scrutiny, D/C workings were also provided with individual fare tables glued and varnished to plywood boards as with the running boards and, on some cars, a purpose-built frame was provided to permit easy visibility for the driver. These boards remained with the running board and the car itself. On some complex workings over many routes there could be three or four separate fare boards provided with the running board. East Kent felt it was not appropriate to force the driver to use the normal fare table book as there was nowhere easily to stand it close to the driving position and it would be difficult to read from a distance due to the size of print. This was unlike sister company M&D, who provided no such aids.

WORKING ARRANGEMENTS

A few other aspects of operation should be described. From an early stage East Kent took on a large number of seasonal staff due to the high uplift of services in the summer. Despite staff shortages by the 1970s, the author's engagement form, when he returned in 1973, still had an option for seasonal or permanent staff – although by then rotas, especially for the D/C sheet, often had rostered work for rest days as more senior drivers covered tours or express work in the summer and the duties could not be covered with normal five-day-week working. A driver could reject these 'WRDs' (work rest day) but that was frowned upon by the detailers and when overtime was scarce those drivers would often be last in line to be considered for extra work. For such ad hoc work you would record your availability for overtime on a sheet for the purpose, which would then be considered by the detailers. Call-outs could also be rejected but this was less likely, as the crew were already working and they were of a short duration.

To cover sickness or 'no-shows' a number of spare 'standby' staff were rostered to cover these unpredictable events. A 'stand-by' was booked on at the first duty start time and others were booked on later; generally at least two early spares and two late spares were included on the rotas, and other work would often be offered as overtime by detailers on the day. To get staff to/from work, a number of garages offered an early turn and late turn staff car. In 1970 that for Folkestone departed Hythe at 4.30 in the morning and then went via Folkestone, Hill Road to arrive at Kent Road garage in time for the first starts, while a late car departing after the final book-off took any staff requiring transport to those points as required.

Spare staff also covered other ad hoc duties such as the 'box car' at Folkestone mentioned earlier. Another regular piece of work would be the 'bank car', taking the previous day's receipts to the company's bank. That at Folkestone had a rather ludicrous air to it, as drivers and conductors together with the cashiers loaded bag after bag of coins onto a spare car commandeered for the purpose at the bus station; then the bus took a small circuit of the town only to arrive at the bank, which was less than 50 yards from the entrance to the bus station! At Thanet it was more of a job, involving a journey from Westwood to Margate, Cecil Square. To the author's knowledge, despite the low level of security there was no theft from these cars; perhaps the weight of the large amount of coins was a dissuading factor.

Conductors and D/C drivers' duties also required them to have charge of parcels, which at one time was a significant business for East Kent; parcels tickets were carried in the conductor's box but later on parcels were normally delivered already stamped via East Kent's many agents or their own offices. A separate waybill was carried on the car if parcels were conveyed. According to a Traffic Notice of 1971, prescriptions were also carried between Greatstone and New Romney for a period. Mail was also conveyed by the company's cars at one time, with post office staff securing mailbags with chains and locks, which were then retrieved at the destination. Canterbury was one of the last locations to receive such traffic and certainly on service 4. Prior to the 1965 reorganization of the 4 and 6 routes, the circa 7.30pm ex Canterbury would receive a mailbag at Whitstable Post Office, thence proceed to Swalecliffe for layover, and on return to Canterbury, Bus Station the bag would be collected by a postman.

Another quirk of East Kent's operations was the need for crews to interchange between cars in service at remote locations due to the imbalance of cars between garages on some routes. The 17 between Canterbury and Folkestone was one of the last services to feature such working as late as 1968 or beyond; the 0705 ex-Canterbury and 0734 ex-Folkestone exchanged D/C drivers at Etchinghill at 0753, which ensured late-turn drivers finished at the correct location, while the cars were stabled away from their home depot on alternate nights.

Seasonal employment was always a feature of East Kent up to the late 1960s. This discharge letter of September 1938 would have been issued to many staff taken on for the summer and was no reflection on their competence or trustworthiness. Compare the letterhead with the author's employment letter of 1968. AUTHOR'S COLLECTION

The remoteness of some routes and length of journey meant that there was a great deal of responsibility upon staff to operate properly and broadly to the rule book, as supervision could not be 100 per cent. In most cases staff provided a good service, but there were cases where boundaries were pushed. One story concerned service 18, which passed through a thick pine forest near Stelling Minnis. One December, a driver, knowing he was likely to have no passengers on the working from Folkestone, allegedly took advantage of the large number of spruce trees growing there which conveniently fitted into the boot, as it was a KFN/LJG-series Reliance. On the return journey from Canterbury the police were encountered checking the boots of motorists' cars for Christmas trees but the bus was waved through without scrutiny; on arrival at Folkestone there was a good trade in trees!

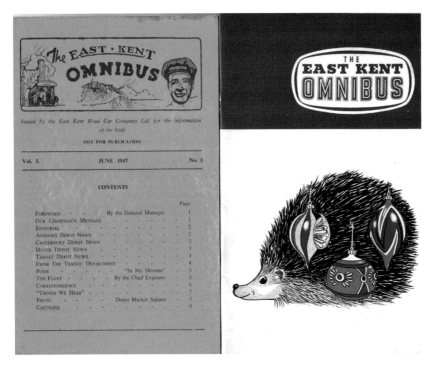

EAST KENT E.K.9
ROAD CAR COMPANY LTD

DAILY TIME SLIP

Name ....

Clock No. .... Date ....

Car No.	Full Description of Work Done	Allocation No.	Hrs.
	Total		

Superintendent ....

Signature ....

ROUTE LEARNING
ONLY N°3/ 3040

EAST KENT
ROAD CAR COMPANY LTD

Employee's Duty Pass

(To be used only on business of the Company)

Name WALLACE PS

Outward Journey:

From WESTWOOD GARAGE

To THANET

On

Return Journey:

From 9 MAY 73

To as above

On

Issued by R. Snould Inspector
PP

R. G. JAMES,
General Manager.

This Pass must be given up on the last section for which
it is made available.

TS 1495

Two essential bits of paper to have at the start of employment 'on the road'. Left is an overtime slip to record any extended hours, while right is a duty pass for route learning. Note that despite being issued in 1973 it still gives Mr James as General Manager although he left in the 1960s. Certainly old stock! AUTHOR'S COLLECTION

The EAST · KENT
OMNIBUS

*Issued by the East Kent Road Car Company Ltd. for the information
of the Staff*

NOT FOR PUBLICATION

Vol. I. JUNE 1947 No. 1

CONTENTS

		Page
FOREWORD	By the General Manager	1
OUR CHAIRMAN'S MESSAGE		1
EDITORIAL		2
ASHFORD DEPOT NEWS		3
CANTERBURY DEPOT NEWS		3
DOVER DEPOT NEWS		3
THANET DEPOT NEWS		4
FROM THE TRAFFIC DEPARTMENT		4
POEM	"In My Dreams"	5
THE FLEET	By the Chief Engineer	5
CORRESPONDENCE		6
"THINGS WE HEAR"		7
PHOTO	Dover Market Square	7
CARTOONS		8

THE
EAST KENT
OMNIBUS

The cover pages of the very first and the very last East Kent Omnibus *staff magazines issued in June 1947 and December 1971 respectively.* COLLECTIONS – J. G. WILSON/AUTHOR

Uniforms provided covered winter and summer attire, the former of black serge with red piping on the collar, trousers and caps, while the summer dust jacket in later days was grey with red cuffs and collars. Earlier dust coats were white. The serge trousers were uncomfortable in the summer, but there was no lightweight alternative. As a conductor, the author took to wearing his own black trousers, which were flared bell-bottoms, the style of the time. On one occasion, Folkestone's District Superintendent, Barry Robinson, a well-respected manager with a sense of humour, accosted him as he came off a bus: looking at the flared trousers he observed, 'Conductor Wallace, with those trousers you would be more at home on a boat rather than a bus!' Point made – uniform trousers were restored to use. As one of his Folkestone colleagues later observed, 'We ran a colourful bus service.'

This enlightened method of operation by some crews was soon to come to an end, probably rightfully so; by 1968 the company had embarked on what was termed 'work study'. Time and motion assessments were the order of the day, and this first affected workshop and engineering functions. The NBC's corporate policy also changed the method of scheduling; in the 1970s timetable preparation was changed and integrated with duty compilation to achieve the most efficient use of crews. At times this required adjustment to journeys to avoid extra duties, despite possible adverse effects on the regular intervals of services. The days of leisurely turn-rounds at termini with, hopefully, refreshments available such as at the Light Railway Café, conveniently placed for services 103/A, would soon become a thing of the past.

SOCIAL LIFE AND UNION MEMBERSHIP

East Kent staff enjoyed a good social life and there was a great community spirit, which lasts to this day. This started at work with canteens run by the local staff associations. Folkestone and Canterbury had canteens in their bus stations, Thanet's was at Westwood Garage; while other canteen locations were provided at Pencester Road, Dover; Rye, opposite the station approach; and at Ashford's social club premises adjacent to the Station Road garage. After the Second World War, from June 1947, a staff magazine was published, titled the *East Kent Omnibus*; initially it appeared monthly but in later days publication became more intermittent until it finished in December 1971 to be replaced by lesser offerings from the NBC corporate stable. Containing articles of general information, news from the social clubs and inter-depot games results, its appearance was always looked forward to.

In the 1960s each depot had a social club; the company supported these as they were seen as essential for good staff relations. Thanet and Dover had modern premises in their garages whilst Folkestone's was refurbished within the existing older buildings in 1970. Other garages had more modest premises; Canterbury's was located away from the depot in Station Road West, opposite the head office. These were used for many social occasions particularly the inter-depot indoor games league, culminating in presentations for the winning depots at an annual celebration held in April, normally at the Winter Gardens, Margate. This event, laid on by the company, was the major celebration of the season. A buffet was provided and free coaches ran from each depot so staff did not have to drive. Another aspect of East Kent's family spirit was the children's Christmas parties laid on by the social clubs at each depot, while another company-wide occasion for staff was the annual long service presentation for those completing more than twenty-five years of service. This first took place in January but from the 1960s moved to November and was normally held at the Leas Cliff Hall, Folkestone. The company's hospitality extended to its passengers as well, and each January a 'Tours Tea Party' was held, partly to reward those customers from the previous year's season but also to advertise the programme for the forthcoming year.

Although East Kent did not have a 'closed shop', requiring road staff to be members of an appropriate union, as was the case at London Transport for example, membership of the former Transport and General Workers Union (TGWU) was the norm in the 1960s, while office staff could avail themselves of the National Association of Clerical and Supervisory Staff (NACSS). Some depots were more active than others and a dispute in 1970 led to a work-to-rule rigidly enforced at Folkestone, which also produced a set of local newsletters on the dispute entitled 'On the Buses'.

A more rigid approach by management, changing perceptions and the obvious conclusion that it was not appropriate to sell alcohol on premises associated with professional driving duties meant that Stagecoach decided to close the remaining clubs. By today's standards it may seem surprising that the company condoned the practice of having bars at its depots but it was a different world in those earlier days. The downside of their closure is that the close friendship between staff engendered by such things as the inter-depot games has been lost for ever; but the happy times spent relaxing at the clubs, often after a long and arduous day's work driving along the roads of Kent, will remain a long-standing memory for all former East Kent staff.

The long-service awards ceremony was the company's way of thanking those employees who had completed twenty-five or forty years continuous service. Illustrated is the programme for the 1966 awards in the Jubilee year. JOHN (FRED) WILSON COLLECTION

CHAPTER FIFTEEN

BUS TICKETING SYSTEMS

At the start, like many companies of the time, East Kent used the Bell Punch ticket system, initially of the geographic format, specific to each route, of differing values also identified by colour with all stages described; later, from the mid-1920s, the simpler stage-numbered version replaced the geographic version. Some early geographic tickets carried a route identifier in letters at the head, for example CF for Canterbury–Faversham, while other examples carried a service number completely unrelated to the later system introduced in 1937.

In the 1930s faster and more advanced ticket machines were developed, although there is also a report of fare boxes with sliding trays being used on some early town D/C services using fourteen-seaters, for example at Canterbury in the 1920s/30s at a fare of 1½d (0.5p). On East Kent, Setright 'Insert' machines were introduced, which involved a card

ticket being inserted into the machine that then printed value, stage boarded, journey and date on the lower, blank, portion. Two versions existed, the short-range, which printed the fare in figures; and the long-range, with the value in words. The tickets were of different colours like the Bell Punch and featured overprints – ½d overprint was used where machines could not record that value, and the 'S' overprint was used for single tickets. Returns were double-ended to enable cancellation, while other variations included exchange tickets. As far as can be ascertained, the Inserts were in use by 1931/2, but around the same time, reportedly in 1932/3, but certainly no later than 1939, the company also took delivery of the more advanced Setright Roll Ticket machine, which printed ticket details on a roll that was blank apart from the company's name and a summary of conditions on the reverse. These new Setrights

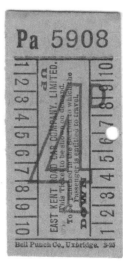

These five examples of East Kent Bell Punch tickets show the many differing varieties used. From left to right: a Folkestone example with a valid route number; one with service 8, which to the author's knowledge was never used for Northbourne; MRC on the third ticket was presumably to designate Margate, Ramsgate, Canterbury; while the last two are simpler numerical designs, the return believed to be the final form. ROGER ATKINSON COLLECTION – COURTESY DAVID HARMAN

Three examples of Setright Insert tickets, that on the left being the earliest with the two others being later examples featuring a single (S) and ½d overprint. The machine with printed 'ONE' for the fare was a long-range; the two others would have been short-range machines. ROGER ATKINSON – COURTESY DAVID HARMAN; AUTHOR'S COLLECTION

were of the 'short-range' version, which had a limited number of fare values of lower denominations. In the early post-war period it is thought that Bell Punch, Setright Inserts and Setright short-range were all in use at the same time.

In 1946 the company bought more Insert machines, but in December 1948 delivery of the new long-range Setright Speed commenced, which could print higher values than the earlier short-range Roll Ticket machines, now having separate shillings and pence dials. In 1949 Thanet depot also gained some experimental TIM machines but these were not used at other depots; the Setright Speed was gradually introduced at all depots commencing with Ashford then extending first to Folkestone and Thanet. It is thought that these deliveries heralded the end of the Bell Punch ticket system on East Kent and it is unlikely to have survived beyond 1948/9. Short-range Setrights probably followed soon after as more long-range machines were delivered, although the Setright Insert machine was retained for use on fare audits as different ticket colours could be used to identify separate fare

values issued, unlike on the early Setright Speed machines. In the 1950s fare audits were necessary to support applications for fare increases to the traffic commissioners, and firm evidence is available to support their use in 1956 and 1958 at least. It is likely that audit requirements accounted for the survival of a large number of blank insert tickets of different colours that were recovered from Hastings depot upon its closure in 1969, some of which are in the author's collection. By the late 1950s and throughout the 1960s, the company had standardized upon the Setright Speed long-range machine, which continued in use, modified for decimalization, up to the end of crew operation. A brief

A variety of Setright 'roll' tickets. Top left is one from a short-range machine, while below that is the reverse of a similar ticket showing the conditions summary. Bottom left is a later Setright Speed long-range ticket, the green colour issued on open-top services. The right column shows the later form of ticket with a conditions summary on the front, allowing the reverse to be used for advertising. Top is a pre-decimal version; in the centre the decimal format; while the bottom one shows the print style used for both M&D and East Kent for a time. AUTHOR'S COLLECTION

experiment was carried out at Dover in 1954 with Ultimate machines but the bulky equipment did not find favour. The pre-printed Setright ticket format changed in the late 1960s: the summary of conditions, now in briefer form, moved to the bottom of the roll front with the company name now only on the top row (previously it had been on top and bottom). This allowed the reverse of the roll to be used for advertising material.

The first use of roll-ticket Setrights required two tickets to be issued for returns, one with the value and another with the letter 'R' and not separated. Upon the return journey the section with the value would be cancelled in the insert slot, the conductor using the value 'X' for the blank ticket issued as a result. The 'R' ticket would be separated from the ticket with the value and retained with the 'X' ticket for audit purposes. It was a somewhat cumbersome method that was eventually replaced by the single-issue return, cancelled by over-stamping using a push-button on a mounting above a pad on the front of the machine. This allowed the conductor to stamp a number corresponding to that which would be printed on the next ticket, thus allowing inspectors to verify if a valid, correctly cancelled return was being used. This could also be used to verify exchange tickets.

Early East Kent Setright Speed machines had a slot similar to the Insert Setright, which required a blank ticket to be issued to cancel the later single-issue returns. This was called a 'double-star' as pre-decimalization machines printed a star to signify no value. Later, once the early machines had been replaced on East Kent, 'double-star' tickets would never normally be issued; the presumption being that these had been issued fraudulently, instead of recording a fare value. However, M&D still used such machines; one day a Folkestone inspector, having just checked an M&D vehicle on service 10, believed he had caught a conductor fiddling by issuing 'double-star' tickets, having found a number littered over the floor of the bus. He was somewhat crestfallen when a colleague pointed out that this was M&D's legitimate way of cancelling returns!

Some more modern Setrights were equipped for use with the electric motor drive on D/C Regents by means of a removable handle. By 1970 the company was experimenting with Almex machines (there had been earlier trials in the mid- to late 1950s and at Folkestone in 1969) and these were gradually introduced for D/C work, commencing with Ashford and Herne Bay depots. The need for more advanced systems saw Wayfarer II electronic ticket-issuing equipment introduced from 1989 at Thanet depot, and by 1990 these had ousted all the remaining Almex machines on the company although they saw use on open-top service

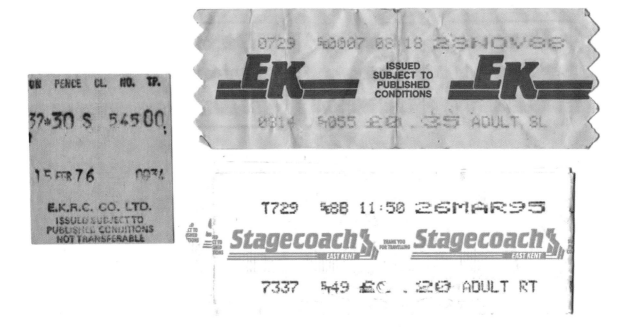

New styles of tickets. The Almex version on the left was used, after a number of trials, from the early 1970s side by side with Setrights, although only for D/C operations. Right are two examples of the modern Wayfarer issue, which replaced the old machines. Top is the East Kent Buses version replaced in 1993 by the Stagecoach version, below. All have now gone. AUTHOR'S COLLECTION

The design of the two season tickets on the right, still in use in the 1960s/70s, was little changed from the pre-war years. The cross signifies scholar (14–18 years). That on the right is an adult ticket. Below right is an experimental design – the holder and validity was on the other side while below left is the design under NBC auspices. AUTHOR'S COLLECTION

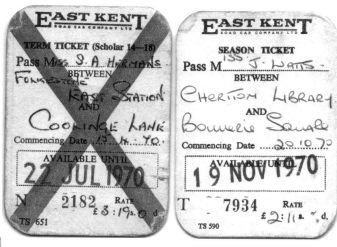

69 in the summer of that year. This was an oddity as Thanet had never used Almex machines in normal service, the Wayfarers directly replacing their Setright Speeds. Tickets for the Wayfarer machines were issued from a cream or white roll overprinted with the new *EK* logo in red –later replaced by the Stagecoach East Kent logo in yellow on a white roll.

Very soon afterwards, the development of Smartcards prompted the need to trial new electronic ticket equipment, and this came in the form of AES-Prodata (later ERG) TP4000 machines first trialled at Folkestone in 1996–7. As a result of their success the new type of machine was rolled out across the fleet, culminating in the introduction of the TP4003 in 1999, although this was replaced by the Stagecoach standard Vix ERG TP5000 series machine from May 2009. All of these machines use a plain square section ticket without any additional pre-printed text.

Today's use of Smartcards, particularly for multi-journey

tickets, using a standard data format is a far cry from the varied ticket types in use over the years although the artwork on Smartcards themselves can of course be extremely varied. It would be impossible to record all the differing ticket types used in a book of this size but some examples of tickets in use, primarily in the post-war period of BET's East Kent, are shown here and overleaf.

Season tickets in the 1960s had three distinguishing features: adult tickets were of a plain, wallet-sized rectangular card detailing the name of the holder, points between which it was valid, price and date of expiry. Scholar's tickets were similar but identified by a single overprinted red band for children under fourteen years or a red cross for those between fourteen and eighteen years. The actual design had not undergone much change for many years, but at the turn of the decade, experimental tickets were trialled and the format then changed from the style that could be traced back to the 1920s. For the large number of colliery

T.S. 685

EAST KENT ROAD CAR COMPANY LTD   L   4063

TRAVEL WARRANT

To EAST KENT ROAD CAR COMPANY LIMITED

Please Issue.........*one*........*Single / Adult* * } Tickets
                                  *Return/ Child * * }

from ...*Chilton*... to *FOLKESTONE POST OFFICE*

or nearest stage points to cover these places, and debit the fares to the Office of
Issue.

Date ......*22 DEC*........ Signature...*JG*... *for Head Postmaster*
                                                Folkestone Kent.
*Delete word not applicable.
Enter number of passengers in words.

ACCEPTED BY CONDUCTOR OR OFFICE	STAMP OF ISSUING OFFICE:
vlc 60 24 91	FOLKESTONE POST OFFICE.

FARE	TOTAL AMOUNT PAYABLE	
1/2	1/2	

This Warrant is not transferable. It must be presented at the commencement of the
journey to the Conductor of the bus (or in the case of an Express Service journey to
the appropriate Booking Office). A ticket or tickets will be issued in exchange subject
to the Company's Conditions of Carriage and Passenger Regulations.

Where a journey necessitates travel on more than one service, separate Warrants must be
issued for each service concerned. In the event of there being no return ticket available
between the points, a separate Warrant must be issued for the return journey.

TS 691   M 1176

EAST KENT ROAD CAR COMPANY LTD

POST OFFICE TRAVEL WARRANT

THIS VOUCHER IS AVAILABLE FOR A FOUR-PENNY SINGLE FARE STAGE.

This Voucher must be handed to the Conductor, who will issue in exchange
an ordinary Single Ticket value 4d.

The Holder of this Voucher is conveyed subject to the Company's
Conditions of Carriage and Passenger Regulations, details of which may
be obtained at any Booking or Enquiry Office.

4D.

*These warrants were
used by postmen and
exchanged for a normal
ticket for the journey
undertaken (although
sometimes not — and
used towards the crew's
'tea money'!). The later
version (right), with
a specific value, was
presumably an attempt
to make the system less
susceptible to fraud.*

AUTHOR'S COLLECTION

services, special tickets were issued to certify legitimate use of them by the miners, while other workers using normal stage carriage services such as post office staff were issued with warrants which were exchanged for a ticket corresponding to the journey indicated on the warrant or, in later, days they had specific values.

In the 1960s staff passes were in the form of a small folded card with full details inside. A Home and Duty pass (blue cover) was provided for free travel to and from work (superseded in 1970 when different arrangements for privilege tickets came in), and privilege tickets (brown cover) allowed reduced rate travel (also issued to spouses and children). Salaried staff were allowed free travel and had a red pass with gold lettering, while long-service staff, with over twenty-five years' service, had a dark green pass. Other duty passes, on paper, were normally issued on a per-journey basis, for example for route learning or for travel on company service.

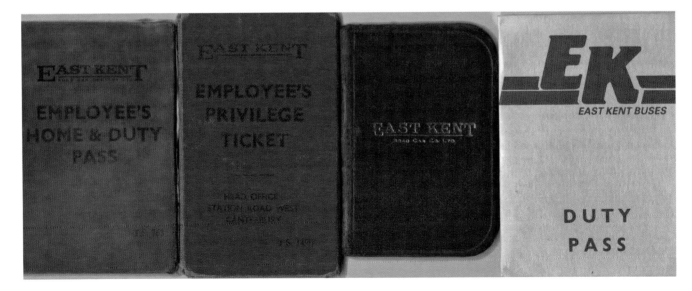

Some tickets not normally seen by the public. Left to right: Home & Duty pass for free travel to and from work; Privilege ticket for reduced rate travel; salaried staff free travel pass (all from the 1960s/70s); and a later East Kent Buses staff pass. AUTHOR'S COLLECTION

Emergency tickets were carried in conductors' boxes and were used in similar fashion to the Bell Punch, by clipping the fare value, although in the 1960s/70s the tickets were folded with the conductor or D/C retaining the rear portion and handing it in with the waybill in order that an auditable record was retained. Up to the 1970s exchange tickets were also carried and these were issued in return for transfers, such as from express services, in order to complete journeys to destinations not served directly by the London express service. The passengers would carry a voucher issued for the connecting journey for which the exchange ticket was issued.

For small goods, parcels tickets, left luggage tickets and carriage-paid-through tickets were all issued at various stages in the Company's history, and a few examples of these and other tickets are illustrated here.

Vouchers were often used by passengers leaving express services and completing their journey by bus. The exchange ticket (right), reminiscent of earlier inserts, was issued in exchange and cancelled by the conductor to validate it in case of inspection. AUTHOR'S COLLECTION

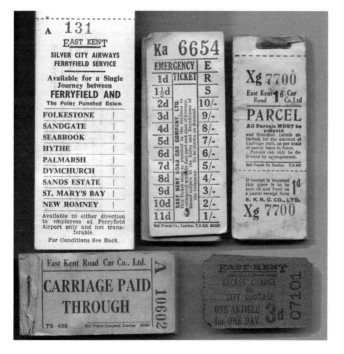

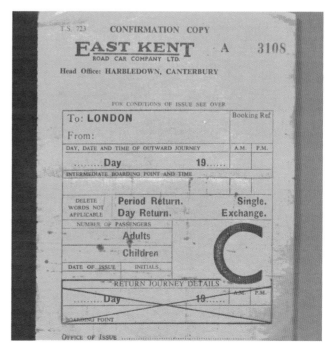

There were myriad other tickets used across East Kent's operations. Here are a few examples from BET times. LEFT: *Top, left to right: a special ticket for Ferryfield airport employees; pre-decimal emergency ticket; and a parcels ticket book. Bottom: 'Carriage Paid Through' ticket also used for parcels; and a left luggage excess receipt.* RIGHT: *an express ticket confirmation issued when the head office was still at Harbledown.* AUTHOR'S COLLECTION

PART VI

CONCLUSION – INTO THE NEXT 100 YEARS

East Kent enters its next century on a very positive note; most recently, as a result of Stagecoach's initiatives, bus ridership on East Kent has seen phenomenal growth from 14.6 million journeys in 2003 doubling to over 28.6 million in 2011, with subsequent increases in the following years of 4.7, 2.2 and 8 per cent. Table 13 (below) gives an insight into the changes over the past 100 years.

Looking back, two of the three bus stations developed by East Kent in the 1950s survive; Folkestone's original design is still recognizable although the parking bays are much modified, while Canterbury was completely redesigned in 2000–1. Two original garages at Herne Bay and Folkestone survive (although Herne Bay is planned to be replaced in 2016) while Westwood is still extant on the same site, although much reduced in size.

The East Kent of today is a forward-thinking company and one that the founder, Sidney Garcke, would be proud of, although the past is not forgotten. The preservation movement in East Kent is very active; over forty vehicles are in operable condition and many others under restoration. They range from an early Tilling-Stevens of 1930, a Leyland Tiger TS8 of 1937, a number of Dennis Lancet

Many East Kent vehicles have been preserved by individuals, including Guy Arab IV MFN 888, once restored by the company but now owned by John Lines and maintained in pristine condition. She is seen here in Ramsgate in July 2009 in the capable hands of ex-Dover driver Ted Hood on a re-enactment of service 9; normally the 8/9 blind would be carried by the car from Canterbury on service 8, connecting with the 9 at Sarre.
AUTHOR

Table 13   East Kent Statistics, 1916–2014

Year	1916–7	1938–9	1966	1990	2014
Vehicles owned	72	544	622	290	354
Employees	200	1,422	2,160	900	921
Mileage (millions)	1.11	14.697	17.625	10.0	14.0
Passengers carried (millions)	4.5	45.5	60	23	33*
Services operated	17	122	137‡	129#	115#
Route miles	185	1,731	1,052	N/A	N/A

Notes: Figures for 1990 and 2014 are estimates. * Estimate based on annual increases from 2011. # Does not include schools services unless part of a normal service timetable. Clockwise and anticlockwise services (for example 4 and 6) counted as one service. ‡ Company-quoted figure based on highest service number. Actual services totalled 139 including suffix variants. Circular services 4/6 and 6/4, 4A/6 and 6/4A counted as one service each. N/A: Not available.

buses and coaches of both pre- and post-war varieties, Beadle-Leyland coaches, numerous Guy Arabs and AEC Regents, including an AEC Bridgemaster, to more modern vehicles, such as a Daimler Fleetline and Bristol VRs. In the forefront of promoting interest in the company has been the M&D and East Kent Bus Club (www.mdekbusclub.org.uk), which has been active for over sixty years, but other groups such as the Friends of the East Kent, and the Dover Transport Museum also contribute to keeping the memory alive. Stagecoach themselves have kept an AEC Regent in traditional colours and the local management have rendered help in providing information and permission for use of former publications in this book as well as being supportive of the MDEK Club's activities.

In conclusion, East Kent is one of the few bus companies that can celebrate its centenary operating very much across the area where it was originally founded and with its original name. It is a name to be proud of and the author considers himself fortunate to have worked for the company. The year 2016 will hopefully see a number of events to celebrate the company's centenary and to keep its memory alive into the next 100 years.

Friends of the East Kent (FotEK) organise many EK running days. Here, one of the Dennis Falcons, EFN 568 is at Deal, South Street, recreating a short-working of the 76 to Betteshanger colliery overseen by ex-Deal driver and Inspector John Conway. Betteshanger was the last of the Kent pits to close, in 1989. The Falcons, like their predecessors the Dennis Aces, had the nickname 'Flying Pigs'. AUTHOR

A wonderful idiosyncrasy of East Kent was the use of specially branded sugar packets in the Canterbury bus station cafeteria even into NBC days. The BET and NBC versions are illustrated here. AUTHOR'S COLLECTION

Where it all started for the author. A suitable postscript to the photograph of AJG 26 in the front papers is this view of MFN 938F, the first car of the last batch of AEC Regents at Hythe Light Railway Station in May 1971. The lower-case via blind display is for the hourly diversion of the 103A via Downs Road Estate; this was a revised and comprehensive display for the route and only delivered with these cars and the later Fleetlines. Note the Henry Greenly-designed bus shelter unique to this location. AUTHOR

EAST KENT SERVICE NUMBER SCHEME FROM 1937 (including major changes up to summer 1938)

Service (1937)	Route	Approximate weekday frequency	Notes
1	Canterbury and Ashford via Wye	60–120 minutes	
2	Herne Bay, Canterbury and Hastings via Ashford, Brookland	2 (winter), 6 (summer) journeys	Only 1 journey to HB plus 2 s/w SO Rye–Brenzett
3	Canterbury and Faversham via Boughton	30–60 minutes	30-minute service SSuO pm & all day summer
4	Canterbury and Tankerton via Whitstable and Blean	15–20 minutes	
5	Canterbury and Whitstable via Chestfield	80 minutes	
6	Canterbury and Herne Bay via Herne	Winter 30 minutes Summer 15–20 minutes	
7	Canterbury and Herne Bay via Broomfield	6 journeys (winter) 8 journeys (summer)	
8	Canterbury and Margate via Sarre and St. Nicholas	30 – 60 minutes	30-minute service SSuO pm & all day summer
9	Canterbury and Ramsgate via Minster, and Manston	120 minutes (winter) 65–105 minutes (summer)	
10	Folkestone and Maidstone via Hythe and Ashford *(joint with M&D)*	30–60 minutes	30-minute service varies – all day summer
11	Canterbury and Preston via Ickham and Grove	2 journeys	
12	Canterbury and Stodmarsh via Ickham	7 journeys, 1 extended to Grove	2 journeys are s/w to Wickhambreaux
13	Canterbury and Deal via Sandwich and Worth Cross roads	Hourly with 13A	Majority of journeys via Eastry as 13A
13A	Canterbury and Deal via Sandwich and Eastry	Hourly with 13	
14	Canterbury and Goodnestone	3 journeys and 4 s/w to Wingham	SO (winter) WSO (summer)
15	Canterbury and Dover via Bridge and Lydden	Hourly	Extra s/w Dover–Lydden SO pm
16	Canterbury and Folkestone via Denton	Hourly	
17	Canterbury and Folkestone via Elham	Hourly	
18	Canterbury and Folkestone via Stelling Minnis	120 minutes (approx.)	
19	Canterbury, Hythe and Dymchurch via Stone St.	3 journeys	Summer only
20	Canterbury and Waltham via Petham	70–120 minutes (approx.)	
21	Canterbury and Adisham	4 journeys	WSO
22	Canterbury and Old Wives Lees	4 journeys	WSSuO
	Canterbury city services		
23	Whitstable Road and Old Dover Road		
24	Wincheap and Sturry Road		
25	London Road and St. Martins Hill		
26	Mandeville Rd and South Canterbury	All every 30 minutes	To K & C Hospital Sep 1937
27	Whitstable Road and Wincheap		
28	Hales Place and Wincheap		
29	St. Martins Hill and Sturry Road		
30	*Spare number*		
31	Faversham and Chilham via Selling	3 journeys	One s/w Faversham–Selling TSO
32	*Spare number*		
	Whitstable town service		
33	Chestfield and Seasalter (Blue Anchor)	Hourly	
34	*Spare number*		

35	Herne Bay and Margate via Upstreet	4 journeys 5 SO (winter)	Introduced March 1937 vice Service 40. Upstreet
		6–7 journeys (summer)	to Margate summer only
36	Herne Bay and Margate via 'Coastal Road' (Thanet Way)	4 journeys (summer)	Summer only
		6 journeys (high summer)	
37	Herne Bay and Faversham via Graveney	120 minutes (winter)	I/w with 38
		60–90 minutes (summer)	
38	Herne Bay and Faversham via Dargate	120 minutes (winter)	I/w with 37
		60–90 minutes (summer)	
39	Herne Bay and Reculver	4 journeys (winter)	
		30-minutes (summer)	
40	Herne Bay and Upstreet	4 journeys 5 SO (winter only)	Replaced by service 35 from March 1937
41	Herne Bay and Whitstable	Intermittent workings (winter)	S/w over 37/38 identified from March 1937
		30 minutes (high summer)	
	Herne Bay town services		
42	Railway station and Hillborough	30–50 minutes	Some s/w to Beltinge
43	Hampton Pier and Beltinge via Blacksole	30 minutes	
44	Hampton Pier and Beltinge via seafront	30 minutes	Summer only
45	*Spare number*		
46	Birchington and Minnis Bay	20 minutes	Summer only
47	Minster, Birchington and Minnis Bay	Did not operate	Summer only
48	*Spare number*		
49	Birchington, Margate, Broadstairs, Ramsgate and Margate via Reading Street and Westwood	20 minutes; enhanced to 10 minutes (Garlinge–Ramsgate Station summer & throughout in high summer 1938)	Introduced March 1937 after tramway abandonment. I/w with 49A
49A	Birchington, Margate, Broadstairs, Ramsgate and Margate via Northdown Hill and Westwood	20 minutes; enhanced to 10 minutes (Garlinge–Ramsgate Station summer & throughout in high summer 1938)	Introduced March 1937 after tramway abandonment. I/w with 49
50	Palm Bay and Birchington station via Margate harbour	20 minutes	Superseded by services 49/A in March 1937
51	Palm Bay (summer), Margate and Westgate	8–10 minutes	Until March 1937 IoTES Route 1 also ran Cliftonville–Margate–Westgate–Birchington
52	Margate and Ramsgate via Westwood, Ramsgate Station	15–30 minutes. Excl. IoTES workings	Joint with IoTES. Superseded in March 1937 by 49/A. Reintroduced summer 1937 only via St Luke's Avenue
53	Margate and Ramsgate via Broadstairs and St. Peter's village	18–36 minutes ex-IoTES workings (20 minutes from March 1937)	Joint with IoTES until March 1937
54	Millmead Road and Garlinge via Cecil Square	30–40 minutes	Ex-IoTES March 1937 l/w with 54A
54A	Arlington Gardens and Garlinge via Cecil Square	30–40 minutes	Ex-IoTES March 1937. Additional journeys from Arlington Gdns to Station 30 minutes SO (summer), 15 minutes (high summer) l/w with 54
55	Margate Station and Broadstairs via Kingsgate, Joss Bay	Hourly; 30 minutes summer & 20 minutes high summer	Ex-IoTES March 1937. I/w with 55A and 55B
55A	Margate Station and Broadstairs via Callis Court Road	Hourly	Ex-IoTES March 1937. I/w with 55 and 55B
55B	Margate and Broadstairs via Lanthorne Road	Hourly	Ex-IoTES March 1937. I/w with 55 and 55A
56	Margate, Birchington, Minster, Cliffsend, Chilton, Ramsgate, Broadstairs, Cliftonville and Margate (circular)	Hourly (45 minutes high summer)	Ex-IoTES March 1937 90 minutes from September 1937
57	Garlinge and Garlinge via Victoria and Cecil Square (circular)	Hourly	Ex-IoTES March 1937
58	Margate and Minster via Manston	Hourly	
59	Margate and Wingham via Minster, Stourmouth	4 journeys. 120 minutes summer	
60	Margate and Deal via Haine and Sandwich	60–105 minutes	Summer only
61	Margate and Dover via Haine, Sandwichand Eastry	3 (winter)–7 (summer) journeys plus 1 s/w Margate–Sandwich	SSuO winter/low season Daily, high summer
62	Margate and Hastings via Ramsgate, Deal, Dover, Folkestone and Rye	4 journeys (winter) 120 minutes (summer) 60 minutes (high summer)	I/w with South Coast Express until May and after October 1937
63	Margate town circular service	Hourly	Ex-IoTES March 1937
64	*Spare number*		
65	Margate and Ramsgate via Manston	Hourly	Summer only
66	Ramsgate and Deal	3 journeys (winter) 80–120 minutes (summer)	
67	Canterbury and Maidstone via Charing (*joint with M&D*)	6 journeys	
68	Ramsgate and Aylesham via Sandwich	4 journeys	SO (SSuO high summer)
69	Ramsgate and Minster via Manston	Every 50 minutes approx. From March 1937 service revised with s/w to Manston and reduced to Minster. Hourly approx. when 65 runs	I/w Ramsgate–Minster with service 9 (winter)
70	Ramsgate and Minnis Bay via Manston and Acol	90 minutes	

Service (1937)	Route	Approximate weekday frequency	Notes
71	Ramsgate, Nethercourt Circus and Broadstairs via Queen Street, Derby Arms, Station, St Lawrence, Hare & Hounds and Rumfields	30 minutes (winter) 20 minutes (summer)	Service replaced former IoTES 8 in 1932
72	*Ramsgate town service*, Royal Victoria Pavilion and Railway Station	30 minutes	Summer only
73	*Spare number*		
"	Ramsgate and Nethercourt Circus via Royal Esplanade *(introduced 1938)*	20 minutes	Summer only
74	Sandwich and Westmarsh via Ash	5 journeys 6 journeys by summer 1938	Plus s/w (SO/FSO) to Woodnesboro' and Ash
75	*Spare number*		
76	Deal and Betteshanger	4 journeys (approx.)	Additional journeys FSSuo pm
77	Deal and Staple via Betteshanger, Eastry	5 journeys plus 1 s/w to Eastry	Additional journey to Eastry SSuO
78	Deal, Eythorne and Barfreston	5 journeys (approx.) Some as s/w to Eythorne	Some s/w to Sutton and SO extensions to Barfreston
79	Deal and Kingsdown	40 minutes (winter) 20 minutes (pm high summer)	Some journeys to Kingsdown Links
80	Deal and Dover via St. Margaret's Bay	30 minutes (winter) 15 minutes (high summer)	
81	Sandwich and Sandwich Bay	7 journeys	Summer only. First/last journey extended from/to Deal via Worth
	Deal town services		
82	South St. and Mill Hill via Gladstone Rd.	⎡	
83	South Street and Mill Hill via London Rd.	All every 30 minutes	
84	South Street and Mil Hill via Park Avenue	⎣	
85	South Street and Sandown	13 journeys (winter) 40 minutes (high summer)	
86	Monument and Elms Vale Road via Tower Hamlets	30 minutes	Introduced July 1937. First registered as 97A
87	Dover and Ramsgate via Eastry and Sandwich	90 minutes	
88	Dover and Elvington via Eythorne	45 minutes	
89	Dover, Shepherdswell and Nonington	9 journeys to Shepherdswell or Barfreston	Additional 2 journeys to Nonington WSO
90	Dover and Folkestone via Capel	10–15 minutes 8 minutes (high summer)	
91	Dover and Folkestone via Alkham	Hourly	
92	Dover and Capel via West Hougham	5 journeys (6 SO)	TFSSuO. Runs all week high summer
93	Dover, Guston and East Langdon	60–90 minutes	Frequency includes s/w to Guston only
93A	Dover and West Langdon	3 journeys	SO
94	Dover and Betteshanger via Whitfield and Northbourne	3 journeys	SO
	Dover town services		
95	Marine station and River	20 minutes	
96	Marine station and Buckland	5 minutes	Combined 95/96 freq.
97	Monument and Maxton	10–12 minutes (1938 i/w 97A)	6 mins March 1937 until 1938
97A	Monument and Elms Vale Road *(introduced 1938)*	12 minutes (i/w 97)	97A introduced 1938 – then combined 6 min. interval (12 minutes to each terminal)
98	East Cliff/Prince of Wales Pier and River	20 minutes	Introduced June 1937
99	Folkestone (harbour) and Shorncliffe Camp	5 minutes. 4 minutes (summer)	
100	Folkestone (harbour) and Sandgate via Junction station, Cheriton and Shorncliffe Camp	Hourly. 30 minutes (summer) 20 minutes (high summer)	
101	Folkestone (harbour) and Newington	9–10 journeys pm only	High summer only
102	Folkestone, Hawkinge Aerodrome, Swingfield and Selsted	Hourly	Only one early and one late journey to/from Selsted
103	Folkestone (Wood Ave.) and Hythe via Junction	10 minutes 8 minutes (summer)	Number used for 103A journeys prior to June 1937. I/w with 103A
103A	Folkestone (Wood Ave.) and Hythe via Foord Road	10 minutes 8 minutes (summer)	Introduced June 1937 to differentiate between routings in Folkestone. I/w with 103
104	Folkestone (harbour) and Dymchurch	5 journeys	Summer only
105	Folkestone (harbour) and Lydd via Hythe, and Dymchurch	60–90 minutes	
106	Folkestone (Wood Ave.) and Cheriton (White Lion) via Junction and Joyes Road	20 minutes	SO afternoons only (winter) All day/week summer
	Folkestone town service		
107	Morehall or Shorncliffe Crescent and East Cliff Pavilion and The Warren	40 minutes western terminals 20 minutes combined	Warren extension summer only
108	*Spare number*		
109	Hythe and Ashford via Brabourne	5 journeys Ashford–East Brabourne plus 2 Ashford–Hythe and 1 more Hythe journey SSuO	SSuO Hythe journey runs all week in summer
	Hythe town service		
110	Saltwood, Palmarsh Estate and West Hythe	50-70 minutes	6 journeys to West Hythe
111	*Spare number*		

112	Rye and Ashford via Appledore	3 journeys	Plus 1 s/w Rye–Appledore WSO
113	Rye and Hastings via Winchelsea	Hourly. 30 minutes (summer)	
114	Rye and Winchelsea Beach	5 journeys (6 SO)	Plus s/w to Winchelsea
		Hourly (summer)	
115	Rye and Rye Harbour	Normally 6 journeys plus 3 SO	Summer only
			Service suspended due to road condition
116	Rye and Camber	120 minutes (winter)	Additional journeys SSuO (winter)
		Hourly (summer)	
117	*Spare number*		
118	Ashford and Wye via Brook	4 journeys	
119	Ashford and Bilsington via Ham Street	7 journeys (8 SO)	Some workings to Ruckinge only
120	Ashford, Canterbury and Margate	2 journeys	High summer only
	Ashford town services		
121	Woodchurch Turning and Hunter Avenue	30 minutes	Plus 30 minutes H. Ave s/w pm ThFSO
122	King's Avenue and South Willesborough	Hourly	
123	Beaver Green and Willesborough Lees	Hourly (30 minutes pm)	
124	High Street and Newtown	30 minutes	
125	Kennington and Kingsnorth	Hourly	
126	*Spare number*		
127	Hastings and Pett, Chick Hill	8 journeys	
128	Hastings and Pett Level	8 journeys (9 WSO)	
		45 minutes (summer)	
129	*Spare number*		
"	Monument and St. Radigund's *(introduced 1938)*	30 minutes	

Notes:

S/w = short-working
I/w = inter-worked
TSO = Tuesdays and Saturdays only
TFSSuO = Tuesdays, Fridays, Saturdays and Sundays only
WSO = Wednesdays and Saturdays only

WSSuO = Wednesdays, Saturdays and Sundays only
ThFSO = Thursdays, Fridays and Saturdays only
FSO = Fridays and Saturdays only
SO = Saturdays only
SSuO = Saturdays and Sundays only

BIBLIOGRAPHY

Commercial Motor (Various reports 1925–75)

East Kent Road Car Co. Ltd, *Silver Jubilee 1916–1941* (*Bus & Coach*, August and September 1941)

East Kent Road Car Co. Ltd, *Omnibus* staff magazine (June 1947–December 1971)

East Kent Road Car Co. Ltd, *Jubilee 1916–1966* (East Kent 1966)

Invicta, *The Tramways of Kent – Volume 2*, East Kent (Light Railway Transport League, 1975)

M&D and East Kent Bus Club, various *Fleet Lists/Enthusiast Guides* (MDEK Club, 1973–2015)

M&D and East Kent Bus Club, *East Kent Illustrated Fleet History 1916–1978* (MDEK Club, 1978)

M&D and East Kent Bus Club, *East Kent in 1937* (MDEK Club 1987/revised edition 2015)

M&D and East Kent Bus Club, *The Open Top Services of East Kent* (MDEK Club, 2004)

M&D and East Kent Bus Club, *East Kent Vehicles & Services 1955* (MDEK Club, 2005)

M&D and East Kent Bus Club, *East Kent Vehicles & Services 1959* (MDEK Club, 2011)

M&D and East Kent Bus Club, *East Kent Vehicles & Services 1972* (MDEK Club, 2012)

M&D and East Kent Bus Club/Wallace, R., *AEC Regents of Maidstone & District and East Kent* (MDEK Club, 2014)

Woodworth, F., *East Kent* (Capital Transport 1991)

INDEX

THE fussy cut SAMPLER

48
quilt blocks
from your
favorite fabrics

NICHOLE RAMIREZ & ELISABETH WOO

Published in 2017 by Lucky Spool Media, LLC

Lucky Spool Media, LLC
1005 Blackwood Lane, Lafayette, CA 94549
www.luckyspool.com
info@luckyspool.com

Text: © Nichole Ramirez and Elisabeth Woo
Photography: © Lehua Noëlle Faulkner
Additional Photography: John Pearson
Props + Styling: Nichole, Erin Dollar + Charlie Wright
Editor: Susanne Woods
Illustrator: Kari Vojtechovsky
Designer: Ashley Tucker

Lucky Spool Media® and its associated marks are registered trademarks owned by Lucky Spool Media, LLC

9 8 7 6 5 4 3 2 1
First Edition
Printed and bound in China

Library of Congress Cataloging-in-Publication Data available upon request

ISBN: 978-1-940655-22-2

LSID 0031

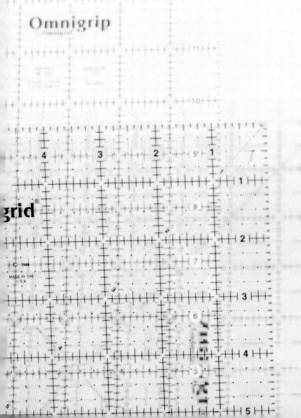

DEDICATION

To Rich, who always takes care of me.
—Elisabeth

To my grandpa, an amazing craftsman who taught me that there's nothing
more fulfilling than creating something with your own hands.
—Nichole

ACKNOWLEDGMENTS

We were privileged to partner with many amazing people and companies as we worked on this book. Thank you to Aurifil for providing thread to piece with and to Prym for sharing the best Omnigrid rulers. Thank you to Lauren of Sew Modern and Kelly of Superbuzzy for generously providing the fabrics for the book—we hope every person has the opportunity to frequent shops as welcoming and wonderful as the ones you have built for us here in Southern California. Many thanks to Erin Dollar for her styling prowess and Charlie Wright for her prop library that we were allowed to pillage. Thank you to Jacqueline of Soak Wash for providing endless Flatter to help keep our blocks flat and manageable, and to Susanne for taking a chance on us and allowing us to share our love of fussy cutting with all of you.

Nichole would also like to thank her family, including Joanne and Glenn, Robert, Anthony, Theresa and Gary, and Bill and Jill. Her boyfriend, Franky, for putting up with a house full of fabric, being the biggest supporter and cheerleader, and taking care of the dog and cats while she was working at all hours. Robert Kaufman for being the best work family. Lauren and Kelly for being inspiring ladybosses and wonderful friends. Carolyn Friedlander for her endless talent and support. Ramona, Jenny, Wendy, Elinor, Charlie, Cathy, Julia, Dana, Kelly and Jeric, Michael and Lindsey, John, Jose, Daniel, April, Paul, Mo and Karl, Taya and Mika, and the rest of the gang for being the best, most talented group of people and the greatest friends I could ask for. Lehua for always being a beacon of positivity and the sweetest person around. And lastly, Elisabeth for being an amazing coauthor, coworker, and dear friend.

Elisabeth would like to thank Valori, Karen, and Julia for being ever-present encouraging voices through this process. Her mom, dad, and all the friends she cancelled plans with to spend time sewing alone, and everyone at Robert Kaufman for the support and encouragement on this project. Without you all, this wouldn't have been possible. And, of course, there's Nichole, the mastermind who said, "We really should write a book."

contents

fussy cutting is fun

WHAT IS FUSSY CUTTING?

If you're reading this, then odds are good you're a confident quilter who enjoys the thrill of hunting for the perfect fabrics for a project. Fussy cutting takes that one step further, adding interesting novelty prints, stripes, text, and other designs to your selection process, then determining just the right way to cut them to showcase that portion of the fabric. There's nothing more satisfying than strategically cutting your fabrics and ending up with a perfect block that frames your favorite element of your most loved print. But fussy cutting encompasses more than just featuring fabrics. Prepare to actively engage your creativity as you meet the challenges of lining up directionality, finding balance in your fabrics, and so much more. Once you master fussy cuts, you can quickly incorporate them into any kind of project—and, believe us, you'll want to!

A LITTLE ABOUT US

Hi! We're Nichole and Elisabeth! We both love quilting, cats, dogs, and looking at cute baby animals on the Internet — we were destined to be friends. When we're not quilting, we like to get together and go to Disneyland, craft fairs, and other fun events around Los Angeles. More than anything, we both love fussy cutting. This technique is what initially brought us together (well, that and fabric shopping), and we're so excited to share with you what we've learned on our quilting journey.

GET TO KNOW NICHOLE

Hello! My name is Nichole and I love fussy cutting! I have always loved to make things with my crafty Mom and started collecting fabric long before I sewed a stitch. I love going to estate sales and thrift stores and have amassed quite a collection of fabric. I have everything from 30's feedsacks to 70's florals, plus lots of new fabric from my favorite designers. I found myself a workhorse of a machine and made a quilt for a friend who was having a baby. It was not the prettiest or the most well made, but the act of making that first quilt was so rewarding. I was hooked. Ever since, I have been sewing non-stop. I tend to do things in extremes. While I love everything about improv's free-form and limitless nature, there is something so great about showcasing my favorite prints in lovely, directional cuts by making a well-crafted block with perfect points.

GET TO KNOW ELISABETH

Hi! I'm Elisabeth, and as you may have guessed, I really like quilting. When I started quilting, I didn't realize how soon the quilty-bug would bite, nor how quickly it would become my entire world. I'm an absolute pro at collecting fabric and my favorites are all different shades of oranges and blues. I love quilting with a limited color palette, and orange/blue combos are my go-to pull for new projects. Whenever I'm stuck in a creative rut, I like to browse through antique shops looking for old quilts. There's nothing better than the craftsmanship you can find in traditional blocks. While staying home and quilting is my favorite, I do love going on vacation so I can explore quilt shops all over the country! When I'm not quilting, I'm hanging out at home with my cute dog, who of course has her very own quilt.

OUR APPROACH

While we both enjoy fussy cutting, we approach our fabrics and block designs differently. If there's one thing we know for certain, it's that not everyone thinks about fabric the same way. In this book, we give you the opportunity to see how we start with the same blocks yet create dramatically different finished quilts. We will walk you through forty-eight unique blocks, each created in two different styles that can easily be adapted to your own personal tastes by adjusting the focal point and fabrics.

Some blocks use a limited palette, others are scrappy, some whimsical or eclectic or vintage. Our hope is that seeing the two blocks side-by-side will inspire you to add fussy cuts to your quilting. These extra-special details will always bring smiles to our faces, and we hope to share that joy with you.

FOCAL POINT: Determining which portion of the block will be the main attraction, where you want to draw the most attention to.

FABRICS: Selecting your main fussy cut fabric, coordinating fabric(s), and background fabric.

THE ANATOMY OF A BLOCK

Fussy cutting showcases all stripes, geometrics, backgrounds, tossed prints and more, in a way that balances the overall look of a block while also drawing attention to the fabric you want to feature.

Coordinating Fabric   Fussy Cut   Background   Focal Fabric

FUSSY CUT: Cutting fabric to selectively feature a portion of the design.

FOCAL FABRIC: The selected motif you want to feature in a fussy cut.

COORDINATING FABRIC(S): The non-focal designs chosen to augment the focal point.

BACKGROUND: The fabric(s) that make up the background of the block, generally of a lighter shade or a neutral color.

GETTING TO KNOW YOUR FABRICS

As quilters, we believe in the same universal truth: there can never be too much fabric! What we love about fussy cutting is how every type of fabric is important. Sometimes when people think about fussy cutting, they just imagine novelty prints, but there's so much more than that!

When you begin incorporating fussy cutting into your projects, you'll start seeing your fabric in new ways. When you browse a quilt shop, instead of just seeing the beautiful colors and wonderful collections, you'll see the seam allowances between designs, the possibilities in an interesting stripe and the size of a design in relation to the project you're working on. For this book you'll need a variety of designs ranging in size, anywhere from a 1" to a 6-7" motifs. We like to look for designs that have some space around them so it's easier to isolate the individual elements of the fabric when fussy cutting.

TO PRE-WASH OR NOT TO PRE-WASH? Once you take your fabrics home, you can pre-wash or not (we know each quilter approaches this differently, so we say do what you're comfortable with). The only time we would not pre-wash is if you purchase a pre-cut bundle. Washing a pre-cut could result is significant shrinkage, and you don't want to lose any of the designs you want to fussy cut! These are a few important guidelines you'll want to keep in mind as you work through this book.

Fabric Requirements

We do not give exact yardage requirements for the blocks in this book because you will be using select pieces from a variety of fabrics. Instead, we give the required cut sizes you will need to sew each block. One of the cardinal truths about fussy cutting is that it uses more fabric and creates more scraps. We think that the finished impact of a fussy cut block is worth this. We completely understand that it can be hard to throw away those precious scraps, so just save them! You never know when you'll be working on a little project and need a tiny scrap. They've come in handy for everything from covered buttons to super tiny pincushions!

Framing

To frame a motif, look at the cut size, then take away your seam allowances. For instance, if a square says to cut at 5" and you know you have a ¼" seam allowance on all sides, the actual visible area of your square will be 4½". The framed motif must fit inside the seam allowances.

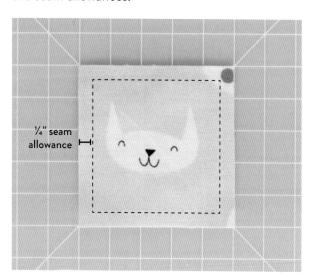

¼" seam allowance

Directionality

Some fabric designs have a clear directionality (for example, arrows all pointing the same way). Being aware of this when fussy cutting will help you maintain a continuous flow in your block.

Design Wall

Make sure that all of the time you spent selecting and cutting your fabrics results in a perfect block. Be sure to arrange the pieces before sewing them all together. Using a small design wall is a great way to check the directionality and fabric placement before you begin sewing.

MAKE A SINGLE BLOCK "DESIGN WALL": Since all of the pieced blocks in this book measure 9½" square (unfinished), purchase a 12" square stretched canvas from your favorite craft or art supply store. Cover it with a piece of batting, pulled taut, and staple it to the back on the board. This is an easy way to arrange your block design before piecing and allows you to stand at a distance when you evaluate your fabric choices.

Seam Allowance

All the blocks in this book use a ¼" seam allowance. You will find your seam allowance is an excellent friend when you are working on a fussy cut block, since it will often let you hide parts of the design you do not want to show.

Fabric Repeats

There are many different types of fabric repeats that each present a challenge for fussy cutting. Several chapters in this book will take a more detailed look at different kinds of repeats and how to use them. Once you are comfortable with the different patterns that we will explore in this book, you'll know just what to grab for any block.

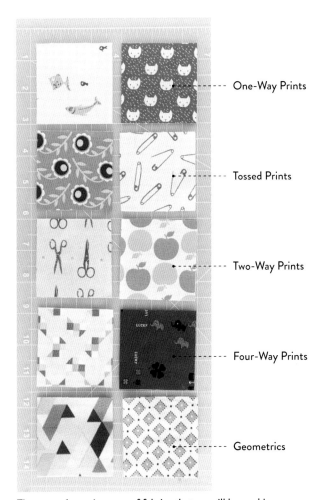

One-Way Prints

Tossed Prints

Two-Way Prints

Four-Way Prints

Geometrics

These are the main types of fabrics that we will be working through with you throughout this book. Each print presents its own challenges when cutting and piecing, so it is a good idea to get familiar with each type in your own stash so that you can follow along with our cutting directions as well as take advantage of all of our tips and tricks!

While any kind of print can be used as a background, we tend to gravitate toward softer, "quiet" designs that blend into the block instead of conflicting with the selected focal fabric. These are also known as 'blenders'.

BLOCK BASICS

SINGLE CUT BASICS

Since the focus of this book is to isolate motifs, some of the speed cutting and piecing you may be familiar with may not be appropriate. Here are one-at-a-time instructions for the Block Basics used frequently throughout the book.

Half-Square Triangles (HSTs), Traditional Method

This method yeilds one unit. Mark a corner the length of your needed size along the wrong side of both squares. Connect with a diagonal line. Cut through the fabrics one at a time on the drawn lines. Position right sides together, stitch a ¼" away from the diagonal edge. Press the unit open and trim to size if necessary.

Quarter-Square Triangles (QSTs)

This method yeilds one unit. Mark a horizontal line the length of your needed size. Mark two diagonal lines from corner to corner. Cut through all marked lines. Arrange the cut pieces in their correct placement. Position right sides together and stitch a ¼" away from a short edge on one triangle pair. Repeat. Align the two units, nesting the seams in the center. Stitch a ¼" away from the diagonal edge. Press open and trim the unit to size.

Flying Geese

This method yeilds one unit. Mark a diagonal line on the wrong side of each of the squares. Position one marked square, right sides facing, with one short side of the rectangle. Stitch along the marked line. Trim away the excess fabric using a ¼" seam allowance. Press open. Repeat for the second square on the opposite short side of the rectangle. Press the unit open.

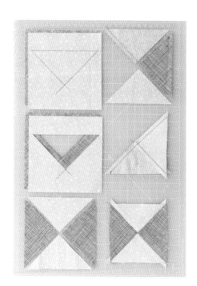

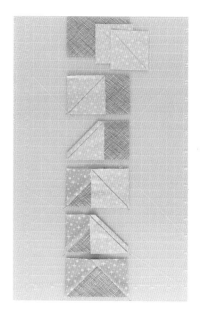

SPEED CUT BASICS

For many of the HSTs, you may be using only background fabrics that are solids or have a fabric repeats that don't require you to fussy cut them. For those occasions, here is the construction technique for speed cutting.

Half-Square Triangle 2-at-a-Time

This method yeilds two units which works well for background fabrics that don't require that directionality be maintained. Begin with your two squares facing right sides together. Mark a diagonal line along the wrong side of the layered squares. Stitch a ¼" away from both sides of the marked line. Cut the unit in half along the cut line. Press both units open and trim to size if necessary.

FINISHING YOUR QUILT

Lucky Spool has a free downloadable PDF of quilt making basics (www.luckyspool.com). We include information about the entire quilting process from cutting to finishing your quilt; however, here are some tips from us that you won't find in the PDF.

BACKING

When it is finally time to back a quilt, both Nichole and Elisabeth prefer to use widebacks. These are 108" wide fabrics that eliminate the need to piece yardage together to cover the entire quilt. A 3-yard cut gives you a 108" square of fabric to work with, which is wide enough for both layout options of our samplers.

QUILTING

If you have a domestic machine and you love quilting at home, then absolutely quilt as desired! If there's nothing you enjoy more than sending a quilt top to your favorite long-armer, we encourage you to do that instead. Nichole partnered with the talented Tanya Heldman of *Free Range Quilter* to work magic on her quilt and Elisabeth worked with Angela Walters, who first inspired her to try free-motion quilting at home.

BINDING

The last step in your quilt is of course to bind it! We both prefer to cut our binding strips to 2¼" and use double fold binding. There is again some debate about whether it is better to hand or machine stitch the binding, and we have a very similar stance to the quilting question. We feel that you should bind your quilt however you prefer. As long as you're having fun, then you're doing it right.

OUR FAVORITE TOOLS

THREAD

We've found Aurifil thread is the best for fine piecing with the least amount of lint build-up. It is super strong and with over 1,400 yards on a spool, you can sew quite a few blocks before you start running low. Plus, we love that there are 270 colors to choose from, so you can always find just the right shade for any project you want to sew!

RULERS

Omnigrid® acrylic rulers are hands-down our favorites. They have a solid grip so they don't slide when you're cutting and the yellow and black printing is easy to see on both light and dark fabrics. Here are our favorites, the ones we used extensively while working on these blocks.

> **4" x 14":** Elisabeth's favorite! This ruler never feels too big or too small. It's always just right.

> **9½" SQUARE:** This ruler is perfect for squaring up final blocks.

> **6½" SQUARE:** Small enough to be manageable, but large enough to grip comfortably.

> **3½" SQUARE:** Nichole's favorite! Perfect for squaring up individual block sections.

- -

A NOTE ABOUT BLOCK SIZE: Each block in this book is 9½" square unfinished, unless otherwise noted. Any blocks finishing larger will have instructions on trimming down to 9½" square.

- -

ROTARY CUTTERS

A sharp rotary cutter is essential for good fussy cuts. There's nothing worse than having your blade skip parts of the fabric when you are cutting!

SCISSORS

We love Kai scissors because they are super sharp and fit comfortably in our hands when you especially need precision. You'll want to make sure you have your favorite pair of scissors is always close at hand.

SEAM RIPPERS

Because we all make mistakes sometimes.

PINS

Always handy for matching and stabilizing seams.

ERASABLE PENS

We like pens such as Frixon, which have a fine point and are erasable with heat. Because precision is very important when fussy cutting, using a pen that will make a fine line makes for more successful marking.

PERMANENT MARKERS

At many points in our book, we ask you to mark your ruler. The red or black fine-tip versions of permanent markers are perfect for precise lines. The lines are easily removed from rulers with isopropyl alcohol (rubbing alcohol). Be careful not to use these on your fabric though!

TWEEZERS

We love having a pair of sharp-pointed tweezers close at hand when sewing. They're very handy for unpicking papers when paper piecing.

WHITE GLUE

Perfect for designs that require glue-basting.

FREEZER PAPER

Available at any local grocery store, this quiet hero makes piecing off-grain items a breeze!

STARCH ALTERNATIVE

We always use a spray starch alternative like Flatter. We love how flat and precise our blocks are when we use it. Alternative starches are often available in several lovely scents for folks who enjoy aromas. For the people with sensitive sniffers, you can easily find excellent scentless options!

IRON

We prefer using a hot, dry iron paired with a spray starch such as Flatter for the best block result.

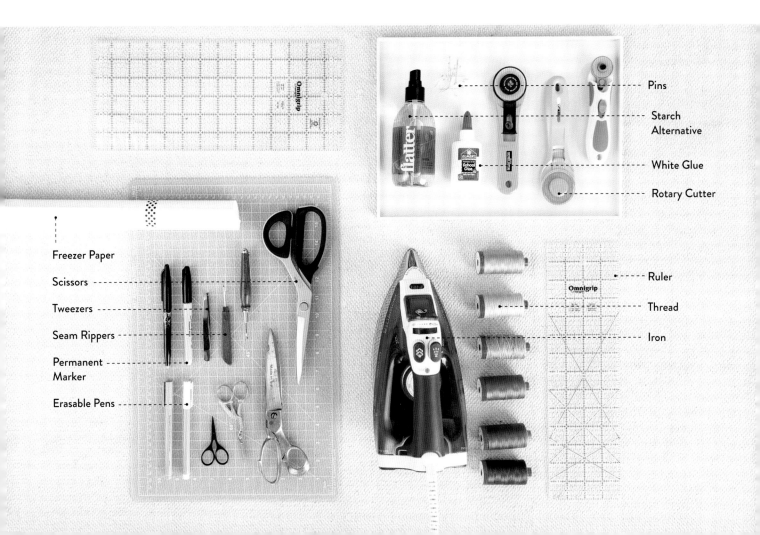

block # 14

background basics

WE ALL HAVE FAVORITE QUILT BLOCKS or can recall blocks that captured our imaginations—what is it about those blocks that makes them special? Some are family heirlooms, some have intricate piecing or elaborate appliqué. One of the most important elements in a block is the often-unsung hero: the background. The featured fabrics or the bright colors wouldn't shine without a perfectly set stage. It adds the balance and the quiet your eye needs to take in the overall design. Often backgrounds are low-volume fabrics or neutral tones, but you can easily work with lighter shades to achieve the same effect.

In this chapter, you will learn about the importance of directionality in the background of a block, how to choose what and where your background will be, and how to perfectly pair backgrounds with other elements in your blocks. This can all seem intimidating at first, but the extra effort put into getting the background just right will be worth it, because in the end you'll have a block that looks exactly like you imagined it.

cutting basics for backgrounds

Squares and rectangles are the easiest shapes to fussy cut, and with these tricks you will create eye-catching, dynamic blocks. This block focuses on directionality. Before sewing your block, arrange the units on your design wall (see page 8) and ensure any pattern in the fabric that you want to feature is consistently facing one direction. If you want to feature a design motif, make sure that the design is inside your seam allowances. Elisabeth often draws the requisite ¼" seam allowance onto her fabric using an erasable pen (see page 12) before cutting to visualize what the fussy cut will look like once pieced. Nichole uses her clear acrylic ruler (see page 12) to see what the ¼" seam allowance will be prior to cutting.

Nichole's Block

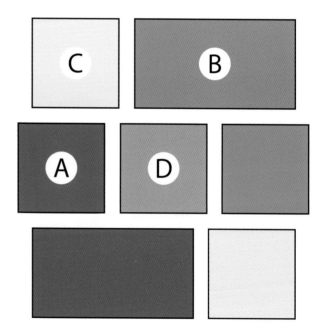

Block Diagram

FABRIC NEEDED

From Fabrics A and B, cut:
(1) 3½" square
(1) 6½" x 3½" rectangle

From Fabric C, cut:
(2) 3½" squares

From Fabric D, cut:
(1) 3½" square

Take Two: Elisabeth's Block

TIP: Remember, no matter what block shape you cut, you must always consider the seam allowance.

BUILD YOUR BLOCK

1. Referencing the Block Diagram, arrange all of the cut units into the final block shape.

   NOTE: This is recommended as the first step for every block in this book to avoid piecing mistakes and to ensure proper unit alignment.

2. For the top row, sew a Fabric C square to the Fabric B rectangle.

3. For the middle row, sew a Fabric A and Fabric B square to either side of the Fabric D square.

4. For the bottom row, sew the Fabric A rectangle to the remaining Fabric C square.

5. Sew the rows together in order and press.

See how important it is to have proper directionality? All the block's shapes are going in the same direction except for the bottom right corner. While there is nothing technically wrong with the block, this error makes the block look disjointed and pulls the eye to that location instead of your focal point.

directionality in half-square triangles and backgrounds

It can be easy to make a directionality mistake when assembling half-square triangles (HSTs). With careful placement and a little planning, you'll be able to create HSTs that keep their directionality and always look great!

Making HSTs using the traditional method (see page 10) will give you the most control over your fabric placement and leaves enough excess fabric to create easily squared-up blocks with little waste. Making HSTs using the two-at-a-time method (see page 11) is faster and by using a simple flip test (see the TIP opposite), you can easily be sure your directionality is consistent.

Elisabeth's Block

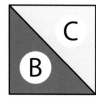

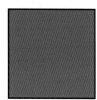

Block Diagram

FABRIC NEEDED

From Fabric A, cut:
(2) 3½" squares

From Fabric B, cut:
(3) 4" squares for HSTs

From Fabric C, cut:
(1) 3½" square
(3) 4" squares for HSTs

Take Two: Nichole replaced her Fabric C square with another Fabric A square.

BUILD YOUR BLOCK

1. Gather the 4" Fabric B and Fabric C squares and create (6) 3½" HST units using the two-at-a-time HST method (see page 11).

2. Ensuring that the fussy cut Fabric A units share a common directionality (see below), sew the top row together using a Fabric A square and 2 assembled HST units.

3. Repeat Step 2 for the bottom row.

4. Sew an assembled HST unit to either side of a 3½" square for the middle row.

5. Sew the rows together in order and press.

TIP: A test flip makes it easy to check on directionality before sewing. After placing the right sides of the fabric together, flip up the bottom left corner and fold along the diagonal to make sure your block has the directionality you desire.

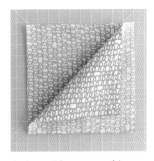

designs with non-matching directionality

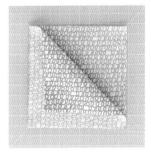

designs with matching directionality

combining block 1 and block 2

This block combines the skills learned from Blocks 1 and 2. Begin by using a background fabric with an all over print to create a cohesive background for both the 4-square and the HST blocks. Once you are comfortable with the piecing style, try using a directional background fabric as used in Elisabeth's block on the facing page.

A great way to make sure your directionality flows through this block is to piece your HST units first, then arrange them with the squares on your design wall. Rotate the remaining background squares until the directionality is consistent throughout. Once everything looks right, piece the final block units together.

Nichole's Block

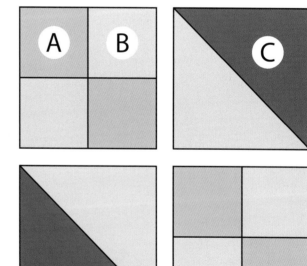

Block Diagram

FABRIC NEEDED

From Fabric A, cut:
(4) 2¾" squares

From Fabric B, cut:
(4) 2¾" squares
(1) 5½" square for HSTs

From Fabric C, cut:
(1) 5½" square for HSTs

Take Two: Elisabeth's Block

BUILD YOUR BLOCK

1. Gather the 5½" Fabric B and Fabric C squares and create (2) 5" HST units using the two-at-a-time HST method (see page 11).

2. Gather the 2¾" Fabric A and Fabric B squares and create (2) 5" 4-square units. Sew 4 Fabric A and B squares together and press. Then sew the 2 units together to create a checkerboard 4-square.

3. Sew the units from Steps 1 and 2 together to form 2 rows of 2 units each.

4. Sew the rows together and press.

matching backgrounds & borders

Now that you've mastered the basics of making your HSTs all go in one direction, let's try a block that's a bit more challenging. Matching the directionality in your background fabrics even when your HSTs are orientated differently, is a quick way to make a block look complete. While this may require a bit more care while cutting your HST units, you'll quickly find that it is an easy adjustment.

When you're working with squares, it's easy to adjust directionality since all four sides are the same—but when you work with rectangles it's a little tricker. You'll often see rectangles in borders, but they can also be found in other parts of a block. You'll notice that this block has rectangles as part of the inner block, as well as the border, so you must take extra care when cutting your directional background. To cut correctly, make sure you cut two background rectangles with the directionality running vertically, and two rectangles with the directionality running horizontally for both the borders as well as the inner block When the block is pieced together, the background fabric will look like one fluid piece, all running the same direction. Magic!

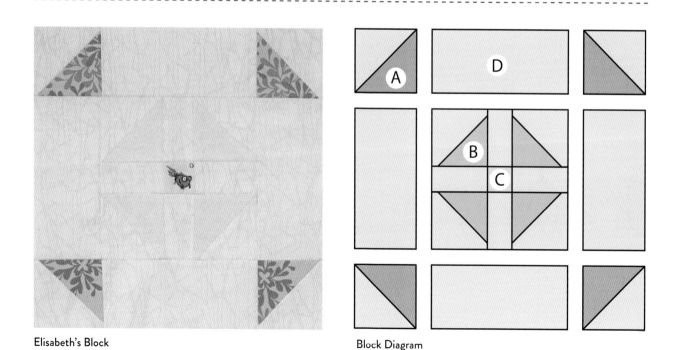

Elisabeth's Block

Block Diagram

FABRIC NEEDED

From Fabric A, cut:
(2) 3" squares for HSTs

From Fabric B, cut:
(2) 3" squares for HSTs

From Fabric C, cut:
(1) 1½" square for the center

From Fabric D, cut:
(4) 3" squares for HSTs
(4) 1½" x 2½" rectangles
(4) 2½" x 5½" rectangles

Take Two: Nichole replaced the Fabric B and C squares with Fabric A. Nichole only used two fabrics whereas Elisabeth used four.

BUILD YOUR BLOCK

1. Gather the Fabric A squares and (2) 3" Fabric D squares and create (4) 2½" A/D HST units using the two-at-a-time HST method (see page 11).

2. Repeat Step 1, using Fabric B squares in place of the Fabric A squares, to create (4) 2½" B/D HST units.

3. Before sewing, arrange the assembled units and the remaining cut units according to the Block Diagram and double-check directionality.

4. For the top and bottom rows, sew a Fabric A/D HST to either side of a horizontal 5½" Fabric D rectangle. Set aside.

5. For the center unit, sew a Fabric B/D HST to either side of a 1½" Fabric D rectangle, paying attention to the fabric placement for directionality. Repeat for the bottom row of the center unit.

6. Sew a 1½" Fabric D rectangle to either side of the Fabric C square.

7. Assemble the rows from Step 5 on the top and bottom of the row from Step 6. Press.

8. Sew a 5½" Fabric D horizontal rectangle to either side of the unit from Step 7. Press.

9. Sew the rows together in order and press.

CHAPTER 2

stripes

STRIPES ARE one of the most versatile (and intimidating) designs to fussy cut. You might be a little worried that stripes are too bold or too hard to work with. But by cutting carefully, you can make a dynamic block with minimal effort. By changing the direction the stripes are oriented, you can create movement, borders, or unity within a block. This chapter will inspire you to add striped fabrics to your favorite blocks to give them an unmistakable flair. Plus, we'll give you some helpful hints to mimic the look of striped fabric using some simple shapes. By the end of this chapter, you will be on the hunt for all the striped fabrics in your stash, or running to your favorite fabric store to buy new ones!

Stripes come in all shapes and sizes. Some of our favorites are hand drawn stripes, bias stripes, pin stripes, and designs that imitate stripes, plus so many more!

cutting basics for stripes

Okay, okay, we know: stripes can be tricky to cut properly. But with a few tips you'll be creating blocks that show off stripes in new and fun ways. By playing with scale, direction, and (of course) fussy cutting, you can create amazing patterns to end up with a dynamic block! If you are mindful of the directionality of your striped fabrics before cutting and piecing, you can showcase a seamless flow in your background fabric or mix in an unexpected secondary design.

Nichole's Block

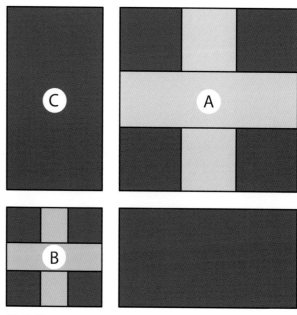

Block Diagram

TIP: If you are using a directional background, be aware of the orientation of the rectangle units and cut in the same direction you'd be piecing them in the block (vertically or horizontally).

FABRIC NEEDED

From Fabric A, cut:
(2) 2½" squares for the large +
(1) 6½" x 2½" rectangle

From Fabric B, cut:
(2) 1½" squares for the small +
(1) 3½" x 1½" rectangle

From Fabric C, cut:
(4) 2½" squares
(4) 1½" squares
(2) 6½" x 3½" rectangles (one cut on the horizontal and one cut on the vertical if using a directional background fabric)

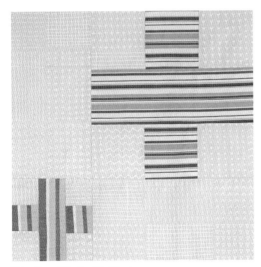
Take Two: Elisabeth's Block

BUILD YOUR BLOCK

1. Before sewing, arrange the cut units according to the Block Diagram and double-check the directionality of your cuts.

2. Sew a 2½" Fabric C square to either side of a Fabric A square. Press and repeat.

3. Sew an assembled unit from Step 2 to both 6½" sides of a Fabric A rectangle. Press and set aside.

4. Repeat Steps 2 and 3 using the 1½" pieces of Fabrics B and C.

5. Sew a Fabric C rectangle to the assembled unit from Step 3 along the 6½".

6. Sew a Fabric C rectangle to the assembled unit from Step 4 along the 3½".

7. Sew the rows together and press.

creating movement with stripes

This block allows you to create a fun border around your chosen fussy cut. There are several options for determining how to incorporate stripes within the block. You can cut the strips of three fabrics all running the same direction and vary the width of them to add interest. You can have the middle stripe running in the opposite direction to the outer borders, creating movement from many directions. You can even just use a stripe for one or two of the three border strips. Deciding upon how much of a stripe effect you want to create will help direct you in your fabric choice and orientation.

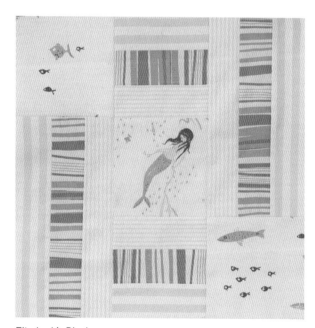

Elisabeth's Block

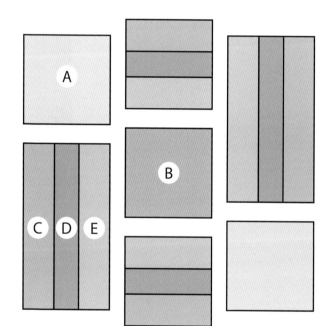

Block Diagram

FABRIC NEEDED

From Fabric A, cut:
(2) 3½" squares

From Fabric B, cut:
(1) 3½" square

From Fabrics C, D, and E, cut:
(2) 1½" x 6½" rectangles from each fabric
(2) 1½" x 3½" rectangles from each fabric

Take Two: Nichole's Block

BUILD YOUR BLOCK

1. Before sewing, arrange the cut units according to the Block Diagram and double-check the directionality of your cuts.

2. Sew a 6½" Fabric C rectangle and a 6½" Fabric E rectangle to either side of 6½" Fabric D rectangle. Press. Repeat and set aside.

3. Repeat Step 2 using the 3½" rectangles.

4. Sew a Fabric A square to one side of an assembled unit from Step 2. Press. Repeat.

5. Sew an assembled unit from Step 3 to the top and bottom of the Fabric B square. Press.

6. Sew the three columns together and press.

TIP: Cutting a long strip of a striped fabric may be tricky, but it is often the best way to create consistent lines. Let the stripes direct your cutting. Pay attention to aligning the stripes and create a single strip that is the length of the combined strips needed. Then cut that strip into subsections, creating pieces that all match!

---

shapes imitating stripes

There are so many fabric pattern repeats that are designed to mimic stripes. They can initially appear to be geometrics (like dots and dashes) or more organic allover prints (like leafy vines and flowers). But when you look closely, you see that those shapes actually produce a striped fabric. Incorporating these designs into your blocks adds the same directional flow as working with stripes, but with the added bonus that they are a little more forgiving when they don't align perfectly. They are versatile designs that work well in everything from small piecing to larger dramatic borders or even quilt binding. So give your prints a second look. They might actually be stripes in disguise!

Nichole's Block

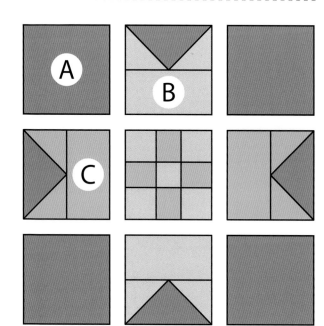

Block Diagram

FABRIC NEEDED

From Fabric A, cut:
(4) 3½" squares
(4) 2¼" x 3¾" rectangles

From Fabric B, cut:
(4) 2¼" squares
(2) 2" x 3½" rectangles
(5) 1½" squares

From Fabric C, cut:
(4) 2¼" squares
(2) 2" x 3½" rectangles
(4) 1½" squares

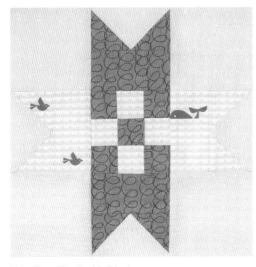

Take Two: Elisabeth's Block

TIP: If you need to trim your Flying Geese units to size, be sure to leave a ¼" seam allowance above the top point. Flying Geese units for this block should be 2" x 3½" unfinished.

BUILD YOUR BLOCK

1. Before sewing, arrange the cut units according to the Block Diagram and double-check the directionality of your cuts.

2. Gather 2 Fabric A rectangles and (2) 2¼" Fabric B squares and assemble 2 Flying Geese units (see page 10). Trim to 2" x 3½".

3. Sew a 3½" Fabric B rectangle to the assembled Flying Geese unit. Repeat.

4. Repeat Steps 2 and 3 with the remaining Fabric A rectangles, (4) 2¼" Fabric C squares and (2) 3½" Fabric C rectangles.

5. To create the 9-patch block in the center, sew a 1½" Fabric B square to either side of a 1½" Fabric C square. Press. Repeat. Sew a 1½" Fabric C square to either side of the remaining Fabric B square. Press. Sew the 9-patch rows together in order. Press.

6. For the top and bottom rows, sew a 3½" Fabric A square to either side of an assembled unit from Step 3, checking your fabric orientation. Repeat.

7. For the middle row, sew an assembled unit from Step 4 to either side of the assembled 9-patch unit from Step 5.

8. Sew the rows together and press.

secondary patterns with stripes

Stripes are one of Nichole's favorite patterns to use in a quilt block. They automatically draw the eye to the movement within the block and are a great way to create striking primary and secondary patterns (especially when making a quilt using multiples of one or two blocks). By paying close attention to how you cut and position your stripes, you can quickly transform a block design and immediately create movement and directionality.

Elisabeth's Block

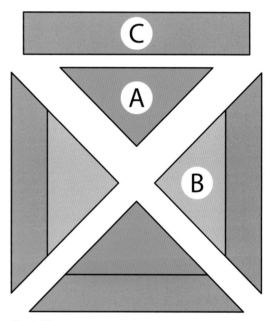

Block Diagram

FABRIC NEEDED

From Fabrics A and B, cut:
(1) 5¼" square from each fabric

From Fabric C, cut:
(4) 11" x 2" rectangles

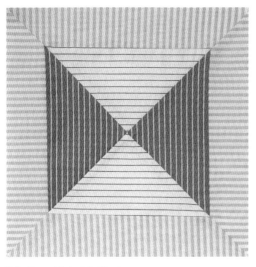
Take Two: Nichole's Block

BUILD YOUR BLOCK

1. Cut the Fabric A and Fabric B squares diagonally from the top left to the bottom right corner.

2. Center a Fabric C rectangle on the long edge of each A and B triangle. Sew and press. The Fabric C rectangle will overlap the triangle by 1½" on either side. Use a square acrylic ruler aligned with the right angle of the Fabric A and Fabric B triangles and trim away the excess from Fabric C (see the Block Diagram for placement).

3. Gather an assembled A/C unit and an assembled B/C unit from Step 2 and sew together along the 7½" side. Repeat for the remaining units, mirroring the color placement.

4. Sew the two assembled units from Step 3 together along the long edge, matching the center seams. Press.

5. Trim the block to 9½" square.

TIP: Depending on how your stripes are aligned on your fabric, you may have to cut them on the bias to get the same effect shown in Elisabeth's and Nichole's blocks. If you pair stripes of similar width, with the contrast of light and dark values reversed where the seams meet, you will trick the eye into thinking the stripes match perfectly . . . even when they might not!

playing with color and value

AS YOU MAY HAVE GUESSED BY NOW, making engaging and fun blocks takes more than just fussy cutting cute designs. One of the most important components of the fabric selection process is understanding when to use a light-, mid-, or dark-valued fabric to create the balance of contrast you want in your blocks. When the fabrics selected for a block are too similar in value, you lose the overall impact of the piecing or the block design. In this chapter, we're going to show you some block designs that illustrate how to use color effectively to achieve a balance of contrast and to add even more focus to your fabulous fussy cuts. Plus, we'll give you some helpful hints on how to mimic the look of a striped fabric using some simple shapes.

What is Value?
Value is used to describe how light or dark a color is. Light value tends to include tints and dark value tends to include shades. The perception of value is often influenced by the saturation of the color as well as the amount of white (tints), gray (tones) or black (shades) added to the primary hue. Try to evaluate where each fabric you choose would fall into the spectrum.

avoiding distracting backgrounds

When working with value, it is important to consider the pattern in your background fabrics. One of the best ways to accentuate bold color in all of your fabrics, is to select a background fabric with a pattern that has a limited color palette. This allows your eye to focus on the more dominant colors. As always, if you select a directional background, be mindful of your cutting.

No matter what prints you select as your background fabrics, make sure that they don't compete too strongly in scale or color with your neighboring fabrics. If your background is too distinct on its own, it will take away from the focal fabric in your block. Look for colors that are different enough to make the focal fabric "pop" while also working well with the other fabrics in the block.

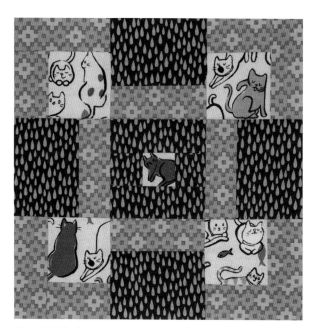

Nichole's Block

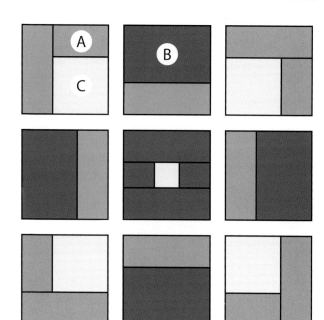

Block Diagram

FABRIC NEEDED

From Fabric A, cut:
(4) 2½" x 1½" rectangles
(8) 3½" x 1½" rectangles

From Fabric B, cut:
(4) 2½" x 3½" rectangles
(2) 1½" x 3½" rectangles
(2) 1½" squares

From Fabric C, cut:
(4) 2½" squares
(1) 1½" square

Take Two: Elisabeth chose to add in a different fabric for her outer edge units and the center-most square. If you'd like to do the same, swap in additional fabrics for (4) 2½" x 3½" rectangles for Fabric B, (4) 3½" x 1½" for Fabric A, and (1) 1½" square for Fabric C in Steps 3 and 4 following.

BUILD YOUR BLOCK

1. Before sewing, arrange the cut units according to the Block Diagram and double-check the directionality of your cuts.

2. Sew a 2½" x 1½" Fabric A rectangle to a 2½" Fabric C square. Referencing the Block Diagram for placement, sew a 3½" x 1½" Fabric A rectangle to the assembled unit. Press. Repeat to create a total of 4 corner units and set aside.

3. Sew a 1½" x 3½" Fabric A rectangle to a 2½" x 3½" Fabric B rectangle. Press. Repeat to create a total of 4 units and set aside.

4. Sew a 1½" Fabric B square to either side of the 1½" Fabric C square. Sew a 1½" x 3½" Fabric B rectangle to the top and bottom of the assembled unit. Press.

5. Referencing the Block Diagram for placement, sew an assembled corner unit from Step 2 to either side of an assembled unit from Step 3. Press. Repeat to create a total of 2 rows.

6. Sew an assembled unit from Step 3 to either side of the assembled unit from Step 4. Press.

7. Sew the three rows together and press.

BLOCK

10 *value basics*

Combining two color families can often make a strong statement. In this block, we will work with two color families, using different values of each color to create interest in the block. Get inspiration from the color wheel, a favorite photo, or the trendiest fabrics of the season to select a great pair of colors. Use fabrics that complement each other and look related based on the scale of print, theme, and/or use of negative space—but it doesn't hurt to use fabrics that have a fun design or visual element, since the squares are big enough to really let the fabrics shine.

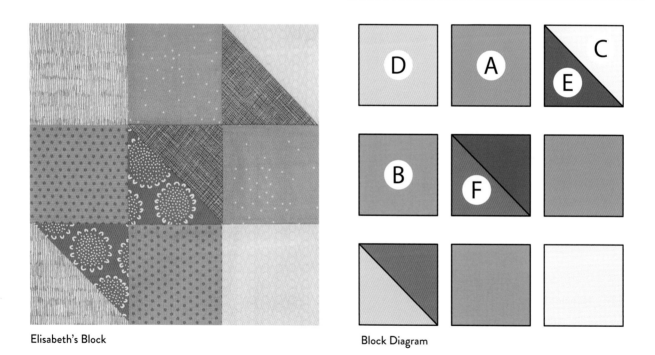

Elisabeth's Block   Block Diagram

FABRIC NEEDED

From Fabrics A and B, cut:

(2) 3½" squares

From Fabrics C and D, cut:

(1) 3½" square
(1) 4" square for HSTs

From Fabrics E and F, cut:

(1) 4" square for HSTs

Take Two: Nichole's Block

BUILD YOUR BLOCK

1. Gather the 4" of fabrics C, D, E and F. Using the HST construction (see page 10) construct one D/F, F/E, E/C unit. Trim each to 3½". You will have one C triangle and one D triangle left over.

2. Referencing the Block Diagram for placement, sew a 3½" Fabric D square to a 3½" Fabric A square. Sew the assembled E/C HST unit to create the top row.

3. Sew a 3½" Fabric B square to the assembled F/E HST unit. Sew a 3½" Fabric A square to create the middle row.

4. Sew the assembled D/F HST unit to a 3½" Fabric B square. Sew the 3½" Fabric C square to create the bottom row.

5. Sew the rows together and press.

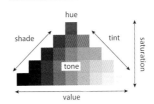

Value Grid

Not sure if you have the right combination? Audition your fabrics before cutting by laying them down next to each other and determining if one is overpowering the others. Work with our Value Grid to build a value scheme for your block. We both chose to work with complementary colors in our individual diamonds, but feel free to use the color wheel as a resource to choose contrasting or harmonious colors for a similar effect.

achieving transparency

Next we want you to try your hand at transparency! This effect is often incorporated into modern quilt designs and creates depth by mimicking woven layers. To achieve transparency, work with a dark fabric, one or two medium fabrics, and a light fabric. The medium fabric(s) should be just the right shade between the dark and light so it looks like the color that results when the light and dark fabrics overlap.

Audition your fabrics using your block diagram before piecing to make sure you are achieving the desired woven effect. If you're not sure your fabric choices work, enlist the help of a few quilty friends who can point you in the right direction, or try posting your fabric audition on your favorite social media platform or online quilting community. Even though we spend most of our quilting time alone, we all have quilty friends we trust to give their honest opinions when we're not sure!

Nichole's Block

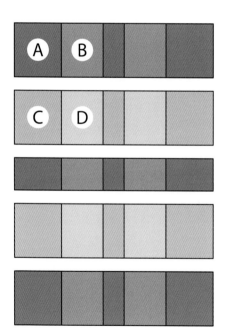

Block Diagram

FABRIC NEEDED

- -

From Fabric A (dark), cut:
(4) 2½" squares
(4) 1½" x 2½" rectangles
(1) 1½" square

From Fabrics B and C (medium), cut:
(4) 2½" squares
(2) 1½" x 2½" rectangles

From Fabric D (light), cut:
(4) 2½" squares

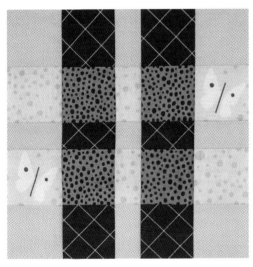

Take Two: Elisabeth exchanged her light fabric for one of Nichole's medium fabrics and her dark fabric for Nichole's second medium fabric. If you'd like to do the same, switch your Fabric C and Fabric D cuts and your A and B cuts.

BUILD YOUR BLOCK

- -

1. Before sewing, arrange the cut units according to the Block Diagram and double-check the directionality of your cuts.

2. Sew a Fabric B square to either side of a Fabric A rectangle. Sew a 2½" Fabric A square to either side of the assembled unit. Repeat and set aside.

3. Repeat Step 2 for Fabrics C and D.

4. Sew a Fabric B rectangle to either side of the 1½" Fabric A square. Sew a Fabric A rectangle to either side of the assembled unit.

5. Press the seams for each row in opposite directions. Nesting the seams, sew the rows together and press.

- -

TIP: This is an excellent block to practice nesting your seams. Piece your five rows but do not press them. Arrange your rows by referencing the Block Diagram for placement. Beginning with the top row, press all the seams to the right; then press all the seams for each subsequent row in different directions. When you sew the rows together, you'll be able to "nest" the seams together, creating a smooth finish.

- -

playing with scale

One of the best ways to make a block dynamic with little effort, is to play with the scale within the prints of your fabrics. By choosing a similar shape in a variety of sizes, a block becomes more interesting than if you only used the same sized motif for the whole block.

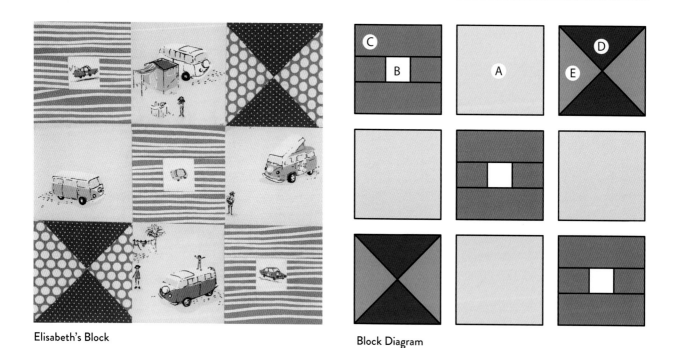

Elisabeth's Block

Block Diagram

FABRIC NEEDED

From Fabric A, cut:
(4) 3½" squares

From Fabric B, cut:
(3) 1½" squares

From Fabric C, cut:
(6) 1½" squares
(6) 1½" x 3½" rectangles

From Fabrics D and E, cut:
(2) 4½" squares for QSTs

Take Two: Nichole's Block

BUILD YOUR BLOCK

1. Before sewing, arrange the cut units according to the Block Diagram and double-check the directionality of your cuts.

2. Gather the Fabric D and Fabric E squares and create 2 QST units (see page 10). Trim the QSTs to 3½" square and set aside. Depending on your cuts, you may only need (1) 4½", but to be safe, we have included two cuts for you to be able to play around with your placement.

3. Sew a Fabric C square to either side of a Fabric B square. Sew a Fabric C rectangle to the top and bottom of the assembled unit. Press. Repeat to create a total of 3 units.

4. Referencing the Block Diagram for order and placement, sew one unit from Step 3, a Fabric A square and one QST together to form the top row. Press. Repeat to form the bottom row.

5. Sew a Fabric A square to either side of the remaining assembled unit from Step 3.

6. Sew the rows together and press.

precision fussy cuts

WHEN QUILTERS THINK ABOUT FUSSY CUTTING, what immediately comes to mind is how to fit a great design into just the right spot of your piecing. This chapter explores strategies for achieving the perfect results we all crave. It can be tricky to determine where you want to feature your favorite fabrics or what motif from your favorite fabric to incorporate into a specific block. It can be even harder to cut into some of your most treasured fabrics for fear of making a mistake. Just remember, fussy cutting is supposed to be fun! Take a deep breath, measure a few times, mark and measure again, then cut. And you know what? Sometimes even after all that measuring and all that marking, your ruler slips, or you realize you were reading the wrong line in the cutting instructions. That's when you go get some ice cream or a cookie or a coffee or just go take a walk. It happens to all of us, but in the end, fussy cutting is worth it. We promise.

ANITA GROSSMAN SOLOMON, our dear friend and quilting hero, recommends drawing directly onto a ruler with a permanent Sharpie pen so that you can see your fussy cut area before you make the cut.

Anita Grossman Solomon is a teacher and author, as well as the innovator behind the Make It Simpler® techniques. She is known for her impressive construction shortcuts for traditional-looking blocks.

MARKING YOUR RULER FOR QST HOURGLASS BLOCKS

To mark on a 6½" square ruler for a 3½" finished QST hourglass block, first draw the 4½" square lines, then a line along each diagonal. Draw in your ¼" seam allowances on each side of the diagonal lines.

The pen marks are easily removed from the ruler with isopropyl alcohol, but because it may damage the surface, always mark on the side of the ruler without the pre-printed measurements. To ensure than none of the ink gets on your fabric, don't forget to clean the sides of your ruler after marking and always place the non-marked side of the ruler on the fabric.

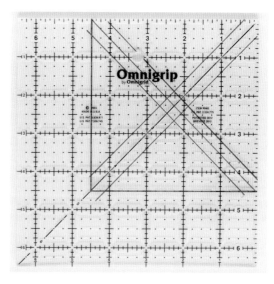

QST markings on the acrylic ruler help you to visualize the final area seen within each fabric when the seam allowance is taken up.

MARKING YOUR RULER FOR HST BLOCKS

To fussy cut a triangle within either side of your HST units, temporarily mark your visible area directly on your ruler as you did for the QST opposite. For this block, draw a 4" square, then draw a diagonal line from one corner to the other. Draw ¼" seam allowances on each side of the diagonal line. This shows the visible area for both triangles of your finished 3½" HST units.

HST markings for this 4" square clearly show the areas you can see on your fabrics.

MARKING YOUR RULER FOR FLYING GEESE UNITS

To fussy cut a rectangle for the Flying Geese units, temporarily mark your visible area directly on your ruler as you have done for the QST and the HST. For this block, draw a 2¼" x 3¾" rectangle. Then, mark a point on the top edge 2¼" from the top left corner. Draw a diagonal line from this point to the bottom left corner. Repeat and mark a point on the top edge 2¼" from the top right corner, then draw a diagonal line from this point to the bottom right corner. The triangle in the center shows the visible area for your finished Flying Geese units.

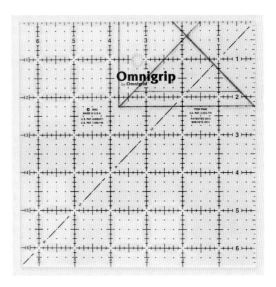

The Flying Geese markings on this ruler will help you visualize the area on the cut rectangle.

centering a motif

One of the easiest ways to make your fussy cuts stand out and look intentional is to center them in the block. By intentionally positioning the fabric away from the edges and leaving more space around the fussy cut to really frame it, you show that you carefully planned your fabric cuts, rather than just getting lucky and cutting your fabric in just the right spot. To end up with a nicely framed motif, take the finished block size you want to fill (for example 3″) and divide that in half. This gives you the center point for your block. Once you select a motif to feature, use your clear ruler to place the center of your block size in the middle of the image. If you cut at this point, you can be sure that the final picture will be centered in the block. Don't forget to add your seam allowance in! Centering motifs is easy, and once you begin including fussy cuts in your blocks, it will quickly become second nature.

Nichole's Block

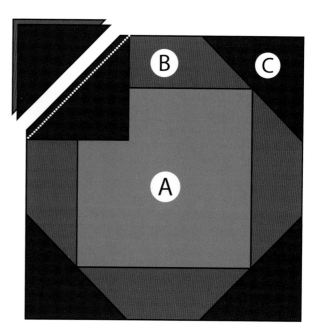

Block Diagram

FABRIC NEEDED

From Fabric A, cut:

(1) 6½" square

From Fabric B, cut:

(2) 2" x 6½" rectangles
(2) 2" x 9½" rectangles

From Fabric C, cut:

(4) 3½" squares

Take Two: Elisabeth's Block

BUILD YOUR BLOCK

1. On the wrong side of each of the Fabric C squares, mark a diagonal line — on two of the squares, mark from the upper left to the lower right; on the other two, mark from the upper right to the lower left. Set aside.

2. Sew a 2" x 6½" Fabric B rectangle to either side of the Fabric A square. Press.

3. Sew a 2" x 9½" Fabric B rectangle to the top and bottom of the unit assembled in Step 2. Press.

4. Using the Block Diagram as a guide, position a Fabric C square right sides together in one of the corners of your assembled unit from Step 3. Sew along the marked diagonal line. Repeat for the remaining three Fabric C squares.

5. Using an acrylic ruler, trim ¼" away from your sewn line on each of the Fabric C squares, cutting through both layers of fabric.

6. Press well and trim to 9½" square.

featuring motifs in HSTs

If you are following along with this book in numerical block order, you already have experience with fussy cutting squares, borders, and background fabrics. Next let's try going one step further and fussy cutting the HST units themselves! These can be trickier because you still need to consider your seam allowance and background fabric directionality when making your cuts, but now you also have to find an accurate seam allowance along a diagonal line. Using the technique of marking the visible fussy cut area on a ruler (see page 47) will allow you to cut your fabric with confidence.

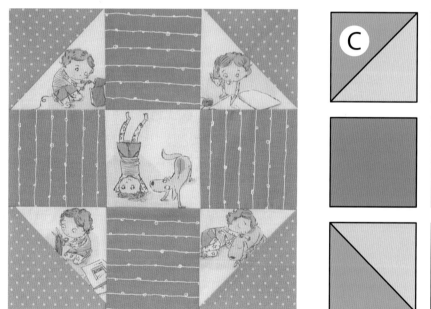

Elisabeth's Block

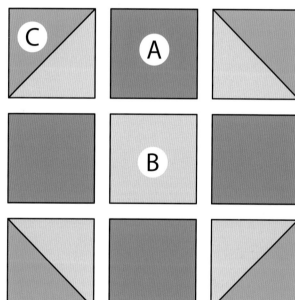

Block Diagram

FABRIC NEEDED

From Fabric A, cut:
(4) 3½" squares

From Fabric B, cut:
(1) 3½" square
(4) 4" squares for HSTs

From Fabric C, cut:
(4) 4" squares for HSTs

Take Two: Nichole's Block

BUILD YOUR BLOCK

1. Paying close attention to the directionality in the fabrics, cut the 4" Fabric B and Fabric C squares in half diagonally. Two of each fabric need to be cut on the diagonal from the top left to the bottom right, and two need to be cut on the diagonal from the top right to the bottom left. Match HST parts and, using the traditional HST method (see page 10), create 4 HST units. Trim to 3½" square if needed.

2. Referencing the Block Diagram for placement, sew an assembled HST unit from Step 1 to either side of a Fabric A square for the top row. Repeat for the bottom row.

3. Sew a Fabric A square to either side of the 3½" Fabric B square for the middle row.

4. Sew the rows together and press.

mirroring motifs

Mirroring is a technique in which the same parts of a fabric repeat are cut multiple times. The identical cut pieces are then arranged in different directions to create a balanced movement within the block. To cut identical pieces of fabric, first cut your focal motif to the required size based on the block instructions you are using, then locate the identical motif on the fabric repeat. Position the cut block exactly on top of the repeat (with the right sides of both fabrics facing up) so that the alignment of the two motifs is exact— holding the two fabrics up against a bright window or using a lightbox will help with this. Being careful not to shift your fabrics, trace around the cut block using an erasable pen, then cut along the drawn line. This simple technique yields matching motifs that will add a 'wow' factor to any block.

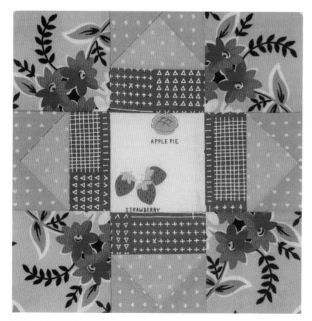

Nichole's Block

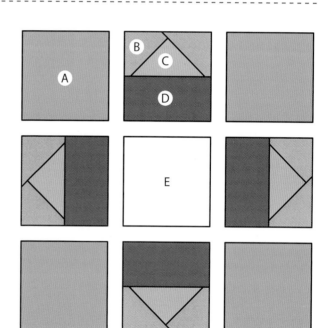

Block Diagram

FABRIC NEEDED

From Fabric A, cut:
(4) 3½" squares featuring mirrored motifs

From Fabric B, cut:
(8) 2¼" squares

From Fabric C, cut:
(4) 2¼" x 3¾" rectangles

From Fabric D, cut:
(4) 2" x 3½" rectangles

From Fabric E, cut:
(1) 3½" square

Take Two: Elisabeth also used the mirroring technique for her Fabric C rectangles.

BUILD YOUR BLOCK

1. Before sewing, arrange the cut units according to the Block Diagram and double-check the directionality of your cuts and the orientation of your mirrored cuts.

2. Gather the Fabric B squares and Fabric C rectangles and create 4 Flying Geese units (see page 10). Trim to 2" x 3½". Referencing the Block Diagram for placement, sew a Fabric D rectangle to the bottom of each Flying Geese unit.

3. Sew a Fabric A square to either side of the assembled unit from Step 2. Repeat.

4. Sew an assembled unit from Step 2 to either side of the Fabric E square.

5. Sew the rows together and press.

border motifs

Sometimes borders can feel pretty boring, like you just spent all this time making a component of an intricate block but then used a neutral border fabric so that you could quickly finish it. But borders don't have to be boring! Use your favorite horizontal fussy cuts to fill one in and make an interesting design. A simple border can become a showstopper with thoughtful and fun fabric placement.

Elisabeth's Block

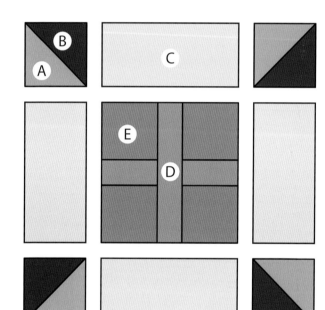

Block Diagram

FABRIC NEEDED

From Fabrics A and B, cut:
(2) 3" squares for HSTs

From Fabric C, cut:
(4) 2½" x 5½" rectangles

From Fabric D, cut:
(1) 1½" x 5½" rectangle
(2) 2½" x 1½" rectangles

From Fabric E, cut:
(4) 2½" squares

Take Two: Nichole's Block

BUILD YOUR BLOCK

1. Before sewing, arrange the cut units according to the Block Diagram and double-check the directionality of your cuts.

2. Gather the Fabric A and Fabric B squares and create 4 HST units using the traditional HST method (see page 10). Trim to 2½" square if necessary.

3. Sew an assembled HST unit to either side of a 2½" x 1½" Fabric C rectangle. Repeat and set aside.

4. Referencing the Block Diagram for placement, sew a Fabric E square to the top and bottom of a 2½" x 1½" Fabric D rectangle. Press and repeat.

5. Sew an assembled unit from Step 4 to either side of the remaining Fabric D rectangle. Press.

6. Sew the remaining Fabric C rectangles to either side of the assembled unit from Step 5. Press.

7. Sew the rows together and press.

mastering motifs

NOW THAT YOU'VE LEARNED THE BASICS of framing fussy cuts in a variety of shapes and using different cutting methods, we're going to take things a step further. In this chapter we will introduce you to the best way to work with complementary fabric prints to reinforce your focal prints; to play with a theme within a block; and to transition from focal print to secondary to background fabrics seamlessly. You'll find that the skills you've learned in the previous chapters come into play in each of the blocks in this chapter. Creating strong fussy cut blocks is like adding layers to a cake—employing one of our techniques on its own is good, but when you use many techniques together in just the right proportions, you have a real showstopper.

And really . . . who doesn't want more cake?

coordinating secondary prints

This technique is about finding a secondary print that coordinates with your focal print by complementing it, not competing with it. Your secondary fabrics should feel like a natural extension of your focal fabric, which means matching their value fairly closely, employing a smaller scale repeat than the focal print(s), or even selecting a color that complements the focal print design motif. By balancing all of these considerations, the final block will further emphasize the focal fabric and you will hardly notice the secondary fabrics. Practicing this can come in especially handy if you don't have enough of your focal fabric to use it throughout an entire block or quilt.

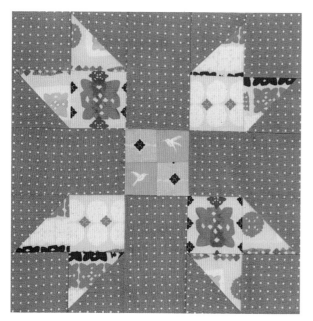

Nichole's Block

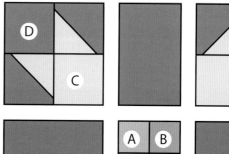

Block Diagram

FABRIC NEEDED

From Fabrics A and B, cut:

(2) 1½" squares

From Fabric C, cut:

(4) 2¼" squares
(4) 2¾" squares for HSTs

From Fabric D, cut:

(4) 2¼" squares
(4) 2¾" squares for HSTs
(4) 2½" x 4" rectangles

Take Two: For Elisabeth's version, she exchanged her four-patch squares and two 2¼" squares with two new fabrics. If you'd like to do the same, substitute for the Fabric C and D 1½" squares and two 2¼" Fabric C squares.

BUILD YOUR BLOCK

1. Gather the 2¾" Fabric C and Fabric D squares and create (4) 2¼" C/D HST units using the two-at-a-time method (see page 11).

2. Referencing the Block Diagram for placement, sew a 2¼" Fabric D square to an assembled C/D HST unit from Step 1. Press. Repeat to create a total of 4 units and set aside.

3. Sew a 2¼" Fabric C square to an assembled C/D HST unit from Step 1 . Press. Repeat to create a total of 4 units.

4. Sew units from Steps 2 and 3 together, being sure to nest the seams. Repeat to create 4 units.

5. Sew an assembled unit from Step 4 to either side of a Fabric D rectangle. Repeat and set aside.

6. To make the center 4-patch unit, sew a 1½" Fabric A square to a 1½" Fabric B square. Press and repeat. Sew together the 2 assembled units to form a 4-patch unit and press.

7. Sew the remaining 2 Fabric D rectangles to either side of the 4-patch from Step 6. Press.

8. Sew the rows together and press.

- -

Refer to page 47 for fitting motifs into an HST unit, but adjust the measurements for your Fabric A and C cuts to 2¾" square for this block.

complementary cutting

Complementary cutting is a fun way to work with multiple colorways of the same fabric design. A colorway is when the same design is printed in different colors. By lining up the directionality in the two fabrics, you create the illusion of a single fabric suddenly changing color. This is an excellent opportunity to practice the directionality skills you learned in Chapter 1 (see page 14), creating large HST units from secondary fabrics that easily complement your focal fabric despite their large cut size. This is an especially satisfying technique because it looks so much more difficult than it is.

Elisabeth's Block

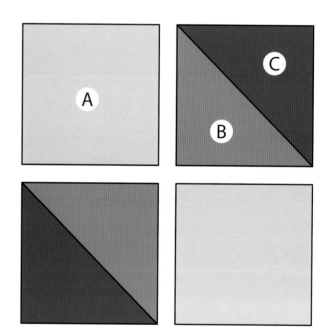

Block Diagram

FABRIC NEEDED

From Fabric A, cut:

(2) 5" squares (consider using the mirroring technique from page 52)

From Fabrics B and C, cut:

(1) 5½" square for HSTs

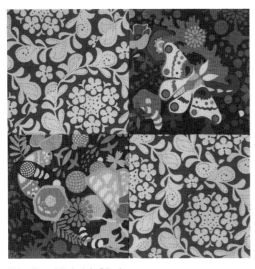

Take Two: Nichole's Block

BUILD YOUR BLOCK

1. Gather the Fabric B and Fabric C squares and create 2 HST units using the two-at-a-time HST method (see page 11). Trim to 5" square if needed.

2. Referencing the Block Diagram for placement, sew a Fabric A square to an assembled HST unit from Step 1. Repeat to create a large 4-patch.

3. Sew the two rows together and press.

TIP: Remember to use the test flip technique from Block 2 (refer to page 19) to make sure your directionality flows smoothly through your block.

BLOCK 19 *fussy geese*

Flying Geese are a fun staple in a quilt-maker's diet. The exaggerated large geese in this block are a great way to frame some of your favorite larger scale prints that do not conform to a traditional square shape. Using the ruler marking method (see page 47 and the Tip opposite), it's easy to find the exact fussy cutting area in a tricky cut shape. Once you take that guesswork out of finding your perfect fussy cut on your focal fabric, you will confidently cut into any of your favorites! This block also offers the chance to select two different coordinating fabrics to create a strong secondary design as the background. This makes the block much more engaging than if you were to pick just one single background.

Nichole's Block

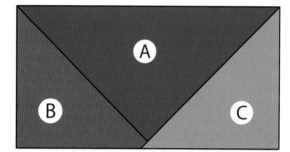
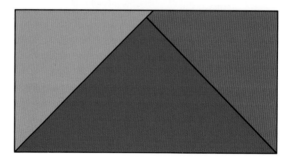

Block Diagram

FABRIC NEEDED

From Fabric A, cut:
(2) 9½" x 5" rectangles

From Fabrics B and C, cut:
(2) 5" squares

Take Two: Elisabeth's Block

BUILD YOUR BLOCK

1. Referencing the Block Diagram for placement, assemble a Flying Geese unit (see page 10) using 1 of each of your fabric cuts. Press. Repeat to create a total of 2 Flying Geese units.

2. Sew the two rows together and press.

TIP: Follow Anita's advice and mark your ruler to see the visible fabric in the finished block. Mark the cut size, 5½" x 9¾", and mark dots 5½" in on the bottom line from both the right and left sides. Draw a diagonal line from the top left corner to the bottom right dot; then repeat on the other side, drawing a diagonal line from the top right corner to the bottom left dot. Your visible area is the triangle between the two lines you made, and ⅜" from the top.

framing motifs

- -

This block is an exercise in finding the right shapes of designs to fit odd sized blocks using the mirroring (see page 52), border (see page 54), and centering (see page 48) techniques from Chapter 4—using coordinating prints that pair well together. This block is a fun challenge with both small and large rectangles to consider, as well as monitoring value and placement to make sure none of the five focal or secondary fabrics is overpowering the block.

- -

Elisabeth's Block

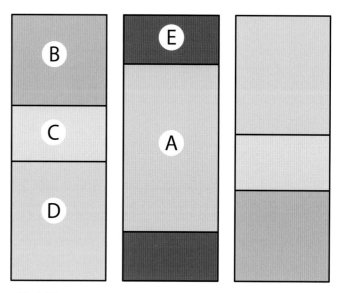

Block Diagram

FABRIC NEEDED

- -

From Fabric A, cut:
(1) 3½" x 6½" rectangle

From Fabric B, cut:
(2) 3½" squares

From Fabric C, cut:
(2) 3½" x 2½" rectangles

From Fabric D, cut:
(2) 3½" x 4½" rectangles

From Fabric E, cut:
(2) 3½" x 2" rectangles

BUILD YOUR BLOCK

- -

1. Before sewing, arrange the cut units according to the Block Diagram and double-check the directionality of your cuts.

2. Sew a Fabric B square to the top of a Fabric C rectangle. Sew a Fabric D rectangle to the bottom of the Fabric C rectangle. Press and repeat to create a total of two columns. Set aside.

3. Sew a Fabric E rectangle to the top and bottom of a Fabric A rectangle. Press.

4. Sew the three columns together and press.

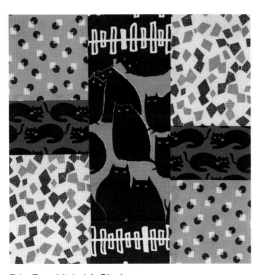

Take Two: Nichole's Block

CHAPTER 6

mixing motifs

IN THIS CHAPTER we're going to explore scale by finding motifs to fit smaller piecing, and practice determining when not to feature a motif in a block. We haven't touched on the importance of building a space in your block construction for your eyes to rest. This can sometimes mean knowing when to use a background fabric even though you really want to use that matching secondary fabric. Just because you have a space that could fit a design, does not always mean it is in the block's best interest to do so. As a general rule, if you are featuring a motif in one space, you should build an area of rest around it. That way the viewer can focus quickly on what you intended to be the focal motif of the block.

sizing to fit

This block is a study in scale, working with progressively larger borders and finding multiple coordinating prints featuring similar motifs in a variety of sizes. Consider your block sizing when selecting your fabrics. Are your designs too large or too small? If you plan to feature a focal fabric or two, keep in mind where you want them to go in the final layout. Do they detract from the design elements you've already worked through, or are they just right to add some interest while leaving the emphasis on your variety in scale? Working through these questions as you select your fabrics will help you build a successful block.

Nichole's Block

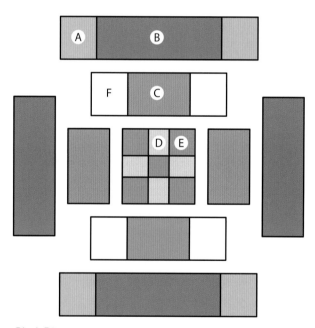

Block Diagram

FABRIC NEEDED

From Fabric A, cut:
(4) 2" squares

From Fabric B, cut:
(4) 2" x 6½" rectangles

From Fabric C, cut:
(4) 2" x 3½" rectangles

From Fabric D, cut:
(4) 1½" squares

From Fabric E, cut:
(5) 1½" squares

From Fabric F, cut:
(4) 2" squares

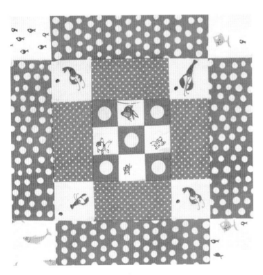

Take Two: Elisabeth's Block

BUILD YOUR BLOCK

1. Before sewing, arrange the cut units according to the Block Diagram and double-check the directionality of your cuts.

2. Sew a Fabric A square to either side of a Fabric B rectangle. Press. Repeat and set aside.

3. Sew a Fabric F square to either side of a Fabric C rectangle. Press. Repeat and set aside.

4. To create the central 9-patch unit, sew a Fabric E square to either side of a Fabric D square. Press and repeat to create the top an bottom rows. Sew a Fabric D square to either side of a Fabric E square. Press. Sew the three rows together in order to make a 9-patch. Press.

5. Sew a Fabric C rectangle to either side of the assembled 9-Patch unit from Step 4. Press.

6. Sew an assembled unit from Step 3 to the top and bottom of the assembled unit from Step 5.

7. Sew a Fabric B rectangle to either side of the assembled unit from Step 6. Press.

8. Sew an assembled unit from Step 2 to the top and bottom of the assembled unit from Step 7. Press.

focused cutting from the same fabric

You know "the fabric"... it has that perfect motif you immediately fall for and can't get out of your head. It's only later that you notice the smaller elements the designer worked into the fabric: a little bunny over there, a cute floral crown here, and is that a martini glass I spy? In fabrics with large and small motifs combined, those little guys can be easily overlooked, and if you were to keep them grouped together in a larger cut in your patchwork, you would continue to see only the large motif. When you isolate those great elements into smaller fussy cuts, however, you draw attention to each of the motifs in a different way and can create a different story through your piecing. Change up the story of your block by using both smaller and larger cuts of your focal fabric.

Elisabeth's Block

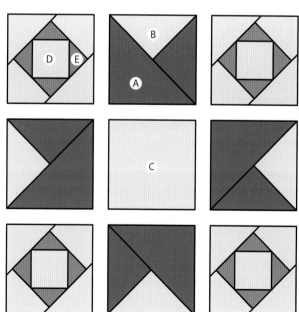

Block Diagram

FABRIC NEEDED

From Fabric A, cut:
(1) 4½" square for the HSTs
(2) 4" squares- subcut diagonally

From Fabric B, cut:
(1) 4½" square for the HSTs
(4) 3½" squares

From Fabric C, cut:
(1) 3½" square

From Fabric D, cut:
(4) 2" squares

From Fabric E, cut:
(4) 2⅝" squares

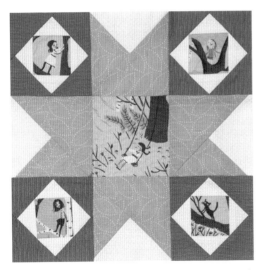

Take Two: Nichole inverted Fabric A and Fabric B in her diamond-in-a-square units.

BUILD YOUR BLOCK

1. From the 4½" Fabric A and Fabric B squares, create 2 HST units using the traditional HST method (see page 10). Press open the seam of one HST, trim to 4" square, then cut along the diagonal, perpendicular to the seam.

2. Sew a subcut Fabric A triangle to a triangle unit from Step 1. Repeat to make a total of 4 units. Trim to 3½" square.

3. Cut the (4) 3½" Fabric B squares along both diagonals, forming a total of 16 little triangles. Repeat with the Fabric E squares.

4. Sew the Fabric E triangles to each side of the Fabric D squares. Press and trim to 2⅝".

5. Sew the Fabric B triangles to the Step 4 unit and press. Repeat for the remaining three units. Square up to 3½".

6. Sew an assembled Step 5 unit to either side of a Step 2 unit to make the top row. Repeat to make the bottom row.

7. Sew a Step 2 unit to either side of the Fabric C square to make the middle row.

8. Sew the three rows together and press.

BLOCK
23 *complementary focal fabrics*

Do you have two fabrics united in theme that you just can't wait to piece together? Never fear! Blocks with more than one focal fabric can work well when you consider a few key design factors. The first thing to consider is whether most of the colors are in the same color family and within a similar range of hue. Next evaluate whether the themes are complementary and feature artwork of a similar style. Once you're confident the fabrics marry well, choose your secondary fabrics to tie the two together more closely. It can be challenging to audition different styles together to achieve an interesting block that isn't too distracting, so take your time when building this block.

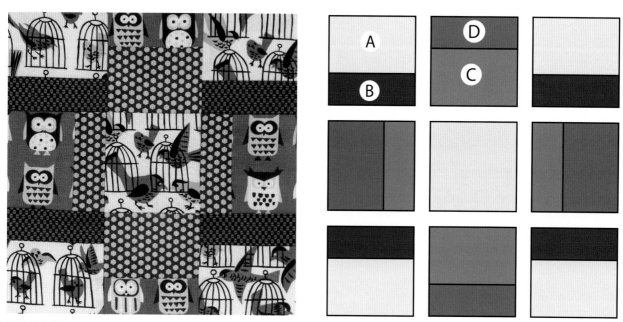

Nichole's Block   Block Diagram

FABRIC NEEDED

From Fabric A, cut:
(4) 2½" x 3½" rectangles
(1) 3½" square

From Fabric B, cut:
(4) 1½" x 3½" rectangles

From Fabrics C and D, cut:
(2) 1½" x 3½" rectangles
(2) 3½" x 2½" rectangles

Take Two: Elisabeth's Block

BUILD YOUR BLOCK

1. Before sewing, arrange the cut units according to the Block Diagram and double-check the directionality of your cuts.

2. Sew a Fabric A rectangle to a Fabric B rectangle. Press. Repeat to create a total of 4 units and set aside.

3. Sew a 2½" x 3½" Fabric C rectangle to a 1½" x 3½" Fabric D rectangle. Press, repeat and set aside.

4. Referencing the Block Diagram for placement, sew the remaining Fabric D and Fabric C rectangles into 2 units. Press.

5. Sew an assembled unit from Step 4 to either side of the Fabric A square and set aside.

6. Referencing the Block Diagram to maintain your fabric directionality, sew an assembled unit from Step 2 to either side of an assembled unit from Step 3. Repeat.

7. Sew the three rows together and press.

complementary directionality in HSTs

You learned the basics of fussy cutting a motif in an HST in Block 14 (see page 50), but this block takes those skills to the next level. Because there are so many places where the same fabric will meet, you must carefully cut your focal fabric so that you avoid introducing a distracting seam. This block is a great way to practice selecting a background fabric that pairs nicely with your focal fabric without creating an accidental distraction. Also, keep the secondary design of this block in mind, since this impacts the directionality of the HST placement.

Elisabeth's Block

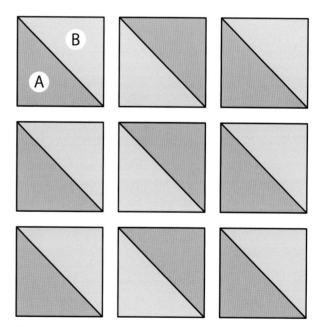

Block Diagram

FABRIC NEEDED

From Fabrics A and B, cut:

(5) 4" squares for HSTs

Take Two: Nichole switched the positioning of the focal fabric and the background fabric.

BUILD YOUR BLOCK

1. Paying close attention to the directionality in both fabrics, use the traditional HST method (see page 10) to create 10 HST units. You only need 9 HSTs for this block, but it's nice to have an extra HST to audition a few different layouts.

2. Arrange the HSTs using the block diagram and photograph for orientation.

3. Sew the HSTs into 3 rows of 3 units each. Stash the extra HST unit for future use or inspiration.

4. Sew the rows together and press.

tossed prints

TOSSED PRINTS are one of the most common quilting fabrics as well as one of the most forgiving fabric designs to fussy cut. A tossed print features motifs that are scattered across the fabric in all directions; as if they've been thrown onto the background and landed wherever they wanted to! Because they are tossed, you don't have to worry about directionality. Still, you need to pay attention to your cutting. While it may seem like you will disrupt a design no matter where you cut, it is possible to identify a focal point within the repeat and to emphasize that in your fussy cuts. These prints are easy to cut and mix and make great additions to your fabric collection.

BLOCK 25 *cutting basics for tossed prints*

In some tossed prints, you truly can cut anywhere, but others have interesting elements in them that you might want to highlight. Consider the fabric in Take Two. There are shapes of squirrels, cats, hearts, and more! When you work with tossed fabrics, your goal may be to get at least one of your focal motifs completely inside the shape you are cutting. Find the element within the fabric that you really like. Before you cut your block pieces, double check to ensure that your chosen element is framed in the fussy cut.

Nichole's Block

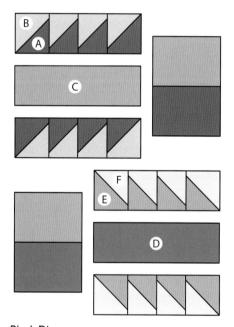

Block Diagram

Refer to Block 14 (see page 50) for fitting motifs into an HST unit, but adjust the measurements to make a 2½" square for this block.

FABRIC NEEDED

From Fabrics A and E, cut:
(4) 2½" squares for HSTs
(1) 2¾" x 3½" rectangle

From Fabrics B and F, cut:
(4) 2½" squares for HSTs

From Fabrics C and D, cut:
(1) 2¾" x 3½" rectangle
(1) 2" x 6½" rectangle

Take Two: Elisabeth switched the positioning of the two assembled rectangle pairs in her block.

BUILD YOUR BLOCK

1. Gather the Fabric A and Fabric B squares and create 8 HST units using the two-at-a-time HST method (see page 11). Repeat with the Fabric E and Fabric F squares. Press and trim each unit to 2" square if needed and set aside.

2. Sew the assembled A/B HST units from Step 1 into 2 rows of 4 blocks each. Press.

3. Sew an assembled row from Step 2 to either side of the 2" x 6½" Fabric C rectangle. Press and set aside.

4. Sew a 2¾" x 3½" Fabric A and Fabric C rectangle together. Press.

5. Sew the assembled unit from Step 3 to the assembled unit from Step 4. Press and set aside.

6. Sew the assembled E/F HST units from Step 1 into 2 rows of 4 blocks each. Press.

7. Sew an assembled row from Step 6 to either side of the 2" x 6½" Fabric D rectangle. Press and set aside.

8. Sew a 2¾" x 3½" Fabric D and Fabric E rectangle together. Press.

9. Sew the assembled unit from Step 7 to the assembled unit from Step 8. Press.

10. Sew the two rows together and press.

finding the focal in a tossed print

It is challenging to isolate a motif in a tossed print. With other types of fabric design, there is usually space so that you can isolate a fussy cut, but tossed prints have so much going on, and in so many directions too! Take your time when choosing and cutting your fabrics. It also helps to select a fabric with motifs that are in close proportion to your cut size so that you can successfully isolate the motif. Keep in mind that with tossed prints the spacing is not always consistent between different motifs, so you may need to be a little more selective with the motifs you want to fussy cut.

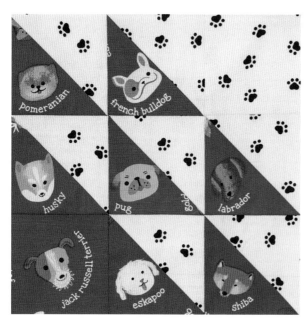

Elisabeth's Block

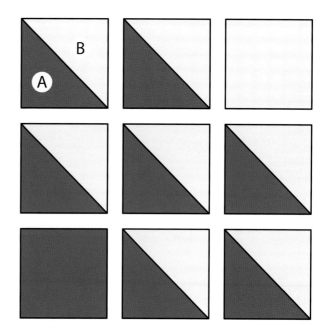

Block Diagram

FABRIC NEEDED

From Fabric A, cut:

(7) 4" squares for HSTs

(1) 3½" square

From Fabric B, cut:

(4) 4" squares for HSTs

(1) 3½" square

Take Two: Nichole reversed her Fabric A and Fabric B placements. If you'd like to do the same, simply switch the two cutting instructions.

BUILD YOUR BLOCK

1. Gather the 4" Fabric A and Fabric B squares and create 7 HST units using the traditional method (see page 10). Trim to 3½" square if needed. You will have one triangle (half square) of each fabric remaining that will not be used.

2. Before sewing, arrange the units according to the Block Diagram and double-check the directionality of your fabrics.

3. Sew an HST unit and a 3½" Fabric B square to either side of one HST unit. Press and set aside.

4. Sew 3 HST units together. Press and set aside.

5. Sew a 3½" Fabric A square and an HST unit to either side of another HST unit. Press.

6. Sew the rows together and press.

Refer to page 52 for fitting motifs into an HST unit, but adjust the measurements to 4" square for this block.

forcing directionality

When you feature a tossed print and want all your designs to face in a single direction, you will probably need to force directionality. This means your cut pieces will be off-grain, or "on the bias." The grain of a fabric is the direction in which the fibers are woven together. They intersect at a 90 degree angle, and generally a one-way, two-way, or four-way design will be printed parallel or perpendicular to the selvage (on-grain). But with tossed prints, the design will go in all directions. These cuts can be tricky to work with because the fabric distorts easily when handled or pressed. Certainly, don't be afraid to use your fabric this way, but do be more gentle as you feed the fabric into your machine and use a light hand when ironing these units. We always like to iron using a starch alternative; you may also find that this is extra-helpful when working on the bias.

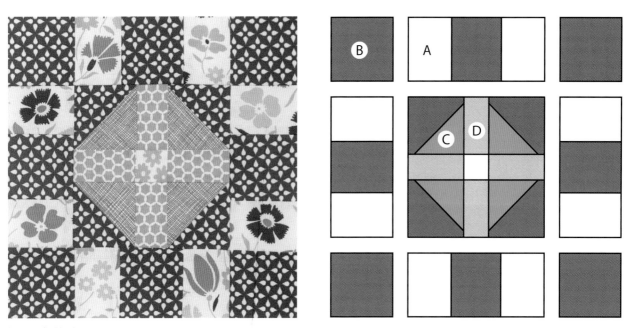

Nichole's Block   Block Diagram

FABRIC NEEDED

From Fabric A, cut:
(8) 2½" x 2" rectangles
(1) 1½" square

From Fabric B, cut:
(2) 3" squares for HSTs
(8) 2½" squares

From Fabric C, cut:
(2) 3" squares for HSTs

From Fabric D, cut:
(4) 1½" x 2½" rectangles

Take Two: Elisabeth's Block

Refer to Block 14 (see page 50) for fitting motifs into an HST unit, but adjust the measurements to 3" square for this block.

BUILD YOUR BLOCK

1. From the 3" Fabric B and Fabric C squares create 4 HST units using the traditional HST method (see page 10). Press, trim to 2½" square and set aside.

2. Sew a Fabric A rectangle to either side of a 2½" Fabric B square. Repeat to create a total of 4.

3. Sew a 2½" Fabric B square to either side of an assembled unit from Step 2. Press and set aside.

4. Sew an assembled HST unit from Step 1 to either side of a Fabric D rectangle. Press and repeat.

5. Sew a Fabric D rectangle to either side of the 1½" Fabric A square. Press.

6. Sew an assembled unit from Step 4 to the top and bottom of the assembled unit from Step 5.

7. Sew an assembled unit from Step 2 to either side of the assembled unit from Step 6.

8. Sew the three rows together and press.

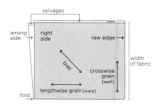

Always check the grainline for bias to avoid distortion in the sewn units. If you must use the motif and cut it on the bias, consider using freezer paper to stabilize (see page 130).

improv-pieced motifs

Now that you've worked with tossed prints, we wanted to share a great trick by Latifah Saafir (see page 86) on how to isolate smaller motifs that may be too close together to fussy cut consistently for the shape you want. This cool technique allows you to isolate smaller motifs in your prints without any distractions. While it looks tricky, all you need is a background fabric in a color that matches the background color in your focal fabric. Then add in a little confidence (you can do this!). This trick opens up new possibilities for using those quirky smaller motifs in larger squares of your block. It's addictive, though—once you get the hang of it, you'll see new possibilities in all of your fabrics!

Elisabeth's Block

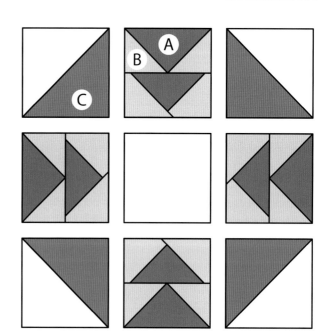

Block Diagram

FABRIC NEEDED

From Fabric A, cut:
(8) 2¼" x 3¾" rectangles for Flying Geese

From Fabric B, cut:
(16) 2¼" squares for Flying Geese

From Fabric C, cut:
(4) 4" squares for HSTs

Focal Fabric: 1 fat quarter

Solid Fabric (that matches the focal fabric background)**:** 1 fat quarter

Take Two: Nichole's Block

Refer to page 47 for featuring motifs in a Flying Geese unit and HST units and page 10 for assembling the units.

BUILD YOUR BLOCK

1. Create your focal fabric using the technique we share with you on pages 86-87.

2. Choose a pieced motif for the center square and trim to 3½" square and set aside. For the pieced motifs to be used in the HSTs, trim each to 4", paying close attention to the fabric placement to allow for the motif to remain in position once the HST is complete.

3. Gather the 4" pieced motif squares and Fabric C squares, and create 4 HST units using the traditional HST method (see page 10). Press trim to 3½" if necessary and set aside.

4. Gather the Fabric A rectangles and Fabric B squares and assemble 8 Flying Geese units (see page 10). Trim to 2" x 3½".

5. Referencing the Block Diagram for placement, sew together 2 of the assembled units from Step 4. Repeat to create a total of 4 assembled units. Press.

6. Sew an assembled HST unit from Step 3 to either side of an assembled unit from Step 5 for the top row. Repeat for the bottom row.

7. Sew an assembled unit from Step 5 to either side of the 3½" pieced-motif square from Step 2.

8. Sew the three rows together and press.

LATIFAH SAAFIR is a pattern and fabric designer, know for her bold and innovative modern quilts and fabric designs that are graphic and contemporary. She co-founded both the Los Angeles Modern Quilt Guild and the worldwide Modern Quilt Guild, and enjoys challenging techniques that need meticulous attention to details.

Latifah loves creating these improv-pieced shapes. It lets her perfectionist side shine and gives her the exact shape she needs using any fabric that has a solid background, without including any competing partial designs from elsewhere on the focal fabric!

STEP 1:
Indentify the motif you want to feature Using an erasable pen, draw lines around the image, leaving as much space as you can without including other motifs. This step can be more than four sides if needed.

STEP 2:
Trace a ¼" seam allowance around the shape you just drew.

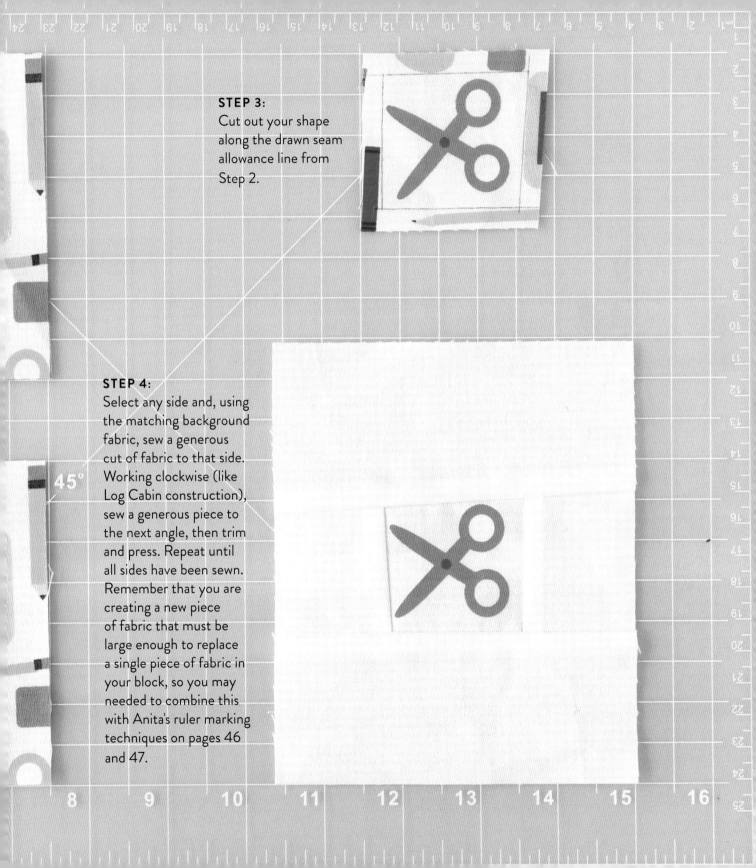

STEP 3:
Cut out your shape along the drawn seam allowance line from Step 2.

STEP 4:
Select any side and, using the matching background fabric, sew a generous cut of fabric to that side. Working clockwise (like Log Cabin construction), sew a generous piece to the next angle, then trim and press. Repeat until all sides have been sewn. Remember that you are creating a new piece of fabric that must be large enough to replace a single piece of fabric in your block, so you may needed to combine this with Anita's ruler marking techniques on pages 46 and 47.

prints with directionality

AS WE LEARNED IN CHAPTER ONE, directionality is so important in fussy cutting. Prints with an obvious orientation of the motifs are easy to use as a focal fabric because they usually all have very well-defined directionality. Directional prints, however, are not as forgiving as tossed prints. You'll know immediately if your piecing is off (even just a little), and precise cutting and pressing are imperative for this group of blocks. We love to use directional prints in our favorite designs. Based on their scale, colors, and motifs, these prints are a solid choice for a focal, secondary, or even a background fabric for any block. From tonal geometrics to strong linear motifs and novelty prints, this category of fabrics holds endless possibilities.

working with one-way prints

The lesson in this block is choosing carefully which portions of the block units to feature your one-way prints within. By combining different one-way prints together in a variety of directions you create a dynamic block. Be mindful of the direction in which you want your design to flow in the finished block by making sure that you're cutting pieces in the appropriate direction. You really need to arrange these units on a flat surface or your design wall beore piecing on this one.

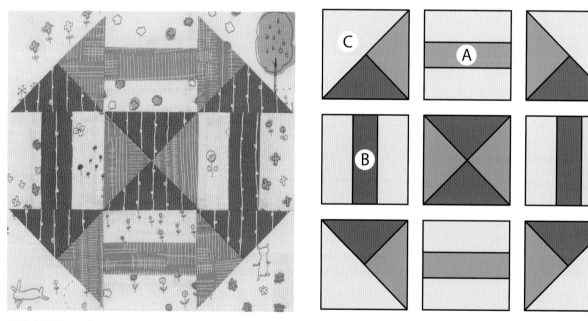

Nichole's Block

Block Diagram

FABRIC NEEDED

From Fabrics A and B, cut:
(3) 4½" squares for QSTs and half-QSTs
(2) 3½" x 1½" rectangles

From Fabric C, cut:
(2) 4" squares cut once on the diagonal
(8) 3½" x 1½" rectangles

Take Two: Elisabeth's Block

Refer to page 46 for fitting motifs into a half-QST unit and to page 47 for fitting motifs into an HST unit.

BUILD YOUR BLOCK

1. Gather the Fabric A and Fabric B squares. Using the technique on page 10 and referencing the Block Diagram for the orientation of the prints, assemble 6 half-QST units. Repeat to form 6 pairs. Note the fabric placement of each A/B pair: 4 are alike, while the remaining 2 are opposites.

2. Referencing the Block Diagram for placement, sew together 2 assembled units from Step 1 to form a full QST unit. Press. Trim to 3½" if necessary and set aside.

3. Sew a Fabric C triangle to an assembled half-QST unit from Step 1. Repeat to create a total of 4 units. Press and set aside.

4. Sew a Fabric C rectangle to the top and bottom of a Fabric A rectangle. Press. Repeat and set aside.

5. Sew a Fabric C rectangle to either side of a Fabric B rectangle. Press. Repeat and set aside.

6. Sew an assembled unit from Step 3 to either side of an assembled unit from Step 4. Repeat.

7. Sew an assembled unit from Step 5 to either side of the assembled QST unit from Step 2.

8. Sew the rows together and press.

two-way motif basics

The lesson in this block is choosing carefully which portions of the block units to feature your two-way prints within. Placing your two-way prints too closely together will draw the eye to any inconsistencies in piecing (like where you may have cut off part of the print) that will look like an error in the final block. Select units where the prints will not be touching directly and consider first cutting wide and long strips to maintain the same distance from the seam allowances. If you position your two-way prints closely together but so that they don't share any long seams, you can get the look of a continuous flow throughout. Remember, if you are featuring your two-way fabric in an HST or Flying Geese unit, you need to be mindful of directionality in your cut units so that you do not end up with a sideways motif.

Elisabeth's Block

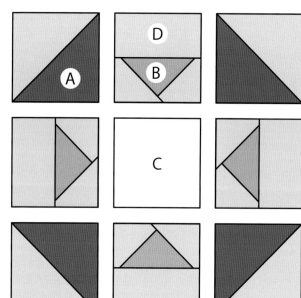

Block Diagram

FABRIC NEEDED

From Fabric A, cut:

(2) 4" squares for HSTs

From Fabric B, cut:

(4) 2¼" x 3¾" rectangles for Flying Geese

From Fabric C, cut:

(1) 3½" square

From Fabric D, cut:

(2) 4" squares for HSTs
(8) 2¼" squares for Flying Geese
(4) 2" x 3½" rectangles

Take Two: Nichole's Block

Refer to page 46 for fitting motifs into a Flying Geese unit and to page 47 for fitting motifs into an HST unit.

BUILD YOUR BLOCK

1. Gather the Fabric A squares and 4" Fabric D squares and create 4 HST units using the traditional HST method (see page 10). Be sure to cut one of the Fabric A squares in half along the diagonal from top left to bottom right and cut the other from top right to bottom left. Trim to 3½" square.

2. Gather the Fabric B rectangles and 2¼" Fabric D squares and assemble 4 Flying Geese units (see page 10). Trim to 2" x 3½".

3. Before sewing, arrange the cut units according to the Block Diagram and double-check the directionality of your cuts.

4. Sew a Fabric D rectangle to an assembled Flying Geese unit from Step 2. Repeat to create a total of 4 units.

5. Sew an assembled HST unit from Step 1 to either side of an assembled unit from Step 4. Repeat. Press and set aside.

6. Sew an assembled unit from Step 4 to either side of the Fabric C square. Press.

7. Sew the three rows together and press.

large scale one-way prints

When you find a perfect photograph, you put it in a frame, right? Why should your favorite prints be any different? Use this block to add an interesting secondary directional print to frame your large-scale one-way focal. You want to find a strong focal fabric that is visually interesting, then select a complementary print to frame it perfectly.

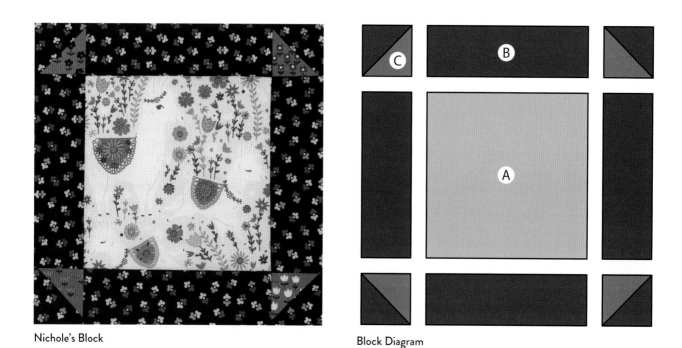

Nichole's Block

Block Diagram

FABRIC NEEDED

From Fabric A, cut:
(2) 2½" squares for HSTs
(1) 6½" square

From Fabric B, cut:
(4) 6½" x 2½" rectangles

From Fabric C, cut:
(2) 2½" squares for HSTs

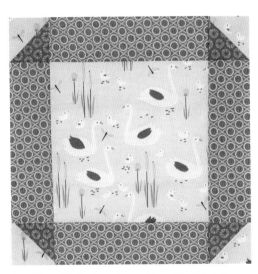

Take Two: Elisabeth exchanged her 2½" Fabric A squares for Fabric B squares. If you'd like to do the same, omit the 2½" squares from the cutting instructions for Fabric A and add it to the cutting instructions for Fabric B.

BUILD YOUR BLOCK

1. Gather the 2½" Fabric A squares and Fabric C squares and create 4 HST units, using the traditional HST method (see page 10). Trim to 2" square if necessary.

2. Before sewing, arrange the cut units according to the Block Diagram and double-check the directionality of your cuts.

3. Sew an assembled HST unit from Step 1 to either side of a Fabric B rectangle. Press repeat, and set aside.

4. Sew a Fabric B rectangle to either side of the 6½" Fabric A square and press.

5. Sew the rows together and press.

Refer to page 47 for fitting motifs into an HST unit, but adjust the measurements to 2½" square for this block.

four-way prints

It can feel like a challenge to work four-way prints into fussy cuts since the designs are generally close together, but they can also be very forgiving! Because the designs are going in so many directions, with four-way prints it can be less difficult to find a motif with a little extra space around it than it is with a tossed print. This makes it fairly easy to force directionality or at least achieve the appearance that your designs in your cut units are all going in the same direction.

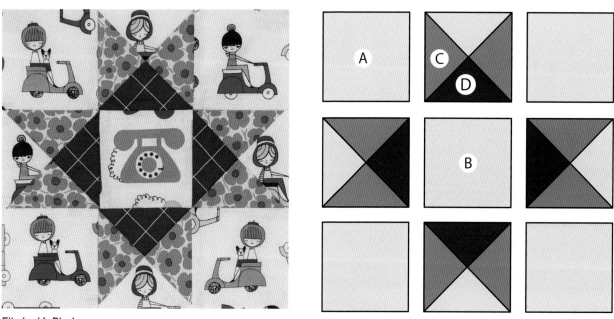

Elisabeth's Block

Block Diagram

FABRIC NEEDED

From Fabric A, cut:
(4) 3½" squares
(1) 4½" square for QSTs

From Fabrics B, cut:
(1) 3½" square

Fromm Fabrics C and D, cut:
(2) 4½" squares for QSTs

Take Two: Nichole used Fabric A for her center square too. If you'd like to do the same, delete the Fabric B square and replace it with a fifth 3½"square from Fabric A.

BUILD YOUR BLOCK

1. Gather the 4½" Fabric A, Fabric B and Fabric C squares, cut each square along both diagonals and assemble 4 QST units (see page 10). Trim to 3½" if necessary and set aside.

2. Before sewing, arrange the cut units according to the Block Diagram and double-check the directionality of your cuts.

3. Sew a 3½" Fabric A square to either side of an assembled B/C QST unit from Step 1. Press. Repeat. Press and set aside.

4. Sew an assembled A/B/C QST unit from Step 1 to either side of the remaining 3½" Fabric A square. Press.

5. Sew the three rows together and press.

Refer to page 46 for fitting motifs into a QST unit and for assembling the units.

CHAPTER 9

geometrics as focal fabric

YOU'LL LIKELY BE SURPRISED by how many geometric prints you have in your stash when you go looking for them. These fabrics are often the quiet ones that may initially seem more like secondary prints, but when you combine a few of them together, they shine all on their own. This chapter is a great example of how you can create stunning quilt blocks by focusing your fussy cuts solely on geometrics. Consider how secondary designs form when you force your stripes to flow in the same direction, or how mixing tiny and giant geometric motifs can make a dramatic impact. Geometrics have an interesting voice to add to any block, and in this chapter we will explore some ways to really let them sing.

BLOCK 33 *cutting basics for geometrics*

When working with geometrics, the best advice is to think of them in the same way as you would any other motif. Consider which portion of the design will be visible, which way your directionality should appear, and make sure you are cutting straight without needlessly cutting off portions of the motifs. This is especially important when the geometric prints are also your focal fabrics, because any cut that is not perfectly straight will be especially noticeable.

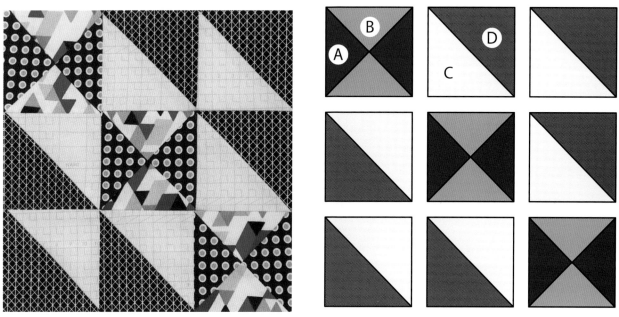

Nichole's Block

Block Diagram

FABRIC NEEDED

From Fabrics A and B, cut:
(2) 4½" squares for QSTs

From Fabrics C and D, cut:
(3) 4" squares for HSTs

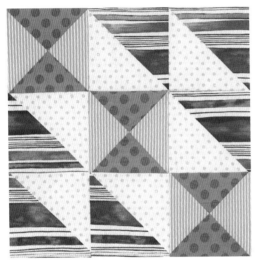

Take Two: Elisabeth's Block

BUILD YOUR BLOCK

1. Gather the Fabric A and Fabric B squares and assemble 3 QST units (see page 10). Trim to 3½" square. Press and set aside.

2. Gather the Fabric C and Fabric D squares and create 6 HST units using the traditional HST method (see page 10). Trim to 3½" square. Press and set aside.

3. Before sewing, arrange the cut units according to the Block Diagram and double-check the directionality of your cuts.

4. Sew 2 assembled HST units from Step 2 to an assembled QST unit from Step 1. Repeat, press and set aside.

5. Sew an assembled HST unit from Step 2 to either side of an assembled QST unit from Step 1.

6. Sew the rows together and press.

Refer to page 46 for fitting motifs into a QST unit and page 47 for fitting motifs into an HST unit.

complementary geometrics

Geometric fabrics can present a challenge if the weave of the fabric is warped, which means the design will shift a little off-grain. So, when you make a straight cut you may end up with a design that has a slight wave or curve in it. This can happen if fabric is torn or if it is distorted too much when ironed. When you are trying to fussy cut a geometric, it is important to get your original cut shape as straight as possible, as this will impact the overall design. Use your ruler to check the accuracy of your print before you cut. If there is any warping of the fabric or if the motifs aren't straight, this distortion will be especially noticeable in your finished block. Finally, select prints that will join nicely at the seam without creating too much conflict. To achieve this, look for prints that aren't too similar in scale or color and avoid strong stripes, since they will look out of place if they don't line up perfectly.

Elisabeth's Block

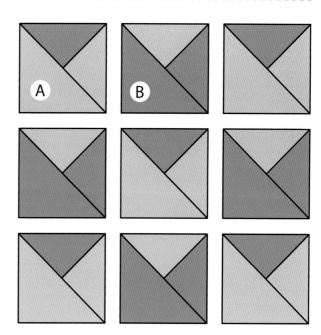

Block Diagram

FABRIC NEEDED

From Fabric A, cut:
(4) 4½" squares for HSTs, cut once along the diagonal
(5) 4" squares for QSTs

From Fabric B, cut:
(4) 4½" squares for HSTs, cut once along the diagonal
(5) 4" squares for QSTs

Take Two: Nichole's Block

Refer to page 46 for fitting motifs into a half-QST unit and page 47 for fitting motifs into an HST unit.

BUILD YOUR BLOCK

1. Using the 4½" squares, assemble 5 HSTs (see page 11). Cut each HST along the diagonal, perpendicular to the seam. Discard one and trim to 4".

2. Construct the half-QST units with 5 units from Step 1 and the 4" Fabric A pieces, creating a total of 5 units, referencing the Block Diagram for placement of the fabrics in the half-HST. Trim to 3½". Press and set aside.

3. Repeat Step 2 using the remaining triangle pairs and the 4" Fabric B pieces, to create a total of 4 units. Press.

4. Sew three half-QST units together to form each row. Repeat for each of the rows.

5. Sew the rows together and press.

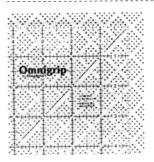

You can quickly test geometric designs to make sure they are not warped by lining up your ruler with the design. You'll notice in this design we used the 45 degree line on the ruler to line up with the print.
This will help make sure your designs are cut correctly so the geometric doesn't warp in your block.

finding secondary designs

Creating secondary repeats with strong geometrics is a fun way to bring a new perspective to a fabric. Look for fabrics that have an interesting design that are almost self-contained when removed from the repeat. Use the mirroring technique (see page 52) to cut multiple pieces of the same portion of a fabric, and work with your layout to make sure that the overall design feels balanced before you sew everything together. If you have trouble visualizing the motif apart from the repeat, cut a single block section so you can test it out before committing to the entire block.

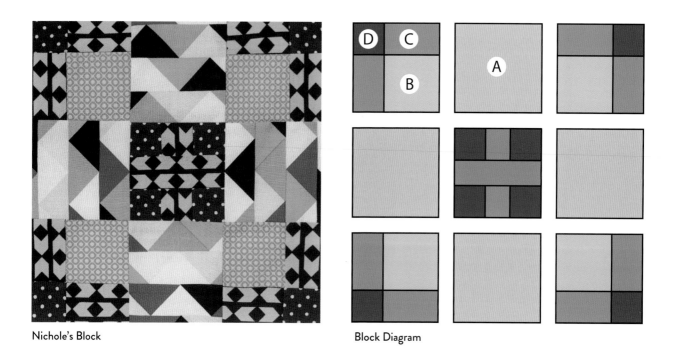

Nichole's Block

Block Diagram

FABRIC NEEDED

From Fabric A, cut:
(4) 3½" squares

From Fabric B, cut:
(4) 2½" squares

From Fabric C, cut:
(1) 1½" x 3½" rectangle
(8) 1½" x 2½" rectangles
(2) 1½" squares

From Fabric D, cut:
(8) 1½" squares

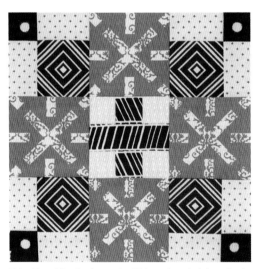

Take Two: Elisabeth used a fifth and sixth fabric for her block. If you'd like to do the same, replace (4) 1½" Fabric D squares with 4 from your fifth fabric for the corner squares, and replace all the 1½" x 2½" Fabric C rectangles with your sixth fabric for Steps 1 and 2.

BUILD YOUR BLOCK

1. Sew a 1½" x 2½" Fabric C rectangle to a Fabric B square. Repeat to create a total of 4 units. Press and set aside.

2. Sew a Fabric D square to a 1½" x 2½" Fabric C rectangle. Repeat to create a total of 4 units. Press and set aside.

3. Sew a Fabric D square to either side of a Fabric C square and press. Repeat for a total of 2 units.

4. Sew an assembled unit from Step 3 to the top and bottom of the 1½" x 3½" Fabric C rectangle. Press.

5. Sew a Fabric A square to either side of the assembled unit from Step 4. Press and set aside.

6. Sew an assembled unit from Step 1 to an assembled unit from Step 2. Repeat to create a total of 4 units. Press.

7. Sew an assembled unit from Step 6 to either side of a Fabric A square and press. Repeat.

8. Sew the rows together and press.

playing with scale

- -

This block initially appears complex because you have similar blocks in a variety of sizes, plus a color layout that is repeated in various units of the blocks that meet unexpectedly in many places. Playing with multiple prints that share the same geometric shape, but in different sizes, really reinforces the complex appearance.

    The trick is using scale to bring balance to the block instead of distracting from the design. Decide which part of the block you want to use your focal fabrics within, then selectively choose your secondary and background fabrics, if any, to enhance that portion. Mixing large, medium, and small prints together will draw more attention to the largest geometric print and will make the smallest one feel like a background. Here, scale is definitely the key, so take some extra time to audition a variety of fabrics for this block.

- -

Elisabeth's Block

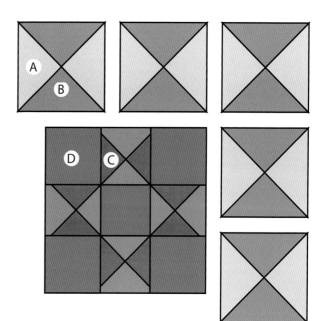

Block Diagram

FABRIC NEEDED

From Fabric A, cut:
(3) 4½" squares for large QSTs

From Fabric B, cut:
(3) 4½" squares for large QSTs
(2) 3½" squares for small QSTs

From Fabric C, cut:
(2) 3½" squares for small QSTs

From Fabric D, cut:
(5) 2½" squares

Take Two: Nichole used an additional fabric for her 2½" QST units. If you'd like to do the same, use a different fabric for the 3½" Fabric B squares, in Step 2 below. Nichole also adjusted the placement of the blocks.

BUILD YOUR BLOCK

1. Gather the 4½" Fabric A and Fabric B squares and assemble (6) 3½" QST units (see page 10). Set one aside for future use or inspiration. Press and set aside.

2. Repeat Step 1, using the 3½" Fabric B and C squares to assemble (4) 2½" QST units.

3. Sew a Fabric D square to either side of an assembled QST unit from Step 2. Press. Repeat.

4. Sew an assembled QST unit from Step 2 to either side of the remaining Fabric D square.

5. Sew the rows together and press.

6. Sew together 2 assembled QST units from Step 1. Press.

7. Sew the assembled unit from Step 6 to the assembled unit from Step 5. Press.

8. Sew the remaining 3 assembled QST units from Step 1 into a row. Press.

9. Sew the assembled unit from Step 8 to the assembled unit from Step 7. Press.

- -

Refer to page 46 for fitting motifs into a QST unit and for assembling the units.

CHAPTER 10

remixed blocks

NOW THAT YOU ARE COMFORTABLE WORKING WITH ALL TYPES OF DESIGNS as well as many types of blocks, let's try mixing it up a bit and combining many of the techniques you've learned in previous chapters. You may have already started doing this in your previous blocks without even realizing it! That's the best part about fussy cutting, once you've mastered a few simple tricks it's easy and quick to add these cuts into all of your blocks!

two-way prints and directional backgrounds

When you begin adding fussy cuts to your piecing, they can quickly define a "top" and "bottom" of your block, and finding ways to add in your stash of multi-directional fabrics can be a challenge. We've included this block with that challenge in mind. Why not create a block that has no clear "up" or "down"?

First, identify a portion of the motif that shows all the directions and highlight it in the center of the block. From there, include fussy cut portions of motifs from the same fabric and have fun positioning them in various directions around the block. Take that one step further by adding in a background with subtle directionality. Look for a design that enhances the block without cluttering the overall design or drawing attention away from the focal fabric.

Nichole's Block

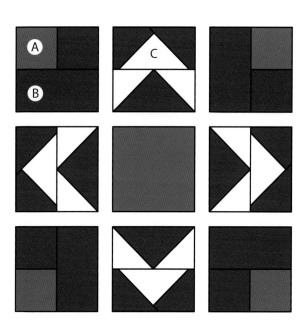

Block Diagram

FABRIC NEEDED

From Fabric A, cut:
(1) 3½" square
(4) 2" squares

From Fabric B, cut:
(4) 2" squares
(4) 2" x 3½" rectangles
(4) 2¼" x 3¾" rectangles for Flying Geese
(8) 2¼" squares for Flying Geese

From Fabric C, cut:
(4) 2¼" x 3¾" rectangles for Flying Geese
(8) 2¼" squares for Flying Geese

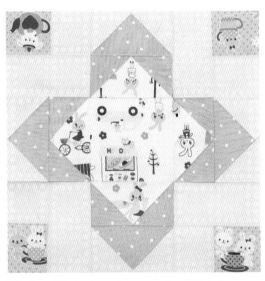

Take Two: Elisabeth used the same focal fabric for her center square and a Flying Geese rectangle. She also used a fourth fabric for her corners. If you'd like to do the same, cut your (4) 2" squares from your Fabric D and use your focal fabric to replace the 4 Fabric B Flying Geese rectangles.

BUILD YOUR BLOCK

1. Gather the Fabric A rectangles and Fabric C squares and assemble 4 A/C Flying Geese units (see page 10). Trim to 2" x 3½". Repeat using the Fabric C rectangles and the 2¼" Fabric D squares to assemble 4 C/D Flying Geese units. Set aside.

2. Sew an assembled Fabric A/C Flying Geese unit from Step 1 to an assembled Fabric C/D unit also from Step 1. Repeat to create a total of 4 units. Press and set aside.

3. Sew a Fabric B square to the left of a 2" Fabric D square. Press. Repeat to create a total of 4 units.

4. Sew a Fabric D rectangle to the bottom of an assembled unit from Step 4. Press. Repeat to create a total of 4 units .

5. Sew an assembled unit from Step 4 to either side of an assembled unit from Step 3. Repeat and press.

6. Sew an assembled unit from Step 2 to either side of the 3½" Fabric A square. Press.

7. Sew the rows together and press.

- -

Refer to page 47 for featuring motifs in a Flying Geese unit.

fitting motifs in multiple shapes

This block gives you multiple opportunities to fit your favorite motifs into different shapes. Explore what you've learned with HSTs, fussy cut geese and finding prints that imitate stripes on a large scale, to make this block a success! Remember that the orientation of this block is not fixed. We used a horizontal fabric as our focal fabric, but if you have a vertical motif that would fit well in this shape, just rotate the block and go with a vertical orientation.

Elisabeth's Block

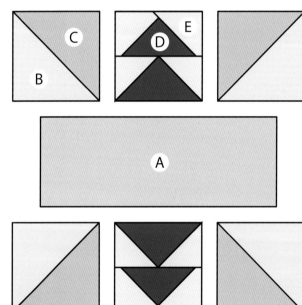

Block Diagram

FABRIC NEEDED

From Fabric A, cut:
(1) 3½" x 9½" rectangle

From Fabrics B and C, cut:
(2) 4" squares for HSTs

From Fabric D, cut:
(4) 2¼" x 3¾" rectangles for Flying Geese

From Fabric E, cut:
(8) 2¼" squares for Flying Geese

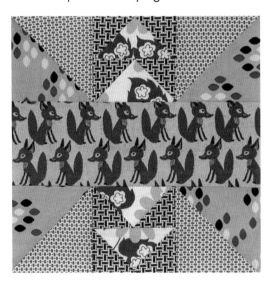

Take Two: Nichole's Block

Refer to page 47 for featuring motifs in a Flying Geese unit and for fitting motifs into an HST unit.

BUILD YOUR BLOCK

1. Gather the Fabric B and Fabric C squares and create 4 HST units using the traditional HST method (see page 10). Trim to 3½" square. Press and set aside.

2. Gather the Fabric D rectangles and Fabric E squares and assemble 4 Flying Geese units (see page 10). Trim to 2" x 3½". Press and set aside.

3. Before sewing, arrange the cut units according to the Block Diagram and double-check the directionality of your cuts.

4. Sew together 2 Flying Geese units from Step 2. Press and repeat.

5. Sew an HST unit from Step 1 to either side of an assembled Flying Geese unit from Step 4. Repeat.

6. Sew the three rows together and press.

TIP: Don't forget to consider directionality in your HST blocks, as well as in the sides of your geese. Often small-scale one-way prints are used as secondary fabrics, but you'll notice in Elisabeth's block that she featured a fussy cut motif in those spaces. If you want to try this as well, remember to fold the motif back frequently to double check directionality.

working with borders and HSTs

While this block looks easy at first glance, the large scale of the focal HST makes it very important to be especially thoughtful in your fabric selection. Whatever motif you choose to feature in this space will be the center of attention, especially when you add in a great border design! Feel free to select any type of fabric, but remember to balance the scale of the prints. In the border section, we chose to use both one-way and two-way designs so you can see how either type of motif can support the finished block in different ways.

Nichole's Block

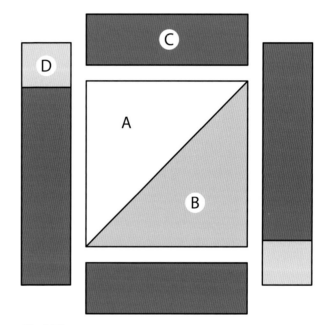

Block Diagram

FABRIC NEEDED

From Fabrics A and B, cut:
(1) 7" square for the HST units

From Fabric C, cut:
(2) 2" x 6½" rectangles
(2) 2" x 8" rectangles

From Fabric D, cut:
(2) 2" squares

Take Two: Elisabeth's Block

BUILD YOUR BLOCK

1. Before sewing, arrange the cut units according to the Block Diagram and double-check the directionality of your cuts.

2. Gather the Fabric A and Fabric B squares and create 1 HST unit using the traditional HST method (see page 10). Trim to 6½" square.

3. Sew a 2" x 6½" Fabric C rectangle to the top and bottom of the assembled HST unit from Step 2.

4. Sew a Fabric D square to the top of a 2" x 8" Fabric C rectangle. Repeat, but sew the Fabric D square to the bottom of the Fabric C rectangle.

5. Sew an assembled unit from Step 4 to either side of the assembled unit from Step 3. Press.

imitating stripes and isolating motifs

Can you believe this is a 9-patch block? Using a one-way directional design to imitate stripes follows the same rules that apply to regular stripes. Pay close attention to your fabric placement before piecing to make sure your directionality is consistent. As long as you are mindful of the alignment in each of your three fabrics, you will create a woven effect. This block also gives you the opportunity to feature a small scale print in the 1" center blocks. Practice isolating nine indivudal motifs to showcase in this space. Because you are working with so many squares, each with an exact direction, it can be easy to mix up which seam you are supposed to stitch. Don't get discouraged if you make a mistake — just take your time, keep your seam ripper close by, and the results will be worth it!

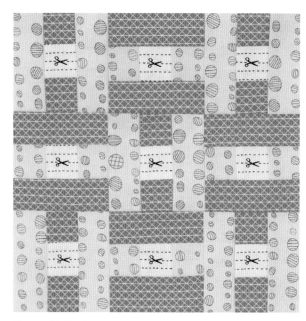

Elisabeth's Block

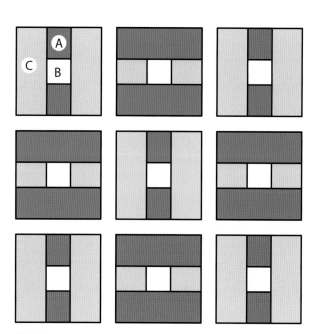

Block Diagram

FABRIC NEEDED

From Fabric A, cut:
(10) 1½" squares
(8) 1½" x 3½" rectangles

From Fabric B, cut:
(9) 1½" squares

From Fabric C, cut:
(8) 1½" squares
(10) 1½" x 3½" rectangles

Take Two: Nichole's Block

Refer to page 47 for featuring motifs in a Flying Geese unit and for fitting motifs into an HST unit.

BUILD YOUR BLOCK

1. Sew a Fabric A square to the top and bottom of a Fabric B square. Repeat to create a total of 5 units. Press.

2. Sew a Fabric C rectangle to either side of an assembled unit from Step 1. Repeat to create a total of 5 units. Press and set aside.

3. Sew a Fabric C square to either side of a Fabric B square. Repeat to create a total of 4 units.

4. Sew a Fabric A rectangle to the top and bottom of an assembled unit from Step 3. Repeat to create a total of 4 units. Press and set aside.

5. Referencing the Block Diagram for placement, sew an assembled unit from Step 2 to either side of an assembled unit from Step 4. Repeat. Press and set aside.

6. Sew an assembled unit from Step 4 to either side of the remaining assembled unit from Step 2. Press.

7. Sew the rows together and press.

TIP: Depending on the design of your directional print, you might try cutting a row longer than you need, then subcut pieces you want from that strip. Use the mirroring technique (see page 52) here if you want exact matches. If there is a design element you'd like to isolate in your focal fabric, make sure to fussy cut around the motif.

creating a narrative in your blocks

HAVE YOU EVER BEEN INSPIRED AND EXCITED to work on a project but not sure where to start? Sometimes looking at a new block can make you feel that way. A blank slate can be intimidating, as you decide what you want the block to say. The beauty of a sampler is that each block is a new opportunity to tell a different story. Pull several fabrics that inspire you, and see what fits that unit. Look for motifs that work well for the shapes within the block you're creating. Everyone's fabric audition process is a little different, but once you find a fabric you're really excited about, use that as a springboard to create a fun world within a single block. If your focal fabric contains fish, then use a secondary fabric that feature the ocean! If your focal fabric contains dogs, do you think of cats next? As you build your fabric selections, you can begin to tell a story. That is what this chapter is about.

Your story can be silly, sophisticated, whimsical, or even a little bit personal . . . and it doesn't even have to make sense. For instance, in Block 41, Nichole fondly remembers her childhood trips to the park where she would feed the local geese and birds.

picking a theme

- -

While it's true that with fussy cutting you can put a motif any place you want, one way to challenge yourself is to select a theme for a block and then try to keep all of your motifs working with that theme. You'll want to gather a variety of motifs and design styles that work well together while also maintaining a good color balance. If you're not sure where to start, look through your fabrics to see if something strikes your fancy and build a theme around that. Make sure you have enough supporting fabrics to communicate your theme, but be careful not to overload your block with too many fussy cuts. Use coordinating prints to add quiet spaces to your blocks. Remember, a good block will give your eye a place to rest.

- -

Nichole's Block

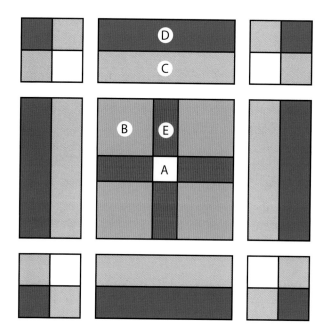

Block Diagram

FABRIC NEEDED

From Fabric A, cut:
(5) 1½" squares

From Fabric B, cut:
(4) 2½" squares

From Fabric C, cut:
(8) 1½" squares
(4) 1½" x 5½" rectangles

From Fabric D, cut:
(4) 1½" squares
(4) 1½" x 5½" rectangles

From Fabric E, cut:
(4) 1½" x 2½" rectangles

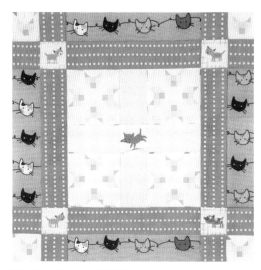

Take Two: For the 1½" Fabric D squares, Elisabeth used her Fabric A. If you'd like to do the same, cut 4 more 1½" squares from Fabric A and delete the squares from the cutting instructions for Fabric D.

BUILD YOUR BLOCK

1. Before sewing, arrange the cut units according to the Block Diagram and double-check the directionality of your cuts.

2. Sew a Fabric C and Fabric D square together and press. Repeat to create a total of 4 units.

3. Repeat Step 2 with the Fabric A and Fabric C squares to create a total of 4 units.

4. Sew an assembled unit from Step 2 to a unit from Step 3. Repeat to create a total of 4 units.

5. Sew a Fabric C and Fabric D rectangle and press. Repeat to create a total of 4 units and set aside.

6. Sew an assembled unit from Step 4 to either side of an assembled unit from Step 5 and press. Repeat to create a total of 4 units and set aside.

7. Sew a Fabric B square to either side of a Fabric E rectangle and press. Repeat.

8. Sew a Fabric E rectangle to either side of a Fabric A square. Press.

9. Sew an assembled unit from Step 7 to the top and bottom of the assembled unit from Step 8.

10. Sew an assembled unit from Step 5 to either side of the assembled unit from Step 9.

11. Sew the three rows together and press.

using one collection

We love to blend multiple fabric collections together when we're quilting, but sometimes it can be nice to work within one collection for a block or two since the fabrics are already designed to coordinate with each other. To find collections that work best for these blocks, look for a line with a variety of interesting designs (novelty and geometric, with both small-scale and large-scale motifs), with enough contrast in the color scheme to make a visually compelling block, but also with enough quiet prints to use as a background so your eye has a place to rest.

When you work with a single collection, the key to a great block is to balance the prints. It can be very easy to get excited about a group and put all your favorite motifs together, but sometimes the most effective use of the fabric is to cut and feature the "background" portion, since it can help add balance and keep the block from becoming too busy or too overwhelming.

Elisabeth's Block

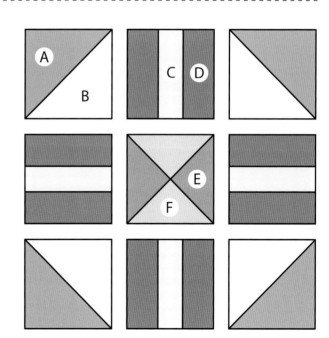

Block Diagram

FABRIC NEEDED

From Fabrics A and B, cut:
(4) 4" squares for HSTs

From Fabric C, cut:
(4) 1½" x 3½" rectangles

From Fabric D, cut:
(8) 1½" x 3½" rectangles

From Fabrics E and F, cut:
(1) 4½" square for QST

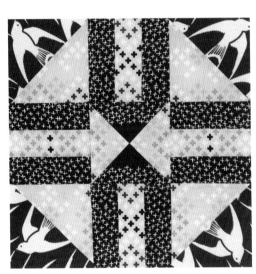

Take Two: Nichole used Fabric B for 2 of her QST triangles and in the stripe blocks. If you'd like to do the same, substitute Fabric B in place of the Fabric F square and the Fabric C rectangles.

BUILD YOUR BLOCK

1. Gather the Fabric A and Fabric B squares and create 4 HST units using the traditional HST method (see page 10). For busy prints, 4 squares per fabric may be necessary for fussy cutting. Press and set aside.

2. Gather the Fabric E and Fabric F squares and create 1 QST unit (see page 10). Set the remaining QST aside for future use or inspiration. Press and set aside.

3. Sew a Fabric D rectangle to either side of a Fabric C rectangle along the longest edge. Press. Repeat to create a total of 4 units.

4. Before sewing, arrange the cut units according to the Block Diagram and double-check the directionality of your cuts.

5. Sew an assembled HST unit from Step 1 to either side of an assembled unit from Step 3. Press. Repeat and set aside.

6. Sew an assembled unit from Step 3 to either side of the assembled QST unit from Step 2. Press.

7. Sew the rows together and press.

Refer to page 46 for fitting motifs into a QST unit and for fitting them into an HST unit.

coordinating other designers

We all have our favorite fabric styles and even our favorite designers, but sometimes putting all of them together ends up looking disjointed in a block, no matter how much we love the fabrics on their own. It can be challenging to pair different fabric lines together while making the block feel cohesive. To audition secondary and background fabrics for this block, consider color palettes that complement your focal fabric. Do the groups you are auditioning look good together as a color family? Next, look for similarities in design style, keeping in mind that you are looking for a similar style in your focal fabric as well as your secondary and background fabrics. Ask yourself questions like: Is there a small element in your focal fabric that repeats in one of your supporting fabrics? Can they help tell the story of your block?

Nichole's Block

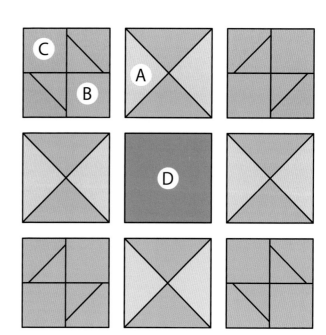

Block Diagram

FABRIC NEEDED

From Fabrics A, cut:
(4) 4½" squares for QSTs

From Fabric B, cut:
(4) 4½" squares for QSTs
(4) 2" squares
(4) 2½" squares for HSTs

From Fabric C, cut:
(4) 2" squares
(4) 2½" squares for HSTs

From Fabric D, cut:
(1) 3½" square

Take Two: Elisabeth chose to add two additional fabrics in place of the Fabric B 2" squares and the 2½" squares for the HSTs.

BUILD YOUR BLOCK

1. Gather the 4½" Fabric A and Fabric B squares and create 4 QST units (see page 10). Trim to 3½" square. Press and set aside.

2. Gather the 2½" Fabric B and Fabric C squares and create 8 HST units using the traditional HST method (see page 10). Trim to 2" square. Press and set aside.

3. Sew an assembled unit from Step 2 to a Fabric B square. Press. Repeat to create a total of 4 units.

4. Sew an assembled unit from Step 2 to a Fabric C square. Press. Repeat to create a total of 4 units.

5. Sew an assembled unit from Step 3 to an assembled unit from Step 4. Press. Repeat to create a total of 4 units.

6. Sew an assembled unit from Step 5 to either side of an assembled QST unit from Step 1. Press. Repeat and set aside.

7. Sew an assembled QST unit from Step 1 to either side of the Fabric D square. Press.

8. Sew the three rows together and press.

Refer to page 46 for fitting motifs into a QST unit and for assembling the units.

you in a block

Imagine if you could put everything you love or everything that speaks to you in a block that perfectly describes your personality. With fussy cutting, you can! For this block, we want you to think about your favorite colors and motifs that represent you. Are you a dog or a cat person? Do you need coffee and donuts in the morning? Can you not live without candy? It's a fun challenge to dig through your stash and find perfect little gems that reflect who you are. We all acquire fabric that speaks to us—this is the opportunity to let that fabric speak about you! If a good friend or loved one can look at your block and say, "Oh, you definitely made that," then you've accomplished your goal!

Elisabeth's Block

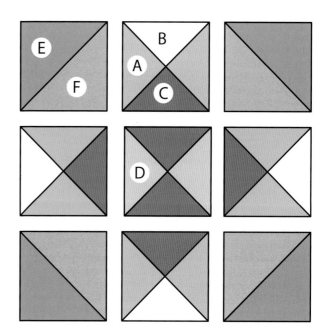

Block Diagram

FABRIC NEEDED

From Fabric A, cut:

(2) 4½" squares cut twice on the diagonal for QSTs

From Fabric B, cut:

(4) 4½" squares cut twice on the diagonal for QSTs

From Fabric C, cut:

(6) 4½" squares cut twice on the diagonal for QSTs

From Fabric D, cut:

(1) 4½" square cut twice on the diagonal for QSTs

From Fabrics E and F, cut:

(4) 4" squares for HSTs

Take Two: Nichole's Block

BUILD YOUR BLOCK

1. Before sewing, arrange the cut units according to the Block Diagram and double-check the directionality of your cuts.

2. Gather four triangles cut from the Fabric A, B, and C squares and assemble 4 QST units (see page 10). Trim to 3½" square. Press and set aside.

3. Gather four triangles cut from the Fabric C and Fabric D squares and assemble 1 QST unit. Trim to 3½" square. Press and set aside.

4. Gather the Fabric E and Fabric F squares and create 4 HST units using the traditional HST method (see page 10). Trim to 3½" square. Press and set aside.

5. Sew an assembled HST unit from Step 4 to either side of an assembled QST unit from Step 2. Press. Repeat and set aside.

6. Sew an assembled QST unit from Step 2 to either side of an assembled QST unit from Step 3. Press.

7. Sew the rows together and press.

For fussy cutting prints, larger quantities of squares per fabric may be necessary. The cutting instructions reflect the final cut sizes. Extra triangles are created when fussy cutting the squares along the diagonal.

Fussy Cutting is Fun

3 / 7 / 2 0 1 6

Elisabeth

advanced directionality

HERE WE ARE AT CHAPTER 12! By now you know almost all of our fussy cut tricks and tools, but there are still a few things we have up our sleeve that are just fun. We want to share our favorite techniques to help make complicated piecing a little easier, and show you how to add a customizable touch to your blocks as well as any future projects you work on.

working with freezer paper

Did you find in a previous block from our book that when you cut your designs slightly off-grain or on the bias that it was challenging to keep them from stretching when you went to piece them or iron them? Try stabilizing those same fabrics using freezer paper instead. It's one of Nichole's favorite tricks! This technique does take a little extra time, but it results in very clean blocks without distortion.

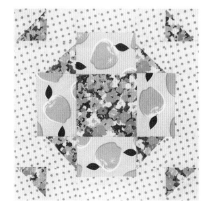

Nichole's Block

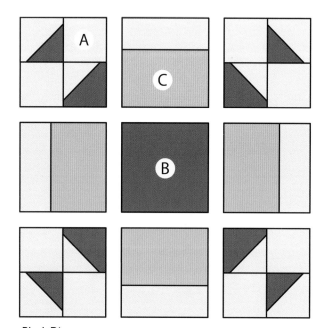

Block Diagram

Take Two: Elisabeth selected a fourth fabric for her center square. If you wish to do the same, substitute a new fabric for the 3½" Fabric B square.

Step 1:
Cut freezer paper to the size needed for your motif.

Step 2:
With a hot dry iron, iron shiny side of freezer paper to the wrong side of the fabric.

Step 3:
With an erasable pen, mark the cut size needed for your block.

Step 4:
Cut to size. Use this for the 2" Fabric A squares and/or the Fabric B rectangles.

FABRIC NEEDED

From Fabric A, cut:

(8) 2" squares

(4) 1½" x 3½" rectangles

(4) 2½" squares for HSTs

From Fabric B, cut:

(1) 3½" square

(4) 2½" squares for HSTs

From Fabric C, cut:

(4) 2½" x 3½" rectangles

Freezer paper

TIP: When sewing with freezer paper, make sure to adjust your stitch length to a short stitch (we recommend 1.4mm). The close stitching will perforate the freezer paper and make it easy to tear off once your block is completed. A pair of sharp tweezers works well to remove the freezer paper from tight spaces.

BUILD YOUR BLOCK

1. Gather the 2½" Fabric A and Fabric B squares and create 8 HST units using the traditional HST method (see page 10). Trim to 2" square. Press and set aside.

2. Sew an assembled HST unit from Step 1 to a 2" Fabric A square. Repeat to create a total of 8 units and set aside.

3. Sew 2 units from Step 2 together to form a 4-patch unit. Repeat to create a total of 4 units.

4. Sew a Fabric A rectangle and a Fabric C rectangle together along their longest sides. Press. Repeat to create a total of 4 units.

5. Sew an assembled 4-patch unit from Step 3 to either side of an assembled unit from Step 4. Press. Repeat and set aside.

6. Sew an assembled unit from Step 4 to either side of the 3½" Fabric B square. Press.

7. Sew the rows together and press.

TIP: When applying freezer paper to the back of your off-grain motifs, use a larger piece of paper than the block size requires. This will then peel off without damaging your fabric. Take extra care to make sure you do not iron on the shiny-side of the freezer paper.

re-creating repeats

Have you ever been so in love with a design in more than one color that you wished you could show them all at the same time? If you said yes, this technique is for you! In this block, we glue-baste color stories together where our Fabric A and B rectangles meet, matching the repeat carefully to make a dramatic block. While this technique has practical applications (like if you purchased a fat quarter and one of the motifs was cut off but you really wanted to use it still), it is also fun to do and will make you feel like a pro!

To create the effect we achieved, make sure you are using a final motif that fits nicely in the center pieced 5″ square (your focal section for this block) and which comes in two different colors. Also check that you have enough of an overlapping repeat so that the technique can work.

Elisabeth's Block

Take Two: Nichole's Block

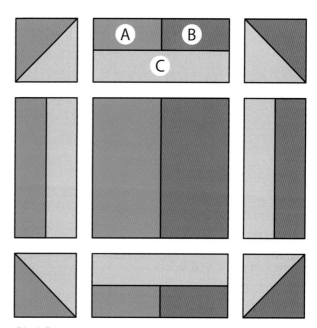

Block Diagram

Step 1: Identify where your Fabric A and B rectangles meet, then position one fabric over the other. Fold back one raw edge so that you have at least a ¼" seam allowance folded in.

Step 2: On the right side, lightly add a thin glue line on the fold.

Step 3: Carefully place your fabric so the designs combine into one repeat, then press with a hot dry iron.

Step 4: Unfold and mark your stitch line (in red) in the crease.

Step 5: Stitch along the drawn line precisely. Any variation will impact accuracy. Trim the excess fabric to a ¼" seam allowance.

FABRIC NEEDED

From Fabrics A and B, cut:
(2) 3" squares for HSTs
(1) 1½" x 5½" rectangle
(1) 4½" x 8½" rectangle

From Fabric C, cut:
(4) 3" squares for HSTs
(4) 1½" x 5½" rectangles

BUILD YOUR BLOCK

1. Gather the 3" Fabric A, Fabric B and Fabic C squares and create 4 HST units using the traditional HST method (see page 10). Create 2 A/C HSTs and 2 B/C HSTs. Trim to 2½" square. Press and set aside.

2. Using the technique at left, sew the 4½" x 8½" Fabric A and B rectangles together. Subcut to yeild (1) 1½" x 5½" top pieced unit, (1) 5½" square center unit and (1) 1½" x 5½" bottom pieced unit

3. Sew a Fabric C rectangle to a 1½" x 5½" Fabric A rectangle. Press and repeat with Fabric B.

4. Sew an assembled HST unit from Step 1 to either side of the assembled top unit from Step 2. Repeat for the assembled bottom unit.

5. Sew the assembled side units from Step 3 to either side of the center of the block.

6. Sew the rows together and press.

TIP: Before cutting, remember that larger quantities of squares per fabric may be necessary for fussy cutting. The cutting instructions here reflect the technique used for the center of the block. Also, extra triangles for HSTs will be created when fussy cutting the squares along the diagonal. Set these aside for future use.

advanced motifs in block shapes

The key to this block is identifying a motif that is almost exactly the same size and shape as the final element in each part of the block. This allows the motif to fill almost the entire portion of the block shape, so instead of seeing a block, you first see the fussy cut motif, then the block shape.

If you want to feature motifs in an HST unit too like we did, it can be helpful to draw out the block size onto tracing paper (or freezer paper or anything see-through) or onto your acrylic ruler, so that you can quickly check the motif size with your finished piece size. As always, don't forget to add in the seam allowances and remember to keep your motif ⅜" in from the trimming edge of the block.

Nichole's Block

Take Two: Elisabeth used the Fabric B print again in the Flying Geese blocks. If you'd like to do the same, cut the Fabric D squares from Fabric B instead.

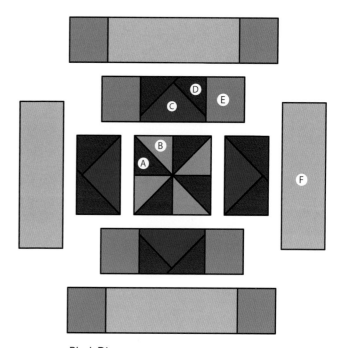

Block Diagram

FABRIC NEEDED

From Fabrics A and B, cut:
(4) 2½" squares for the HSTs

From Fabric C, cut:
(4) 2¼" x 3¾" rectangles for the Flying Geese

From Fabric D, cut:
(8) 2¼" squares for the Flying Geese

From Fabric E, cut:
(8) 2" squares

From Fabric F, cut:
(4) 2" x 6½" rectangles

Refer to page 47 for featuring motifs in a Flying Geese unit and for fitting motifs into an HST unit, but adjust the measurement to 2½" square.

BUILD YOUR BLOCK

1. Gather the 2½" Fabric A and Fabric B squares and create 4 HST units using the traditional HST method (see page 10). Trim to 2" square. Press and set aside. Discard the remaining triangles.

2. Gather the Fabric C rectangles and the Fabric D squares and assemble 4 Flying Geese units (see page 10). Trim to 2" x 3½". Set aside.

3. Sew the 4 assembled units from Step 1 into a pinwheel. Sew an assembled Flying Geese unit from Step 2 to either side of the pinwheel. Press and set aside.

4. Sew a Fabric E square to either side of an assembled Flying Geese unit from Step 2. Repeat. Press and set aside.

5. Sew an assembled unit from Step 5 to the top and bottom of the Step 4 unit. Press.

6. Sew a Fabric E square to either side of a Fabric F rectangle to form the top row of the block. Repeat to form the bottom row. Press and set aside.

7. Sew a Fabric F rectangle to either side of the assembled unit from Step 6 to form the middle row. Press.

8. Sew the rows together and press.

signing off: creating your custom label

Quilt labels have been around as long as quilts. Some quilters label each quilt they make, and others never label any. We fall somewhere in the middle. Fussy cutting letters into custom words and sentences is a fun way to piece your messages into your blocks as a reminder of your work. This is an ideal spot to tell someone you love them, or to leave secret messages or reminders, like a special date or maybe you just want to put your name on it. This block allows a 3½" x 9½" space for your message. If your text is smaller than that, get creative and use a coordinating fabric to add height and width, then trim to the required size.

Elisabeth's Block

Take Two: Nichole used the same fabric for her 2" squares and her HST units. If you'd like to do the same, cut 2" squares and (6) 2½" squares from one fabric and (6) 2½" squares from another fabric.

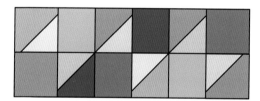

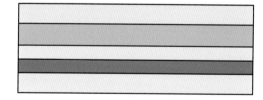

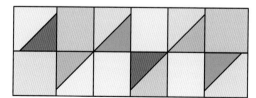

Block Diagram

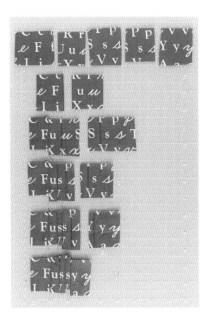

Step 1: Cut out the letters you need for your special message. Make sure to leave room on all sides so you have room to work.

Step 2. Starting with the first letter of your word, use an erase-able pen to mark ¼" away from the end of the right side of the letter. DO NOT CUT THIS LINE. Mark a secondary line just a tad to the right. This will be your cut line, and will keep the letters from touching once they are all pieced together. Repeat this process on the left side of your second letter.

Step 3: Cut along the lines you identified as your cut lines in step 2.

Step 4: Sew your first two letters together using a ¼" seam allowance then press.

Step 5: Repeat Steps 1-4 for the rest of your desired word.

FABRIC NEEDED

- -

From assorted scraps, cut:
(12) 2½" squares for HSTs
(12) 2" squares

For 3½" x 9½" custom label, cut:
letters to spell out your chosen message
coordinating fabric for background, if needed

BUILD YOUR BLOCK

- -

1. Gather the 2½" squares and arrange in pairs of contrasting values, then create 12 HST units using the traditional HST method (see page 10). Trim to 2" square. Press.

2. Gather 3 assembled HST units from Step 1 and (3) 2" squares, then sew together to form a row of alternating HSTs and squares as in the Block Diagram. Repeat to form a total of 4 rows. Press.

3. Sew 2 assembled rows from Step 2 together. Repeat. Press and set aside.

4. Piece letters as desired to form your custom label. Trim to 3½" x 9½".

5. Sew the rows together and press.

- -

TIP: If you want to re-create the look of the typewriter keys in Elisabeth's block, cut each letter piece a consistent size, making sure the letter is centered in the cut. This will result in evenly spaced letters.

TIP: For additional accuracy—or to create a secondary design, such as cursive writing—glue-baste letters together using the technique from Block 46 (see page 133).

- -

CHAPTER 13

building your quilt

IF YOU'VE BEEN WITH US THROUGH EVERY CHAPTER OF THIS BOOK, you now have 48 fussy cut blocks, so let's talk about finishing your quilt! As you have likely noticed by now, we both have very distinct styles, so of course we prefer different layouts for our final block placement. There is a traditional layout with sashing and cornerstones (Elisabeth's preference), as well as a more modern grouping (Nichole's favorite). There is no right or wrong way to put your blocks together. You have taken the time to create them all and you should enjoy putting together the final layout!

Elisabeth's quilt

Finished Size: 67" x 88"

TRADITIONAL LAYOUT

FABRIC NEEDED
Sashing and borders: 2¼ yards
Cornerstones: ⅛ yard
Backing: 5½ yards*
Binding: ½ yard

*see Backing (page 11) for wideback options

CUTTING
From the sashing/border fabric, cut:
(21) 2" x WOF strips
Subcut:
    (82) 2" x 9½" sashing strips
    (9) 3" x WOF border strips
From the cornerstone fabric, cut:
(2) 2" x WOF strips
Subcut:
    (35) 2" squares
From the binding fabric, cut:
(8) 2¼" x WOF strips

BUILDING YOUR QUILT

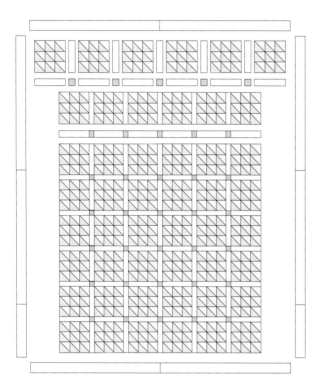

3. Sew 6 sashing strips and 5 cornerstones together to form a sashing row, alternating the strips and squares and beginning and ending the row with a sashing strip. Press seams toward the sashing. Repeat to make 7 sashing rows.

4. Sew a sashing row to the bottom of the top block row. Pin at all seam intersections to ensure sharp points! Sew the remaining rows together, alternating block rows and sashing rows. The bottom block row will not have a sashing row sewn to the bottom. Press all seams toward the sashing rows.

5. Piece the 3" border strips together, end-to-end, in pairs. Cut the remaining strip in half and sew each half to a strip pair.

6. Center, pin, and sew the longer 3" border pieces to the right and left sides of the quilt center. Press toward the sashing and trim the excess sashing to the length of the quilt center.

7. Center, pin, and sew the shorter 3" border pieces to the top and bottom of the quilt center. Press toward the sashing and trim the excess sashing to the width of the quilt center.

1. Lay out your blocks in 8 rows of 6 blocks each, balancing the fabrics and piecing in a pleasing arrangement.

2. Sew a sashing strip between each block in the row, beginning and ending the row with a block. Press seams toward the sashing. Repeat to assemble all 8 block rows.

Nichole's quilt

Finished Size: 79" x 79"

MODERN LAYOUT

FABRIC NEEDED
Sashing and filler blocks: 2½ yards
Backing: 7¼ yards*
Binding: ¾ yard

*see Backing (page 11) for wideback options

CUTTING
From the sashing/filler block fabric, cut:
(4) 9½" x WOF strips
Subcut:
    (16) 9½" square filler blocks
    (28) 1½" x WOF strips—set aside 14
    sashing strips
From the remainder, subcut:
    (56) 1½" x 9½" block sashing strips
From the binding fabric, cut:
(9) 2¼" x WOF strips

TIP: The filler blocks will create a
secondary design. Be mindful of the
filler block placement as you piece the
rows together.

BUILDING YOUR QUILT

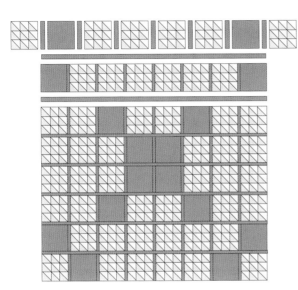

1. Lay out your pieced blocks and filler blocks in 8 rows of 8 blocks each, balancing the fabrics and piecing in a pleasing arrangement and placing the filler blocks to create a secondary design.

2. Sew a block sashing strip between each block in the row, beginning and ending the row with a block. Press seams toward the sashing. Repeat to assemble all 8 rows.

3. Sew the sashing strips together, end-to-end, in pairs to create 7 sashing strips.

4. Center, pin, and sew a sashing strip to the bottom of the top block row. Sew the remaining rows together, alternating block rows and sashing strips. The bottom row will not have a sashing strip sewn to the bottom. Press all seams toward the sashing.

RESOURCES

FABRIC AND NOTIONS

Fancy Tiger Crafts (Denver, Colorado):
www.fancytigercrafts.com

Superbuzzy (Ventura, California):
www.superbuzzy.com

ADDITIONAL SUPPLIES

Soak Wash (for Flatter):
www.soakwash.com

Kai Scissors:
www.kaiscissors.com

Aurifil 50wt Cotton Thread:
www.aurifil.com

Omnigrid Rulers:
www.prym-consumer-usa.com/brands/omnigrid

Pilot Frixion Pens:
www.pilotpen.us/brands/frixion/

Olfa Rotary Cutters: and Mats:
www.olfa.com

Clover Notions:
www.clover-usa.com